T0291303

Indigenous Peoples and Mining

Indigenous Peoples and Mining

A Global Perspective

Ciaran O'Faircheallaigh

OXFORD
UNIVERSITY PRESS

OXFORD
UNIVERSITY PRESS

Great Clarendon Street, Oxford, OX2 6DP,
United Kingdom

Oxford University Press is a department of the University of Oxford.
It furthers the University's objective of excellence in research, scholarship,
and education by publishing worldwide. Oxford is a registered trade mark of
Oxford University Press in the UK and in certain other countries

Published in the United States of America by Oxford University Press
198 Madison Avenue, New York, NY 10016, United States of America

British Library Cataloguing in Publication Data
Data available

Library of Congress Control Number: 2023932246

ISBN 978-0-19-289456-4

DOI: 10.1093/oso/9780192894564.001.0001

Printed and bound by
CPI Group (UK) Ltd, Croydon, CR0 4YY

To Carol

The love of my life

Acknowledgements

This book is the result of over 30 years' research and professional practice in which I have been supported by numerous colleagues, friends, and research collaborators.

I express my profound gratitude to the many Indigenous people without whose generosity and willingness to share their knowledge and experience the book could not have been written. I have enormous admiration for their courage, determination, optimism, and good humour in dealing with what to an outsider often seem like overwhelming challenges. My fervent hope is that the information contained in this book helps to support them in dealing with those particular challenges associated with the relentless pressures for exploitation of mineral resources on Indigenous lands.

I wish in particular to thank Wayne Bergmann, who has shared much of my journey in seeking to understand the dynamic of relationships between Indigenous peoples and the miners who set out to exploit Indigenous territories. I also acknowledge the comradeship of the many Indigenous and non-Indigenous people who have worked with me on impact assessments of mining projects and on negotiations with mining companies. Tony Corbett provided invaluable support in much of my research on these negotiations and read and commented on every page of the book.

My thanks to Griffith University and my colleagues in its School of Government and International Relations for their invaluable support for my research and my engagement with Indigenous communities over many years.

Above all, my thanks to my family. My parents instilled in me a love of knowledge and a sense of social justice that I hope are reflected in the following pages. My children and grandchildren have been an endless source of inspiration, and an invaluable source of support in difficult times.

Above all, none of the work that generated this book could have been possible without my wife Carol. She tolerated my long absences in the field over most of our married life with remarkable good humour and was the rock on which our family rested. She was an unfailing source of counsel in every challenge I faced during my career. I cannot express my sadness that Carol did not live to see the end result of the research in which she played such an indispensable part.

Contents

List of Tables and Figures   ix
List of Abbreviations   x

1. Introduction   1

I.   THEORY AND CONTEXT

2. Theoretical Perspectives on Interactions between
   Indigenous Peoples and Mining   9

3. History: Indigenous Peoples and Mining in the
   Nineteenth and Twentieth Centuries   22

4. Forces for Change: International Recognition of
   Indigenous Rights   39

II. KEY ACTORS

5. Indigenous Peoples: Diversity and Shared Experiences   59

6. The Mining Industry: Wealth, Influence, and Pressures
   for Change   77

7. The State, Indigenous Peoples, and Mining   90

III. STRATEGIES, COSTS, AND OPPORTUNITIES

8. Indigenous Engagement: Negotiation and Agreements   107

9. Indigenous Opposition: Resistance and Refusal   122

10. Managing the Negative Impacts of Mining on Indigenous
    Lands and Peoples   138

11. Maximizing Mining's Economic Potential for Indigenous
    Peoples   153

IV. CASE STUDIES

12. Chile: Indigenous Strategies of Resistance and
    Engagement   175

13. Botswana and South Africa: A Contrast in Indigenous
    Strategies and Outcomes   201

14. Indigenous Rights and Mining in the Philippines   219

15. Australia and Canada: A Test for Indigenous Engagement
    Strategies   238

16. Not Just Mining: Cumulative Impacts and Sami Reindeer
    Herders in Sweden   259

17. Analysis and Conclusion   281

References   294
Index   325

List of Tables and Figures

Table 11.1 Points in project economic structure where payments can be extracted   161

Figure 12.1 Mining locations in the Salar de Atacama, Chile   188

Figure 13.1 San resettlement from the Central Kalahari Game Reserve   206

Figure 16.1 Sami reindeer herding areas in northern Sweden   262

List of Abbreviations

[Sp.] indicates that an abbreviation relates to the Spanish name for the entity.

AANDC	Aboriginal Affairs and Northern Development Canada
ABC	Australian Broadcasting Commission
ABS	Australian Bureau of Statistics
ACC	Amadiba Crisis Committee
ACHPR	African Commission on Human and Peoples' Rights
AGM	Annual general meeting
AIHW	Australian Institute of Health and Welfare
ALC	Anindilyakwa Land Council
APWLD	Asia Pacific Forum on Women, Law and Development
ASM	Artisanal and small-scale mining
ATP	Authority to Prospect
BC	British Columbia
BCA	Bougainville Copper Agreement
BHP	Broken Hill Proprietary
BRA	Bougainville Revolutionary Army
CAB	Country Administrative Board (Sweden)
CADC	Certificate of Ancestral Domain Claim
CADT	Certificate of Ancestral Domain Title
CDAs	Community development agreements
CERD	Committee for the Elimination of Racial Discrimination
CIGI	Centre for International Governance Innovation
CKGR	Central Kalahari Game Reserve
CMZ	Compania Minera Zaldivar
CONADI	National Corporation for Indigenous Development [Sp.]
CONAMA	National Environmental Commission [Sp.]
CPA	Council of Atacamanian Peoples [Sp.]
CRA	Conzinc Rio Tinto of Australia Ltd
CSR	Corporate social responsibility
DENR	Department of Environment and Natural Resources (Philippines)
DMR	Department of Mineral Resources (South Africa)
ECC	Environmental Clearance Certificate (Philippines)
EIA	Environmental impact assessment
ELI	Environmental Law Institute
ERM	Environmental Resources Management
FECONACO	Federation of Native Communities of Rio Corrientos [Sp.]
FPIC	Free prior and informed consent
FPK	First Peoples of the Kalahari
FTAA	Financial or Technical Assistance Agreement
GEAT	Groote Eylandt Aboriginal Trust
GEBIE	Groote Eylandt and Bickerton Island Enterprises

GOS	Government Offices of Sweden
IA	Impact assessment
IACHR	Inter-American Commission on Human Rights
IAIA	International Association for Impact Assessment
IBA	Impacts and benefits agreement
ICCs/IPs	Indigenous cultural communities/Indigenous peoples
ICCPR	International Covenant on Civil and Political Rights
ICERD	International Convention on the Elimination of All Forms of Racial Discrimination
ICESCR	International Covenant on Economic, Social and Cultural Rights
ICIA	Indigenous controlled impact assessment
ICMM	International Council on Mining and Metals
IDA	Indigenous Development Area (Chile)
IFC	International Finance Corporation
IFI	International financial institution
IFPIC	Indigenous free prior and informed consent
IGF	Intergovernmental Forum on Mining, Minerals, Metals and Sustainable Development
IIED	International Institute for Environment and Development
ILO	International Labour Organization
IPACC	Indigenous Peoples of Africa Coordinating Committee
IPN	Indigenous Peoples of the North
IPRA	Indigenous Peoples' Rights Act (Philippines)
IWGIA	International Working Group on Indigenous Affairs
IWIMRA	Indigenous Women in Mining and Resources Australia
KLC	Kimberley Land Council
LIA	Labrador Inuit Association
LNG	Liquefied natural gas
LRC	Legal Resources Centre (South Africa)
MEL	Minera Escondida Limitada
MILF	Moro Islamic Liberation Front
MMSD	Mining, Minerals and Sustainable Development
MNC	Multinational corporation
MPSA	Mineral Production Sharing Agreement
MRC	Mineral Resources Commodities
NCIP	National Commission on Indigenous Peoples
NGO	Non-government organization
NMG	Nickel Mountain Group
NNTT	National Native Title Tribunal
NPA	New People's Army
OECD	Organisation for Economic Cooperation and Development
OPC	Occidental Petroleum Company
OPIC	Overseas Private Investment Corporation
PFII	Permanent Forum on Indigenous Issues
PH-EITI	Philippines Extractive Industries Transparency Initiative
PIWC	Pauktuutit, Inuit Women of Canada
PKKP	Puutu Kunti Kurrama and Pinikura

PNG	Papua New Guinea
QIA	Qikiqtani Inuit Association
RCA	Environmental Qualification Resolution [Sp.]
RCMP	Royal Canadian Mounted Police
RDS	Royal Dutch Shell PLC
RTIO	Rio Tinto Iron Ore
SBML	Special Bauxite Mining Lease
SCL	Chilean Lithium Society [Sp.]
SI	Survival International
SMA	Superintendency of the Environment [Sp.]
SMI	Sagittarius Mines, Incorporated
SN	Squamish Nation
SQM	Sociedad Química y Minera de Chile SA
SSAI	Siocon Subanon Association, Incorporated
SSR	National Union of the Swedish Sami
TEM	Transworld Energy and Mineral Resources
TOTF	Traditional Owner Task Force
TVI	Toronto Ventures, Incorporated
UDHR	Universal Declaration of Human Rights
UN	United Nations
UNDESA	United Nations Department of Economic and Social Affairs
UNDRIP	United Nations Declaration on the Rights of Indigenous Peoples
UNESC	United Nations Economic and Social Council
UNESCO	United Nations Educational, Scientific and Cultural Organization
UNHRC	United Nations Human Rights Council
UNOHCHR	United Nations Office of the High Commissioner for Human Rights
VBNC	Voisey's Bay Nickel Company
WA	Western Australia
WEL	Woodside Energy Limited
WCCC	Western Cape Communities Coexistence
WGDD	Working Group on the Draft Declaration
WGIP	Working Group on Indigenous Peoples
WMC	Western Mining Corporation
WNG	Woodfibre Natural Gas
XolCo	Xholobeni Empowerment Company

1
Introduction

Indigenous peoples have occupied their territories for thousands of years, territories increasingly being mined by an industry applying the most modern extractive, marketing, and transport technologies on a scale that can be difficult to comprehend. Mining reshapes landscapes, literally moving mountains and diverting rivers, landscapes that their Indigenous owners often believe were originally shaped by ancestor beings that still reside at sites where they completed their work. This book seeks to understand the political, social, economic, and cultural dynamic that is created by the relentless expansion of mining into Indigenous territories. Contributing to such an understanding involves a task of global significance. Indigenous peoples manage or have tenure rights over an estimated 25 per cent of the world's land surface. Their territories intersect with about 40 per cent of all ecologically intact landscapes and protected areas, and contain a large proportion of the world's mineral resources (Dowie 2009; Gustafsson and Schilling-Vacaflor 2022).

The dynamic between Indigenous peoples and mining is often presented in academic and activist writing as inevitably involving the destruction of Indigenous peoples, territories, and cultures. Despite the overwhelming economic and technological power that modern mining wields, caution must be exercised in accepting this perspective. Indigenous peoples have survived for millennia because they possess remarkable resilience, and we should not assume this resilience will desert them in dealing with modern mining. Indeed, empirical research that involves serious engagement with relations between Indigenous peoples and mining points to a picture much more complex than a fundamental incompatibility between the advent of mining and the survival of Indigenous peoples and cultures.

Mining is a diverse industry operating in virtually every corner of the globe, and Indigenous peoples are highly diverse in their histories, beliefs, and social and cultural practices. Given this diversity, in seeking to offer a 'global' perspective I make no claim to comprehensiveness. I do make two other claims. First, much of the existing literature focuses on one or two aspects of the relationship between Indigenous peoples and mining: for example, on the implications of international legal recognition of Indigenous rights; the role of the state in facilitating exploitation of Indigenous lands; regulatory regimes for assessing mining projects or for negotiating agreements between Indigenous communities and mining companies; the negative environmental and cultural impact of mining on Indigenous territories; the impact of resource revenues on Indigenous societies; or the corporate social responsibility policies of mining corporations. In any specific context in which Indigenous peoples deal with the mining industry, most or all these factors are likely to be at play, and to interact

Indigenous Peoples and Mining. Ciaran O'Faircheallaigh, Oxford University Press. © Ciaran O'Faircheallaigh (2023).
DOI: 10.1093/oso/9780192894564.003.0001

with each other in shaping outcomes. This book seeks to address *all* these dimensions of the relationship between Indigenous peoples and mining and to do so in an integrated way.

Second, most scholars in the field, and this applies to my own previous work, limit their geographical focus to one or two countries. This book seeks to achieve a considerably wider focus, drawing on the experience of Indigenous peoples in some 15 countries and offering detailed case studies of First Peoples from different regions of the globe (Canada, Chile, Australia, the Philippines, Sweden, Botswana, and South Africa). In addition to achieving geographical breadth, the choice of cases is designed to allow further analysis of general issues that shape relations between Indigenous peoples and mining. For example, most existing research deals with the impacts of mining in isolation from those caused by other development activities on Indigenous territories. In reality, the effects of mining can be seriously compounded when it coincides with the impact of, for example, windfarms, tourism, agribusiness, and infrastructure development. Including a case on Sami people in Sweden allows these interconnections to be explored, as the Sami's capacity to continue reindeer husbandry is threatened precisely by the cumulative effects of multiple industrial activities. Negotiation of agreements is increasingly important in relations between Indigenous peoples and the mining industry throughout the globe. Australia and Canada have for three decades used negotiated agreements as the foundation for managing those relations. Analysis of their experience allows the implications of the expanding practice of agreement making to be analysed in depth. Similarly, the case study of the Philippines allows a consideration of the impact on Indigenous peoples of militarization and the criminalization of opposition to mining, phenomena evident in many other countries.

The book also seeks to incorporate the distinct experiences and perspectives of Indigenous women. I draw on the limited literature in this area in Chapter 5 to consider separately the implications of mining for Indigenous women. In addition, in the case studies and the thematic chapters—for example, those on Indigenous protest and on negotiation of agreements—I include a focus on the specific role of Indigenous women and on the impacts and issues affecting them.

Personal and ethical standpoint

I am Irish by birth, Irish (Gaelic) is my first language, and I lived in Ireland until my early twenties, when I moved to Australia to pursue my postgraduate education. My doctoral thesis was on multinational mining companies and their relations with governments in mineral-rich countries, and it involved extensive research on taxation of mineral resources and on corporate pricing and marketing practices. I then taught at the University of Papua New Guinea in the early 1980s, where a formative aspect of my work involved field research at the Panguna mine on the island of Bougainville, a mine closed by armed rebellion in 1989, leading to a civil war that lasted a decade.

For the last 30 years I have spent many months working and living in Indigenous communities throughout northern Australia and in Canada and, during 2011–16, in Bougainville. In addition to conducting research, I have been extensively involved in managing community-controlled impact assessments for Aboriginal communities in Australia and assisted Indigenous communities in Australia, Canada, and Papua New Guinea to negotiate contractual agreements with mining and oil and gas companies. My understanding is that Aboriginal communities initially sought my participation in this latter work because they hoped that my knowledge of multinational mining companies would help address a serious imbalance in information that hampered communities in their negotiations with industry. As my experience working with Indigenous communities grew, they drew on my advice regarding a range of negotiation issues and in organizing community consultations to prepare for negotiations.

I have at times provided information jointly to Indigenous communities and mining companies at their request. I have not worked solely for a mining company at any point in my career, and have declined invitations to do so. My position in this regard does not arise from a philosophical or ideological opposition to mining. Most of the amenities, comforts, and securities of modern life rely directly or indirectly on the extraction of minerals, including energy minerals such as oil and gas. In my view we do not, on a global scale, have a choice not to mine. This reality will not change as the world moves away from a carbon economy, with production of lithium and silica sand, for example, required to grow rapidly to supply batteries and solar panels. The relevant questions relate to where mining should occur and should not occur, and the conditions under which it should occur. My position in declining to work for the mining industry arises from a belief that the imbalance in resources and information faced by Indigenous communities constitutes an injustice and is likely to lead to outcomes that harm them and society as a whole, and that Indigenous peoples should be supported in making informed decisions about proposed developments on their territories. Further, since the mining industry has no need of my knowledge regarding itself, the only basis on which it might seek to retain my services is to gain access to my knowledge of Indigenous communities, knowledge often provided to me based on confidentiality and trust. The only ethical course in my view was to make whatever knowledge I possess, other than that in the public domain through my research publications, available only to Indigenous communities.

The position I have adopted in my professional practice does not mean that this book is a polemic. Most of my research has been the subject of formal peer review designed to ensure a rigorous and balanced approach to collection and analysis of research data. I have been careful to draw on a wide range of sources that present a variety of perspectives, ensuring that I present as full and accurate a picture as possible of the events I describe and the issues I analyse. To the extent possible I have drawn on the voices and testimonies of Indigenous peoples in discussing their experience. No matter the extent of my engagement with Indigenous communities, I make no claim to speak on their behalf or to share their position in the world. I am white, male, and have enjoyed a level of privilege few Indigenous people are able to experience. Growing up in Ireland, I had a strong sense of what it was to be a colonized people. But the Ireland I grew up in had achieved its independence from Britain a generation earlier, Gaelic was an official language, and Gaelic speakers like myself were privileged. I was awarded extra marks in my high school exams because I completed subjects such as maths and chemistry through Gaelic. This is a long way from the experience of many Indigenous peoples.

The foundation of my ethical position is that I should do no harm to the Indigenous communities I work with and conduct research about and, to the extent possible, that my research should help advance their interests. From this starting position, I have only undertaken research in Indigenous communities or involving Indigenous people with their consent; where possible I have sought their views on my findings prior to publication; and I have ensured that the results of my research are available to Indigenous organizations that contribute to it. In drawing on primary data and published sources, I have sought to ensure the reliability of the sources involved and that the context of Indigenous actions and choices is fully explained. In addition to these general principles and practices, my research has in many cases been governed by formal research agreements with the Indigenous communities concerned that deal with matters such as confidentiality and intellectual property. It has also been subject to clearance by university ethics committees.

A specific comment is required on the issue of confidential information. In cases where a formal research project has been involved, I have given a written commitment not to publish information identified as confidential. However, where I have previously worked with an Indigenous community, my participation in negotiations and community consultations is often governed by a relationship of trust rather than by formal documentation. My Indigenous hosts or employers may provide access to a great deal of information without indicating what part of it, if any, is confidential or sensitive. In these cases I have observed a precautionary principle, not publishing information that I judge *might* be confidential or sensitive.

I wish to express my sincere gratitude to the many Indigenous people who have shared information and knowledge with me. Their generosity has been indispensable not just because the knowledge they provide constitutes a key component of my published work, but because this knowledge is also invaluable, even where I cannot use it directly, in allowing me to interpret, and to gauge how much weight to attach to, information already in the public domain. In acknowledging their generosity, I also recognize there is knowledge that Indigenous people have not shared with me: for example, because I am male; because I am not Indigenous; or because I cannot fulfil the cultural requirements that must precede access to certain categories of knowledge. In some cases, I *know* that knowledge has not been shared because I have been told of its existence. As a general principle I always *assume* that some knowledge may not have been shared. This places a limitation on my ability to represent fully the motivations, goals, and strategies of Indigenous actors who feature in some of the narratives that follow. It is a limitation that Indigenous people have themselves chosen to impose and whose acceptance is thus central to a recognition of Indigenous peoples as the owner of their knowledges, and so to the ethical conduct of research (Smith 2021: 167).

The book begins by discussing theoretical perspectives on the relationship between Indigenous peoples and mining. The focus here is on academic theory. As I note later, Indigenous knowledge also generates theoretical perspectives, often starting from a very different premise. Two chapters follow that outline key aspects of the context for contemporary relations between mining and Indigenous peoples, the history of engagement between the two in the nineteenth and twentieth centuries, and the growing international recognition of Indigenous rights in the decades after 1945. This is followed in Part 2 by a chapter devoted to each of the three key actors that are always centrally involved in mining on Indigenous territories—Indigenous peoples, the state, and mining corporations. Despite claims by some authors that the state has recently absented itself through the adoption of neo-liberalism, in fact the state always affects outcomes, by setting the legal and policy framework within which Indigenous peoples interact with the mining industry, and by influencing, through its absence or presence, the distribution of power between the other parties. The role of other actors, including environmental and civil society groups, is discussed in the case studies and in analysing Indigenous strategies for dealing with industry and the state. These strategies are the focus of Part 3, in chapters that review approaches focused on engagement with industry designed to minimize the negative effects of mining and maximize its economic benefits for Indigenous peoples; and strategies that focus on refusal of mining on Indigenous territories. In Part 4 I present case studies of Chile, Botswana, South Africa, the Philippines, Australia, Canada, and Sweden. These provide opportunities to examine how the issues, influences, and strategies discussed earlier in the book have manifested in a variety of contexts, and to critically assess the utility and relevance of contending concepts and theories.

A note on COVID

When I began writing this book in 2020 the COVID-19 pandemic had only just started. COVID-19 has serious implications for Indigenous peoples. It is especially dangerous for people with underlying health issues and limited access to medical services, and many Indigenous people belong to this group. Older people, who play critical leadership roles in Indigenous societies, are especially vulnerable. Some First Peoples—for example, in Alberta, Canada, and in the Brazilian Amazon— have incurred significant fatalities and negative social and cultural impacts from COVID-19 (IWGIA 2021). There may also be implications more directly for Indigenous engagement with the mining industry. For example, mines and their workforces may become entry points for COVID-19 into Indigenous communities, leading them to put sanitary cordons in place and to prevent outsiders from accessing mining sites. It may be more difficult for communities to come together to make decisions related to mining and their access to consultation forums may be restricted. For instance,

Chilean regulatory authorities have sought to complete consultation processes for environmental impact assessment remotely, ignoring the limited access of Indigenous communities to digital infrastructure and the cultural inappropriateness of using a computer interface to consult with them (IWGIA 2021: 350–1). Community access to information or to the media may be compromised, as may be the ability of academic analysts, sympathetic civil society groups, and the media to obtain information regarding what is happening at mines on geographically remote Indigenous lands. Transparency regarding the actions of state agencies and extractive industries may be diminished (Bainton et al. 2020). An extreme case of this last point is represented by Brazil's Minister of the Environment, Ricardo Salles, who spoke of simplifying rules and processes for developers to access Indigenous territories 'in this calm moment in terms of press coverage, because they are only talking about COVID' (cited in Menton et al. 2021: 3).

It is also likely that the need to foster economic recovery 'post COVID' will be used as a justification for quickly developing extractive projects on Indigenous lands (IWGIA 2021: 257–9, 291, 296). For example, in July 2020 the then Philippines President, Rodrigo Duterte, launched a large number of 'economic stimulus' projects on Indigenous lands, and the country's Department of Natural Resources announced 'plans to advance mining and river dredging in order to spur on the country's economic recovery programme' (IWGIA 2021: 296).

The political ramifications of COVID-19 for Indigenous peoples are complex and not easily predictable. For example, in Brazil, while the pandemic has seen intensification of attacks on Indigenous peoples and their territories and associated environmental conflicts, these have in turn increased Indigenous capacity for active resistance, strengthened community ties and the national Indigenous movement, and mobilized a new cohort of Indigenous youth with access to higher education, considerable capacity to utilize social media and to lead Indigenous cases in the courts (Menton et al. 2021: 1).

I recognize the possibility that COVID-19 may be bringing about change which it is not possible to reflect fully in what follows.

PART I
THEORY AND CONTEXT

2

Theoretical Perspectives on Interactions between Indigenous Peoples and Mining

Introduction

This chapter examines theories that have been applied to examine the relationship between Indigenous peoples and mining, or which seem potentially useful in understanding that relationship. It focuses on the research literature, recognizing that there are alternative theories that emerge from Indigenous cosmologies and ways of experiencing the world (see Chapter 5). It also focuses on theories that examine the overall relationship between mining and Indigenous peoples. In addition there are 'meso-level' theories that focus on specific aspects of that relationship: for example, the negotiation of agreements between mining companies and Indigenous communities, or on the role the state plays in structuring company–Indigenous relations. These are examined in the relevant thematic chapters.

This chapter begins by reviewing two theories that offer directly opposing understandings of what is involved in the relationship between Indigenous peoples and mining. Marxist/mode of production theory regards the relationship as inherently and unavoidably exploitative of Indigenous peoples. Modernization theory, in contrast, sees mining and other forms of industrial activity as the only basis on which Indigenous peoples can advance their economic and social welfare. The following section examines regulation theory, which argues that both Marxist and modernization theories are flawed, that contemporary capitalism is fluid and dynamic, and that nations and communities can engage with the world capitalist economy in quite different ways depending on their 'modes of social regulation'. I then discuss neoliberal governance theory, which considers that the world is in a particular juncture in which Indigenous peoples are being offered the opportunity to engage with the mining industry, but that because the state is failing to protect the interest of its Indigenous peoples, this engagement is only available on terms deleterious to them. In the following sections, I consider three theoretical perspectives that are broad in focus but which might offer insights into the relationship between mining and Indigenous peoples. These are racism and whiteness; colonialism and postcolonialism; and gender theory. In concluding the chapter, I consider a fundamental issue on which all of the theories discussed adopt a position, which is the relative influence on outcomes for Indigenous peoples of 'structure' (material, institutional,

Indigenous Peoples and Mining. Ciaran O'Faircheallaigh, Oxford University Press. © Ciaran O'Faircheallaigh (2023).
DOI: 10.1093/oso/9780192894564.003.0002

and ideological factors that create the framework within which individuals, communities, and societies function); and 'agency', which refers to the ability of individuals and communities to take decisions and actions which shape their current and future livelihoods.

Much writing on Indigenous people and mining is primarily empirical and lacks explicit theory. It is therefore sometimes necessary to deduce underlying theoretical foundations from the way in which empirical analysis is undertaken and empirical findings are interpreted.

Marxism and modes of production

Drawing on Marxist concepts, this framework argues that the mining industry and Indigenous peoples represent fundamentally different and conflicting modes of production. Indigenous peoples, despite the many changes affecting their lives over recent centuries, engage in a mode of production that is based on consumption of resources they extract on a sustainable and long-term basis from areas of land and sea with which they have had an intimate association for generations. Their social and cultural relations reflect, and help sustain, shared connection with their ancestral lands. There is no drive to expand production beyond these lands, and there is a compelling need to sustain their productivity as this is the key to economic and social survival. Indigenous modes of production are place-based, social, autonomous, and sustainable.

The mining industry is part of a very different, capitalist mode of production that depends for its survival on continued expansion, and on 'primitive accumulation' which involves in part the extraction of wealth, in the form of minerals, from Indigenous lands. The industry's endless and growing demand for minerals also reflects the inherent and necessary tendency of capitalism to expand production. Unlike Indigenous peoples, the mining industry has no enduring connection to specific areas of land, and indeed the finite nature of mineral resources means the industry must inevitably move on to new sites of exploitation. Neither is the industry embedded in social relationships, and it is driven by individual and corporate pursuit of wealth. The mining industry's mode of production has no attachment to place; is individualistic and acquisitive; and its use of resources is unsustainable, involving the destruction of land and waters through the physical act of mining or as a result of the widespread pollution it causes (Hall 2013; Howlett et al. 2011; Kulchyski and Bernauer 2014: 6–7).

When two such diametrically opposed modes of production encounter one another, the inevitable result is conflict (Acuna 2015; Samson 2017). Mining literally consumes the land on which Indigenous livelihoods rely (Orihuela 2012: 693). The large influx of outsiders that typically accompanies mining, combined with the introduction or expansion of wage incomes, undermines Indigenous social and cultural practices, including food production and sharing (Dalseg et al. 2018: 148–9).

Given the superior economic and organizational resources available to the international mining industry, the outcome of conflict is the triumph of capitalism. This outcome is rendered even more certain because the state supports the expansion of mining at the expense of its Indigenous citizens. The state's role in this regard reflects the structural power of business under capitalism; the immediate incentives created for state agencies by the prospect of growing revenues from mining on Indigenous lands; and the political and electoral marginality of Indigenous peoples in all but a handful of states (Orihuela 2012: 694; Procter 2020).

There are some variations among 'mode of production' analysts, depending on whether or not they admit of any role for Indigenous agency. For those who do, this agency may allow Indigenous peoples to capture some of the wealth produced by mining in the form of jobs or of royalties paid to affected communities. It may also mean that some of this wealth is utilized to support continuation of elements of the Indigenous mode of production in the short term, as for instance where wages from mining are used to purchase equipment and fuel for use in subsistence hunting and fishing (Kulchyski and Bernauer 2014: 7–8). However, exercise of Indigenous agency has an impact only at the margin and in the longer term the Indigenous mode of production succumbs if mining is allowed to proceed (Howlett and Lawrence 2019).

Modernization theory and developmentalism

Modernization theory and developmentalism rest on the belief that there is an historical process, both inevitable and desirable, through which all parts of the globe are absorbed into industrial society on the model that characterized the transition of western Europe and the United States from agriculture to industry. Linked to concepts of progress as a linear and universal phenomenon, this approach envisages the disappearance of earlier cultural, social, and economic forms and their replacement with forms characteristic of Western industrial society. The latter include private rather than communal ownership of property, and more broadly the adoption of capitalist market systems, associated legal regimes, and liberal democratic political systems; social organization based on nuclear families, rather than on extended social networks based on kinship and/or cultural affiliation; and large urban centres rather than dispersed, small-scale communities (Natcher 2019; Samson 2017).

This approach underpins a great many corporate and state approaches to the issue of mining and Indigenous peoples (Dalseg et al. 2018; Samson 2017: 6–7; Sawyer 2004: 8), though it is rarely articulated as an explicit theoretical position. It suggests that mining constitutes a bastion of progress, by offering Indigenous peoples the opportunity to engage in market-based economic activity. Its underlying assumption is that use of labour, land, and resources is more productive in mining than within a subsistence economy, producing a surplus that is sufficient both to repay mining investors and to improve the material well-being of Indigenous peoples. Considerable emphasis is placed on the role of wage employment, both directly in mining and indirectly in industries supplying it with goods and services, as a mechanism for generating Indigenous incomes (Dalseg et al. 2018: 153). Wages are assumed to more than compensate for any loss of subsistence production resulting from the effects of mining (VBNC 1997: 49). Educational and employment opportunities associated with mining are understood to increase the underlying skills base of Indigenous peoples, which can then be applied in other projects or sectors when a particular mine runs out of ore (Natcher 2019).

Developmentalism and modernization theories pay little attention to the impact of mining on Indigenous cultural or social relations. It is assumed that the primary questions regarding development are economic, and that if the net economic impact of mining on Indigenous peoples is positive, its overall implications will also be positive. In addition, to the extent that mining does alter existing social and cultural forms, this is assumed to be an inevitable effect of 'progress' (Natcher 2019; Samson 2017).

Regulation and 'hybrid' theories

Regulation theory suggests that neither 'mode of production' nor 'modernization' theory accurately describes the current state of the global political economy or the choices available for states, communities, or peoples in engaging with it. A key argument is that there *are* choices in this regard, denying the determinism of both 'mode of production' and 'modernization' approaches (Corbridge 1990; Hirst and Zetlin 1991). Corbridge (1990: 633), for instance, argues that 'there is a powerful trend in post-Marxist circles toward theories of capitalist development which emphasize contingency, disorganization and structuration. In place of a topheavy structuralism, there is a new emphasis upon human agency … Side-by-side with this, post-Marxism is proving more sensitive to questions of gender, ethnicity and ideology'. This theoretical reorientation, according to Corbridge, reflects dramatic changes in the world economy, from a system that in 1950 'exhibited a seemingly simple order and division of labour', dominated by the United States and a few financial centres and national regulatory systems, and in which the 'Third World' provided only a source of cheap labour and raw materials. This world order has been replaced by a 'truly internationalized economy' in which trillions of dollars move around the world daily outside state control and in which 'a world of inter-dependent yet rival regional capitals and a system [of] multiple players' compete for influence (Corbridge 1990: 626).

Regulation theory argues that in this much more fluid and dynamic system 'modes of social regulation' determine the nature of engagement with the world capitalist economy, whether engagement occurs based on an acceptance of capitalist values of accumulation, or on alternative values that mobilize economic engagement towards other goals including environmental sustainability and self-determination. A mode of social regulation is 'a complex of institutions and norms which secure, at least for certain periods, the adjustment of individual agents and social groups to the overarching principles of the [capitalist] accumulation regime' (Hirst and Zetlin 1991: 19). Modes of social regulation are based on such things as habits and customs, social norms, laws, and institutional forms, and unique modes can exist at local, regional, national, or global scales. Regulation theory thus suggests that Indigenous groups can 'opt into' the global economy but do so on terms that reflect their own values, priorities, and ambitions (Anderson et al 2006; Bainton and Macintyre 2013).

A related approach, referred to as hybrid theory, has been applied by several scholars in Australia and Canada. They argue that there is no inherent incompatibility between mining specifically and capitalism in general, on the one hand, and Indigenous economies and peoples, on the other. This is because Indigenous peoples can utilize the elements of capitalist ventures that suit their purpose without compromising the integrity of their economies and societies. In one formulation of the hybrid approach, Altman and his colleagues (Altman and Kerins 2012) argue that Aboriginal peoples in north Australia have been able to combine wages and business income derived from commercial activities; land-based and cultural activities such as subsistence food production and sale of cultural artefacts; and public sector provision through welfare payments and subsidies for housing and other services. This melding of 'traditional' and 'modern' sources of livelihood is considered to be compatible with the long-term survival of Indigenous cultures and societies in forms that are different from those of earlier centuries or decades, but which are nevertheless distinctively Indigenous and vibrant (see also Natcher 2019: 229–30; Southcott 2015).

Regulation theory focuses mainly on modes of regulation at the national level (Hirst and Zetlin 1991: 18–19, 38), and while some writers acknowledge the significance of sub-national and civil society groups and institutions, they have little to say about how their characteristics or the strategies they adopt interact with the global political economy to bring about particular outcomes. Corbridge (1990: 633), for instance, notes the growing interest of regulation scholars in 'ethnicity', but does not explain its relevance or otherwise expand on this point. Similarly, hybrid theory focuses on establishing the principle that traditional or subsistence modes of production can still help provide viable livelihoods for Indigenous peoples within national market economies (Atman and Kerins 2012; Buchanan and May 2012). It is less concerned with exploring the efficacy or impact of 'hybrid' strategies that also involve engagement with the market economy, including extractive industries. Neither does regulation theory address the issue of whether, or at what point, specific 'modes of social regulation' may become incompatible with capitalism. Rather it is assumed that the concrete variability of different modes of engagement with capitalism is consistent with retaining the concept of capitalism as a dominant global mode of production that retains certain fundamental characteristics (Hirst and Zetlin 1991: 28). Particularly given the significant tensions between Indigenous and market-based economic and social systems (see Chapter 5), the question of whether the two are compatible remains open. The implications of specific Indigenous 'social formations' for the success or otherwise of engagements with capitalism is not addressed and also requires careful attention (on both points, see Bainton and Macintyre 2013).

In applying regulation theory to the entrepreneurial and business development activities of specific First Peoples in Canada, Anderson et al. (2006) claim that the two are compatible. They argue that the groups involved engage in the capitalist economy in a manner that generates economic surpluses in the form of business profits, but that these profits are not distributed to individuals but used for social purposes. Specifically, they are invested in developing Indigenous capacity for self-determination: for instance, through fostering Indigenous human capital, building and protecting an Indigenous land base, facilitating cultural transmission between generations, and reducing reliance on government funding. Anderson et al. (2006) argue that in combination with growing state recognition of Indigenous rights in land and Indigenous political autonomy, this approach means that engagement with capitalism need not lead to Indigenous marginalization and to external exploitation of Indigenous resources, but can rather support rising Indigenous living standards and growing Indigenous autonomy. Anderson et al. do not delve into the specific social formations of the First Peoples they discuss and consider how these might have affected the business investment and social outcomes they describe (Anderson et al. 2006: 51–4).

Neo-liberal governance theory

In relation to mining and Indigenous peoples, neo-liberal governance theory suggests that recent decades have seen a restructuring of relationships between the state, industry, and Indigenous peoples. It is argued that the state, intent on reducing regulation and public spending at the behest of business, has largely devolved responsibility for governance to industry. It has done this in particular through the use of contractual agreements under which terms for development of minerals on Indigenous land are negotiated between mining companies and Indigenous communities, rather than being established by the state (see Chapter 8). Yet at the same time the state creates legal and political frameworks that favour the mining industry and establishes a profound inequality in relations between the industry and Indigenous peoples (Howlett et al. 2011; Laforce et al. 2009). This occurs in particular because the ultimate power to allocate land and mineral resources remains with the state (Procter 2020). As a result, Indigenous peoples cannot stop mining from occurring on their ancestral lands, and so they lack the sanction that would create an equitable negotiation arena with industry (Laforce et al. 2009: 67; Scott 2020: 279).

Neo-liberal theorists also emphasize the unstable and finite nature of industrial activity based on mineral resources. Even if Indigenous communities can capture a significant share of the economic surplus generated by mining, the potential benefits are undermined in the short term by the erratic nature of mineral markets and prices, and in the longer term by the inevitable closure of exhausted mines. In the meantime, the material base that can support Indigenous livelihoods is seriously, and often fatally, compromised (Scott 2020: 280). Another problem is that mining creates or exacerbates divisions within Indigenous societies: for instance, on the basis of gender, given that women rarely have access to employment opportunities generated by the industry, or because Indigenous elites are able to appropriate benefits for themselves or their immediate families (Samson 2017: 15–16). These divisions undermine the wider familial and community relationships that are at the heart of Indigenous societies, further compromising their viability.

Bhatt (2020) argues that neo-liberalism is reflected in, and that its impacts are heightened by, contemporary financing arrangements in relation to large development projects, including mining projects, in the Global South. She contends that the contracts that states enter with international financial institutions and private developers involve states agreeing not to exercise their normal powers in areas such as taxation, trade controls, and environmental and labour regulation. In some cases, states agree that projects will be governed by the laws of the financier's home country, and will not be subject to international law (Bhatt 2020: 50). In her view this 'contracting out' by the state can be highly detrimental to the interests of affected Indigenous communities, which are left without the protections that domestic and international law would normally provide, heightening their vulnerability and increasing inequality (Bhatt 2020: 162–83).

Critics of neo-liberalism argue that government must again become involved in relations between industry and Indigenous peoples if continued exploitation is to be avoided. This position seems inconsistent with the reality that state authorities have rarely acted to protect Indigenous interests in the past, and so there is little reason to assume that they would so in the future (Procter 2020).

Racism and whiteness

Race theories, which posit that individuals derive core personal characteristics from membership of racial or cultural groups, can be seen as providing ideological support for the dispossession of Indigenous peoples and exploitation of their lands and resources for the benefit of dominant societies. The view that Indigenous peoples are inherently less intelligent, are amoral, lazy, and fail to make effective use of land and resources was used in colonial times as justification for driving them from their ancestral lands and denying them economic and political rights. In Australia, for instance, the legal doctrine of *terra nullius* or 'empty land' was based on the assumption that while Aboriginal people were present across the continent, they were incapable of making productive use of land. This was used as a justification for confiscating all territory that could be exploited for Western economic activity, in particular agriculture and mining. Some scholars argue that racism is still a powerful force. Orihuela (2012), for instance, shows how in Peru urban elites associate being 'white' with hard work and wealth, and being Indian with laziness and poverty.

Racism can thus be used to justify Indigenous dispossession and marginalization. It can be used, for instance, to trivialize the importance of Indigenous cultural heritage and justify a failure to modify mining practices so as to avoid its destruction. It can also be used to excuse mining companies from investing in Indigenous employment and training programs, on the basis that Indigenous people are incapable of the learning required to perform skilled roles or are incapable of sustained employment (Norris 2010). Racism can also be used to explain away continued Indigenous poverty, as mineral wealth is extracted from Indigenous lands, on the basis that poverty is an inherent feature of the Indigenous condition. On the other hand, if Indigenous people do acquire wealth, this can be used to argue that they have left behind what made them distinctive, and so there is no longer any need to recognize that they possess inherent Indigenous rights or interests that need to be addressed by the state or industry (Cattelino 2010).

Colonialism and postcolonialism

Theories of colonialism and postcolonialism focus on political and governing structures as these affect Indigenous peoples, particularly structures created by settler societies such as Australia and Canada. They stress that the denial of Indigenous sovereignty that was at the heart of the colonial enterprise continues today and is the defining issue in terms of relations between Indigenous peoples and dominant societies. The latter cannot accept the concept of Indigenous sovereignty because to do so would strike at the heart of their existence. 'Australia' or 'Canada' could not exist but for the denial of Indigenous sovereignty and the dispossession that accompanied it. In fact, Indigenous peoples never acceded to this denial of sovereignty. When they signed treaties in the eighteenth and nineteenth centuries in Canada, New Zealand, and the United States, for example, Indigenous peoples understood they were agreeing to share land and resources but believed they would continue to exercise sovereignty over their own affairs and the territories they retained. Settler states could not accept this interpretation as it would impose unacceptable constraints on the expanding colonial enterprise. They did everything in their power to undermine not only Indigenous sovereignty but the viability of Indigenous societies: for example, removing children, suppressing languages and cultural practices, and replacing existing modes of governance with patriarchal and elitist structures mirroring those of the colonial powers (Alfred 1999; Simpson, A. 2017; Simpson, L. B. 2017).

Efforts to deny and undermine Indigenous sovereignty continue. Even where states appear to accept claims for greater Indigenous autonomy, as in the settlement of land claims or the devolution of local governance and of public service provision, this inevitably involves a recognition by the Indigenous peoples concerned of the legitimacy of colonial settlement. Such recognition strikes at the heart of Indigenous identity and culture, and the prospects for the survival of distinct Indigenous peoples. Arrangements that embody recognition of colonial states also frequently involve extinction of inherent Indigenous rights in land, in return for grant of non-Indigenous forms of title over limited parts of ancestral territories. The result is continuing dispossession, making way for exploitation of Indigenous lands, especially for mineral extraction (Alfred 1999; Simpson, A. 2017; Simpson, L. B. 2017).

Colonial and postcolonial theories can be seen as linked to a mode of production approach in that colonial and postcolonial regimes open the way for and promote mineral extraction on Indigenous lands. However, Indigenous theorists in particular often deny the inevitability of the triumph of colonial and capitalist regimes. They argue that Indigenous individuals, communities, and peoples have the option of 'refusal', of denying the legitimacy of colonial regimes and refusing to recognize them or engage with them in any way. Such an approach, they argue, can provide a basis for the eventual recognition of Indigenous peoples as sovereign entities within the states concerned. They acknowledge that in the short term 'refusal' may well require individuals and communities to forgo the material benefits that can be extracted from engagement with the state and industry, and may impose on Indigenous people heavy costs associated with the repression that constitutes the state's response to resistance and refusal (Alfred 1999; Simpson, A. 2017; Simpson, L. B. 2017; see also Sawyer 2004). This position has obvious implications for the strategies of Indigenous engagement which are the focus of Part 3.

Other analysts embrace a less radical mode of 'refusal' and advocate an engagement with the state and industry but a rejection of the terms on which that engagement is usually offered. For example, Procter (2020) describes how Innu peoples have consistently refused to engage with Canada and the Province of Newfoundland and Labrador on the basis of state historical narratives and state definitions of 'Indigeneity' and Indigenous interests. For example, in negotiations regarding land claims and approvals processes for major projects, the Innu have refused 'settler-colonial narratives that identify indigeneity solely through past-tense cultural characteristics or limited economic need, [but rather] instead continuing to reshape environmental governance by defining their indigeneity in their own terms, as elsewhere and otherwise' (Procter 2020: 8). Similarly, Cattelino (2010: 249–50) describes how Florida Seminoles have for over a century refused to accept the US government's approach to Indian sovereignty and celebrate historical incidents of this refusal. At the same time the Seminoles are deeply involved in the capitalist economy via casinos, using the revenues they derive from gaming to fund the practical exercise of their sovereignty.

Gender theory

Gender theory takes as its starting point the existence of structural inequalities in access to power and resources between men and women, inequalities that define relationships between the two and shape the way in which families, kinship groups, and organizations function. These inequalities are reflected, for instance, in dominant societal norms regarding the relative abilities and needs of the genders;

in assumptions about what roles are appropriate for each in the private and public spheres; in their relative access to educational and employment opportunities; in the way in which the activities and work of each are valued and rewarded; and in the legal rights men and women are entitled to exercise (Acker 1990; Dalseg et al. 2018). Capitalist societies in particular 'are built upon a deeply embedded substructure of gender difference', with the result that 'power at the national and world level is located in all-male enclaves at the pinnacle of large state and economic organisations' (Acker 1990: 139). Feminist theorists use gender as an analytical category to understand the way in which gender inequality is created and maintained, and to provide a basis for action designed to bring about gender equality.

A fundamental implication of a gendered perspective is that it is insufficient and inappropriate to focus only on the interaction between mining and Indigenous 'peoples' or Indigenous 'communities'. It is also essential to focus separately on the impacts of mining on Indigenous men and women, because the nature of those impacts may be very different, reflecting inequalities based on gender (see Chapter 5 for a detailed discussion). For instance, men may have much greater access than women to employment opportunities in mining, and the impact of mining on the environment and on subsistence resources may affect men and women differently. Men may have a greater say then women in the distribution of financial benefits from mining, and where both have influence in this area, the outcomes that emerge may differ depending on the gender of decision-makers. Women may bear a heavy burden in maintaining domestic life, including care of children, when men work in mines. On a more structural level, over time the arrival of mining may alter existing gender relations within affected Indigenous societies, resulting in changes to the relative power of men and women in areas not directly related to mining, further marginalizing women from decision-making power, increasing inequality, and adversely affecting their quality of life (Dalseg et al. 2018; Lahiri-Dutt 2011; Macintyre 2011).

These issues are of particular importance when the source of change is the mining industry, which is male dominated and hierarchical, and evinces a 'macho' culture that is particularly indifferent or hostile to women and their interests and needs (see Chapter 7). As Dalseg et al. note (2018: 139) 'The masculine culture of these industries has meant that nearly all spaces associated with resource extraction, such as workplaces, boardrooms, or community meetings, are antagonistic to the participation of women.' One result of this situation can be a blindness to gender issues, a 'gender-blind, male-centred conceptualisation of development' (Lahiri-Dutt 2011: 2), and an assumption that 'the interests of some people within a community can be equated with the interests of all' and that 'if the benefits of mining extend to men they will automatically trickle down to women' (Lahiri-Dutt 2011: 4). In this context, decision makers may not even be aware of gender issues and so fail to address them, and may take actions that seriously exacerbate inequality.

Structure and agency

Underlying these theoretical approaches are assumptions about the relative power of structure and agency. 'Structure' refers to underlying material, institutional, and ideological factors that are generally slow to change and create the framework within which individuals, communities, and societies function. 'Agency' refers to the ability of individuals and communities to take decisions and actions which reflect their goals and values, and shape their current and future livelihoods. The theories reviewed above can be seen as sitting on a spectrum in terms of their approach to the agency of Indigenous peoples. At one end of the spectrum, 'mode of production' theories emphasize structure, in this case the core features of capitalism, and leave little room for the exercise of Indigenous agency, or for agency on the part of any entity that exists in opposition to capitalism. The world *must* conform to the needs of capital (Corbridge 1990: 623, 625). Neo-liberal governance theory comes to similar conclusions, arguing that opportunities that have recently emerged for Indigenous peoples to engage in consultation and negotiations constitute a chimera designed to give the appearance of Indigenous influence but leaving power relations and outcomes unchanged. If Indigenous people participate, they are being duped. If they do not participate, they have no opportunity to influence outcomes. In either case, they are powerless to shape their fate (Howlett and Lawrence 2019; Scobie and Rodgers 2019).

At the other end of the spectrum, 'hybrid' theory suggests that Indigenous agency is powerful. Indigenous peoples are able to pick and choose elements of capitalist and Indigenous modes of production to create livelihoods that maintain key elements of their culture and society, while providing access to material benefits offered by Western capitalism. Regulation theory would also assign significant agency to Indigenous communities and First Peoples through the impact of their social formations on the nature of their engagement with capitalism.

Colonial and postcolonial theories could be seen as falling in between, recognizing the power of the structural forces aligned against Indigenous peoples but arguing that they do have the choice and the capacity to resist those forces, albeit at considerable cost to themselves. A similar approach is adopted by some South American scholars who believe that an accumulation of historical forces has created structural tendencies that predispose a nation or region to generate specific outcomes for Indigenous peoples. For instance, Orihuela (2012) argues that Peru's current political system is especially prone to conflict. This reflects its colonial history, the ethnic structure resulting from this, the impact of racism, economic dependence on a small number of primary export industries, poorly functioning institutions, and the position of its coastal capital, Lima, as an elite-dominated enclave exploiting the peoples and industries of the hinterland. In his view this is a context which, even though Indigenous peoples constitute a large proportion of Peru's population, fosters 'subtle racism [which] reconstructs indelible inequalities', and which explainscontinuing

Indigenous marginalization and the extent and severity of the conflict that accompanied expansion of mining into Indigenous territories from the 1990s. Orihuela does not view this outcome as predetermined, but rather as resulting from a series of policy choices made by political elites which could have been otherwise and created a 'counterfactual' with different outcomes for Peru, including its Indigenous peoples (2012: 701–2).

The nineteenth-century German theorist Tonnies (1887/2001) addresses the structure versus agency debate in the context of small communities and the global capitalist system. His work has been used recently, for example, in analysing the relationship between Aboriginal communities and fly-in, fly-out uranium projects in northern Canada (Jensen and Sandström 2020). Tonnies used the concepts of *Gemeinschaft* and *Gesellschaft* to examine the relationship between community and capitalism. Tonnies believed that while *Gesellschaft*, or capitalism, is global in its reach, its triumph is far from inevitable. It is essential to recognize that the impact of structural forces is mitigated or countered by *Gemeinschaft*, or human agency and discretion on the ground. *Gemeinschaft* and *Gesellschaft* are not mutually exclusive, and indeed he argued that structural forces have their origins in, and structural change is driven by, human agency. The result is that as capitalism spreads across the globe, the bonds of community are not sundered, and the possibility of agency remains, with the result that quite different consequences may result from the introduction of capitalist forms of production in different locations and social contexts (Jensen and Sandström 2020: 79).

Conclusion

This chapter has reviewed theoretical perspectives that can inform analysis of relationships between Indigenous peoples and extractive industries, and whose validity and utility can be tested in seeking to apply them in this way. Some of the theories are antagonistic and mutually exclusive: for instance, mode of production and modernization theories, or each of these theories and regulation theory. Gender theory could be seen as irrelevant to mode of production theory as the latter suggests that mining will destroy Indigenous society, and so gender relations within that society become moot. Gender theory, on the other hand, might be applied alongside modernization theory, suggesting that if the latter's assumption is correct and the benefits of mining do 'trickle down' to Indigenous men, they will not trickle down to Indigenous women. Gender theory could also be applied in conjunction with colonialism and postcolonialism, arguing that the racism and marginalization experienced by Indigenous men affects Indigenous women even more severely as a result of being reinforced by patriarchy and sexism. Like Indigenous scholars who espouse the possibility of refusal in the face of colonial regimes, feminist theorists would argue that despite the deeply embedded nature of gender inequality in capitalist society, it is possible for women to identify the sources of that inequality and fight to remove them.

In applying the theories in later chapters, the goal is not to pick one theory regarded as superior in every respect. Rather it is to assess the relative power of theories, alone or in combination, in explaining the patterns that can be observed in interactions between Indigenous peoples and mining across different parts of the globe.

3

History

Indigenous Peoples and Mining in the Nineteenth and Twentieth Centuries

Introduction

This book is about contemporary interactions between Indigenous peoples and the mining industry. The history of relations between Indigenous peoples and miners provides a critical part of the context for these interactions, setting patterns whose impact is still evident today. In this regard, two periods of history are especially significant.[1] The first involves the 'gold rushes' that occurred in different parts of the globe in the mid-nineteenth century, because they played a key role in defining the relative power of, and relations between, Indigenous peoples, miners, and states. They also helped form the foundations of the legal systems that govern mining to this day. The second is the rapid expansion of mining in the decades after 1945 in response to the long post-war economic boom. This period saw the emergence of the modern global mining industry, which is characterized by mines that are massive in physical and economic scale and dominated by powerful corporations operating across national boundaries and industry sectors. It also saw the state develop a much more active role in encouraging and facilitating, rather than adjusting to, mining in Indigenous territories (Carvalho 2017).

The gold rushes were characterized by violence against Indigenous peoples and their dispossession and marginalization—violence which in many cases was facilitated or condoned by the state. At the same time, Indigenous people often displayed considerable agency, ingenuity, and persistence in resisting marginalization and, faced with the destruction of Indigenous economic resources that mining wrought, in finding ways to earn livelihoods within the new economy. Indeed, Indigenous people were responsible for or assisted in major mineral discoveries during the gold rushes, and they mined on their own behalf, worked in the industry, or traded with miners. This engagement, ignored in mining history until recently, is highlighted using recent research in North America, Australia, and New Zealand (Cahir 2012; Carpenter 2016; Ellwood 2014; Ellwood and Wegner 2019).

---

[1] This is not to suggest that exploitation of mineral resources on Indigenous lands only started with the nineteenth-century gold rushes. See, for example, Santayo (2002: 20–1) on Spanish exploitation of gold and silver resources in the sixteenth century.

Indigenous Peoples and Mining. Ciaran O'Faircheallaigh, Oxford University Press. © Ciaran O'Faircheallaigh (2023).
DOI: 10.1093/oso/9780192894564.003.0003

Dispossession and marginalization continued well into the twentieth century, as indicated by the experience of Indigenous peoples with the post-Second World War mining boom, illustrated here with examples from Australia, Indonesia, and the former Soviet Union. At the same time, the opportunities for Indigenous peoples to gain alternative livelihoods from mining were much more limited than during the gold rushes, as large-scale mining of industrial minerals such as copper, iron ore, and bauxite required huge capital investments that could only be undertaken by multinational mining companies and state industrial enterprises.

The experiences of specific First Peoples must be seen in the context of dominant attitudes towards Indigenous peoples among Europeans and European settlers in the nineteenth and the first half of the twentieth centuries. Social Darwinism provided an overarching ideology in this regard. The world's human population was seen as arranged in a hierarchy of intelligence, progress, and moral worth, with Europeans at its pinnacle and all other peoples occupying lower places on the pyramid. Indigenous peoples were generally regarded as occupying its base, and were often seen as barely human, 'beasts in human shape' according to one British settler's description of Australian Aboriginal people. They were seen as lacking intelligence, lazy, unable to make productive use of land and other resources, and, like other species lacking the ability to compete and survive, destined for extinction. Such beliefs provided a justification for depriving Indigenous peoples of their lands and resources, for cheating them of their gold, for killing or forcibly relocating any who resisted, and for a refusal by the state to render them any assistance on the basis that this would be wasted on peoples who were believed to be dying out (Cahir 2012: 122–3; Rawls 1976: 36).

Before focusing on relations between Indigenous peoples and outside forces, it is important to note that Indigenous people often engaged in mining prior to their contact with Europeans. The oldest ochre mine identified in Australia was worked from around 32,000 to 13,000 years ago (Ellwood 2014: 61). Aboriginal people in Victoria quarried for crystal, greenstone, sandstone, obsidian, kaolin, ochres, and basalt, at times digging shafts to a considerable depth, and they traded extensively in quarried stone (Cahir 2012: 7–9). Minerals and mining were far from an unknown quantity, which helps explain the ability of many Indigenous peoples quickly to take advantage of economic opportunities provided by the arrival of European gold miners.

The gold rushes

In terms of mining activity whose impact can clearly be seen in the contemporary period, an appropriate starting point is with the gold rushes of the mid-nineteenth century, including California (1848–50), the Australian colonies of Victoria and New South Wales (1851–5), New Zealand (1857–64), and the Canadian province of British Columbia (1858–9). Their impact on Indigenous peoples and territories was devastating, involving the sudden arrival of tens of thousands of miners who were often entirely unrestrained by government regulation. They were driven by a determination to make their fortunes, and regarded Indigenous peoples as primitive or even subhuman and lacking any legal or moral standing. The impact of the California gold rush was especially brutal and severe, according to Wilson (1998: 228) 'probably the most destructive episode in the whole history of Native/Euro-American relations'. Castillo (1998) describes the California gold rush:

> Within a year a hoard [sic] of 100,000 adventurers from all over the world descended upon the native peoples of California with catastrophic results ... Thinly spread government officials were overwhelmed by this unprecedented deluge of immigrants and all effective authority collapsed. A virtual reign of terror enveloped tribesmen in the mining districts ... Numerous vigilante type paramilitary troops were established whose principal occupation seems to have been to kill Indians and kidnap their children ... The handiwork of these well-armed death squads combined with the widespread random killing of Indians by individual miners resulted in the death of 100,000 Indians in the first two years of the gold rush. A staggering loss of two thirds of the population. Nothing in American Indian history is even remotely comparable to this massive orgy of theft and mass murder. Stunned survivors now perhaps numbering fewer than 70,000 teetered near the brink of total annihilation [see also Starr 1998].

Contemporary accounts also document the routine perpetration of sexual violence by miners against Indian women and the murder of Indian men who sought to prevent such assaults or retaliated against white perpetrators (Rawls 1976; Wilson 1998: 228–9).

The scale and severity of the destruction reflected a specific set of historical and political factors, including the fact that California had only recently been annexed from Mexico by the United States and had no effective government (Allen 2007: 17); the weakening of Indigenous societies and populations already caused by centuries of Spanish and Mexican colonization, including decimation of Indigenous populations by disease and systemic labour exploitation; and the fact that many of the miners seem to have been driven by a deep-rooted racial hatred. It also reflected the general approach of the United States to its Indigenous peoples, based on deliberate and systematic extermination and relocation to remote barren areas of no interest to white farmers or industrialists (Castillo 1998; Wilson 1998: 228–9). This last factor was evident from the fact that state and federal governments eventually reimbursed the paramilitary groups for expenses incurred in their murderous activities. It is also reflected in the attitude of California's first governor after the establishment of US rule, who in his maiden speech to the state legislature promised that 'a war of extermination will continue to be waged between the races until the Indian race becomes extinct' (cited in Castillo 1998).

A contemporary commentator on the California gold rush placed the situation there in a national context:

> The late emigrants from across the mountains, and especially from Oregon, had commenced a war of extermination upon them, shooting them down like wolves, men and women and children, wherever they could find them ... Thus has been

renewed in California the war of extermination against the aborigines, commenced
in effect at the landing of Columbus, and continued to this day, gradually and surely
tending to the final and utter extinction of the race. (cited in Rawls 1976: 42)

California Indians resisted the incursion of miners and squatters into their lands,
at times inflicting significant casualties. However, their efforts were futile given the
numerical superiority of the invaders and the consistent failure of state and federal
governments to render them protection or support. They were relegated to tiny and
impoverished corners of their ancestral estates (Castillo 1998; Rawls 1976: 38).

In other settler colonies and in particular where government rule was established
prior to the discovery of gold, the extreme excesses of California were generally
avoided (Allen 2007: 8–9). (An exception was the gold rush on the Fraser river
in southern British Columbia in 1858 when American miners crossed the border
and used violence in a systematic and organized way, reminiscent of California, to
'remove impediments' in the form of Indian opposition: Marshall 2002). This did
not mean that killings of Indigenous people and sexual violence against Indigenous
women were absent. They certainly were not (Cahir 2012: 109; Canadian Museum
of Immigration and the University of Western Ontario 2020). However, murder was
less systematic, on a smaller scale, and less likely to be officially sanctioned.

Regardless of the specific context, the impact of mining on Indigenous livelihoods
was dramatic and often irreversible. This occurred because of the devasting effect
of diseases introduced by miners; the destructive impact of extensive placer mining
on land and waters that were essential to Indigenous survival; and the widespread
depletion of wild flora and fauna by miners who often lacked access to other sources
of fresh food. Mining's impact in this regard is illustrated by contemporary accounts
from the Australian state of Victoria, where Aboriginal people were able to participate actively in gold mining and large-scale organized killings were rare. One traveller
described how 'The diggers [miners] seem to have two especial propensities, those of
firing guns and felling trees … every tree is felled … every feature of Nature is anni-
hilated' (cited in Cahir 2012: 118). The colonial government board responsible for
Aboriginal administration warned of 'vast quantities of fish destroyed annually by
netting and the swivel gun … Both fish and game are ruthlessly killed in such a manner as to injure, not only the interests of the blacks but those of the colonists generally'
(cited in Cahir 2012: 118). Numerous contemporary sources attest to the disappearance of Aboriginal people from their traditional lands as these were damaged by gold
mining and as wild game was exterminated (Cahir 2012: 119).

Mining also brought adverse social and cultural impacts. In some cases, introduction of alcohol resulted in breaches of social norms, fostered internal conflict,
led to the abandonment of cultural activities and food production, and adversely
affected people's health. Cultural sites were desecrated by miners, whose liaisons with
Indigenous women also often led to conflict. Outsiders sometimes interfered with
ceremonial and cultural activities, and the commercialization of those activities in
order to generate income from entertaining miners was a further source of internal
tensions (Anderson 1983; Cahir 2012: 112–17).

As in California, Indigenous peoples elsewhere resisted the depredations of miners as best they could. In Victoria, Aboriginal people tried to assert their status as landowners and their right to exercise control over what happened on their land, and to insist on sharing the benefits from exploitation of their resources. One government official was rebuked by an Aboriginal man who had been accused of theft in the following terms: 'What for you say I steal? What for you steal my country? *You* big one thief. What for you quamby [camp] along o'here? Geego along o' your country, and let blackfellow alone' (emphasis in original; cited in Cahir 2012: 88). Aboriginal landowners threatened trespassers, forcibly removed Aboriginal women from miners who had absconded with them, and at times met violence with violence.

Yet as in California they were unable to stem the relentless wave of dispossession that accompanied both the earlier phase of agricultural settlement and the influx of gold miners. The profound nature of their dispossession is reflected in the response of one Aboriginal man when a magistrate asked him if he had any children: 'Why me have lubra [wife]? Why me have piccaniny [children]? You have all this place, no good have children, no good have lubra, me tumble down and die very soon now' (cited in Cahir 2012: 90).

The participation of Indigenous peoples in the gold rushes has often been relegated to, literally, a footnote (see, for example, Allen 2007: 5, n. 12). An image of the gold rushes as excluding Indigenous peoples entirely would be misleading, especially in misrepresenting their agency in the face of often profound external impacts. Even in the California gold rush, they played an important and active role in the early phases of mining. They were involved in the first discoveries and provided a large portion of the labour involved in the initial phase of gold mining (Wilson 1998: 228). However, reflecting the existing system of labour exploitation established by Spain and continued by Mexico, they were initially paid only in food and other provisions. Indians did also work as free agents, bartering the gold they won for trade goods, though these exchanges were often highly exploitative. Numerous contemporary reports discuss Indians exchanging gold for beads and other trinkets, and describe cheating by white traders: for example, tampering with weights to understate the amount and value of gold presented by Indian miners. As time passed, they became more savvy traders and began to bargain to extract greater value from their gold (Rawls 1976). However, the participation of Indians miners was short-lived, contemporary commentators noting that within two years they had virtually disappeared from the goldfields. This seems to reflect the growing violence against them, particularly by newly arriving miners from other parts of the United States, and the consequent tendency of Indians to avoid contact with Europeans. It also reflected the exhaustion of surface gold deposits easily accessible to miners with no capital, and the growing dominance of mechanized mining that required substantial investment beyond the reach of Indian miners (Rawls 1976).

Recent research based on contemporary accounts by miners and government officials and the diaries and sketches of travellers and artists has led to a reappraisal of the role of Aboriginal people in one of the nineteenth century's great gold rushes, in the Australian colony of Victoria in the 1850s. As their land and food supplies were usurped, Aboriginal people found ways of earning a livelihood from the mining industry. They helped miners find new sources of gold; undertook mining on their own behalf; took jobs as cooks, laundry workers, and child minders; and sold food, blankets made from possum skins, building supplies, services, and entertainment (in the form of corroborees or traditional displays of singing and dancing) to the miners. In doing so they displayed considerable commercial acumen. As occurred with some Europeans, they sometimes found it more lucrative to trade with miners than to undertake the laborious work of mining themselves (Cahir 2012: 68–9, 73–83). One traveller reported an encounter with Dja Dja Wurrung people, whose descendants are in 2022 involved in negotiating agreements with multinational gold-mining companies, in the following terms: 'Even the Aborigines are wealthy. I met a party of them at Bullock Ck well clothed, with a good supply of food, new cooking utensils and money in their pockets. One remarked with a becoming expression of dignity "me no poor blackfellow now, me plenty rich blackfellow"' (cited in Cahir 2012: 24).

Aboriginal people also worked for the colonial administration. Armed Aboriginal police, who were originally recruited to track escaped convicts and lost or stolen livestock, were regularly used to escort gold shipments from the Victorian goldfields to Melbourne, the state capital. They were also used to enforce mining laws and collection of licence fees from miners, earning the wrath of the latter (Cahir 2012: 47–55). It is rare to find Indigenous people enforcing state law on miners, but its occurrence warns against oversimplified characterization of the engagement of Indigenous peoples with mining.

Cahir summarizes the situation of Aboriginal peoples affected by the gold rushes in Victoria as follows: 'Not only has the traditional story of gold (characterized by a mistaken assumption that the "Aborigines were swept aside") been shown to be untrue, there is now clear evidence that Aboriginal people were conscious actors and active participants in Australia's economic history, rather than passive spectators or pawns in another culture's game' (2012: 2–3). The specific context is important in this regard. Frontier warfare, earlier widespread, had now largely ceased, and many Aboriginal people had prior experience of wage labour and of dealing with white employers in the pastoral industry (Cahir 2012: 9, 11). Conditions for Indigenous participation were often less favourable elsewhere, as the discussion of California indicates. It should also be noted that some Aboriginal people refused to have any dealings with mining or miners, went out of their way to avoid them, and indeed publicly expressed their distaste for the 'whitefellow all gone mad digging holes and washing stones' (Cahir 2012: 89, 124). This of course reinforces Cahir's point about Aboriginal people not being pawns in someone else's game. Indeed, Cahir's description of the Aboriginal response to mining is reminiscent of the 'hydrid' school of thought's approach to contemporary Indigenous engagement with capitalism: they were 'actively choosing to be two-way people—opting to balance their traditional lifestyles with some participation in the non-Indigenous economic milieu ... [they] were neither dependent on non-Indigenous people's material goods nor willing to forgo their Aboriginal cultural imperatives for a life of dreary servitude' (Cahir 2012:

106; see Ellwood and Wegner 2019 for the experience of Aboriginal miners in other, later gold rushes in Australia).

The situation in New Zealand was similar to Victoria, with Maori people responsible for important gold discoveries, undertaking mining on their own behalf, and supplying miners with goods and services. They also travelled to California and Australia to take part in gold mining. At the same time, some Maori wanted nothing to do with mining and refused to disclose locations where they knew gold was to be found (Carpenter 2013, 2016). However as in California, in both Australia and New Zealand Indigenous participation faded rapidly when easily accessible surface gold deposits were exhausted and mining required substantial capital investment in equipment such as water sluices, dredges, and stamping machines to crush rock (Cahir 2012; Carpenter 2016).

The very particular nature of the gold rushes, involving huge influxes of miners who were driven by the lure of quick riches and frequently did not stay long before moving on to the next 'rush', must also be stressed. Other forms of mining—for example, of tin—involved much longer-term commitments by miners, who often worked the same claims on a continuous basis for years and even decades. This form of mining led to quite different types of relationships with, and impacts on, Indigenous peoples. For instance, Anderson (1983) has shown how in the decades after 1885 tin miners in far north Queensland established relations of mutual dependency with local Aboriginal clans. Indeed, the employment opportunities provided by tin mining allowed Aboriginal people to stay on their ancestral estates, maintain cultural practices, and avoid removal by the Queensland government to distant mission reserves, a fate that befell many Aboriginal people in adjacent regions where mining was absent.

Two specific aspects of the portrayal of Indigenous engagement with mining both in popular accounts and in much of the literature deserve to be highlighted. The first involves the tendency to credit non-Indigenous miners with discoveries that were actually made by Indigenous peoples, a tendency which, it should be noted, persisted into the era of large-scale industrial mining of iron ore and other minerals in the twentieth century (Boutet 2014). In New Zealand, for example, a rich discovery on the Arrow river which led to a major gold rush in 1862 was claimed by a miner called William Fox and the field became known as 'Fox's Rush'. In reality, the discovery was made by a Maori man, Jack Tewa, known at the time as 'Maori Jack', in the previous year (Carpenter 2016: 94). Similarly, a number of key discoveries in north Queensland from the 1860s to the 1920s were made by Aboriginal people but attributed to white miners (Ellwood 2014). One of these, a woman miner called Altengen and known as Kitty Pluto, was especially successful, finding several large gold nuggets and making discoveries that resulted in the establishment of mining fields. In her case recognition did eventually come, with the Queensland government awarding her a full pension for discovering a goldfield. She is the only Aboriginal woman recognized in this way, though not the only one to discover a goldfield (Ellwood 2014: 71, 79).

The second aspect is the frequent suggestion that Indigenous people were fundamentally disinterested in gold and the economic benefits it could create and that any involvement they had in mining was ephemeral and often accidental. For instance, in 2012 residents of the historic gold-mining town of Arrowtown erected a plaque finally recognizing the role of Jack Tewa in the discovery of gold on the Arrow river. Part of the text states: 'In August 1862, Jack Tewa, known as Maori Jack, found gold near the spot … Tewa was not particularly interested in gold mining but the word of his find got out to those that were' (Carpenter 2013: 112). In fact, in 1865, four years after discovering gold on the Arrow river, Jack Tewa banked £400, worth about A\$50,000 in 2021, from gold he had extracted from just one claim. He told an acquaintance he hoped to use some of the money to travel to England and seek an audience with Queen Victoria (Carpenter 2016: 94). As will become apparent in later chapters, the assumption that Indigenous people are inherently disinterested in benefiting from the wealth created by mining is a view that still has considerable currency.

The state and the gold rushes

The presence and role of state authorities varied considerably from one context to another. As noted, the state was virtually non-existent when the California gold rushes started and whatever regulation and legal framework existed was created by the miners themselves (Allen 2007). The same initially applied in southern British Columbia (Marshall 2002). In Australia, white settlement had started a generation before the gold rushes with the pastoral industry, and the state apparatus was well established. Despite the remoteness of the Klondike gold rush in Canada's Yukon territory in the 1890s, Royal Canadian Mounted Police (RCMP) were quickly despatched once the rush started, and they immediately established and enforced a regulatory system for mining (Allen 2007; Cahir 2012).

Whatever the specific circumstances, the state showed an unwillingness in every case to support the rights or interests of Indigenous peoples against the mining onslaught, and a disinterest in helping them to build alternative livelihoods as they lost their land and food supplies. If any justification was provided for this reluctance, it was that Indigenous peoples were doomed to extinction and so there was no point in 'wasting' resources on them. The attitude of state officials was typified by the direction given by the Canadian government to the RCMP officer it despatched to the Klondike to help regulate the gold rush there. The Han Indigenous landowners had been forcibly relocated to clear the way for a new mining town, and the officer was told not to treat the Han 'in any way which would lead them to believe that the Government would do anything for them as Indians' (cited in Canadian Museum of Immigration and the University of Western Ontario 2020). The colonial administration in Victoria had adopted a similar stance during the 1850s gold rush (Cahir 2012: 121–2).

Even where meagre and entirely inadequate allocations were made by government to help relieve destitute and at times starving Indigenous peoples, they were often spent on the wages of white officials or appropriated for their own benefit by corrupt government officers (Cahir 2012: 121; Castillo 1998).

A key action that all state authorities did take was to establish a system of 'free entry' for miners, or to give legislative effect to such a system that miners had already established. This meant that miners could enter and occupy any land, regardless of land tenure; 'stake' claims by marking the boundaries of the relevant area with corner posts; exclude other miners; look for minerals within that area; and, if they located any, have the right to exploit them (see Hoogeveen 2015 for the ideological and legal foundations of this approach and details of how it functioned). Underlying the free entry system was an assumption that mining constituted the optimal use for land, regardless of how it was currently employed and, following on from this, that miners should be permitted to enter land even where the owner objected. Its establishment was of enormous significance. Variants of the free entry system, and the associated ability to buy and sell mining tenures once granted by the state, came to form the fundamental basis of mining and land law in settler states: for instance, in British Columbia's Gold Fields Act (1859) and the American General Mining Law (1872), as well as in many other contexts (see, for example, Santayo 2002 on Colombia's mining law). The priority afforded to mining over other land uses is still a feature of the legal and political landscape in most modern states (Hoogeveen 2015; Lander 2020: 109), an issue we return to at many points in the book. The priority attached to mining underpinned not only the free entry system but government resource allocation systems generally. For instance, Boileau (2016: 131) shows how in New Zealand legislation gave priority to mining in allocating water, and how local authorities and market gardeners were forced to undertake lengthy legal battles to try and ensure access to sufficient water for their needs.

The Post-Second World War mining boom

In the decades after 1945, as the world experienced a sustained economic boom, the global mining industry expanded rapidly. The value of Australia's mineral production, for instance, grew more than eightfold between 1952 and 1978 (Govett and Govett 1980: 89). Higher-grade ore deposits closer to industrial markets were largely exhausted by this time, requiring exploitation of lower-grade orebodies in more geographically remote and climatically extreme parts of the world. These were the same regions where Indigenous peoples had been better able to retain control and use of their ancestral lands, because they were generally unsuitable for European agriculture for environmental reasons or because of their distance from major markets. The 1950s, 1960s, and 1970s saw the development of numerous large-scale mining projects on Indigenous lands, enthusiastically supported by governments anxious to cash in on the new resources boom. Indigenous peoples were largely unable either to stop mining or to benefit from it. Indigenous people had been able to participate at least in the initial phases of the earlier gold rushes because gold was easily accessible using human labour and the simplest of equipment. The new phase of mining expansion required massive capital investment in sophisticated technology and complex infrastructure, ruling out active Indigenous participation. The Indigenous experience can be illustrated by the following examples from different parts of the globe and a variety of political and legal contexts.

Bauxite mining, far north Queensland, Australia

In 1955 the exploration arm of the Melbourne-based company Consolidated Zinc was issued Authorities to Prospect (ATPs) to explore for bauxite over an area of 2,585 square miles of Western Cape York in far north Queensland. Extensive bauxite deposits were located and in 1956 Comalco Ltd was established as the vehicle that would develop them. Shortly afterwards Consolidated Zinc merged with Rio-Tinto Mining, and Conzinc Rio Tinto of Australia Ltd became the Australian component of the new entity, with the London-based Rio Tinto-Zinc Corporation as its major shareholder.

ATPs allowed the mining companies that held them to negotiate Special Bauxite Mining Leases (SBMLs), each covered by dedicated legislation. Under the Comalco Act (1957), the Queensland government awarded Comalco a mining lease in western Cape York covering an area of 2,380 square miles. Its term extended to January 2042, with an option to renew for a further 21 years, a combined term of 106 years. Comalco's lease was granted over an area that had previously been an Aboriginal reserve set aside for the exclusive use of its Aboriginal inhabitants, with the mining lease constituting 93 per cent of the area of the reserve. Comalco's SBML was excised from the reserve without any reference to the wishes or interests of its Aboriginal inhabitants. This action was consistent with a general policy and legislative regime in Queensland and Australia, which at this time failed to recognize the fundamental human, democratic, and property rights of Aboriginal people (O'Faircheallaigh 2016: 50–4).

Over the period 1961–4, Comalco developed large-scale mining operations, power and transport infrastructure, and a port to ship its bauxite on the Weipa peninsula. It also established the Weipa township, complete with new shops, hospital, schools, and recreational and sporting facilities, to house non-Aboriginal workers and associated service personnel such as teachers, medical staff, and police. By the early 1970s Comalco was producing 10 million tonnes of bauxite per annum. The Weipa bauxite operations provided the platform for Comalco to develop as a fully integrated producer of alumina, aluminium metal, and manufactures, with refineries, smelters, and factories in Queensland, Tasmania, New Zealand, and Sardinia.

The archaeological evidence indicates that Aboriginal people have lived in western Cape York for some 30,000 years. By the early 1960s most Aboriginal people in the area were resident at mission settlements at Aurukun, Napranum, and Mapoon, all located on or close to Comalco's lease, for at least part of the year. Many still continued to hunt, fish, and gather on their traditional country. No attention was paid to their needs or interests in the establishment of Comalco's operations. For instance, while the Comalco Act (1957) required the company to ensure that it did not deplete regional water resources so as to undermine the operations of other explorers or miners, no mention was made of the needs of Aboriginal people who relied on access to water for their livelihoods. While large areas of Aboriginal land were handed over to Comalco, Aboriginal people gained little from its operations. For instance, few of them were employed in the mine, with the bulk of the workforce comprised of non-Aboriginal people recruited from outside the region. Twenty-five years after the mine was established, fewer than one in ten workers were Aboriginal (Cousins and Nieuwenhuysen 1984: 2). As occurred throughout Australia, no rents or royalties were payable to Aboriginal landowners.

The Queensland government's destruction of the Aboriginal community of Mapoon in 1963 illustrates the complete disregard with which Aboriginal people and their property were treated. It was initially envisaged that Comalco would need to build a second port to ship its bauxite, in a bay north of Weipa on which Mapoon was located. Over the period 1957–63, the Queensland government sought to close the Mapoon community to make way for the port: for example, shutting the only store in the town, and falsely claiming that parasites present in beach sand in the community constituted a health hazard. Many residents left, but over a hundred refused to yield to pressure and remained. On the night of 15 November 1963, armed Queensland police forcibly removed the remaining Mapoon residents to a location hundreds of kilometres away at the tip of Cape York, on the lands of other Aboriginal peoples. They burned down all buildings at Mapoon, including the church and people's private houses and the possessions they contained, to stop people returning to their community. It was to be over a decade before some former residents returned and began to re-establish Mapoon (Holden 1996). To add insult to injury, the second port was never built.

The experience of Aboriginal people in Cape York was replicated at numerous other projects across Australia in the 1960s and 1970s. The title of a paper by Richie Howitt on the goldfields of Western Australia, 'All they get is the dust', expresses very well the way in which Aboriginal peoples were relegated to the fringes of Australia's post-1945 mining boom (Howitt 1990).

Copper and gold in Indonesia

In 1967 the American company Freeport McMoran ('Freeport') began development of a large copper/gold orebody called Ertsberg, located at a height of 4,100 metres and some 170 kilometres from the coast in West Papua (also known as Irian Jaya), which comprises the western half of the island of New Guinea. Formerly a Dutch colony, the administration of West Papua was transferred to Indonesia in 1963. Freeport built a road and slurry pipeline to transport copper/gold concentrate to the coast, where it constructed a port, an airstrip, and a new town called Tembagapura. Commercial production started in December 1972. Freeport subsequently discovered an even larger orebody, Grassberg, adjacent to its initial find. Grassberg was to become the world's largest gold mine and its second biggest copper mine, and one of the world's richest mining operations (Ballard 2001). Freeport disposes of massive quantities of waste, known as tailings, from its ore-milling operations directly into the Agabagong river, which flows into the Aijkwa river and thence into the Arafura Sea. At times waste has overflowed the banks of the Aijkwa river, as for example in 1990 when tailings inundated an area of 30 square kilometres of lowland forest (Ballard 2001: 23).

The land on which Freeport made its discoveries belongs to a Melanesian people called the Amungme, and the coastal area where the town and port were built to the Kamoro people. Prior to Freeport's arrival they engaged in a subsistence lifestyle, combining garden cultivation with hunting and fishing. Under Indonesian law, traditional land or *adat* fell into the category of lands not 'effectively used', and so was designated as state-owned land to be used for the welfare of the nation (Soares 2004: 122). Neither Indigenous group was consulted by the company or the Indonesian government regarding plans to develop the mine and to relocate people whose land would be required by Freeport, or regarding the contract between Indonesia and Freeport which allowed its development. The mountain tops where Freeport's orebodies are located are sacred to the Amungme, and when Freeport arrived in the area the Amungme set up *salib* signs, crosses of wood that traditionally indicated that trespass beyond the point indicated was not permitted by the owner of the land (Ballard 2001: 24). These were ignored, and as the Freeport mine and coast infrastructure were developed Amungme and Kamoro were forcefully relocated from land required for the project.

The Amungme and Kamoro endured the environmental effects of the project, and witnessed the destruction of numerous sites of ritual and spiritual significance, including sacred pandanus groves, pools and lakes, and the actual mountain peaks of Ertsberg and Grasberg (Ballard 2001: 30). They were also overwhelmed by outsiders as the Indonesian government encouraged migration into the area from regions of Indonesia experiencing population pressure. Large numbers of people from other parts of the West Papua highlands also migrated to the vicinity of the mine. By 1990 the population of the area reached more than 100,000, compared to several thousands of Amungme and Kamoro before Freeport's arrival (Ballard 2001; Soares 2004: 123). While Freeport quickly became one of Indonesia's largest corporate taxpayers, none of this revenue was directed to the Amungme or Kamoro, while most of the jobs generated by Freeport were taken by expatriates or migrants.

The Amungme and Kamoro continued to express their opposition to Freeport's activities and those of the Indonesian government, including by posting anti-trespassing signs around Freeport's operations, writing formal letters of complaint to the government, public demonstrations, and raising the Morning Star Flag of the West Papua Liberation movement. In 1977 the Amungme joined province-wide protests against Indonesian rule, including by sabotaging the company's copper

slurry pipeline. The Indonesian military attacked the Amungme communities, straf-
ing villages with ground-attack aircraft, shelling them with mortars, and killing scores
of villagers. Amungme and Kamoro settlements around the mine site and on the coast
were razed to the ground (Ballard 2001: 25).

Throughout the life of Freeport's project, the Indonesian armed forces have played
a key role in suppressing opposition and in maintaining security, with up to 1,800
troops stationed in the area. Under the contracts with Indonesia which allowed
establishment of the mine, Freeport is required to provide accommodation, transport, and wages for all Indonesian government officials located at the project,
including paramilitary police and soldiers. Freeport constructed barracks and other
facilities for troops, who are regularly transported in company vehicles and helicopters. Military suppression of opposition from the Amungme and Kamoro has
been consistently brutal, and Indonesian forces were guilty of numerous breaches
of human rights during the 1970s and 1980s. A later report by Indonesia's National
Human Rights Commission documented 'indiscriminate killings, torture and inhu-
man/degrading treatment, unlawful arrest and arbitrary detention, disappearance,
excessive surveillance, and the destruction of property' (Soares 2004: 129; see also
Ballard 2001: 26–7, for specific details of disappearances, torture, and the arbitrary
killings of several hundred Indigenous people).

Freeport's mine in West Papua displayed features that were characteristic of many
large projects established in the developing world in the 1960s and 1970s. These
involved state support for new mining projects, without any consideration of Indigenous interests; forced relocation of Indigenous landowners; an absence of measures
to limit negative environmental impacts; destruction of culturally and spiritually
important sites; suppression of Indigenous dissent, often using military force; large-
scale migration of non-Indigenous people, swamping the Indigenous population;
and a failure to include affected Indigenous peoples in the financial and other economic benefits generated by mining (see, for example, Albert 1992; Moody 1992;
Regan 1998).

Diamonds, oil and gas in the Soviet Union

During the early years of the Soviet Union, initiatives were proposed to allocate territories in the country's north to 'national minorities', as Indigenous peoples were
known, to protect them from the impact of settlers and to give them a degree of control over their own affairs. These initiatives were unable to gain traction as pressures
grew to develop the north's resources and to set class concepts above nationality concepts, eliminate ethnic differences, and merge all peoples into a unified Soviet people
(Vakhtin 1998: 82). In the 1930s, the territories and resources of Indigenous peoples were confiscated for the use of state departments or included in collective farms
and enterprises, nomadic peoples were forced to convert to a settled way of life, and
their ability to exercise cultural and economic autonomy was severely compromised

(Hele n.d.; Taksami 1990). After the Second World War, the momentum to settle the north and exploit its resources gathered apace, and no attention was paid to the interests of affected Indigenous peoples. Any mention of Indigenous peoples, even in the names of the regions in which they lived, was excluded from official documents. To give an indication of the scale of settlement of Indigenous lands, the Indigenous population of the Khanty-Mansiysk region, which was 20 per cent of the total in 1961, fell to between 1 and 3 per cent in 1988 (Pika and Prokhorov 1989: 124; Vakhtin 1998: 85–6). In terms of resource extraction, Vakhtin's (1998: 89) description of the situation in the 1950s and 1960s was as follows:

> During the decades [after the 1950s] the North has not so much been developed as looted. The principal targets have been forests, gold, nonferrous metals, coal, oil, and natural gas. … no laws existed for either geologists or construction workers. A decision by the central government to develop a new deposit or cut down new tracts of forest could be initiated at any time and in any place; any amount of land could be confiscated from the IPN [Indigenous Peoples of the North] with the stroke of a pen.

A major issue for Indigenous peoples was the lack of attention paid to limiting the environmental impacts of mining, oil extraction, and transport, as this resulted in damage to land and waters that threatened or destroyed their capacity to support Indigenous livelihoods. As Vakhtin notes (1998: 89), 'fragile northern ecological systems and Indigenous peoples could not withstand this pressure, this "unceasing ecological aggression"'. By the late 1980s, the impacts had been so severe that some analysts and Indigenous leaders considered that the continued existence of affected Indigenous peoples was threatened (Aipin 1989; Hele n.d.: 259; Pika and Prohorov 1989: 123; Taksami 1990: 23).

Two examples illustrate the experience of Indigenous peoples with resource extraction in the Soviet era. The first involves diamond mining and the Indigenous Sakha people (or the Yakut, their official designation). Sakha live in what was the Autonomous Soviet Socialist Republic of Yakutia (now the Republic of Sakha within the Russian federation), and in the 1950s accounted for about a third of its population and relied for their livelihoods on reindeer herding and fishing. Yakutia lies in the north-eastern part of Russia, much of it is located above the Arctic Circle, and it occupies an area 2,000 kilometres north to south and 2,500 kilometres east to west. Industrial development of diamond mining commenced in 1957. During the following decades, diamond mines heavily contaminated rivers because of drainage of polluted waters from mines, waste dumps, and processing facilities. The industry used highly toxic liquids including thallium, and waste waters were disposed of on to the surrounding open countryside without any processing to extract toxins. High concentrations of metals including aluminium, chromium, nickel, cobalt, barium, and strontium have been found in the bottom sediments of a number of rivers, some far away from the diamond mines. The building of a hydroelectric station to supply power to the diamond mines created a water reservoir that covered an area of

1,960 square kilometres, which became significantly polluted through accumulation of hydrogen sulphide and phenols. The creation of the reservoir and the pollution it and the diamond mines created had serious impacts on the lives of the Sakha, forcing some to leave their land, putting an end to reindeer breeding, and resulting in a large fall in catches of fish. None of the considerable profits generated by diamond mining flowed to the Sakha (Yakovleva et al. 2000: 322–5).

The second example involves the development of gas and oil resources on the Yamal peninsula, a large area of land jutting out into the Kara Sea above the Arctic Circle and home to the Nenets and Khanty peoples. Here during the 1970s and 1980s extensive areas of forest were cut down, reindeer pastures were destroyed by the tracks of cross-country vehicles and burning, and rivers suffered severely from oil pollution (Chance and Andreeva 1995: 226; Pika and Bogoyavlensky 1995; Taksami 1990: 24–5). Major environmental problems were created by construction of roads and pipeline without any attention to the need to adjust conventional construction and land restoration methods to working in permafrost. Again, the Nenets and Khanty received no compensation for the destruction of their livelihoods and no share of the revenues created by oil and gas exploitation (Pika and Prokhorov 1989: 128–89; Prokhorov 1989). Dredging of rivers for sand and gravel needed for construction also had serious economic, social, and cultural consequences. Pika and Prokhorov (1989: 129) describe the impact on the Khanty of large-scale dredging of a subsidiary of the Ob river as follows:

> The local people fished here, and trapped animals or birds. Many places in the river were always considered 'sacred' and it was categorically forbidden to catch fish, go hunting or make fires ... In such a way the fish-spawning periods, hibernation quarters and the nests of water fowl were preserved. And what surprise, indignation and confusion there was among the Khanty several years ago when powerful equipment began to excavate the bed of the Sob ... the sig and salmon disappeared from the river and people who had been fishermen all their lives lost the natural basis of their livelihood.

Pika and Prokhorov (1989: 130–1) also document the way in which loss of livelihood forced Indigenous peoples into poorly paid and unskilled work, and resulted in a reluctance on the part of young people to continue with traditional economic activity, growing problems with alcohol abuse, a rising incidence of murders and suicides, and a breakdown in family structures (see also Aipin 1989; Chance and Andreeva 1995: 226–8).

Conclusion

Several features distinguish the post-Second World War mining boom from the gold rushes of the mid-nineteenth century. The first involves the technology and scale of operations involved in mining. In the 1960s and 1970s, mining was dominated by large-scale, mechanized operations involving investments in the tens or hundreds of millions by multinational corporations and state-owned enterprises. This contrasts sharply with the gold rushes, especially with their initial stages when mining was dominated by individuals and small groups using technology that required minimal capital. The contrast had two implications, both negative, for Indigenous peoples. Opportunities that Indigenous peoples had to become involved in, or otherwise benefit from, the gold rushes did not exist in the post-war boom. Second, the much larger scale of operations in the latter period meant that individual mining operations had the potential to transform landscapes and affect Indigenous livelihoods on a massive scale, as illustrated by copper/gold mining in West Papua and diamond mining in Yakutia.

The second major difference between the two periods involves the role of the state. In the gold rushes, the state was often initially playing catch-up, following miners into areas where it had been absent or its sway had been limited. The state did, in the wake of the gold rushes, create a legal framework based on the 'free entry' system which privileged mining over other land uses, an approach whose legacy persists to this day. In the post-war boom, the state played a much more central role. It financed and operated mines as in the Soviet Union, or created the legislative framework to attract private mining investment and removed any obstacles in the form of Indigenous peoples, as occurred in Queensland and West Papua. Indigenous people no longer had to contend only with rapacious miners. They had to deal with two dangerous and allied adversaries simultaneously, miners and the state. As in the nineteenth century, Indigenous peoples fought against incursion into their territories, through protest, litigation, and, in some cases, armed conflict (Moody 1988, 1992). But the combined forces of industry and the state were very hard to resist.

The history of gold rushes highlighted the agency of Indigenous peoples. It demonstrated their commercial acumen, and their ability to extract wealth from mining activity that they might have preferred had never arrived on their doorstep, but to which they were able to adapt, and from which they could derive an alternative source of income as the lands and resources on which their livelihoods depended were despoiled by mining. It also highlighted the complexity of relations between miners and Indigenous peoples, and the fact that these relations could take many different forms depending on the specific time and place, and the motivations and choices of Indigenous people.

Between the Second World War and the 1980s, the globe was divided into three great blocks, the capitalist West, the communist states, and what was then called the Third World, each different in terms of its ideological orientation, its economic structure, and its standard of living (Corbidge 1990: 625–6). However, when the opportunity to exploit minerals arose, all three had an identical approach to Indigenous peoples. They pushed them aside with ruthless indifference; showed little care for the impact of mining on Indigenous lives, resources, and culture; refused to share the wealth taken from Indigenous lands; and did nothing to assist Indigenous people to take advantage of the opportunities created by mining. The examples discussed here are provided by way of illustration, with similar outcomes occurring across Indigenous lands in South America, Africa, the Indian subcontinent, and the Pacific Islands.

The remainder of the book considers whether this situation has fundamentally changed in the decades since 1980.

4
Forces for Change

International Recognition of Indigenous Rights

Introduction

Before the Second World War, the only laws relevant to mining and Indigenous peoples operated at the national or sub-national level. After 1945 an international legal regime began to emerge dealing with universal human rights, some of which had a bearing on the situation of Indigenous peoples. From the 1980s, international legal instruments were developed dealing specifically with Indigenous rights and ter- ritories. Only states can ratify such instruments, and states were not going to enact international law on their own initiative that constrained their freedom to exploit Indigenous lands and resources, and to rule Indigenous peoples as they wished. Inter- national law on Indigenous rights developed as a result of a sustained campaign by Indigenous peoples and their allies (Anaya 1997; Havercroft 2010).

International legal instruments dealing with Indigenous rights offer the *possibility* of outcomes from mining on Indigenous lands different from those described in the previous chapter. The question of whether this possibility is being realized is exam- ined at various points later in the book. Here the focus is on outlining key milestones in Indigenous campaigns to achieve recognition of their rights in the global arena, and to highlight the relevance of international treaties, conventions, and declarations for relations between Indigenous peoples and mining.

While states are the primary actors in the formal recognition of Indigenous rights in international law, the private sector plays a key role in determining the extent to which those rights are given expression as miners interact with Indigenous peo- ples. The final sections consider international initiatives to encourage corporate compliance with human and Indigenous rights.

There is much debate about the status of international legal instruments in rela- tion to domestic laws and the obligations they impose on states. 'Treaties' usually do have legal effect in domestic law, in that states signing treaties are required to introduce or amend national legislation to give them effect. 'Conventions' (some- times referred to as 'covenants') bind countries that ratify them to comply with their terms under international law. Within the United Nations (UN) system, signatories of conventions must report on their compliance, and can be censured by the UN for non-compliance. However, states cannot be pursued for non-compliance in domes- tic courts. 'Declarations' are statements of principle and do not involve agreement by

Indigenous Peoples and Mining. Ciaran O'Faircheallaigh, Oxford University Press. © Ciaran O'Faircheallaigh (2023).
DOI: 10.1093/oso/9780192894564.003.0004

states that adopt them to be bound under international or domestic law. This does not mean that declarations may not have moral or political force and so lead to change in the behaviour of states and corporations (Havercroft 2010: 137). As Barsh notes (1994: 75):

> Censure and publicity are the principal weapons of human rights advocacy, and they are equally available whether the underlying standards repose in a treaty or in a declaration … A declaration with a highly visible, popular, and well-publicized review mechanism is more likely to generate diplomatic and public pressure than a treaty that is discussed in the shadows. Likewise, promotional activity creates public expectations of state compliance, and an eloquent declaration is more easily promoted than a treaty couched in legal jargon.

Indigenous rights and international law

International legal instruments recognizing human rights began to emerge in the late 1940s, and a series of key conventions and covenants came into effect in the 1960s. Human rights that had obvious relevance to Indigenous peoples included those related to the self-determination of peoples; the right to equality and non-discrimination; the right to property; and the right to practise and maintain culture and religion. Important instruments include the Universal Declaration of Human Rights (UDHR) (1948); the International Convention on the Elimination of All Forms of Racial Discrimination (ICERD) (1965); the International Covenant on Civil and Political Rights (ICCPR) (1966); and the International Covenant on Economic, Social and Cultural Rights (ICESCR) (1966). Article 1 of both ICCPR and ICESCR provides that:

1. All peoples have the right of self-determination. By virtue of that right they freely determine their political status and freely pursue their economic, social and cultural development.
2. All peoples may, for their own needs, freely dispose of their natural wealth and resources … In no case may a people be deprived of its own means of subsistence.

It is difficult to see how a people can exercise 'the right of self-determination' and 'freely pursue their economic, social and cultural development' if their lands are confiscated or polluted, they are forcefully relocated away from their ancestral territories, or they are subject to violence and confiscation of property, as occurred in many parts of the world in the decades after 1945. Such outcomes, and the extraction of enormous mineral wealth from their territories without their consent, also appear inconsistent with the ability of Indigenous peoples to 'freely dispose of their natural wealth and resources'. The large-scale destruction of land, pollution of waterways, and decimation of fish and wildlife that accompanied much mineral development seems incompatible with the imperative that 'In no case may a people be deprived of its own means of subsistence.'

One of the first instruments focused solely on Indigenous peoples is the International Labour Organization (ILO) Convention C107 on Indigenous and Tribal Populations (1957). The guiding principle of this document was that Indigenous peoples should, and would, become integrated into majority national populations over time. The Convention is described as being concerned with 'the protection *and integration* of indigenous and other tribal and semi-tribal populations' (emphasis added) (Preamble); the goal of governments was assumed to be 'their progressive integration into the life of their respective countries' (Article 2); and the goal of education was to 'help [Indigenous] children to become integrated into the national community' (Article 24). Indigenous cultures and ways of governance would be tolerated but only to the extent they did not represent a barrier to integration. Indigenous people 'shall be allowed to retain their own customs and institutions where these are not incompatible with the … objectives of integration programmes' (Article 7). It is also evident that the goal was integration of Indigenous peoples as individuals, not as viable and enduring communities, as indicated by the statement that 'The primary objective of all such [government] action shall be the fostering of individual dignity, and the advancement of individual usefulness and initiative' (Article 2). Assumptions about the inferiority of Indigenous peoples were evident, for example, from the description of them as being 'at a less advanced stage than the stage reached by the other sections of the national community' (Article 1).

The Convention did call for recognition of 'the right of ownership, collective or individual, of the members of the populations concerned over the lands which these populations traditionally occupy' (Article 11). Indigenous peoples should 'not be removed without their free consent from their habitual territories except in accordance with national laws and regulations for reasons relating to national security, or in the interest of national economic development …' (Article 12). Given that the Australian, Indonesian, and Soviet governments would no doubt have cited 'the interest of national economic development' to justify the removals of Indigenous peoples discussed in Chapter 3, such provisions can hardly have offered much comfort to Indigenous peoples. Those removed should be entitled to 'lands of quality at least equal to that of the lands previously occupied by them, suitable to provide for their present needs and future development' (Article 12), a provision which entirely ignores the way in which Indigenous health, identity, and survival are embedded in connections to *specific* areas of land and water (see Chapter 5).

While ILO C107 was significant as the first international instrument to acknowledge that Indigenous rights might warrant recognition, its focus on integration of Indigenous peoples into dominant societies and the priority it afforded national development undermined its potential utility and meant it would not become a focus for Indigenous peoples in pursuing recognition and protection of their rights.

During the 1960s and 1970s, Indigenous peoples, especially those in settler states such as Australia, Canada, and the United States, were escaping from the most blatant constraints on their political freedom, such as the denial of voting rights and limits on their freedom of movement and of organization. They established organizations at community, regional, and national level to push for equality of treatment before the law and in government policy, and for recognition of their land rights (see Chapter 5). Some of these organizations quickly concluded that gains in the domestic sphere were unlikely to be substantial unless pressure could also be generated at the international level. A key part of their calculations was that by basing their claims to recognition in international fora on their distinct status as Indigenous peoples, they could counter attempts by states to rebut their demands by treating them as merely minorities, as just another ethnic group defined by their poverty. They would 'no longer accept being recognized as anything less than distinctive members [of nation states] with special rights' (Dyck 1985: 22).

Starting in the 1970s with a number of international conferences on Indigenous rights and on discrimination against Indigenous peoples, Indigenous groups started to work together and to consider how they might pursue recognition of their rights through fora such as the UN, and through recognition of Indigenous rights in international law. As the 1980s and 1990s progressed, Indigenous groups from settler states such as Australia and Canada were joined by organizations from South America, Asia, and Africa (Igoe 2006), creating an Indigenous rights movement that gained increasing presence and impact on the international stage. That movement was driven by bodies such as the US-based International Indian Treaty Council, the World Council of Indigenous Peoples (based in Canada but drawing membership from 19 countries at its establishment), and numerous national Indigenous organizations. It was supported by international non-government organizations (NGOs) dedicated to promotion of Indigenous rights, such as the International Work Group on Indigenous Affairs and the World Council of Churches; and by sympathetic officials and advisers of international organizations, especially the UN and the Organization of American States (Anaya 1997; Corntassel 2007; Feldman 2002; Morgan 2007).

Initially, considerable emphasis was placed on elimination of discrimination against Indigenous individuals, with efforts directed at drawing attention to breaches of the UDHR and the ICERD. This resulted in 1980 in the United Nations Economic and Social Council (UNESC) authorizing a study to examine the 'Problem of Discrimination against Indigenous Populations'. The focus of Indigenous activities quickly expanded to include an emphasis on communal rights, on the rights of Indigenous *peoples*. Here a key focus was the provision of the ICCPR and ICESCR providing that 'All peoples have the right of self-determination.' Indigenous organizations argued that this provision should apply to *all* peoples, and that efforts by many states to limit its applicability to peoples who formed majority populations in overseas European colonies, and deny its protection to Indigenous peoples, were discriminatory. They also argued that self-determination was justified on the basis that they were self-governing prior to European colonization. Self-determination was seen as of fundamental importance in that so much else flowed from this right, including the ability of Indigenous peoples to govern themselves; to negotiate with states and other parties on a basis of equality; to participate in international fora which made decisions affecting their communities; to control development on their ancestral lands; to maintain their cultures and languages; and not to have policies or decisions on land use and management imposed on them (Anaya 1997; Havercroft 2010; Morgan 2004: 485–7; Muehlebach 2003). Perhaps most importantly, by definition a right to self-determination is not in the gift of any other entity and, equally, is not in the power of another entity to take away. Given the long history of states depriving Indigenous peoples of their rights and property, this was a central consideration for Indigenous leaders (Muehlebach 2003: 252–3).

By the 1980s, Indigenous organizations were engaging with a range of international bodies, including the ILO, the World Bank, the Organization of American States, and a range of UN institutions. In organizational terms, the movement had developed a regional dimension, manifested for instance in the establishment of the Asia Indigenous Peoples Pact and the Inuit Circumpolar Conference (Feldman 2002; Morgan 2007). The UN constituted the key focus for Indigenous political mobilization, and Indigenous organizations quickly established a significant and permanent position for themselves within its institutions. Important milestones in this regard included the establishment in 1982 of the UN Working Group on Indigenous Peoples (WGIP), comprised of member-state experts rather than Indigenous people and with a mandate to review developments in relation to the human rights of Indigenous peoples and the evolution of standards concerning their rights; the declaration of the First UN Decade of the World's Indigenous Peoples (1995–2004); and the establishment of the UN Permanent Forum on Indigenous Issues (PFII) in 2000. The PFII, which advises the UNESC, has equal numbers of Indigenous and non-Indigenous members and the former are accorded parity in all deliberations and decision making, the first UN body to allow such standing to Indigenous representatives. The PFII became a key focal point for numerous and diverse Indigenous organizations to come together, achieve consensus on key issues, develop strategies, and undertake lobbying of UN bureaucrats and country delegations (Feldman 2002; Muehlebach 2003).

Participation by Indigenous peoples in the UN grew dramatically during the 1980s and early 1990s, as indicated by an increase in the number of organizations involved from 48 in 1983 to over 500 by 2005. While only 22 NGOs and Indigenous organizations participated in the first WGIP in 1983, 169 such organizations and over 1,000 representatives participated in the WGIP session held in July 2004. Despite this growth in participation in key events, Indigenous participation overall was hampered by scarcity of resources. The modest funding provided by the UN was important in facilitating Indigenous participation, especially as priority was given to Indigenous organizations from countries with little experience in international mobilization, particularly those from the South (Morgan 2007: 276, 280). However, many countries, including the United States and Canada, made no or only token contributions to the UN Voluntary Fund for Indigenous Peoples which was established to allow more broadly based Indigenous participation. As a result, only a small proportion of eligible Indigenous organizations that applied for UN funding received support (Corntassel 2007: 154–5).

By the time the ILO ratified its second Convention on the Rights of Tribal and Indigenous Peoples (ILO C169, 1989), the growing influence of Indigenous organizations and agendas was already evident. There was no longer talk of 'integration' or of 'individuals'. The Convention recognized the collective aspiration of Indigenous peoples to 'exercise control over their own institutions, ways of life and economic development' (Preamble), and stated that governments have the responsibility to promote 'the full realisation of the social, economic and cultural rights *of these peoples*' (Article 2, emphasis added). There was a new stress on Indigenous autonomy, and on the need for governments to consult with Indigenous peoples regarding policies that affect them directly. Indigenous peoples 'shall have the right to decide their own priorities for the process of development as it affects their lives, beliefs, institutions and spiritual well-being and the lands they occupy or otherwise use, and to exercise control, to the extent possible, over their own economic, social and cultural development'; and government should allow them to 'participate in the formulation, implementation and evaluation of plans and programmes for national and regional development which may affect them directly' (Article 7).

Indigenous peoples should be 'consulted whenever consideration is being given to their capacity to alienate their lands or otherwise transmit their rights outside their own community'. Studies should be carried out in cooperation with Indigenous peoples 'to assess the social, spiritual, cultural and environmental impact on them of planned development activities. The results of these studies shall be considered as fundamental criteria for the implementation of these activities' (Article 7). There is also a requirement for government to 'take measures, in co-operation with the peoples concerned, to protect and preserve the environment of the territories they inhabit' (Article 7). Under Article 15, the rights of [Indigenous peoples] to the natural resources pertaining to their lands shall be specially safeguarded. These rights include the right of these peoples to participate in the use, management and conservation of these resources.'

Consultation regarding proposed developments of Indigenous lands would not extend to a requirement for governments to seek Indigenous consent for them, except in the cases where their relocation is considered necessary. Relocation should only occur with the 'free and informed consent' of Indigenous people, though where that consent could not be obtained relocation could still occur following 'appropriate procedures established by national laws and regulations ... which provide for effective representation of the peoples concerned' (Article 16).

Despite the limited ambit of the requirement for 'free and informed consent', its inclusion in ILO C169 is significant. As discussed in the next section, this concept, with the addition of 'prior' ('free prior and informed consent' or FPIC) was to become central to Indigenous demands for greater recognition of their rights in the years that followed, as FPIC constituted a basis on which Indigenous peoples could be given real control over proposed developments on their territories.

Recognition of Indigenous rights was also beginning to feature in conventions and treaties with a broader focus on environmental and cultural issues. For example, the Convention on Biological Diversity (1992), which has been ratified by more than

170 countries, calls on states to 'respect, preserve and maintain knowledge, innovations and practices of indigenous and local communities embodying traditional lifestyles relevant for the conservation and sustainable use of biological diversity' (Article 8.j). The 'Bonn Guidelines on Access to Genetic Resources', developed pursuant to the Convention, requires that access to genetic resources should only occur 'with the prior informed consent of Indigenous and local communities and the approval and involvement of the holders of traditional knowledge … obtained in accordance their traditional practices …' (Article 31).

Indigenous people also began to use general provisions of human rights conventions to try and halt exploitation of their land and resources without their consent. An example involved the Awis Tingi people of Nicaragua who successfully argued in the Inter-American Court of Human Rights, established by the American Convention on Human Rights, that Nicaragua had breached articles of the Convention relating to non-discrimination, the right to use and enjoyment of property, and the right to judicial protection. The government had allowed a Korean company to harvest timber on Awis Tingi land without seeking their consent and ignored Supreme Court directions that logging should cease (Bankes 2004).

Indigenous free prior and informed consent

During the 1990s and the 2000s, discussion of Indigenous rights was increasingly couched in terms of the Indigenous right to free prior and informed consent (IFPIC). IFPIC requires that Indigenous people should have the right, free from duress and in possession of full information regarding proposed developments on their ancestral lands, to provide or withhold their consent to those developments prior to any authorization of development activity by state authorities or developers. In summary, Indigenous people should have the right to decide whether and in what form development occurs on their lands (UNESC 2004a; UNDESA 2004). The norm is grounded in a growing international recognition of the relationship between the ancestral lands of Indigenous peoples and their cultural, economic, and social survival.

The ability to live on, care for, and utilize resources from their ancestral lands is central not only to the economic and social well-being of Indigenous people but also to their survival. Land is critical to physical sustenance, but it is also the foundation for social relationships, which in Indigenous societies are bound up with relations to land; and for law and culture, which are interwoven with use of the land and its resources. It is also central to spirituality and religion, which have as their basis beliefs about the creation of the land and the way in which creation spirits continue to occupy the land and influence contemporary life. All of these dimensions of Indigenous life revolve around specific areas of land and the sites, features, and landscapes they contain (UNESC 2004b). Given the historic tendency of governments to allow uncontrolled mineral exploitation on Indigenous territories, it is argued that Indigenous people can only protect their lands and so ensure their survival by themselves deciding whether development should proceed and, if it should, the extent and form of development that should occur. Application of the norm of IFPIC would allow them to do so (UNESC 2004a, 2004b; MacKay 2004).

The right of IFPIC is closely linked to the principle of self-determination of peoples. If peoples are self-determining, no one else can tell them whether their resources or territories are to be developed, or on what terms they should be developed, or how they should live their lives. If self-determination is to be real, IFPIC must apply to proposed activities that can affect those resources or territories and Indigenous ways of life. The link between self-determination and IFPIC was expressed very clearly by one Indigenous activist from Burundi who said: 'Self-determination [means that it is for] us to say "We want it this way". It is within our right, our human rights to say no. To say yes. And not to be pushed around' (cited in Muehlebach 2003: 259).

Control of natural resources and their development is also critical for states, and IFPIC represents a threat to that control. As Muehlebach comments (2003: 256), IFPIC raises the question of:

> whether states should be regarded as the sole, sovereign proprietors of the natural resources that lie within their borders and under what circumstances this general state of affairs might be put to question. The importance of this question cannot be underestimated in its implications for future relationships between states, the groups living within them, and transnational corporate interests.

The United Nations Declaration on the Rights of Indigenous Peoples

The right to IFPIC is central to arguably the most important international legal instrument dealing with Indigenous rights, the United Nations Declaration on the Rights of Indigenous Peoples (UNDRIP) (Pitty and Smith 2011). It was adopted by the UN General Assembly in September 2007 after nearly 20 years of negotiations and campaigning by Indigenous and NGO representatives at the UN. Work on the Declaration began in 1985, and over the next decade over 400 Indigenous delegations had input into its drafting. According to Muehlebach (2003: 248) the Draft Declaration was 'unprecedented as the only international human rights instrument that has ever been produced with the consistent, direct and constructive involvement of the very people it is meant to benefit'.

In 1994 a Draft Declaration on the Rights of Indigenous Peoples was adopted by the UN Sub-Commission on Prevention of Discrimination and Protection of Minorities, and in 1995 the Commission on Human Rights established an Intersessional Working Group (known as the WGDD) to assist in reviewing the Draft Declaration for consideration by the UN General Assembly. While normally NGOs are not permitted to submit formal proposals to such working groups, in this case Indigenous organizations were granted procedural equality with member states (Corntassel 2007: 150; Havercroft 2010: 119). A sustained insistence on being allowed to participate fully in international fora usually restricted to state representatives was a hallmark of the Indigenous campaign during the 1980s and 1990s. This insistence was aimed both at increasing the efficacy of Indigenous representations, and at highlighting Indigenous claims for self-determination, which meant that reliance could and should not be placed on states to properly represent Indigenous interests (for examples of this approach, see Barsh 1994: 56–9; see also Morgan 2007: 279–80; Muehlebach 2003: 248).

At this point there was strong state opposition to many aspects of the Draft Declaration, and only two of its 43 substantive clauses were agreed. Particularly contentious was the Draft Declaration's opening statement affirming the rights of Indigenous *peoples* to self-determination. Numerous states opposed its inclusion on the basis that it would result in secessionist movements by Indigenous groups and the dismemberment of states. This was despite repeated assurances by Indigenous leaders that they had no interest in secession but only in controlling their own destinies within the boundaries of existing nation states, and in being able to develop relationships with existing state authorities on a basis of equality. On the other hand, Indigenous organizations were unwilling to accept any qualification on the right of self-determination because this would relegate them to a position inferior to that of other 'peoples' and because, as mentioned earlier, self-determination was seen as the key to recognition and exercise of an array of rights critical to Indigenous survival and welfare (Corntassel 2007; Havercroft 2010; Morgan 2004, 2007; Muehlebach 2003). Some states, including Australia and Canada, were also opposed to the Declaration on the more fundamental basis that rights in relation to land and natural resources should be addressed by individual states and their Indigenous populations, rather than being subject to a universal declaration on Indigenous rights (Corntassel 2007: 150).

The WGDD met each year for the decade after 1995 to review the Draft Declaration and hear proposals from states and Indigenous organizations. States were not able to override the Indigenous position on self-determination and other key issues, because the chair of the WGDD guaranteed Indigenous activists that a declaration would not be finalized until consensus was reached between Indigenous and state representatives, providing Indigenous delegates with a *de facto* veto and resulting in a stalemate that lasted a decade (Muehlebach 2003: 249). Sustained Indigenous lobbying and negotiations led to more and more states and regional blocks of states supporting the Indigenous position on self-determination (Havercroft 2010; Morgan 2004: 487–8). The Draft Declaration was finally approved by the United Nations Human Rights Council (UNHRC) in June 2006, and forwarded to the UN General Assembly for ratification in September 2007. Only four countries voted against its adoption in the General Assembly: Australia, Canada, New Zealand, and the United States. Each subsequently reversed its position, with the USA withholding its approval of some key provisions.

The UNDRIP begins by affirming that 'Indigenous peoples are equal to all other peoples', and provides that 'Indigenous peoples have the right to self-determination. By virtue of that right they freely determine their political status and freely pursue their economic, social and cultural development' (Article 3). On this basis the

Declaration requires application of the norm of IFPIC to a wide range of areas including relocation of Indigenous people, taking of their property, and adoption of legislative and administrative measures affecting Indigenous peoples (Articles 10, 11, 19, 28, and 29). Articles 26 and 32 are of particular importance in the context of mining:

Article 26

2. Indigenous peoples have the right to own, use, develop and control the lands, territories and resources that they possess by reason of traditional ownership or other traditional occupation or use.
3. States shall give legal recognition and protection to these lands, territories and resources.

Article 32

1. Indigenous peoples have the right to determine and develop priorities and strategies for the development or use of their lands or territories and other resources.
2. States shall consult and cooperate in good faith with the indigenous peoples concerned through their own representative institutions *in order to obtain their free and informed consent prior to the approval of any project affecting their lands or territories and other resources, particularly in connection with the development, utilization or exploitation of mineral, water or other resources* (emphasis added).
3. States shall provide effective mechanisms for just and fair redress for any such activities, and appropriate measures shall be taken to mitigate adverse environmental, economic, social, cultural or spiritual impact).

Provisions designed to protect and facilitate the exercise of cultural and spiritual rights and their connection to land are also of particular significance in the mining context, given the long history of destruction of sites and areas of cultural and spiritual significance by the industry.

Indigenous peoples have the right to practise and revitalize their cultural traditions and customs. This includes the right to maintain, protect, and develop the past, present, and future manifestations of their cultures, such as archaeological and historical sites, artefacts, designs, ceremonies, technologies, and visual and performing arts and literature (Article 11).

Indigenous peoples have the right to maintain and strengthen their distinctive spiritual relationship with their traditionally owned or otherwise occupied and used lands, territories, waters and coastal seas and other resources, and to uphold their responsibilities to future generations in this regard (Article 25).

While much attention was focused on global initiatives such as the Declaration, parallel efforts were pursued at the regional level (Barsh 1994: 70–4; Crawhall 2011). These led, for instance, to the adoption in 2016 of the American Declaration on the Rights of Indigenous Peoples by the Organization of American States.

Enforcement, implementation, and the private sector

Application of the Declaration in practice would lead to outcomes from mining very different to those outlined in Chapter 3. The extent to which the Declaration and other developments in international law have actually had or are having this effect, or contributed to it, is considered in Parts 3 and 4 of the book. It is appropriate to recognize at this point that ratification of international legal instruments by states offers no guarantee that their provisions will be adhered to. Some authors assume that all such instruments have binding or at least normative effect, in that states *should* adhere to them in their dealing with Indigenous peoples (ELI 2004: vii; MacKay 2004: 19; UNDESA 2004: 12; UNESC 2004b: 13). Others stress that much of international 'law' is in fact not binding and is declaratory or aspirational in nature, and that as a result it has little or no impact on state behaviour towards Indigenous peoples (Corntassel 2007: 161–2). Saugestad (2011: 52) argues that 'A basic lesson for all indigenous peoples is that the ultimate solution to whatever problems they may experience must involve the state within whose border they reside … States may choose to ignore their indigenous minority, but the power of the state cannot be ignored.'

There is certainly no guarantee that government agencies or commercial interests operating in their jurisdictions will respect norms enshrined in international legal instruments in their dealings with Indigenous peoples (ELI 2004: 36; CIGI 2018; Corntassel 2007). For example, the Inter-American Human Rights Court has encountered major problems in enforcing its decisions on member countries. In relation to the case of the Awis Tingi mentioned above, the Court ordered Nicaragua to adopt relevant measures to protect Awis Tingi interests in 2002 but Nicaragua had failed to respond a year later (Baluarte 2004). This example highlights the gap that can exist between state policy at the international level and state practice in the domestic sphere, as Nicaragua was among a number of Latin American states that pushed for adoption of the UNDRIP (Morgan 2004: 487–8, 491). Issues of compliance have also arisen in relation to countries that have ratified ILO C169 (Baluarte, 2004; Warden-Fernandez, 2001). In many cases, recommendations from UN and other international bodies 'to cease or to at least address documented violations of Indigenous rights, are for the most part ignored [by states] and remain largely without effective remedy' (Corntassel 2007: 158; see also MacInnes et al. 2017: 156).

The issue of enforcement and implementation also raises the role of the private sector. While international legal instruments involve state actors, many of the activities that affect Indigenous rights and interests are conducted by corporations, and especially so in the mining sector. The extent to which international law changes outcomes for Indigenous peoples also thus depends on the responses to it of corporate actors.

The issue of corporate attitudes towards Indigenous rights must be seen in the wider context of the concept of corporate social responsibility (CSR). CSR is discussed in detail in Chapter 7 in relation to corporate policies and behaviour in specific domestic contexts. Here the focus is on international initiatives to secure corporate recognition of Indigenous rights and compliance with international legal instruments dealing with those rights. For this purpose, it is sufficient to define CSR as a belief that corporations have a duty to create benefits for society in ways that *go beyond* what they cannot avoid doing because of legal obligations, or/and what they would do in any case purely on the basis of economic self-interest (O'Faircheallaigh and Ali 2008). One way of fulfilling this duty may be to base their behaviour towards Indigenous peoples not only on what is required under domestic law, but on recognition of Indigenous rights claimed by Indigenous peoples themselves, including those recognized in international law.

Three distinct strands can be identified in international initiatives dealing with corporate recognition of Indigenous rights. The first involves work channelled through the UN to secure corporate recognition of and compliance with human rights generally, components of which would affect corporate behaviour towards Indigenous peoples. The second involves application of conditions regarding recognition of Indigenous rights to loans provided by international financial institutions such as the World Bank to help finance development projects. The third involves initiatives taken by mining companies themselves through their peak industry bodies.

Business and the United Nations

During the 1990s the responsibilities of business in relation to human rights became a matter for increasing debate. The role of the private sector in the global economy was growing significantly as a result of the collapse of the Soviet Union, economic liberalization in many developing economies, and the rapid growth in world demand for minerals and other raw materials. Corporations were increasingly operating in geographically remote areas, often inhabited by Indigenous peoples and frequently beyond the effective administrative control of states. Concern about corporate breaches of human rights grew apace (IIED 2002; United Nations 2010). In 2004, the UN Commission on Human Rights produced a set of 'Draft Norms on the Responsibilities of Transnational Corporations and Other Business Enterprises with Regard to Human Rights'. These sought to impose as binding obligations on companies directly under international human rights law the same range of duties that states have accepted for themselves. Business was vehemently opposed to this approach, while some human rights advocacy groups strongly favoured it. The Commission on Human Rights declined to adopt the Draft Norms. Instead the UN Secretary-General in 2005 appointed John Ruggie as a Special Representative on the issue of human rights and transnational corporations. His brief was to move beyond the stalemate and clarify the roles and responsibilities of states and companies in the human rights sphere (United Nations 2010).

In 2008, after three years of consultations, Ruggie presented a 'Protect, Respect and Remedy' Framework setting out the broad responsibilities of states and business in relation to human rights, which was adopted by the UNHRC. In this framework, the role of states is to 'to protect against human rights abuses by third parties, including business enterprises, through appropriate policies, regulation, and adjudication'.

Business has the responsibility to respect human rights, which means that 'business enterprises should act with due diligence to avoid infringing on the rights of others and to address adverse impacts with which they are Involved' (Ruggie 2011: 4). The term 'responsibility' rather than 'duty' 'is meant to indicate that respecting rights is not currently an obligation that international human rights law generally imposes directly on companies, although elements of it may be reflected in domestic laws' (United Nations 2010: 2). Ruggie was then asked to 'operationalize' the Framework by developing a set of guiding principles, which he did after a further three years of consultations with governments, business enterprises and associations, communities directly affected by the activities of enterprises, civil society, and experts in law and policy (Ruggie 2011)

In June 2011, the UNHRC adopted the 'Guiding Principles on Business and Human Rights' (UNOHCHR 2011). The Principles do not create new international law obligations but elaborate the implications of existing standards and practices for states and businesses and integrate them 'within a single, logically coherent and comprehensive template' (Ruggie 2011: 5). States must 'protect against human rights abuse within their territory and/or jurisdiction by third parties, including business enterprises', and 'should take additional steps to protect against human rights abuses by business enterprises that are owned or controlled by the State, or that receive substantial support and services from State agencies' (UNOHCHR 2011: 6). Business enterprises should 'In all contexts … respect internationally recognized human rights, wherever they operate' UNOHCHR 2011: 21). They should 'avoid infringing on the human rights of others and should address adverse human rights impacts with which they are involved'. This responsibility 'exists independently of States' abilities and/or willingness to fulfil their own human rights obligations … and it exists over and above compliance with national laws and regulations protecting human rights' (UNOHCHR 2011: 13). It extends to the rights of Indigenous peoples (UNOHCHR 2014: 17). The responsibility to respect human rights applies to all enterprises regardless of size, requires a policy commitment to meet their responsibility, a human rights due diligence process to identify and address impacts on human rights, and development of operational policies and procedures necessary to embed respect for human rights throughout the enterprise. It also requires 'meaningful consultation' with potentially affected groups to understand the specific impacts on specific people. Enterprises should also track the effectiveness of their responses to any impacts on human rights and provide remediation for impacts that occur (UNOHCHR 2011: 16–21).

As noted earlier, the Principles are, by design, only a statement of 'responsibility' and do not create any new legal obligations. The UN denies that this means they are voluntary, arguing that 'Protecting human rights against business-related abuse is expected of all States, and in most cases is a legal obligation through their ratification of legally binding international human rights treaties containing provisions to this effect.' The UN also states that failure to comply with the Guidelines 'can subject companies to the "court of public opinion"—comprising employees, communities, consumers, civil society, as well as investors. So there can be legal, financial, and reputational consequences if companies fail to respect human rights as set out in the Guiding Principles' (UNOHCHR 2014: 8–9). Such consequences may be more likely to eventuate where companies make a public commitment to implement the Principles (see, for example, Rio Tinto 2019).

International financial institutions

Many of the major development projects that affected Indigenous peoples after 1945 were funded or partly funded by international financial institutions (IFIs) such as the World Bank, the International Finance Corporation (IFC) (the Bank's private investment arm), and the Asian Development Bank. As the disastrous impact of some of these projects on Indigenous peoples became clear, pressure grew on the IFIs to impose conditions on loans they granted, requiring borrowers to avoid, minimize, or compensate for negative impacts on Indigenous peoples. A 1982 internal study drew the World Bank's attention to the negative impact of large-scale projects on Indigenous peoples, but it was almost a decade before the Bank introduced an 'Operational Directive' which required planners of World Bank projects to ensure that Indigenous did not suffer adverse effects, enjoyed 'culturally compatible social and economic benefits', and were 'accorded full respect for their dignity, human rights, and cultural uniqueness' (World Bank 1991: 1–2). In addition, planning should involve 'full consideration of the options preferred by the indigenous people affected' (World Bank 1991: 3; see also Anaya 1997; Barsh 1994: 68–9).

The World Bank undertook a major review of its Indigenous Peoples Policy in 2011–12, and pressure was placed on the Bank to include recognition of the principle of IFPIC as part of its revised policy. The World Bank Policy on Indigenous People as revised in 2013 (World Bank 2013) does not require that IFPIC applies to projects it finances, but rather that 'free, prior, and informed *consultation* results in *broad community support* to the project by the affected Indigenous Peoples' (emphasis added). The Policy seeks to ensure that development 'fully respects the dignity, human rights, economies, and cultures of Indigenous Peoples', and states that Bank-financed projects must include 'measures to (a) avoid potentially adverse effects on the Indigenous Peoples' communities; or (b) when avoidance is not feasible, minimize, mitigate, or compensate for such effects'. Bank-financed projects must also be designed 'to ensure that the Indigenous Peoples receive social and economic benefits that are culturally appropriate and gender and intergenerationally inclusive' (World Bank 2013: 1). The Policy requires borrowers to establish:

an appropriate gender and intergenerationally inclusive framework that provides opportunities for consultation at each stage of project preparation and implementation ... [using] consultation methods appropriate to the social and cultural values of the affected Indigenous Peoples' communities and their local conditions [and] ... provide the affected Indigenous Peoples' communities with all relevant information about the project. (World Bank 2013: 10)

There are additional requirements on a borrower where a project involves the commercial development of natural resources such as minerals. For example, the borrower must inform affected communities of their rights to such resources under statutory and customary law, the scope and nature of the proposed commercial development, and the potential effects of such development on the Indigenous peoples' livelihoods and environments. It must establish arrangements to enable the Indigenous peoples to share equitably in the benefits to be derived from development (World Bank 2013: 18).

The Policy does not identify mechanisms or processes to guarantee that 'broad community support' for a project exists; that potential effects are correctly and fully identified; that measures are in place to avoid or mitigate potentially adverse effects and ensure that Indigenous people receive social and economic benefits that are culturally appropriate; and that effects are monitored and benefits provided throughout the life of a project.

More broadly, significant problems have arisen in ensuring that World Bank Operational Directives are put into practice, as is evident from a Review of the Implementation of the World Bank's Indigenous Peoples Policy over the period 2006–8 (World Bank 2011), undertaken by the Bank's own Quality Assurance and Compliance Unit. Among numerous problems the review identified was the failure of many projects to address issues related to land and resource rights important to the well-being of Indigenous peoples, and failure to identify any negative impacts on Indigenous peoples, an omission the Review found 'particularly striking in projects that mention risk factors which, by definition, would generate negative impacts if risks materialize' (World Bank 2011: 21). There was an absence of evidence indicating broad community support in more than half of all projects; and a general absence of monitoring indicators designed to measure project performance regarding Indigenous peoples (World Bank 2011: 21, 23, 26).

Other IFIs have been more willing than the World Bank to go beyond a requirement for 'consultation' and accept the principle of IFPIC. In 1998 the Inter-American Development Bank, following the approach adopted by the ILO, adopted a policy requiring prior informed consent in the case of Indigenous people possibly affected by involuntary resettlement as part of a Bank-financed project. When it revised its Indigenous peoples policy in 2012, the IFC, the branch of the World Bank that provides finance for private sector projects, included a requirement for free prior informed consent by Indigenous peoples where projects have an impact on 'lands and natural resources subject to traditional ownership or subject to customary use' (IFC 2012: 1, 3).

Mining industry initiatives

The mining industry became increasingly embroiled in conflicts and controversies from the 1970s onwards. It was extending its operations more and more into Indigenous territories; those operations were constantly growing in scale and so in impact; and Indigenous peoples were increasingly able to resist the industry's incursions. The growth of electronic media meant that the impacts of mining in far-flung corners of the globe were often immediately evident to the public in the home countries of multinational corporations (see, for instance, Evans et al. 2001; Moody 1992). Criticism of the mining industry's engagement with Indigenous peoples constituted part of a wider debate about its record on environmental and social issues, and its potential to play a role in the world's transition to environmental sustainability (IIED 2002; O'Faircheallaigh and Ali 2008). As part of the industry's response to this debate, nine of the world's largest mining companies established an initiative called Mining, Minerals and Sustainable Development (MMSD) in 1990. This undertook an extensive programme of research, consultation, and discussion, concerning the industry's future and how it might better meet demands for greater accountability, and focus more strongly on societal goals, while ensuring its ability to find and profitably exploit minerals (IIED 2002). One outcome from MMSD was the creation of the International Council on Mining and Metals (ICMM) based in London, whose members now include 27 of the world's largest mining and metals companies and 35 national and regional industry associations. ICMM company members undertake to adhere to the ICMM's Mining Principles. In relation to Indigenous peoples, the two key principles are:

3.6 Respect the rights, interests, aspirations, culture and natural resource based livelihoods of Indigenous Peoples in project design, development and operation; apply the mitigation hierarchy [i.e. 'minimise, mitigate, compensate'] to address adverse impacts and deliver sustainable benefits for Indigenous Peoples.

3.7 Work to obtain the free, prior and informed consent of Indigenous Peoples where significant adverse impacts are likely to occur, as a result of relocation, disturbance of lands and territories or of critical cultural heritage, and capture the outcomes of engagement and consent processes in agreements. (ICMM 2020)

These provisions fall short of a commitment not to proceed with mining projects in the absence of IFPIC, and leave open the question of how and by whom it is determined whether 'significant adverse impacts are likely to occur'. In addition, the Principles constitute a guide for company behaviour rather than mandatory requirements, and the ICMM does not itself have a grievance mechanism that Indigenous peoples can use if they believe that member companies have breached the Principles, which, according to MacInnes et al. (2017: 154) has occurred on numerous occasions. They must instead rely on any internal grievance mechanisms operated by the individual company that is believed to have breached the Principles. MacInnes et al. (2017: 155) also note that the ICMM only includes the world's largest companies and that many others, especially smaller companies that undertake a large proportion of mineral exploration, are not subject to ICMM policies. There can also be significant issues regarding the compliance of the operating subsidiaries of large companies with policies adopted at a corporate level (O'Faircheallaigh 2016: 104).

Conclusion

Recognition of Indigenous rights has emerged as a major international issue since the 1970s. This is indicated by the amount of resources and attention devoted to its promotion by Indigenous peoples and organizations, and the prominent position it now occupies in international legal instruments. Indigenous rights were barely mentioned in such instruments in 1980 but are now the specific focus of treaties and declarations emanating from the UN, the ILO and regional bodies such as the Organisation of African States. They are also a focus of business and human rights initiatives generated by the UN, and of international financial institutions and the global mining industry. As James Anaya notes (1997: 61), the movement for recognition of Indigenous rights has been very much driven by Indigenous peoples themselves and is a testimony to their agency and efficacy at the international level. Several authors have argued that the capacity of Indigenous peoples to operate effectively in the international arena is unsurprising. They engaged in treaty making before contact with Europe, and during the colonial period many Indigenous peoples, including those from Australia, New Zealand, Canada, the United States, the West Indies, and South America, sought to engage with the monarchs and governments of the colonial powers, including through petitions and by sending delegations to their capitals to plead their case (Corntassel 2007; De Costa 2006; Feldman 2002; Moody 1988; Naipaul 1989).

For Indigenous activists, acceptance of the closely related principles of the right of Indigenous peoples to self-determination and of IFPIC have been central to their campaign for international recognition. Only the right to self-determination can ensure that their ability to defend their interests and exercise their freedom to develop in the way they wish is not subverted by states. Only the exercise of IFPIC in relation to whether development occurs on their territories, and if so, to the terms under which it occurs, can allow them to ensure that the principle of self-determination is translated into control over state and corporate practices as these affect their lands, communities, and cultures.

Acceptance of these two principles by states and industry has been reluctant and has proceeded at a pace that has always been slow and at times glacial. Only in the UNDRIP do states commit unreservedly to both, and the Declaration does not bind states in their domestic legal jurisdictions. IFIs have generally been reluctant to commit to IFPIC. Business, whether through the UN Framework for Business and Human Rights, or industry initiatives such as the ICMM's Mining Principles, acknowledges in principle the need to respect Indigenous rights and engage with Indigenous peoples. However, it has been unwilling to support this acknowledgement by undertaking to restrict investments only to projects that have the free and informed consent of affected Indigenous peoples.

There remains the important issue of whether recognition of Indigenous rights in the international arena affects relations between mining and Indigenous peoples 'on the ground'. As noted in discussing individual instances of recognition, there can be no assumption that the signing of a treaty or adoption of a declaration by a state, or adoption of a policy or a principle by a bank or an industry association, means that states or individual corporations will act on their commitments. On the other hand, it can be argued that the ratification of a treaty or adoption of a policy is just a first step, and that what determines impact is the way in which Indigenous peoples and their allies subsequently use these commitments to improve their political leverage and achieve more positive outcomes, including by framing their local struggles as part of a global movement for recognition of Indigenous rights (Barsh 1994; Igoe 2006). Later chapters on Indigenous political strategies and on Indigenous experiences with mining in specific jurisdictions provide the opportunity to assess whether this potential of international recognition to bolster Indigenous political power has been realized.

PART II
KEY ACTORS

5

Indigenous Peoples

Diversity and Shared Experiences

Introduction

Indigenous peoples constitute the key focus of the book, and this chapter seeks to give a sense of who they are, of their diversity, but also of the commonalities that provide the basis for writing a book about their shared experience in dealing with mining. Diversity must be a starting point. Indigenous people live in all regions of the world; according to the United Nations (UN) they occupy or use some 25 per cent of global land area, number 370–500 million, and represent the greater part of the world's cultural diversity. They speak the major share of the world's almost 7,000 languages (UNESCO 2022; see also Garnett et al. 2018). They live in cities and in the world's most remote regions, in its richest countries and its poorest. They also share values and key characteristics. They define their identity and their social relationships through their connections to *specific* areas of land and water; they have been dispossessed and marginalized by dominant societies, which are often colonial in origin; and in material terms they tend to be disadvantaged compared to majority populations. It is these shared characteristics that create the basis for a complex and at times contradictory relationship with the mining industry. Mining represents a threat to their lands, waters, values, and cultures, but at the same time offers access to economic opportunities that can help overcome material disadvantage and provide resources to support Indigenous livelihoods (Tahltan First Nation/IISD 2004).

The next section discusses definitional issues involved in discussing Indigenous peoples. The following sections identify key shared characteristics of Indigenous peoples, focusing on those most likely to be affected by large-scale mineral development, and considering their values, social organization, histories, and current circumstances. This discussion highlights the need to avoid simplistic characterizations of Indigenous peoples in terms of their likely attitudes towards and engagement with the mining industry.

Indigenous Peoples and Mining. Ciaran O'Faircheallaigh, Oxford University Press. © Ciaran O'Faircheallaigh (2023).
DOI: 10.1093/oso/9780192894564.003.0005

Defining 'indigenous peoples'

Given the variety of historical, political, social, and ecological circumstances that exist throughout the globe, it is no simple matter to find a neat and universally applicable definition of 'Indigenous peoples'. The definition employed by the UN is:

> Indigenous communities, peoples and nations are those which, having a historical continuity with pre-invasion and pre-colonial societies that developed on their territories, consider themselves distinct from other sectors of the societies now prevailing on those territories, or parts of them. They form at present non-dominant sectors of society and are determined to preserve, develop and transmit to future generations their ancestral territories, and their ethnic identity, as the basis of their continued existence as peoples, in accordance with their own cultural patterns, social institutions and legal system.

This definition still leaves some room for ambiguity and uncertainty about whether or not specific populations should be regarded as 'Indigenous' (Keal 2007; Muehlebach 2003). For instance, at a national level, customary landowners in Papua New Guinea own over 90 per cent of its land and constitute more than 90 per cent of its population, and so could hardly be described as 'non-dominant sectors of society'. On the other hand, specific groups of customary landowners, such as the Ipili owners of the land on which the Porgera gold mine is located, might well regard themselves as 'distinct from all other sectors of society' and as meeting the other elements of the UN definition. In terms of their relationship to the Porgera mine, they might be indistinguishable from other peoples who unequivocally conform to the UN definition. Indeed, had the border between what are now Papua New Guinea and Indonesia been drawn differently by colonial authorities, the Ipili would be in Indonesia and they would conform with the definition. Given this point, it seems illogical and counterproductive to exclude the experience of the Ipili from the analysis on the basis that they are not 'Indigenous'. Fortunately, these sorts of definitional issues arise only at the margins. In the large majority of cases dealt with in the book, there it is clear that the peoples involved meet the UN definition of 'Indigenous'.

Numerous states have sought to control and apply particular definitions of 'Indigenous' for their own administrative and political purposes. For instance, historically this was done by certain states in relation to individuals, formed a basis for their differential treatment, and in some cases was part of a strategy for the eventual disappearance of Indigenous peoples (Perry 1996; Simpson 2017; Tully 2000: 40–1). In Australia, individuals deemed to have less than a certain proportion of 'Aboriginal blood' were defined as 'half castes' and not as 'Aboriginal natives'. 'Half castes' were deemed suitable for integration into the mainstream and so for having their Aboriginal identity expunged ('assimilation'). 'Natives' were denied citizenship rights and sent to isolated mission or government reserves where they and any descendants were expected eventually to 'die out' (Chesterman and Galligan 1997: 12–13; Rowley 1970: 320–1).

States have also denied that specific peoples are Indigenous, or that Indigenous peoples reside on particular territories. For example, the Soviet Union from the 1930s onwards refused to use 'Indigenous' or any related term and instead applied any differential policy approaches or resource allocation only to 'small minorities'. The latter were defined on the basis that their numbers had to fall below a specified ceiling, with the result that the Soviet Union's largest Indigenous peoples, including the Yakuts, the Komi, the Nenets, and the Sami, were, for legal, policy, and budgetary purposes, defined out of existence (Dahl 1990). After what was regarded as a period of transition, 'small minorities' were deemed to have disappeared as distinct peoples, to have 'completed the full construction of socialism and thereafter the history of their development in no way differed from that of other peoples in the USSR' (cited in Vakhtin 1998: 87). Some African states, intent on emphasizing the homogenous nature of their populations as part of nation-building strategies, have similarly denied the very existence of Indigenous peoples (Igoe 2006; IWGIA 2020: 37, 74; and see Chapter 13). In other cases, including the Province of Labrador and Newfoundland in Canada, state authorities have denied that Indigenous groups continue to reside, or maintain their cultural practices, in areas earmarked for resource development. On this basis they have sought to deny Indigenous people a say in decisions about, or a share of the benefits from, development (Procter 2020). On a more systemic level, Australia's legal regime for recognizing inherent Indigenous rights imposes onerous burdens on Aboriginal claimants to demonstrate an unbroken connection to ancestral lands since the time of first colonization. The result is that they may be unable to achieve legal recognition of their claims to land and be denied procedural rights in relation to development on their territories (Strelein 2003; on the same issue in Canada, see Tully 2000: 47–8).

A final point relates to self-identification of Indigenous people as 'Indigenous'. A characteristic of Indigenous peoples is that they define their cultural and social identities in relation to specific areas of land, and so their primary identity is likely to be expressed in terms of that association, rather than the much broader and generic concept of 'Indigenous'. In my experience, Aboriginal people in Australia, for instance, will describe themselves first as 'Wik', or 'Dja Dja Wurrung', or 'Mirrar', because they define themselves in terms of their connection to Wik, or Dja Dja Wurrung, or Mirrar *lands*. They will also, but secondarily, identify as 'Aboriginal', for instance in the context of a national campaign for recognition of Aboriginal land rights in Australia; and may identify as 'Indigenous', for example in expressing solidarity with associates in Canada or Peru or support for the United Nations Declaration on the Rights of Indigenous Peoples.

It is also the case that peoples may not even be aware of their potential identity as 'Indigenous', until the dynamic of their domestic economic and political situation, combined with initiatives for international recognition of Indigenous rights, makes them appreciate the potential leverage they can gain by articulating an Indigenous identity. Igoe (2006) documents just such a process in relation to Maasai peoples in Tanzania, who had not articulated an 'Indigenous' identity before the 1990s. They started to do so then as part of a strategy to mobilize external resources and support in the face of serious threats to their pastoral way of life arising from loss of their territories to national parks, to rapidly growing commercial agriculture following Tanzania's economic liberalization, and to small-scale subsistence agriculturalists displaced from neighbouring areas. Maasai leaders first combined with other pastoralists to set up a national network of Pastoralist and Indigenous non-government organizations (NGOs), and moved to engage with the international Indigenous movement. They undertook exchanges with Indigenous communities in Canada, Australia, and Latin America; sponsored events to celebrate the UN Decade for Indigenous Peoples; and participated in the UN Forum on Indigenous Issues (Igoe 2006: 399–400).

Apart from the concept of 'Indigenous', a number of other terms require definition. An important one is 'traditional'. 'Traditional' is used extensively in connection with 'Indigenous'. In Australia, for instance, it is widely used as part of the term 'traditional owners', which refers to Aboriginal people who have cultural responsibility for, and often legally recognized interests in, specific territories. It is frequently used in combination with 'knowledge' or 'environmental knowledge' to refer to the distinctive understandings that Indigenous peoples have, based on accumulation of knowledge over multiple generations, of interactions between humans and the environment. It is used in combination with 'territory' or 'lands' to denote the estates of Indigenous peoples prior to contact with colonizers. The difficulty with the term 'traditional' is that it can wrongly imply a lack of dynamism, that Indigenous people are fixed in some prior time and lack the ability to, or interest in, adjusting to the realities of the contemporary world. Thus, except in cases where it has a neutral or purely descriptive purpose (for instance, 'traditional owner' in the Australian context), its use is avoided here. Indigenous lands, for instance, are described as 'Indigenous territories', and the term 'Indigenous ecological knowledge' is used in preference to 'traditional knowledge'.

A final term frequently encountered in association with 'Indigenous' is 'community'. As used here, it has two distinct but related meanings. The first consists of Indigenous people residing in a location adjacent to, or affected by, a project. They share a place of residence and an experience of impact, though the nature of that experience may vary between individuals and groups within a community. The second type involves people who share economic, cultural, and social ties through their connection with, and responsibilities for, an area of land or water affected by mining. They may not reside in one place, and indeed may be widely dispersed. Yet they represent a social and cultural community and, again, an experience of impact, the nature of which may vary.

Use of the term 'community' in either of these two senses does not imply a single attitude or approach to mining among community members, or a single and shared set of interests in relation to a project or to distribution of its costs and benefits, or exclude the possibility that elites may exist whose interests do not coincide with those of the majority (Igoe 2006: 416; Sanz 2019; Schilling-Vacaflor and Eichler 2017). Indeed, as we will see in later chapters, many Indigenous communities are divided in relation to, for instance, their attitude to mining, and political contests around distribution of benefits can, especially where they result in inequitable outcomes, sharpen existing community divisions or create new ones.

Indigenous peoples and cultures

This section draws on an extensive review of relevant academic literature and documentary sources, referenced elsewhere in the book; on my experience over 35 years in working with and living in Indigenous communities and building relationships with Indigenous peoples; and on interactions with numerous Indigenous people in conferences, workshops, and training programmes in different parts of the globe.

There are substantial differences between Indigenous peoples as a whole and the non-Indigenous societies within which they are located. To make this point is not to deny the existence of important differences *within* Indigenous societies. Not all members of any Indigenous society will share the same attitudes to land, to personal economic gain, to kinship obligations, or to Indigenous cultural and spiritual practice.

Central to the identity and survival of Indigenous peoples are the connections between land, kinship and social relations, and culture and spirituality. Connection to ancestral land or 'country' (defined here to include fresh and sea waters and air) is fundamental. Land is traditionally the source of physical survival and since time immemorial has sustained life and health. Many Indigenous communities still rely heavily on the land for production and income, and harvesting of the land's resources is often intimately associated with cultural and social activity and knowledge transmission. Land creates identity. A person is a member of a specific Indigenous group because they have an intimate connection, usually through blood ancestors but sometimes through their place of birth or by adoption, with a particular *country*. To see one's ancestral lands destroyed, to be forcefully separated from them, or to lose the ability to influence what happens on and to them, is not just to lose the source of physical sustenance. It is to lose one's identity or have it threatened. Thus, even if Indigenous people have alternative sources of income with which they can purchase the physical necessities of life, damage to or separation from their ancestral lands still represents a profound threat.

Indigenous peoples tend to have an understanding of 'land' that is very different from the commodity-based approach of contemporary 'mainstream' societies. Land is often understood to have been formed by ancestor spirits as part of creation processes that also involved the creation of peoples. Features of today's landscapes may embody those creation spirits: for example, because those features are their resting places after the work of creation has finished. Land may not be seen as the 'property' of people, and indeed land may be seen as 'owning' people associated with it, rather than as being 'owned' by those people.

The process that resulted in the creation of land and people also resulted in the establishment of a moral order, of rules about how members of a group should and should not relate to each other, about how groups should relate to each other, and about appropriate consequences for breach of the moral order. In many Indigenous societies, reciprocity and balance are central to the moral order, and embodied, for instance, in gift exchange and trade cycles in mundane (everyday) and spiritual items. Group autonomy is also often a central moral principle. Given that a people's land, social relations, and moral order are the result of the actions of creation spirits or ancestors, no external party has the right to overrule a group's decisions in relation to its land and its law. This emphasis on autonomy is a powerful theme across what in some other respects may be quite different Indigenous societies.

Kinship is central to social organization. Extended families or groups consisting of a number of linked families tend to be the basic unit of social and cultural (and often of political) organization. The nature of interpersonal behaviour and social interaction will be heavily influenced by the precise nature of kin relationships. Primary loyalties tend to be felt and expressed towards one's kin or 'clan', and in many contexts other loyalties will have to take second place. Kinship is, of course, intimately connected to land. It is kin relationships to ancestors that provide an Indigenous person with connections to land, and in turn the existence of that common connection and its expression (for example, through economic production or cultural practice) reinforce ties of kinship.

The persistence and importance of kinship and of ties to land as a basis for social relationships and for political action is difficult to overstate. This is not to suggest that there are rigid landowning and kinship structures and social rules that survive from pre-contact Indigenous societies and dictate contemporary behaviour in a mechanistic way. This is far from the case. Both connections to land and kinship systems are dynamic, they have adjusted extensively to the impact of colonization, and they continue to evolve, develop, and adapt. However, kinship and connection to land are still fundamental in defining Indigenous responses to issues such as mineral development.

Culture and spirituality are also closely linked to land. Much of Indigenous cultural practice revolves around caring for and extracting resources from the land, while Indigenous spiritual beliefs are often related to the existence of a creator-being or beings who are believed to have shaped the landscape and created people and other living creatures. Sites of cultural and spiritual significance are often associated with landscape features linked to those creation processes and to the spiritual entities involved in them. For many Indigenous peoples, those entities continue to reside in the land.

Fundamental to Indigenous welfare is the ability to care for the land and the cultural or spiritual sites that form part of it. Such activity ensures that the land maintains its capacity to support people and at the same time protects the spiritual well-being of the individuals concerned because it allows them to fulfil their spiritual obligations. It follows that physical damage to the landscape, or an inability to carry out essential land management practices, can have serious cultural, spiritual, and physical ramifications. The fact that damage is caused by external agencies in the face of opposition from Aboriginal custodians or that custodians are physically prevented from caring for country does not reduce the gravity of the situation. Custodians will still have to answer to other Indigenous people with interests in that country and to the relevant creator- or spirit-beings.

Despite their diversity, many Indigenous peoples have shared understanding of the nature of the universe and of peoples within it, which can be very different from those that underpin Western 'science' and thought. Many Indigenous peoples do not accept the fundamental Judeo-Christian assumptions that humankind is separate from, superior to, and entitled to exploit, the environment or 'nature'. This can be reflected, for instance, in a belief that all nature (including rocks, trees, and rivers) is alive and comprises sentient beings. Rivers can have persona and exercise agency; in some cultures, animals or fish, rather than humans, are seen as having responsibility for managing parts of the environment. It can also be reflected in a belief that humans are not just involved in social relations with each other, but also with animals, birds, rivers, and seas. Within this understanding of the universe, *relationships* are key— with other people, with other creatures, with land and water in all their aspects. In some cultures, for example, individual animals and fish are believed to give them-selves voluntarily to hunters as part of a relationship in which hunters maintain an ecology in which animal and fish species can thrive.

There is often no distinction of the type found in dominant societies between 'law' and 'morality'. The 'law' comprises rules for a moral life; the creation of land, people, and law is understood to have occurred through inextricably related pro-cesses, often referred to in the context of Aboriginal Australia, for instance, as 'the Dreamings' (Rose 1984). While these processes of creation occurred in the past, they also continue to exist and to have an impact today, indicating another way in which many Indigenous societies can differ from Western ones: that is, time is not seen as constituting a single, linear process. This lack of a linear time process may also man-ifest itself in a belief that ancestors have a continued existence and interact with and influence the current generation.

In talking separately about the past and the present, and separately about land, about people (kinship and social relations), and about culture and spirituality, this discussion treats distinctly matters that Indigenous people see in a holistic manner and as inseparable. They not only place a different emphasis on these matters or understand them differently from non-Indigenous people. They do not believe they can be separated in the way that often occurs in non-Aboriginal society (Brody 2000; Stoffle and Evans 1990).

Drawing this discussion together and repeating the need to recognize diversity between and within Indigenous societies, it is nevertheless evident that Indigenous peoples are likely to view 'development' and its impacts in ways fundamentally differ-ent from the dominant society. What may be regarded as an acceptable 'impact' from a mining project, for example, will be very different if humans are in social relations with birds and animals, if rocks and rivers are sentient, and if creation-beings are still present in the landscape. Whether it is possible to compensate people for impacts and, if it is, what is required to effect compensation may also be seen very differently. Financial compensation for loss of land, for example, may be entirely inadequate where land is the basis for peoples' social identity and relationships, and contains the embodiment of creation-beings. Taking resources from their lands and taking decisions without their consent may not just cause economic or political grievances for Indigenous peoples, but also offend the *moral* order by breaching the principles of reciprocity and autonomy.

In drawing this profile of Indigenous societies, it is essential not to fall into the trap of creating a stereotype that sees Indigenous peoples as 'Guardians of Nature' (Vel 2014) who are disinterested in material well-being, altruistic and indifferent to individual interests, egalitarian, and committed to consensual and inclusive decision making. Ramos has coined the concept of 'The Hyperreal Indian' to describe this approach. She has documented how non-Indigenous activists in NGOs in Brazil operated on assumptions regarding what is appropriate Indigenous behaviour and responses to development, and then 'punished' Indigenous people who did not live up to this ideal by withdrawing NGO financial and political support (Ramos 1994; see also Horowitz 2002). The 'authenticity' of Indigenous communities who seek to engage with mining to obtain much-needed economic opportunities or to mitigate negative environmental impacts is questioned, while opposition to mining can be taken as automatically establishing Indigenous 'credentials' (Butler et al. 2021: 20; Gerbrandt and Westman 2020; Lyons 2018). Sehlin MacNeil (2017: 7) argues that essentializing Indigenous peoples in this way tends to feed:

> notions of cultures as stagnant and … makes the conflicted interface between connection to Country and life in a modern world even more difficult to navigate, as Indigenous peoples are then expected to live in ways that the dominant society views as traditional. On the contrary, the people that possess a particular connection to a particular Country must be allowed to determine what connection to Country means and involves.

In analytical terms, an assumption that Indigenous communities, if they are genuinely Indigenous, will naturally be united in their opposition to mining can result in analysis based on an 'idealised pageantry of extractive conflicts' (Lander et al. 2021) and create 'black boxes' which 'may hide the more complex dynamics, interactions and negotiations of power which occur at multiple scales around extractive industries' (Szablowski 2007: 137). It may prove to be the case that mining has seriously detrimental impacts which may threaten the survival of Indigenous peoples. However, it is a mistake to assume that simply because a people engage with the industry in the hope of achieving a more favourable (or at least less damaging) outcome, their Indigeneity is in question. In addition, patterns of engagement can be varied and complex. For example, it may be that an Indigenous community has a strong interest in pursuing economic opportunities, but will be completely opposed to a specific mining project because it would threaten ecological and cultural values on which the community is not prepared to compromise (Kunkel 2017).

Indigenous peoples are just as capable as anyone else of single-mindedly pursuing their specific interests. The point is that they define those interests in a way that is different from most mainstream societies. Indigenous societies were typically small in scale and lacked formal, institutionalized leadership positions, with the result that decision making tended to be consensual. But this does not mean for a moment that they were egalitarian. In creating a consensus, the weight of some individuals always counted for more than others. Neither is there any reason to believe that Indigenous peoples are any less interested in economic prosperity than anyone else. Indeed, the whole purpose of much cultural and spiritual activity is to ensure the ongoing ability of land and waters to provide sustenance and prosperity (Kuokkanen 2011). It is also important to recall the way in which Indigenous peoples adjusted rapidly to the changes wrought by the gold rushes of the mid-nineteenth century and used the opportunities they offered to create significant wealth. Above all, Indigenous societies have survived for thousands and in some cases for tens of thousands of years. That would not have been possible if Indigenous peoples were not pragmatic and adaptable, within the fundamental structures created by their value systems and connections to land. One would expect them to demonstrate the same adaptability and pragmatism, within the limits of their fundamental belief systems and long-term economic interests, when faced with large-scale mineral development in the contemporary world (Bainton and Jackson 2020; Ghostkeeper 2004: 168–70; Horowitz 2002).

A final point to make involves the cosmologies and ontologies of Indigenous peoples and their implications for theory and explanation. As noted above, many Indigenous peoples believe that creation-beings and spirits inhabit the earth, that landscape features such as mountains and rivers are sentient, that these beings and landscape features have agency, and that the exercise of this agency can explain phenomena in the human sphere. For instance, Li (2015: 107–8) recounts the statements of an Indigenous woman in northern Peru that the sacred, sentient mountain Cerro Quilish would have to 'give its consent' before mining could take place on the mountain, that it was a 'fierce' mountain, and that during the exploration phase 'many mine workers lost their lives, "eaten" by the mountain'. Jacka (2018: 68) describes how landowners around the Porgera mine in Papua New Guinea described ancestral python spirits that live at the base of mountains, cause earthquakes, and are believed to have created the gold deposits in the region (see also Sanz 2019: 214).

The way in which the existence and actions of spirit-beings can provide alternative theoretical and explanatory frameworks is illustrated by events at the Argyle diamond mine in Western Australia, a major global source of diamonds which operated between 1983 and 2020.[1] Argyle had a strong safety record that was recognized through several awards. Its good record was blighted in May 2003 when a large mining truck that had broken down rolled into another truck, crushing its cabin and killing the truck's 21-year-old driver. A coronial inquest attributed the accident to

[1] I was assisting Argyle's traditional owners to negotiate a new agreement with Argyle Diamonds Ltd during the period covering these events, and participated in the *manthe* ceremony discussed here. This account is based on my conversations with traditional owners about what for them was the deeply troubling death of a young mine worker; and on court reports regarding the accident.

the failure of several Argyle employees to follow proper safety procedures. The Aboriginal traditional owners of the Argyle mine considered this explanation inadequate. They had arranged, in cooperation with the mine's operator and as part of its standard induction process, that before commencing work every person coming to the mine site went through a ceremony performed by traditional owners and called *manthe*. Through this ceremony the traditional owners welcomed the new arrivals to country, introduced them to the spirit-beings who live under the ground at the mine, and invoked the protection of the spirits for the workers. Due to an administrative error, the young man killed in the accident had not undertaken *manthe* before starting work. The traditional owners did not consider the breaches of safety procedures irrelevant, and they welcomed company action designed to prevent their reoccurrence. However, they invoked a higher-level explanation in the form of the failure to ensure the protection of the sprits and the consequent exposure of the worker to danger. Avoiding safety breaches would not on its own have prevented the accident. Only invoking the protection of the spirits through the *manthe* would have done so.

A major problem for Indigenous peoples is that dominant societies are generally dismissive of their knowledge and their explanations. As a Sami reindeer herder expressed it, 'if we argue something, if we say that something is a certain way, it is not viewed as legitimate' (cited in Sehlin MacNeil 2017: vi).

Colonial impacts and Indigenous marginalization

Indigenous experiences of colonization varied from region to region, depending in particular on the extent to which their territories were deemed suitable for settler agriculture and industry, and on the timing of settlement. For example, the territories of the Mapuche in southern Chile are well watered and fertile, leading to successive waves of dispossession. These started with the Spanish conquest and continued through to the large-scale appropriation of forest resources by foreign investors after Chile's economic liberalization in the 1980s, with the result that the Mapuche lost a large part of their territories (Carruthers and Rodriguez 2009). In Chile's northern desert region, one of the most arid places on earth, Atacama peoples were better able to retain possession of their lands and many do so to this day. Timing was also important. In the late twentieth century, in liberal democracies, at least, the widespread violence that accompanied settlement in the previous century was largely absent. Yet despite these differences there are elements of the colonial experience that are common across nearly all Indigenous peoples. Paul Keal (2007) has argued that it was the 'shared experience of colonization' that made possible the emergence of the international Indigenous movement in the 1970s (see also Perry 1996: 3–4). Keal (2007: 44) cites Australian Aboriginal leader Mick Dodson's response when he first attended the UN Working Group on Indigenous Peoples:

We were all part of a world community of Indigenous peoples spanning the planet; experiencing the same problems and struggling against the same alienation, marginalisation and sense of powerlessness. We had gathered there united by our shared frustration with the dominant systems in our own countries and their consistent failure to deliver justice.

In many cases, the most obvious and dramatic impact of colonization on Indigenous peoples was rapid population loss due to settler warfare, introduced diseases, loss of land, and social disruption. Some peoples did not survive this impact and disappeared for ever (Cocker 1998; Naipaul 1989). In almost all cases, its effect was profound, as indicated by Australia's experience, where the Aboriginal population fell from about 500,000 when European settlement began in 1788, to 93,000 a century later (O'Faircheallaigh 2017: 19). In what is now California, the Indian population fell from an estimated 700,000 at contact to less than 200,000 in the mid-1840s (Wilson 1998: 226; see also Perry 1996: 231–2).

Colonization in all cases was characterized by racism, by an underlying belief that Indigenous societies and cultures were inherently inferior and lacked value. Such beliefs were used by settlers and colonial governments to justify a range of actions and policies that were destructive of Indigenous societies, including theft of land, removal of children, suppression of Indigenous cultures and languages, and, in some cases, attempts to physically eradicate particular Indigenous groups. Racism was also used to justify a refusal by state authorities to recognize Indigenous forms of governance and decision making or to accept that Indigenous peoples had either the capacity or the right to influence decisions which affected them, including decisions regarding development of minerals on their ancestral lands. From a settler perspective, the marked inferiority of Aboriginal societies meant it was obvious that decision making should be in the hands of non-Indigenous government officials or settlers. Such beliefs were used to justify decisions that accorded neatly with non-Indigenous economic and political interests (Åhrén 2004: 82–3; Cocker 1998: parts 2 and 3; Orihuela 2012; Perry 1996: 30–1; Sawchuk 1998, chapter 5; Wilson 1998).

Indigenous peoples were not only denied the capacity to govern themselves, they were also denied the opportunity to participate in 'mainstream' political processes, because one specific manifestation of racism was the denial of political and constitutional rights enjoyed by non-Indigenous citizens. In many countries, Indigenous peoples were, for various lengths of time, excluded from the census, prohibited from voting, had their movements controlled, were denied access to part or all of personal wage income, and were prohibited from establishing formal organizations (Chesterman and Galligan 1997; Kidd 1997; Sawchuk 1998: 7). This denial of fundamental human and political rights prevented Indigenous peoples from using mainstream political channels to pursue their goals, and limited their opportunities to develop the skills required to operate effectively in a non-Indigenous political context. One result of this situation, in combination with colonial policies that denied the legitimacy and relevance of Indigenous forms of governance, is that some Indigenous communities have limited organizational capacity (including internal decision-making capacity) to support effective interactions with non-Indigenous society, including the mining industry.

Blatant manifestations of racism towards Indigenous peoples, including physical segregation, denial of voting rights, confiscation of property, and widespread violence, are still evident in some parts of the world (IWGIA 2020: 74–90, 361–2). Even where they are not, Indigenous peoples still suffer the effects of racism at many levels. These include the influence of racist attitudes in the electorate and so on the formulation of policies affecting Indigenous interests; the dismissal of Indigenous knowledge and ways of knowing; and the impact of racist beliefs on the individual experiences of Indigenous peoples in the workplace and in their communities (Althaus and O'Faircheallaigh 2019; IWGIA 2020; Orihuela 2012).

A specific impact of colonization that is particularly relevant in the current context is Indigenous dispossession or diminution of Indigenous rights to land, including ownership of mineral rights and control over their disposition. As noted above, the degree and nature of impact in this area varied from region to region, but it was significant everywhere. Dispossession was highly destructive in ways that went well beyond the economic, given the role of land in Indigenous identity, social relations, culture, and spirituality.

Colonization had differential impacts on Indigenous men and women. It disrupted established gender roles and relations, with settlers imposing patriarchal structures on societies in which women had exercised significant power. Pre-contact Indigenous societies were often far from achieving gender equality (Anderson 1983), but in many of them women played prominent and influential roles in public life and politics (Anderson and Lawrence 2006; Salmond 2017; Simpson 2017). In New Zealand's pre-contact hierarchical Maori society, for instance, women were often chiefs, including war chiefs who led warriors into battle. In 1840 the colonial government negotiated the Treaty of Waitangi with tribes across the north and south islands, a treaty intended as the foundation document for future relations between Maori and settlers. It was signed by more than 500 chiefs from across New Zealand, but very few were women because British officers refused to allow women chiefs who attended signing ceremonies to add their signatures to the treaty (Salmond 2017). In Canada, federal legislation governing Indigenous peoples, and in particular the Indian Act (1876) and its subsequent iterations, discriminated systematically against women. For instance, it excluding them from appointment to band councils and deprived them (and their children) of band membership if they married non-Indigenous men. Aboriginal men, on the other hand, lost none of their membership rights if they married non-Indigenous women. Leanne Betasamosake Simpson (2017) has documented in detail the negative impact of colonization on the roles, status, and power of Aboriginal women in Canada, and the way in which this impact continues to resonate today on many dimensions of gender and of sexual identity.

Another shared experience of Indigenous peoples stemming from colonization is their low economic status and poor access to public services, such as health and education, relative to non-Indigenous populations. On average, Indigenous incomes are substantially lower and unemployment substantially higher than national averages; levels of formal education are relatively low; and access to physical services such as housing, sewage, and clean water is poor. Health status also tends to be poor, as indicated, for example, by high infant mortality rates and low life expectancy. In many countries, Indigenous people are hugely overrepresented in the criminal justice system and indicators of social trauma such as youth suicide are very high by national standards. It is reported that in the late 1980s the average life expectancy for Indigenous peoples in northern Russia was 16–18 years below the Soviet national average, and that suicide rates were 34 times higher than the national (Taksami 1990). Tragically, similar statistics could be cited for many other Indigenous populations around the globe during the last decade (ABS 2012; Government of Canada 2013; Health Council of Canada 2013; IWGIA 2020: 54, 148, 275, 388; 2021: 181, 311; McGlade 2012). The advent of the COVID-19 virus is likely to worsen this situation, and not only because of its direct impact on the health of vulnerable Indigenous populations. Limited availability of information technology is inhibiting access to education as classes go online; local travel restrictions are preventing people from reaching markets where they sell food; and suspension of international travel is decimating cultural tourism (IWGIA 2021).

The reasons for Indigenous disadvantage are complex. They include the fact that government expenditure on service provision for Indigenous peoples has historically been extremely low and is often still inadequate, and the undermining of Indigenous law, society, and culture as a result of dispossession and policies such as the forced removal of children. They also include the effect of limited organizational skills and capacity on the ability of Indigenous groups to deal with the economic, cultural, and social issues they confront; and the continued unwillingness of governments to work with Indigenous peoples to develop and implement policies that reflect Indigenous values and priorities (O'Faircheallaigh 2017). In economic terms, dispossession has often denied Indigenous peoples access to physical resources required to sustain life and health and, combined with government policy, has stopped them from benefiting from European economic activity on their ancestral lands. In the specific case of mining, for instance, most Aboriginal peoples have until recently not been able to share in the revenues and the direct and indirect employment generated by the industry.

Reflecting the nature of their experiences with government over many generations, Aboriginal peoples are often highly suspicious of, if not openly hostile towards, state authorities. Governments have alienated their lands, taken away their children, suppressed their culture, denied them access to rights and services available to other citizens, and denied them the opportunity to share in the economic benefits created by exploitation of their ancestral land.

Indigenous women and mining

The diversity that characterizes Indigenous peoples also applies to the role and status of women in public life within individual Indigenous societies, with major differences evident between and within countries. In some regions and countries, Indigenous women play a prominent role in relation to the mining industry, whether in engaging with it or resisting it. For example, in western Cape York in north Queensland, the mayors of two of the three Aboriginal communities affected by Rio Tinto's bauxite mines are currently (April 2022) women. Women chair the boards of directors of both Aboriginal trusts that receive bauxite royalties, and the entire board of one of these trusts are women. In other parts of Australia, Aboriginal societies are more patriarchal and women play a limited role in public life, a situation that also applies in some Inuit communities in northern Canada (Dalseg et al. 2018: 145). (This does not necessarily mean that women do not influence responses to mining—a point I return to below.) There is a large literature suggesting that women in Melanesian societies are often excluded from decisions about mining and the use of monetary benefits it generates (Bainton and Jackson 2020; Horowitz 2017). Yet on Bougainville Island in Papua New Guinea, women played and continue to play a prominent role in events surrounding the (now closed) Panguna copper mine, including as leaders of influential landowner associations.

The diversity in the situation of Indigenous women today reflects in part differences that existed between pre-contact Indigenous societies. Contrast, for example, the subjugation of women described by Horowitz (2017: 1426) in pre-contact Kanak society in New Caledonia, with the requirement in certain Bolivian Indigenous societies to have two sets of leaders, female and male (Fernandez 2020: 35), and the central role women played in the economies and governance of many North American Indigenous peoples (Gunn 2018: 33–5). The current situation also reflects diverse contact histories, and contemporary influences including the actions of state agencies and mining companies and the agency exercised by Indigenous peoples in responding to these (see, for example, Fernandez 2020; Horowitz 2017; Kuokkanen 2011; Morales 2018: 82–3; PIWC 2015: 13, 17).

What is common across the wide variety of Indigenous contexts is that women can be affected by mining, and may respond to mining, quite differently from men (see Fernandez (2020) on Bolivia; Horowitz (2017) on New Caledonia; Morales (2018) on northern Canada; Glynn and Maimunah (2021) on Indonesia; Manning (2016) on Papua New Guinea; and Torrado 2022 on Colombia). This point must be recognized at the outset, and I return to it in analysing specific aspects of the Indigenous experience with mining and in the case study chapters.

The literature suggests that there are three main ways in which Indigenous women may be affected by mining in ways different from Indigenous men. First, the social, economic, cultural, and health impacts of mining may be experienced differently. For instance, if women play roles in food production not performed by men, and the resources they use are adversely affected by mining, they will experience its impacts differently (Fernandez 2020: 27). The same will apply if resources or places that have special cultural significance for women are damaged by mining or have their values degraded by the presence and activities of non-Indigenous people (Morales 2018: 76, 78–9). The social value of women's work in food production may be undermined by the premium placed on wage labour in mining and the use of wages and royalty payments to purchase store-bought food (Kuokkanen 2011). The relative economic status of women may decline where employment and business opportunities are monopolized by men or where women can secure only temporary and/or unskilled work (PIWC 2016: 48, 56). The likelihood of this outcome is increased by the fact that mining is a male-dominated industry where barriers to female employment have historically been high (Cox and Mills 2015; Manning 2016: 578; Morales 2018: 77) and because male managers may prefer to engage with Indigenous men, or may be required to do so by established cultural norms (Horowitz 2017: 1420–2, 1427).

Second, women may face impacts or risks of impacts to which men are immune or are much less exposed. These include a higher risk of violence from male relatives, which escalates where wages or royalties are spent on alcohol or drugs, and additional childcare responsibilities when male partners are absent at a mine site, the latter exacerbated when childcare services are inadequate. Women may also experience sexual harassment when they gain employment in mines; and face the risk of violence, including rape and murder, at the hands of male immigrants employed in mines or seeking work in them (Carreon 2009: 107–8; Dalseg et al. 2018: 139; Manning 2016: 579–81; Morales 2018: 75, 82; PIWC 2015: iii–iv, 14–15; 2016: ii, 8, 46).

Third, the social and political influence of women may be undermined because they are excluded from participation in processes that influence outcomes from mining and have profound consequences for them, their children, and their communities. This exclusion can occur in relation to environmental impact assessment because the consultation methods used by companies are inimical to women's involvement (Dalseg et al. 2018). It can also happen in relation to monitoring of project impacts because male on-site company personnel do not seek or welcome women's participation and may subject women monitors to demeaning behaviour or harassment (Gerbrandt and Westman 2020: 1303). Women may also be excluded from management of corporations that determine use of mining royalties (Bainton and Jackson 2020: 372). Negotiation and implementation of agreements is another arena from which women may be excluded (Morales 2018: 74).

This last example highlights the need to consider fully the different ways in which influence may be exerted over decisions. O'Faircheallaigh (2013a) shows how Indigenous women influenced the agendas for and outcomes from mining negotiations in Australia and Canada, despite not being members of formal negotiating teams. Their influence was exerted, for example, through their roles in community consultation processes that shaped Indigenous goals for negotiations, and through the critical part they played in the implementation of agreements, including management of royalties, so shaping the ultimate impact of mining (see Kuntz (2012) for similar findings in relation to women's role in environmental impact assessment in Canada's Northwest Territories). The need to be aware of different ways of exercising influence was brought home to me when I attended as an observer a meeting of an Aboriginal negotiating team involved in discussions with a coal-mining company in British Columbia, Canada. The team was entirely composed of men. At a particular point in the meeting, the team reported on progress in negotiations to the First Nations band council, whose President was a woman, and negotiating team members then discussed possible positions and outcomes on key negotiation issues. After some time, the President laid out for the negotiating team very firmly the outcome she would and would not accept on each key issue. When she had finished speaking and before leaving the meeting, she asked: 'Are you very clear on this?' The male negotiating team members responded that they were.

More generally, it is important to avoid casting women as victims who lack agency when they encounter the mining industry. Gunn (2018: 35) argues that the 'literature too often portrays Indigenous women as victims in need of special assistance, thus perpetuating the deficit model in which Indigenous women are found lacking the ability to help themselves … this approach fails to support Indigenous women's agency and fails to identify the problem as the gendered impacts of colonialism' (see also Großmann et al. 2017: 19–20).

Where exclusion of women from decision making does already occur, it may be exacerbated by the strategies of mining companies as they seek to deflect and control any resistance to their activities. Horowitz (2017) explains how Vale, one of the mine's largest mining companies, excluded from decision making women who were opposed to company plans to remove mangroves from a coastal development site in New Caledonia. Vale then justified the exclusion on the basis that 'custom' did not allow the inclusion of women in public forums. At the same time, Vale ignored custom when it suited the company. It signed a pact with men who had violently attacked company installations to forestall their continued opposition, even though customary chiefs complained that the men involved lacked authority to negotiate with the company (Horowitz 2017: 1432–3). In this way, Vale 'undermined Kanak women's social and political gains by reinforcing a "customary" static vision of Kanak women's social position as inferior, in order to silence them' (Horowitz 2017: 1434–5).

The exclusion of women from decision making shapes the impacts of mining (Dalseg et al. 2018: 150). For example, their exclusion can mean that mining companies, state regulators, and Indigenous negotiators pay less attention to minimizing mining's negative impacts on Indigenous culture, society, and economy; and that less effort is made to provide for future generations and to include women in benefit sharing.

Another issue involves values and priorities, and how these affect attitudes to mining and weighing of its costs and benefits. In some cases, men appear to place greater value than women on short-term, material gains from mining in terms of cash incomes, greater access to consumer goods such as vehicles and opportunities for travel, and the prestige attached to these. Women may be more interested in sustaining subsistence activity and providing future opportunities for their children and grandchildren. They may be strongly negative in their assessment of damage to health and cultural and environmental resources, or of family and social tensions generated by mining and by inequality in distribution of its benefits (Dalseg et al. 2018; Horowitz 2017: 1420, 1433; PIWC 2016). Again, it is important to avoid overgeneralization and essentializing Indigenous women by assuming that they all combine a strong relationship with the environment with a disinterest in the economic benefits of mining, including employment as mine workers (Großmann et al. 2017: 19–20). Matters are more complex. For example, women may have a strong interest in employment but at the same time be more aware of some of mining's negative impacts than are men, affecting their overall assessment of a mining project.

Linked to the issue of values is the nature of responses to mining, where gender may also be a differentiating factor. Some analysts argue that women are often at the forefront of resistance to mining, reflecting the fact that they are especially susceptible to negative impacts which are inherently gendered. Participating in protest action against mining can further increase the exposure of Indigenous women to retribution, including ostracism, imprisonment, and violence (Carreon 2009: 108–9; Fernandez 2020: 35–6; Jenkins 2017; Landén and Fotaki 2018: 26, 28; Morales 2018: 80; Torrado 2022).

The chapters on Indigenous strategies and the case studies in Parts 3 and 4 will provide opportunities to assess the extent to which differentiation based on gender is a key aspect of how Indigenous peoples experience and respond to mining.

Conclusion

Indigenous peoples live in many different environments and each people has its own history. As a result, they display considerable diversity. They also share much in common. Their identities, livelihoods, social relations, and cultural and spiritual lives are intimately connected to specific areas of land and water. Indigenous peoples also share a history of colonization characterized by decimation of their populations, dispossession from their territories, concerted efforts to extinguish their cultural and social identities, and systemic racism and denial of civil and political rights. State actors have been central to this experience of colonization, with the result that many Indigenous peoples have a profound and enduring distrust of the state.

Not all Indigenous peoples have survived colonization. But many have, their numbers are again growing, and even in areas heavily impacted by non-Indigenous settlement they have maintained distinctive social, cultural, and spiritual values and practices, and understandings of the world and the place of humans within it. At the same time, the legacies of colonization are profound and Indigenous peoples experience serious economic and social disadvantage and much diminished life chances, compared to non-Indigenous populations in the states in which they live.

This combination of characteristics, values, histories, and current circumstances creates a very particular dynamic in relation to the mining industry. It represents a source of environmental and social impacts that are threatening to Indigenous lands, cultures, and peoples, but can also generate great wealth, a share of which could support Indigenous peoples in pursuing their own goals and improving their lives. Indigenous peoples are likely to bring to their encounter with the industry both a determination to defend their lands, cultures, and values, and also the pragmatism and adaptability that allowed them to survive as peoples for thousands of years before colonization, and that has allowed them to survive its profound impacts on them. Before focusing on that encounter between Indigenous peoples and mining, I turn now to discuss the other key actors involved in the encounter: the global mining industry and the state.

6

The Mining Industry

Wealth, Influence, and Pressures for Change

Introduction

The mining industry produces fuel and non-fuel minerals without which modern industry and society could not exist. These include uranium, coal, and oil sands; precious metals such as gold, silver, and platinum; non-ferrous metals including copper, nickel, zinc, and lead; bulk materials such as bauxite, the raw material for aluminium, and iron ore which, blended with manganese and non-ferrous metals, is used to produce iron and steel; silica, rutile, zircon, and ilmenite that are extracted from minerals sands; diamonds and other precious stones; lithium, extracted from salt or from rock; and construction materials including sand, gravel, and stone. The industry operates in virtually every corner of the world, and its activities can have a massive impact on the environment and on societies and cultures, and so have profound implications for Indigenous peoples.

The scale of mining operations varies considerably, from projects operated by large corporations, covering hundreds of square kilometres, involving investment of billions of dollars, and employing tens of thousands of people, to mining carried out by individuals or small groups using primarily hand tools and small items of machinery (artisanal and small scale mining or ASM). The focus here is on industrial-scale mining undertaken by corporations. Occasional reference is made to oil and gas projects on Indigenous lands, where these raise issues identical to those involved in mining.

The next section provides information on the structure and mode of operation of the contemporary global mining industry. The following sections discuss the mining industry's approach to engagement with society. I first consider initiatives that the industry refers to as 'corporate social responsibility' (CSR), designed to secure support for its operations from affected communities and to create social benefits beyond those required by a company's legal obligations. I then review literature that offers a critical perspective on the practices of mining companies as they engage with communities and suggests that these are often driven solely by pursuit of profit and pay little heed to the needs or long-term interests of communities and their members. The chapter considers the issues involved in relations between the industry and affected communities at a broad level, to provide a framework for the case study analysis that examines mining company policies and actions in specific Indigenous contexts.

Indigenous Peoples and Mining. Ciaran O'Faircheallaigh, Oxford University Press. © Ciaran O'Faircheallaigh (2023).
DOI: 10.1093/oso/9780192894564.003.0006

Mining industry structure

The most important and distinctive feature of the mining industry is that the distribution of the resources it exploits is a given. Orebodies occur wherever geological processes have placed them, and they cannot be relocated. From this arises a second core characteristic, the industry's global nature. The demand for minerals is often distant from their initial location, and so they must be shipped between states and continents. The funds for their extraction are often not available in the countries where they are found, and so capital must also flow internationally.

The life cycle of a mine involves four stages: discovery of a mineral deposit; construction of a mine and associated infrastructure such as roads, railways, ports, pipelines, and power and water supplies; mine operations; and closure. The mine life cycle for major deposits typically covers several decades, and often longer. Some of the mines discussed later in the book have already been operating for 50 years and are not near to the end of their lives. At the same time, mine life is unpredictable because mineral prices are highly volatile and orebody characteristics are only fully defined as a deposit is extracted, with the result that mines may close before initially planned or, alternatively, have their lives extended if prices and mining conditions are favourable.

Thousands of companies are involved in exploring for minerals because relatively little capital is required to fund exploration and because access to markets is not needed at this stage. The development and operational phase of the industry is highly concentrated with a small number of companies dominant, reflecting the fact that capital costs are very high (up to US$20 billion for a large mining project distant from existing infrastructure), and that access to global mineral markets is now essential. Small or medium-sized companies that discover a deposit will often be taken over by a larger firm. A handful of companies now dominate many sectors of the industry. For instance, just three producers, Rio Tinto, BHP, and Vale, account for nearly a half of total world iron ore output.

The industry is ruthlessly competitive, with firms competing on international markets where supply periodically exceeds demand, and with firms that fail to minimize costs and maximize profits going out of business or facing takeover by more profitable rivals. This point is well illustrated by the fate of six resource companies used by the author as a basis for a study of human rights and CSR, completed in 2002 (O'Faircheallaigh and Kelly 2002). Three of them, Western Mining Corporation, Normandy Ltd, and Mount Isa Mines, have since been taken over by BHPBilliton, Newmont, and Xstrata, respectively. (Xstrata itself later merged with Glencore.) A fourth, Pasminco Ltd, ceased trading in 2004 as a result of depressed zinc prices and foreign currency losses. A fifth, Rio Tinto, might also have ceased to exist as a separate entity if the sixth company, BHPBilliton, had not abandoned a takeover attempt for Rio in 2008 because of a global economic downturn. In such a competitive environment, cost minimization is not just important or even critical. It is a matter of survival.

Historically, mining has been dominated by private sector firms based in Europe and the United States, a dominance reduced in the 1960s and 1970s as a number of major producing countries in Africa and South America, including Chile and Zambia, nationalized their mining industries. Many of these nationalizations were later reversed and the industry is now again dominated by private firms, with the exception of a small number of Chinese and Indian state-owned companies.

The largest mining companies in the world (BHP, Rio Tinto, Vale, and Glencore) are diversified enterprises mining a range of commodities in multiple jurisdictions, exploring for minerals in dozens of countries, and employing tens of thousands of people. BHP's operations, for instance, include mining of copper, zinc, nickel, iron ore, coal, and potash in Australia, Canada, Chile, Peru, the United States, Colombia, and Brazil. The company employs more than 80,000 people, and spent US$517 million on exploration in 2020. It generated revenue of US$43 billion in 2020 (BHP 2020a), larger than the 2019 gross domestic product of more than 100 nations. The mining industry also includes a wide range of other entities, including single-commodity firms operating on a very large scale, such as the Coal Company of India, one of the biggest mineral producers in the world by volume; medium-sized companies operating a handful of mines and with one or two new projects in the pipeline at any one time; and exploration companies which have a few employees, buy in technical expertise as it is required, and rely on a series of small capital raisings from speculative investors to fund their operations.

Significant differences can exist between different industry sectors in terms of their structure and market organization. Gold, for example, is produced by thousands of mines and is almost exclusively sold on open, competitive markets driven by global supply and demand. The products sold are highly standardized (for example, gold bullion, which is 99.5 per cent pure), and it is possible to establish a 'world price' for gold at any time and from virtually any place on earth. I have watched small-scale gold miners in Bougainville, Papua New Guinea, operating in an area several hours' walk from the nearest road, use satellite phones to check the current gold price in London or New York. In contrast, minerals such as bauxite (the raw material for aluminium) and silica sand (used in manufacturing high-quality glass) are highly diverse in their physical and chemical composition, with different percentages of, for instance, organic matter and impurities such as iron, magnesium, and lead. No two bauxite or silica mines produce an identical product. In addition, a high proportion of sales of these commodities take place between subsidiaries of the same company, not on open markets. There is consequently no 'world price' for silica or bauxite. This can create problems for Indigenous communities seeking to obtain an equitable return on minerals extracted from their lands.

What virtually all mining companies have in common is that their primary driver is profit, and that they move capital and resources between projects and locations, and open or close exploration projects or mines, as the need for profit dictates. Mining companies establish connections with particular territories or places, and then sever those connections, purely on the basis of commercial imperatives. They have no intrinsic or enduring ties to any specific place. In this regard, they are the exact opposite to Indigenous peoples.

Reflecting the wide diversity that characterizes mining companies, they vary greatly in their internal structures, and specifically in how they organize for their engagement with Indigenous peoples, and in where responsibility for that engagement lies (Kemp and Owen 2020). Smaller companies will usually not have a separate department or employ dedicated staff to deal with Indigenous peoples, may lack written policies or procedures regarding their Indigenous engagement, and may not participate in industry initiatives designed to improve engagement with Indigenous communities (MacInnes et al. 2017: 155). For example, I was involved in negotiations with a single-project company in Australia in 2021 which had no relevant policy documents and whose relationship with affected Indigenous peoples was handled by the company's chief executive officer. Most large multinational companies will have a dedicated 'community relations' or 'social engagement' department which will employ scores or hundreds of dedicated, professionally qualified staff (250 in Rio Tinto's case in 2020). They will have a hierarchy of policies relevant to Indigenous peoples that operate at corporate, national, and mine site levels. An important consequence of this diversity is that the seniority and authority of the company employees whom Indigenous peoples deal with can vary greatly. At one end of the spectrum, with small companies they may deal with a chief executive officer who is only one step removed from the ultimate decision-maker, the board of directors; who may well be a director and a significant shareholder; and who can make commitments that bind the company. At the other end of the spectrum, many Indigenous interactions will be with community relations staff whose roles will not even bring them into contact with senior company executives, and who will have no capacity to commit the company.

Diversity exists not only across the industry, but within mining companies, especially larger ones. In much of the literature, mining and oil companies are portrayed as monolithic entities united in a highly rational and concerted effort to maximize profits (see, for example, Evans et al. 2001; Frederiksen and Himley 2019; Moody 1992). In reality, like any large organization, companies can have within them multiple interests and perspectives: for example, as between units responsible for operations, finance and marketing, and community relations, or subsidiaries or divisions that focus on production of different commodities. The various elements of a company do not necessarily communicate effectively, let alone act in unison, and the extent of their influence on corporate decision making can vary considerably (Kemp and Owen 2013). For example, Szablowski (2002) documents a case in South America where the corporate unit responsible for planning and production failed to inform community relations staff when the unit redrew the design plans for the project, which in turn changed the land that was required for the project and when it needed to be available. When they were finally informed of the change, community relations staff had to effect a relocation of landowners immediately which had been expected to occur over a period of time, and the company's commitment to make alternative land available to residents could not be met. These events ended the peaceful relations that had existed between the company and affected communities, and meant that the favourable local popular opinion of the company 'was replaced by outrage and distrust' (Szablowski 2002: 263). The existence of diverse and sometimes conflicting interests within organizations is important to keep in mind when considering the interests and actions of corporations and their implications for mine-affected communities (see Welker (2014) for a detailed discussion of these points in the context of one mining company).

The nationality of companies or of their personnel, and the specific national context within which they operate, may also influence their policies and behaviour. Lawrence and Motitz (2019), for example, discuss how a conviction that Sweden is a strong upholder of human rights internationally has been used by Swedish mining companies and their Swedish managers to deny that they might be guilty of transgressing human rights at home because of the way they treat Sami peoples.

A final point that should be made regarding the mining industry is that its personnel, especially its senior technical staff and managers, are overwhelmingly male, with very few women holding decision-making roles at operational or corporate level. Women do work as miners, and have long done so, but as noted in Chapter 2 in discussing gender theory, the industry is dominated by gender-blind, male-centred conceptualizations of development that are often associated with marginalization of women at every stage of the mine life cycle (Lahiri-Dutt 2011; Hill et al. 2016). This may have a major impact on the prospects that Indigenous women will share in employment and other economic benefits associated with mining, deter women who are recruited from staying in employment, and influence the industry's approach to engaging with Indigenous women and their communities (Hipwell et al. 2002: 11–12). The industry's failure to address gender bias and exclusion of women is often condoned by national legislation which fails to require gender equality, to acknowledge women as active participants in mining, or to deal with health hazards and gender-based violence that affect women (IGF 2016).

The industry has taken a range of initiatives in seeking to address exclusion and mistreatment of women (see, for instance, IGF 2016; Anglo American 2022). However, the extent of the barriers that women still face in participating in the mining workforce, and the cultural context that prevails in mining companies, is dramatically illustrated in a report published in January 2022 by Rio Tinto, one of the world's largest companies, on workplace culture in the organization (Rio Tinto 2022). Based on surveys and interviews involving a third of the company's staff globally, among the study findings are that in Rio Tinto:

- Bullying is systemic, experienced by almost half of the survey respondents.
- Sexual harassment and everyday sexism occur at unacceptable rates.
- Racism is common across a number of areas.
- Employees do not believe that the organisation is psychologically safe which impacts on their trust in the reporting systems.
- Unique workplace features, such as the hierarchical, male dominated culture, create risk factors.

- Harmful behaviour is often tolerated or normalised [and] … is often an open secret.
- Employees believe that there is little accountability, particularly for senior leaders and so called 'high performers', who are perceived to avoid significant consequences for harmful behaviour. (Rio Tinto 2022: 4)

While some women reported positive experiences of working with Rio Tinto, the report found that:

> For the majority of women, however, their lived experiences in the organisation were very different to those of men and these experiences impacted their ability to thrive. They spoke of everyday sexism, a corrosive and demeaning phenomenon which, when allowed to flourish, can be fertile ground for more serious sexual misconduct to occur. Further, the harm that everyday sexism causes can be both significant and lasting, taking a personal toll on women's self-esteem, their personal relationships and general health. It also perpetuates unhelpful and outdated gender stereotypes and can be an obstacle to women's career progression. (Rio Tinto 2022: 38)

One woman commented that for male employees of the company 'Apparently the majority of women … are ball breakers, bitches and pieces of work … There is a sense that women who have children are discounted from promotion, particularly in operations. Rio Tinto has seen a raft of female leaders leave for differing reasons, and this is speculated to be at the crux of it' (Rio Tinto 2022: 39).

There is no reason to believe that the problems illustrated by this report are unique to Rio Tinto. Indeed, the company's willingness to publish such a critical study may indicate an awareness of gender issues and a willingness to address them that may not be shared by others in the industry, especially smaller companies that lack the policy infrastructure developed by large multinational mining companies.

Corporate social responsibility

Until recent decades, the mining industry had little need to engage directly with the communities affected by its operations. As illustrated in the historical discussion in Chapter 3, the industry could rely on the state to ensure its ability to locate and develop mineral resources, and any opposition was dealt with either by removal of the communities concerned or by suppression of dissent. Matters have changed in recent decades, for several reasons. Growing national and international recognition of Indigenous rights has imposed legal obligations on companies to engage with Indigenous peoples or/and provided them with legal remedies which they can pursue if companies ignore their interests. Populations in the home countries of corporations and in other countries in which they operate are better educated and better informed than in the past, in part because of the global reach of television and the internet. Global communication networks also assist in organizing consumer boycotts across multiple markets, as happened with Shell after it was accused of causing widespread pollution in Nigeria and colluding with the Nigerian government to suppress popular protests against its operations (Mirvis 2000; Vanclay and Hanna 2019).

Corporations also face greater scrutiny and resistance at the local level from communities affected by their actions. Alliances between non-government organizations (NGOs), which increasingly operate globally, and local groups mean that the latter also have a capacity to press their case internationally. During recent years, people in countries as diverse as Papua New Guinea, Nigeria, Peru, and Canada have taken direct action to delay the projects or disrupt the operations of companies they believed were failing to protect the environment, foster economic and social development, or involve local communities in decision making. It is important to note that in many cases local action is not based on accusations of illegality. Compliance with the law offers no guarantee that a project will be allowed to proceed or operate smoothly. Local opposition can lead to major delays in developing industrial projects, to their temporary closure, or to their abandonment, and the costs for companies and investors can be enormous. Numerous examples of project delays and company losses due to opposition from affected communities are documented in the literature (Day and Affum 1995; Franks et al. 2014; Gao et al. 2002; Humphreys 2000; Richards 2006; Trebeck 2007).

Another important development relates to the growing capacity of individuals or groups who have been adversely affected by a company's operations or products to take legal action against the company in its home country. Historically, such legal action tended to be restricted to the country in which the relevant events or activities occurred, and a company's liability was limited to the assets it held in that country. In recent years, important legal precedents have been established that allow a parent company (and its assets) to be pursued in the courts of its home country. So, for instance, during the 1990s Papua New Guinea villagers affected by pollution of the Ok Tedi and Fly rivers, caused by BHP's Ok Tedi mine, took action in Australian courts to seek compensation. BHP sought a ruling in the Federal Court that Australian courts did not have jurisdiction but, having lost that action, reached a settlement with the villagers which included cash payments in the tens of millions of dollars, dredging of the Ok Tedi river and future containment of tailings. As the risks of being sued increase and now involve multiple legal systems, many companies feel it is better to use CSR policies to try and avoid problems that cause legal suits in the first place.

The increasingly global nature of funding for major industrial projects represents another important factor. Even the largest companies rarely fund major investments from their own resources. Funding typically comes from international banking consortia and international financial institutions (IFIs) such as the International Finance Corporation, the private investment arm of the World Bank. Particularly for projects in developing countries, banks and IFIs require political risk insurance for their investments, provided for example by the World Bank's Multilateral Investment Guarantee Agency or national organizations such as the US Overseas Private

Investment Corporation (OPIC). International financiers and investment insurance agencies are increasingly reluctant to fund projects unless the companies developing them address environmental and social issues in the countries in which they operate (see, for instance, OPIC 2016). This will often require companies to go beyond complying with local laws. If those laws fail to protect the environment or meet the aspirations and concerns of local communities, and projects are delayed or their operations disrupted, it is no comfort to banks or insurers that project operators were operating legally.

In combination, these factors have changed the world in which mining companies operate and provide strong incentives not just to obey the law, but to engage with communities in ways that create benefits for them and minimize negative project impacts. In this way, companies seek at least to minimize community opposition to their operations and, hopefully, secure community consent for mining projects. This form of company engagement with communities is generally referred to as 'corporate social responsibility', and community support as conferring on mining companies a 'social licence to operate' (Dashwood 2012; O'Faircheallaigh and Ali 2008; Owen and Kemp 2013).

In the wider context of relations between business and society, there is extensive debate regarding the concept and practice of CSR, which can be defined as involving policies, actions, and resource commitments that are designed to create benefits for society in addition to those that would be created in any case by a firm seeking to maximize its profits and meet its legal obligations (Ali and O'Faircheallaigh 2007; Carroll 1999). Some analysts see CSR simply as a public relations exercise designed by companies to persuade governments and citizens that they are not only interested in maximizing profits, but also have the public interest at heart. In this view, CSR represents a cynical exercise designed to protect companies from public pressure to behave in a publicly spirited manner, and will involve them spending as little as possible and focusing what they do spend on publicity material such as glossy 'sustainability reports' and highly visible and tangible projects such as construction of buildings or support for the arts or for sports (see, for instance, Ballard 2001; Frederiksen and Himley 2019).

A second approach sees CSR as a holistic and long-term view of what is required to allow a company to survive and continue to generate wealth into the future. CSR is thus not simply a public relations exercise, but will require a company to pay careful attention to societal values and to potentially forgo profits in the short term in order to protect its 'social licence to operate'. However, it does so as part of a rational calculation of self-interest, as an integral part of a strategic approach to maximizing profits over the longer term (Cragg and Greenbaum 2002; Gilberthorpe and Rajak 2017: 198).

Others emphasize that CSR must involve activities that would not be dictated by a purely selfish calculation of corporate interests. CSR refers to a duty or obligation on corporations to create benefits for society in ways that *go beyond* what they cannot avoid doing because of legal obligations and/or what they would do in any case based purely on economic self-interest. Carroll (1999), for example, states that society expects business to use economic resources efficiently, to oper-ate profitably, and to obey all applicable laws, but also to behave ethically, which may require going well beyond what is demanded by the law; and to make volun-tary donations to socially worthy causes (philanthropy), reducing corporate profits (Carroll 1999: 10–11).

There are two major grounds on which business may be expected to behave in ways that do not simply reflect economic self-interest. The first involves the argu-ment that corporations receive substantial benefits from society. For example, they have important legal privileges that are not enjoyed by individual citizens, including limited liability, and they benefit from public expenditures in areas such as education, infrastructure, and scientific research. In return for these benefits, it is argued, they owe society a debt, which they should help to repay by taking societal interests into account in corporate decision making (Donaldson and Preston 1995). The second involves the claim that corporations are not separate from the societies in which they operate, that they are run by human beings who are just as capable of making deci-sions on moral and ethical grounds as other individuals, and that ethics and social values as well as economic self-interest should therefore play a key role in corporate decision making (Crawley and Sinclair 2003).

The argument that corporations owe a duty to society to behave in socially respon-sible ways raises the issue of whether such behaviour should be *required* of companies and enforced by public regulation or by other mechanisms that compel compliance, or whether relevant standards of corporate behaviour should be established only through voluntary mechanisms such as adherence to industry codes of conduct. For some, fundamental changes can only be achieved if companies internalize values that result in socially responsible behaviour, and such an outcome cannot be achieved through attempts by regulators or other actors external to corporations to impose standards. For others, there is little prospect that CSR can result in fundamental change unless effective mechanisms exist to hold companies accountable for their behaviour, and voluntary mechanisms are incapable of providing this accountability (Coumans 2002).

Critics of CSR argue that if it requires anything other than a focus on maximiz-ing profits, it involves real risks not just for corporations and shareholders but also for society. Milton Friedman, for example, identifies two such risks. The first is that productivity will decline as firms fail to focus on efficiency. The second involves a threat to the economic freedom of shareholders, as company managers and direc-tors apply profits to their preferred social purposes rather than distributing them to shareholders and allowing the latter to decide how they should be applied (Friedman 1990). Other critics of CSR focus not on the risks for corporations, but for society. They argue that large corporations already wield enormous economic power, and that as CSR practices become more widespread companies will start to accumulate social power as they use their wealth to intervene in social, political, and cultural affairs. From this perspective, it is preferable for governments to take responsibil-ity for promoting the good of society because, unlike corporations, they can be held accountable by the electorate (Cannon 1992: 47–8).

Whatever the merits of these debates, a review of major mining company and industry association websites reveals the widespread acceptance of the concept of CSR, and the scale of activities and expenditures companies undertake to demonstrate their support for CSR principles (BHP 2020b; ICMM 2020; Responsible Mining Foundation 2020; Rio Tinto 2020). In 2019, for example, BHP spent US$93.5 million on 'social investment' (BHP 2020b), while Rio Tinto spent US$49 million on 'community investments' and 'development contributions', and in addition made payments of US$147 million under agreements with affected landowners or communities (Rio Tinto 2020).

There are contrasting views in the literature about whether company CSR policies drive the responses of communities they seek to influence, or whether those policies are shaped by local contexts and the agency of the communities involved. For instance, Haslam (2021) argues that company policies constitute an exogenous influence which shapes local responses and, in particular, determines the likelihood that resistance to mining will emerge. He states that policies that channel benefits through legitimate institutional forums and distribute them broadly increase perceptions among community members that the cost of protest against companies will be high, and so deter resistance. Where legitimate institutions are not involved and benefits are of limited value and distributed narrowly, the perceived cost of protest is reduced and resistance is more likely. In contrast, Amengual (2018) found that political structures and organization in the localities in which firms operate create distinct incentives for them to distribute benefits in either targeted or inclusive ways, and so shape CSR policies. The case studies will provide an opportunity to assess these alternative approaches.

Mining company engagement practices

One problem with research on CSR is its heavy reliance on company sources of information, including interviews with company officials (see, for example, Dashwood 2012; Haslam 2021). As Campbell (2007: 950) notes, much of the literature in the field focuses on 'the rhetoric of socially responsible corporate behaviour [as expressed] in corporate reports, advertising, websites and elsewhere', and fails to address the question of whether 'corporations are actually behaving in socially responsible ways or simply making hollow claims to that effect'. Reliance on company sources is especially problematic given that an extensive review of mining company reporting on CSR concluded that it provides 'no real measure of ... whether policy statements are applied in practice in any meaningful way; further research is needed to develop such measures in order that performance against intention can be calculated' (Jenkins and Yakovleva 2006: 282).

It is certainly not difficult to find gaps between company rhetoric and delivery (Sarker 2013). For example, the Canadian-based mining company Hudbay Minerals espouses a commitment to protection of human rights, stating: 'Hudbay's Human

Rights Policy clearly articulates our commitments to human rights. Key aspects include commitments to practicing ethical business practices, respecting rights of labour practices and labour relations and promoting and welcoming community participation' (Hudbay Minerals 2015).

Yet Hudbay has faced legal action in the Superior Court of Ontario by Mayan people who assert that private security forces hired by Hudbay engaged in numerous human rights violations, including killing and rape, at its Guatemalan operations in 2009 (for details, see Superior Court of Ontario 2013). Another example involves the major energy producer and distributor, Enbridge. Enbridge states that it is fully committed to developing a strategic approach to environmental management, an approach that the company says is intended to benefit all of Enbridge's stakeholders and society at large (Enbridge 2011). In conducting impact assessments for a proposed oil pipeline across northern British Columbia, Enbridge analysed the ability of a caribou herd to cope with the pipeline's impact, which was a key environmental issue. The company implied in its submission to the environmental review panel assessing the pipeline that this analysis was based on peer-reviewed scientific evidence. In fact, it was based on a single slideshow about another caribou herd in Canada's Yukon Territory, where the ecological context and existing industry impacts were very different (Hume 2012).

A further problem is that companies may abandon CSR initiatives and extra-regulatory environmental activities as a result of change in company ownership, the changing priorities of a new chief executive, or shifts in economic conditions (Goodland 2012). For example, a number of companies in Australia severely curtailed their community engagement activity after commodity prices fell in the wake of the global financial crisis (Kemp and Owen 2018). This may reflect an underlying failure of mining companies to accept that social engagement is a core part of their function, in the same way that exploration, raising finance, and extracting minerals are core functions. It is rather seen as an 'add on' that can be jettisoned or severely pruned when priorities change, or times are hard. In the words of Kemp and Owen (2013), CSR has not yet become part of 'core business'.

Communities have no mechanisms at their disposal that would allow them to prevent such changes in corporate priorities and the negative consequences they bring. There can be consequences of company failure to honour existing commitments or the dilution of CSR policies in terms of 'community backlash' and negative publicity (BBC 2020). Yet it can be argued that at their core CSR commitments are essentially voluntary (RDS 2012, 5; Sarker 2013, 7), and as such can offer communities little assurance that their interests will be protected, particularly over the longer term.

There is also an extensive literature which suggests that, when it comes to engagement on the ground, company personnel, driven by pressures and incentives to ensure speedy project development, maintain operations, and disarm community opposition, resort to practices that have little relation to CSR or to a principled commitment to secure the consent and support of affected communities (Welker 2014). These practices include the use of force and intimidation against project opponents, often in conjunction with state security forces (Ballard 2001; Frederiksen and

Himley 2019; Soares 2004; Li 2015); the co-option of community leaders and elders by offering them preferential access to financial and other benefits (Bernauer 2011: 101–10; Luning 2012: 209; MacKay 2002: 66–9; Rajak 2007); failing to make commitments in writing so they cannot be held to account; bypassing community representatives and legal advisers; and withdrawal of funding or contracts from media or community organizations expressing criticism of a company or project (Frederiksen and Himley 2019: 57; Lowe 1998: 181–2). It is also claimed that many companies are only prepared to support community projects which provide opportunities for favourable publicity, such as physical infrastructure, rather than those that support long-term community goals (Kunanayagam and Young 1998: 151).

Companies have been accused of undermining existing authority structures in communities to weaken opposition to mining and the capacity of communities to demand an equitable share in projects' benefits and effective damage mitigation measures (Christensen 1990, 100–1; UNESC 2002: 23). They are known to create or fund parallel representative organizations more favourably disposed to support company operations, in the process seeking to weaken existing organizations and create divisions within communities. Freeport, for instance, established new community organizations to channel funding for community projects, bypassing traditional authority structures and creating confusion among community members. The company also fomented internal division by favouring some communities over others in the allocation of funding (Soares 2004: 134–6; see also Ballard 2001: 29). Sawyer (2004: 66–80) has documented in detail how during the 1990s the US oil company, ARCO, used a variety of tactics to undermine Indigenous opposition to its operations in Ecuador's Amazon region, and to support individuals or communities well disposed towards the company. ARCO directed employment opportunities, at well above prevailing pay rates, to individuals who were supportive; facilitated registration of land titles by its allies, excluding other groups with shared interests in the land concerned; and set up an organization which supported ARCO's activities as a rival to the well-established Indigenous regional association, which opposed oil development. The company offered incentives including the building of school houses, medical dispensaries, and monthly stipends to communities that left the existing regional association and joined its pro-ARCO rival (Sawyer 2004, 66–80; for an account of similar practices in Bolivia, see Schilling-Vacaflor and Eichler 2017).

Conclusion

The mining industry has experienced unprecedented growth in recent decades, expanding into virtually every corner of the globe to meet growing world demand for minerals. In the process, the industry has become more concentrated and more capital intensive, with a small number of firms investing billions of dollars into projects which are massive in scale and that account for a high percentage of global mineral output. At the same time, small and medium-sized companies persist, especially in the exploration and early development phases of the mine life cycle, warning against any tendency towards overgeneralization. Also warning against such a tendency is the fact that diversity exists within mining companies. This reflects differences in organizational structure, including in how companies organize themselves to engage with society, and differences in perspectives and interests between, for instance, operational and corporate units and staff responsible for planning, finance, production, environmental management, and community engagement. It follows that it is essential to examine the character and behaviour of individual corporations, and of different subsidiaries of the same corporation, in specific contexts (Gunningham and Sinclair 2009). This approach is applied in the case studies.

Historically the mining industry, strongly supported by the state, had little need to concern itself with the impacts of its operations on Indigenous communities. This situation has changed as a result of growing community activism, including through access to the judicial system and recognition of Indigenous rights, combined with much greater public access to information about what occurs at mining sites via television and the web, and the emergence of alliances between affected communities and NGOs, including NGOs in the home countries of multinational mining companies. The industry has responded by adopting initiatives, often under the rubric of CSR, that purport to value societal interests as well as those of shareholders. These initiatives include sharing the wealth extracted from mines with adjacent communities, involving them in company decision making, working with them to protect them from the potentially harmful effects of mineral extraction, and recognizing the need for specific initiatives to address the exclusion and mistreatment of women. Questions remain about the extent to which the rhetoric of CSR is converted into practice at the locations where extraction occurs, and the degree to which CSR policies respond to, or seek to shape, political, social, and cultural characteristics of affected communities. Case studies spanning a range of jurisdictions will help to address these questions, and in particular to identify circumstances in which the mining industry has been more willing, or less willing, to accommodate societal and community interests.

7

The State, Indigenous Peoples, and Mining

Introduction

States are diverse, reflecting their different histories, the political cultures of the societies in which they are situated, and past choices about institutions and organizational forms. It is possible to identify core characteristics that an entity should display to be classified as a 'state': a defined territory and people over which the entity claims exclusive jurisdiction; recognition of that jurisdiction by other states; a system for collecting and reallocating financial, human, and physical resources; and a system for taking and implementing decisions in relation to its populace and territory (Heywood 2007: 90–1). However, such a definition still leaves room for enormous variation. For example, under this definition Papua New Guinea became a 'state' in 1973 when it achieved self-government from Australia. Papua New Guinea then consisted of an agglomeration of numerous peoples speaking some 700 different languages, many of whom had little experience of the departing Australian colonial administration or any other external government authority, and who relied entirely on their own resources for their livelihoods. The very concept of 'Papua New Guinea', let alone of the state of Papua New Guinea, had limited currency (Amarshi et al. 1979). In 1973 the Australian state, in contrast, had its origins in penal settlements where the state initially *was* society; the vast majority of its citizens spoke the same language, and traced their ancestry to Europe; and most of those citizens placed a heavy reliance on the state for access to basic services including health, education, and communications. A landowner for the Lihir mine could say, a decade after its creation as a legal entity, that the state in Papua New Guinea was 'only a concept' (Filer 1996). At the inception of the Australian state, one could say it was society that was only a concept.

All contemporary states do display a common organizational form, including a central or coordinating agency, typically headed by a prime minister, president, or chairperson of a dominant political party. The necessity for central coordination goes to the very definition of the state, as it is not possible to give effect to claims of jurisdiction across a territory without it. Central coordination is also essential to collect and reallocate resources. The efficacy of central coordination activity may, of course, vary considerably. Very few states exist on a scale that can be governed by a single organizational entity, and so nearly all states have functional units which are allocated responsibility for acting on behalf of the 'centre', with responsibilities allocated

Indigenous Peoples and Mining. Ciaran O'Faircheallaigh, Oxford University Press. © Ciaran O'Faircheallaigh (2023).
DOI: 10.1093/oso/9780192894564.003.0007

on a spatial basis (regions, districts, areas), a functional basis (transport, housing, environment, education, Indigenous affairs), or a combination of the two. Typically, states also include institutions with judicial and dispute settlement functions such as courts, which will have some autonomy from the structures of government so they can perform their roles, though the extent of this autonomy may differ markedly.

This introduction to the state, brief and general though it is, cautions against two potential errors in dealing with the state and Indigenous peoples. The first is to assume that one can speak of 'states' in an undifferentiated way and assume that what holds for one state or a group of states will hold for all states. The second is to assume that 'the state' will necessarily act in a unified and consistent manner in dealing with Indigenous peoples. Different elements of the state (central versus local, one functional element versus another, administrative versus judicial) may define the state's interests in relation to Indigenous peoples quite differently.

Theories of the state

There is an extensive literature which theorizes the role of the state, based largely on analysis of states in capitalist, economically advanced countries. Theories can broadly be classified in terms of: (1) the degree of autonomy the state is deemed to have to act independently of societal interests; (2) the identity of the societal interests it responds to, if it lacks autonomy, or the identity of the societal interests it decides to benefit or privilege, if it does have autonomy.

Marxist theories posit that the state has little autonomy. To quote Marx and Engels, 'The executive of the modern state is but a committee for managing the common affairs of the whole bourgeoisie' (Marx and Engels 1969 [1888]: 82). Marx's position reflects his conviction that the mode of production, the way in which economic production is organized, is the fundamental determinant of the political, social, and cultural characteristics of a society. It follows inevitably that in a capitalist economic system the state acts in the interests of capital. Marx did not assume that the outcome of every political contest could therefore be predicted or that individuals or groups were incapable of having any impact on the course of events. However, he believed that the choices facing individuals and interests in society were limited, being fundamentally constrained by previous and current modes of production: 'Men make their own history, but they do not make it as they please; they do not make it under self-selected circumstances, but under circumstances existing already, given and transmitted from the past' (Marx 1972 [1869]: 10). In any society, only by fundamentally changing the mode of production could radical social or political change be achieved. Only by destroying the capitalist mode of production could the exploitation which characterized capitalist society be ended.

Neo-Marxist theorists such as Nicos Poulantzas (1969) and Fred Block (1987) modified Marx's approach to some extent, arguing that the state must maintain a degree of autonomy, 'relative autonomy' in Poulantzas's words, for two reasons.

First, the state engages not with an undifferentiated entity, 'capital', but with fractions of capital such as manufacturing, mining, agriculture, and finance, which have
different and at times conflicting needs. For example, mining is focused on minimizing costs of its inputs, including those purchased from the manufacturing sector, and
may favour reducing import tariffs to increase competition and reduce input prices.
Manufacturers may want the opposite. The state needs a degree of freedom to mediate
between fractions of capital, and impose its preferred outcomes on them (Poulantzas
1969).

Second, in determining those 'preferred outcomes', the state responds to the fundamental and long-term requirements of the capitalist system, rather than to the
short-term demands of capital at a specific point in time. Here also the state needs a
degree of autonomy to overcome the resistance of capital, or of powerful fractions
of capital, to measures that are essential for the long-term survival of capitalism.
Examples could include introduction of worker safety and environmental regulations, which limit the worst excesses of capitalism and deflect popular demands
for radical change, and so protect the capitalist system. Referring back to the earlier discussion of state structures, in responding to such long-term system needs the
state may create functional agencies whose whole rationale involves activities—for
instance, environmental regulation—that require a capacity to act with a degree of
autonomy.

Poulantzas (1969) highlighted the fact that different fractions will struggle for
dominance and that capitalists will also be engaged in struggles with other elements
or classes in society. The degree of autonomy the state enjoys will vary over time
as a function of these struggles. For example, if one fraction is clearly dominant
within the capitalist class and if capitalists are in a dominant position relative to
other classes, the state will have little power. If the position of one fraction of capital is waning and another is in the ascendant but has not yet achieved dominance,
and if capital is involved in intense power struggles with other groups, the state may
have considerable autonomy.

Block (1987) further develops the concept of the state's relative autonomy and in
particular focuses on how it is that the state can pursue goals which are often opposed
by capital (for example, taxation, social welfare measures, and environmental regulation), or which suit one part of capital and not another. In addressing these issues,
Block focuses on politicians and senior bureaucrats, whom he calls 'state managers'.
He stresses the necessity for state managers to maintain a high level of economic
activity, for two reasons. The first is that buoyant economic activity is essential for
the re-election prospects of government and in the longer term for the legitimacy of
political systems. The second is that the resources available to the state depend on the
level of economic activity. If it is buoyant, the state's revenues will be high, and state
managers will have sufficient resources at their disposal to pursue the various activities they need and wish to pursue. The state is thus compelled to maintain a general
climate of business confidence and to sustain business investment, which will make
the state responsive to the needs of capital. But state managers will also act to meet
other societal demands: for example, by stabilizing business cycles and so minimizing

unemployment and poverty among the population at large. This is because the state's interventions are shaped by the desire of state managers to maintain economic and social systems as a whole in a healthy state so they can generate the resources the state requires to function effectively. Block believes that state managers do not simply respond to pressure from capital or other interests in society. They have their own interests in maintaining the system and will make their own calculations as to what is required to do so. Thus, Block regards the state as a set of institutions which have their own interests and agendas.

Block (1987) also argues that while state managers will in general maintain a system which is favourable to capitalist interests, the nature and extent of constraints they face in doing so will vary from case to case and from time to time—for instance, with prevailing economic conditions. So, for example, during the period of extended economic growth from the 1950s to the 1970s, the state had considerable autonomy, and introduced extensive social welfare systems based partly on raising taxes from capital and spending them on social security payments and services for the working class. After the 'oil shocks' of the decade after 1973 the pendulum swung back, with the state again pursuing strongly pro-business policies.

Despite the qualifications they introduce and the complexities they recognize, for neo-Marxists as for Marx, ultimately the state will function, including in exercising whatever autonomy it possesses, so as to protect the interests of capital. In Poulantzas's terms, the economic level remains 'determinant in the last instance'. The state is not the tool of the capitalist class to use at it wishes, whenever it wishes. On the other hand, over the long term the state will inevitably act in a way that corresponds to the broad interests of the dominant (capitalist) class.

Pluralist theories, initially identified with American political scientists such as Robert Dahl and Ricard Polsby (Dahl 1961; Polsby 1971), see the state as exercising an essential neutral role, 'holding the ring' while a range of interests in society (for example, various components of industry, trade unions, religious and charitable groups, and nature conservation groups) engage in a contest in which they seek to mobilize resources and form alliances that allow them to determine outcomes in the range of policy issues addressed in a modern nation state. The role of the state is twofold. It develops and enforces the 'rules of the game', including by protecting fundamental rights such as the right to organize and to exercise free speech, and by creating a legal system to enforce contracts and prevent violence and theft. Its second role is to give effect to the outcomes of the contest between competing groups and policy positions. For example, if labour wins out in a contest regarding safety standards in the mining industry, the state will legislate this outcome and provide mines inspectors to ensure that the new standards are being enforced.

All significant interests are represented in the political contest because they are themselves organized into interest groups such as trade unions or business associations, or because they could so organize and, aware of this potential, the state recognizes and accommodates their interests. Power is dispersed in that no single interest or group can dominate decisions across multiple policy areas or over time, for two reasons. First, different interests can deploy significant resources in the political contest, though these resources will differ. Business, for instance, can draw on substantial financial resources that can be used in lobbying and media campaigns. Religious groups may have little money, but may have large numbers of members whose votes constitute important political leverage. Second, various interest groups combine in alliances whose composition changes over time, depending on the policy issues involved. A specific group may be a member of a winning alliance on one issue, but will be part of a losing alliance on another.

The state must maintain a degree of autonomy and neutrality in the pluralist system, just as referees must do in a sporting contest. But the state's autonomy is designed only to enforce the rules of the game and give effect to the outcomes of the contest. The state does not have substantive policy outcomes that it consistently pursues of its own volition (Dahl 1961; Polsby 1971).

In 1977 Charles Lindblom suggested a variation on the pluralist model which is of particular relevance to a study focused on the global mining industry. In a book whose title, *The Privileged Position of Business*, aptly described his thesis in relation to the state, Lindblom agrees with pluralists that no one interest has a monopoly of power in a capitalist society, but that the interests of one group, business, are consistently prioritized. This does not mean that the state never enacts polices that favour other groups at the expense of business, but rather that business is consistently given more favourable consideration. The most fundamental reason for this is that the decisions business makes have an enormous impact on the lives of all citizens. Its decisions regarding whether to invest capital and regarding the specific activities it will undertake determine whether people have jobs and the level of their incomes, and the availability and cost of key commodities and services that are indispensable to modern society. The state must ensure that business makes the 'right' decisions, or it will be faced with a stagnant or declining economy, falling employment and incomes, shortages or poor quality of goods and services, and inflation.

A key element in Lindblom's argument is that in a capitalist economy business cannot be forced to invest. It has to be persuaded to invest in the areas and at levels which the state considers essential, particularly as capital (unlike labour) is highly mobile and can switch its investments to other jurisdictions if it does not get the support it seeks from a particular state. As a result, state officials have to listen to business with special care, to try and ensure that its needs are met. No other interest occupies an equally critical position in capitalist societies. This means that if the interests of business conflict with those of other groups, the state will treat interests of these other groups as secondary (Lindblom 1977).

According to Lindblom, business has several other resources that add to its political leverage. It can often persuade citizens that its interests equate with the national interest. It can argue that the national economy will only be healthy if business invests, and that the alternative to persuading business to invest is a greater economic role for the state. This is likely both to be inefficient and to represent a threat to people's individual freedom, on the basis that free enterprise and individual freedom are inextricably bound up. In addition, business can utilize human, financial, organizational, and promotional resources that its operations provide for political purposes and, further, much of this cost is defrayed by the taxpayer because the expenditures involved are tax deductible (Lindblom 1977).

Policy community or policy network theory constitutes a further variant of pluralism which argues that while power is certainly diffused throughout political systems, it is inaccurate to conceive of polices as emerging from 'the state' or from responses of 'the state' to society. Rather, state actions result from the *interaction* in policy-making institutions of specific elements of the state with responsibility for different policy areas, and societal interests with a particular interest in these same policy areas. Government agencies with portfolio responsibilities in areas such as health, education, housing, and agriculture conceive of initiatives which they canvass with interest groups that are active in the relevant policy area. Based on this engagement, an agreed policy is then guided by the responsible state agency through the government system to obtain the budget support, cabinet approval, and legislative enactment required for its formal adoption and implementation. Alternatively, interest groups may bring forward a demand and lobby a state agency for its support in developing and implementing a policy that meets these demands. The 'policy community' refers to the grouping of government agencies and societal interests that populate policy-making institutions in specific policy areas. Policies are initiated and developed within this community, approved by the central political executive (parliament, cabinet, treasury) and then jointly given effect by the members of the policy community. In either case, state agencies may exercise a significant degree of autonomy both in relation to societal groups, but also in relation to the central apparatus of the state. In this latter regard, the support of societal interest may bolster the ability of individual state agencies to resist central direction where this is not consistent with the policy community's interests (Smith 1990).

The term 'community' is apt because the interest groups and government agencies operating in a policy area tend to share fundamental values, assumptions, and interests; have a common view about the underlying objectives of policy; and act together in a cohesive way. Their cohesion is reinforced by constant interaction between them as policies are developed and implemented, and in many cases by movement of personnel backwards and forwards between interest groups and the state: for example, as the groups hire former public servants as consultants and as interest group leaders take up positions on government advisory bodies and statutory boards.

Use of the term 'community' is also seen as appropriate because participants define themselves as being 'insiders', as part of the community, and others as 'outsiders' who are excluded from a role in that area of policy. Barriers are created against participation in policy making by 'outsiders' who might prove disruptive because they do not share the community's underlying interests and values. For example, Smith (1989, 1990, 1991) shows how government food and agriculture agencies combined with farmers' organizations and the food-processing industry in the UK to exclude groups with an interest in public health, animal welfare, consumer rights, and the environment from any significant say in food and agriculture policy over several decades. A key element of policy community theory is that components of the state which are members of the 'community' (in this case, the British Ministry of Agriculture, Food and Fisheries) will be just as keen to exclude components of the state that may not share their interests (in this case, the UK's Departments of Health and of Environment) as they are to exclude interest groups that may be regarded as hostile.

Policy community theorists share with pluralists an assumption that power is dispersed throughout political systems—in this case, between communities controlling different policy areas—and that organized groups, state and private, play a central role in decision-making groups. They explicitly accept a proposition which is inimical to pluralism, that some groups and interests are systematically excluded from influence over policy making and resource allocation. This may even apply over extended periods of time to groups which are well organized and have access to substantial resources, but which are not regarded as 'acceptable' or 'legitimate' by the players who dominate the policy community. A qualification to this final point is that an interest group or state agency could be an 'outsider' in one policy community and an 'insider' in another: for example, a health department which is an outsider in agriculture policy may be very much an insider in aged care policy.

Statist theory regards the state as an autonomous entity, which has powers and resources of its own which are independent of economic or other societal forces. The state does not just respond to interests in society, but rather seeks to shape society in ways that suit the state's own interests. Thus, state interests and actions are not reducible to, or understandable as, the result of social forces. The state autonomously defines and pursues its own goals. Given the significance of the state as an actor, it is very important to understand state institutions in their own right, to focus on the capacity of the state to achieve its goals and the resources it can mobilize in seeking to do so, and to establish what are the goals the state chooses to pursue and why it chooses certain goals over others (Skocpol 1981).

A final perspective on the state emerges from international relations rather than political science literature. This starts with a recognition that states operate not only individually within their own boundaries, but also as actors in a society of states where they constantly interact with each other. These interactions, it is argued, can lead states to accept international norms and laws that limit and shape their behaviour in ways that would not occur if they existed in isolation. This perspective is particularly associated with the work of constructivist scholars inquiring into the adoption of international norms in areas such as human rights and the use of military technology—for example, mines and chemical warfare. Constructivist theorists argue that processes of argumentation, persuasion, and social learning associated with interaction between state actors, multilateral institutions, and international non-government organizations (NGOs) lead state actors to define and redefine their interests in ways that lead them to adopt international norms. Pressure for change at an international level grows until a 'tipping point' is reached when a critical mass of states adopts a norm, followed by a 'norm cascade' when many state actors quickly become convinced of the desirability of adopting a norm. Particularly important in reaching a 'tipping point' are the activities of intellectual entrepreneurs and NGOs who promote new ideas and exert moral pressure on states that ignore the values they advocate (Finnemore and Sikkink 1998; Kelley 2008; Nelson and Dorsey 2007).

As a general summary, these theories of the state do not appear promising for the likelihood that Indigenous peoples dealing with the mining industry will gain a great deal of support from the state. Given the state's alignment with capital, Marxist and neo-Marxist theorists would expect it to support the mining industry in gaining access to Indigenous lands. Lindblom would expect business's 'privileged position' generally to bring about a similar outcome. Given that Indigenous peoples generally account for only a small proportion of voters and have limited money at their disposal, they do not appear likely to win pluralist contests for control, though they might have some capacity to do so on policy issues where they are able to build coalitions with other interests. For similar reasons they appear unlikely to be able to establish themselves as dominant forces in policy communities, unless they can forge alliances with sympathetic state agencies to create and control a policy community dealing specifically with Indigenous affairs. Given their small numbers and paucity of resources, they are also likely to struggle to gain the favourable attention of state managers, whether managers are focused on maintaining state systems in the wider public good or on building empires for their own benefit. Constructivist international relations theory offers perhaps the clearest opportunities for Indigenous peoples to gain from state actions, where learning processes encouraged by the activities of NGOs and norm entrepreneurs result in diffusion of human rights norms that operate in their favour. The extensive efforts of Indigenous peoples to achieve recognition of their rights in international fora suggest they support this last proposition.

Indigenous peoples *in* the state

One way in which Indigenous peoples could possibly influence state action in their favour would be to occupy positions of authority within the state apparatus. In general, Indigenous peoples played little role in the institutions of the state until recent decades. Few were employed as public servants, especially at senior levels, and very few indeed achieved political office. This situation, which reflected their general exclusion from civil and political life, did begin to change in the 1970s as governments in many states introduced affirmative action programmes to increase diversity in their public services. By the first decade of this century, Indigenous representation in the bureaucracies of several countries, including Australia and Canada, was close to their share of population. However, their potential influence was limited by the small size of that share (4 per cent in Australia, 5 per cent in Canada); by the fact that they were overrepresented in the lower levels of public services and had very low numbers at senior executive levels; and by their concentration in service delivery agencies that have a high proportion of Indigenous clients (health, child protection, social welfare), and almost entire absence from economic and central coordination agencies where many crucial policy decisions are made. Illustrating these points, in the Australian state of Queensland, for instance, in 2015 only 3 per cent of Indigenous public servants held senior executive appointments, compared to 7 per cent of non-Indigenous public servants, whereas 27 per cent of Indigenous public servants held positions at the lowest level of service, compared to only 14 per cent of non-Indigenous public servants (Althaus and O'Faircheallaigh 2019: 71). In the Canadian province of British Columbia, for example, the two largest employers of Indigenous peoples are the Ministries of Aboriginal Relations and Reconciliation and of Child and Family Development, whereas numbers employed in central agencies and economic ministries were so small that they were not published under confidentiality guidelines. In 2015 both the Office of the Premier and the Ministry of Trade and Development had fewer than three Indigenous employees (Althaus and O'Faircheallaigh 2019: 66).

This does not mean that Indigenous public servants have no impact on state actions and their consequences. Althaus and O'Faircheallaigh (2019: 199–212) document the way in which Indigenous public servants exert influence through their advocacy of specific policies within the bureaucracy and to government ministers; their impact on the attitudes and understandings of their non-Indigenous colleagues; their engagement with Indigenous communities to ensure they take advantage of resources and services available from government; and, in the longer term, by facilitating the further recruitment advancement of Indigenous employees. However, their low representation at executive levels and their virtual exclusion from central and economic agencies, including those that develop policies most relevant to the mining industry, limit their influence.

A small number of countries with large Indigenous populations have seen Indigenous people serve in high political office, including as president in Bolivia and deputy prime minister in New Zealand. These are exceptions. The situation in Australia is much more typical. Indigenous people have only won political office in very recent years, their numbers are small, and they typically occupy portfolios linked to their Indigenous identities. Illustrating these points, it was not until 2019 that the first Indigenous person was appointed to federal cabinet, and he was appointed as Minister for Indigenous Australians.

Institutional arrangements for mining and Indigenous peoples

Most major mineral-producing states have separate agencies, typically titled departments or ministries of mines, or mines and petroleum, that are responsible for allocating and managing mineral resources and tenements. At a professional level they are staffed mainly by mining engineers, geologists, and resource economists. Their remit is usually to ensure the orderly and rapid development of a state's mineral resources, which typically involves collecting and publishing geological data; maintaining systems for awarding and recording exploration and mineral leases, and ensuring that leaseholders comply with their terms; helping to avoid or resolve disputes between explorers or miners; and providing technical advice to the mining industry. In some cases—for instance, Papua New Guinea—separate entities may be responsible for development of mining policy and regulation of mining activity. 'Mines departments' may also be responsible for regulation of safety standards in mining or, less commonly, for environmental regulation. The latter is more often located within departments of the environment, which will manage the environmental assessment and environmental approval systems that apply to new mining projects; monitor the environmental performance of operating mines and advise on requirements for operators to lodge financial sureties to guarantee environmental performance; and review plans for mine rehabilitation and closure.

Some states have no agencies identified as responsible for Indigenous policy or delivery of services to Indigenous communities, or include them in agencies dealing with disadvantaged or marginalized groups (IWGIA 2020: 131). Where separate institutional arrangements are created for managing Indigenous affairs, they vary considerably. In federal systems, responsibility for Indigenous affairs is in some cases allocated to the national level (for instance, Canada), in others to the state or provincial levels (for example, Australia). Most jurisdictions have a specific bureaucratic entity which is allocated the task of managing Indigenous policies and the administration of Indigenous affairs. Until the 1970s these agencies were often poorly funded. They frequently relied for their operating revenue on selling or leasing Indigenous lands to non-Indigenous interests; or confiscating or garnishing wages earned by Indigenous people under their control; or they outsourced their funding and administrative roles to private entities, especially Christian missions. The roles of 'Indigenous departments' were heavily focused on preventing Indigenous peoples from creating any obstacles to non-Indigenous economic activity, and segregating them from the dominant populations. They often exercised stringent and indeed draconian control over Indigenous peoples, including through the systemic use of violence and imprisonment, and afforded them very little influence over state policy and actions (Alfred 1995: 56–8; Kidd 1997). From the 1970s onwards, some states increased financial allocations to agencies dealing with Indigenous peoples, increased Indigenous employment in those agencies, and, in some cases, created representative structures that allowed for Indigenous input into policy making and resource allocation.

Despite these recent changes, agencies responsible for Indigenous affairs have continued, with few exceptions, to occupy a marginal position within the structures of the state. This is indicated by the fact that responsible ministers are often allocated other portfolios in addition to Indigenous affairs; that ministers for Indigenous affairs are usually junior in rank, and are often not members of cabinet; and that major spending decisions that affect Indigenous peoples are frequently taken in other departments or ministries such as health, education or housing (Cross 2021; IWGIA 2020: 429–30).

As noted earlier, there should be no assumption that the various state agencies involved in mining policy and administration and in Indigenous affairs policy will work closely and cooperatively either within each of these portfolio areas or across them. There may be quite different perspectives on policy issues affecting Indigenous peoples between national and state or provincial government, leading to pursuit of inconsistent and even conflicting policies. In northern Alaska, for example, US and Alaskan governments have pursued conflicting policies in relation to energy development and allocation of land for subsistence, issues Inuit leaders believe significantly influence the quality of native life in Alaska (Chance and Andreeva 1995). Proposals developed by Indigenous affairs departments to achieve a limited accommodation of Indigenous interests may be abandoned by central authorities based on their own political and economic calculations. For example, in the mid-1980s Australia's federal Labor government abandoned a proposal for limited national recognition of Indigenous land rights in the face of concerted pressure from commercial interests and their allies in state governments. In the late 1990s, Canada's federal government, having enshrined recognition of Aboriginal rights in Canada's constitution, rejected Aboriginal requests to have land claims settled and so the nature of Aboriginal rights defined, before approving major mining projects in the Northwest Territories, and Newfoundland and Labrador (O'Faircheallaigh 2016: 40).

State Indigenous policies

Each year the International Working Group on Indigenous Affairs (IWGIA), an NGO based in Copenhagen, publishes a review of developments in relation to Indigenous peoples in over 60 countries, with a particular emphasis on state policies and actions (IWGIA 2020, 2021). This illustrates the wide range of policies that states adopt, and the fact that in a large majority of cases they are actively hostile to Indigenous peoples or inimical to their interests. At one extreme, there are a small number of countries that use systematic violence in an effort to expel Indigenous peoples from their territories or even to eliminate them. For example, Eritrea has used killings, disappearances, torture, rape, and arbitrary arrests and detention to force the Afar and Kunama Indigenous peoples from their territories and destroy their means of livelihood. The Eritrean military and Eritrean government entities have used Indigenous slave labour to build a mine, with those compelled to work subjected to constant threats of physical punishment, imprisonment, torture, and degrading treatment. United Nations agencies have now called for the perpetrators to be charged with crimes against humanity (IWGIA 2020: 76–9).

In other cases, Indigenous people are subject to police harassment and imprisoned on trumped-up charges, and Indigenous activists are subject to violence and arbitrary killings. IWGIA reports that 500 Indigenous people have been killed since 2017 in just 19 countries, over 400 arbitrarily detained, more than 200 illegally arrested, and over 1,600 threatened and intimidated (IWGIA 2020: 12). Violence is often targeted against Indigenous women. In Bangladesh, for instance, violence against Indigenous people in 2019 included the killing of five women and the sexual and physical assault of nearly 100 others (IWGIA 2020: 18).

In many countries, Indigenous peoples' customary rights are ignored and their land and resources appropriated for commercial development without compensation. Indigenous people are moved off their farms and expelled from forests, and their water is diverted to dams. For example, in February 2019, India's Supreme Court ordered 21 state governments to evict thousands of Indigenous forest-dwellers whose rights in land are not recognized under the country's Forest Rights Act. Establishment of sugarcane, oil palms, and rubber plantations have led to the loss of hundreds of thousands of hectares of Indigenous land. In Africa, removal of Indigenous people and exclusion of their herds to make way for game reserves and conservation zones has had a particularly severe impact. In Asia, a number of states have declared shifting cultivation illegal, thereby criminalizing Indigenous peoples' traditional practices (IWGIA 2020: 13).

In other cases, the target of state repression is Indigenous culture. Algeria and Tunisia, for instance, seek to impose a monolithic Arab and Muslim identity on their Amazigh populations, with any public expression of Amazigh identity facing censure and intolerance, and Algeria's police arresting and imprisoning anyone displaying an Amazigh flag (IWGIA 2020: 29, 181). In Bangladesh, the government has required all NGOs with 'Indigenous' in their names to remove the term and has imposed sanctions if they fail to do so. Some states simply ignore their Indigenous populations. They do not take active steps against them, but also fail to deal with threats to them, such as forest fires, deny them access to decision-making forums, and fail to offer them services and support available to other sections of the population.

Another issue is that where courts do recognize Indigenous rights, the executive arm of government engages in ongoing litigation in attempts to reverse court decisions, or refuses to implement them. For example, Barabaig Indigenous people in Namibia took court action after the government illegally fenced areas of their territory and made them available to commercial farmers, winning judgments in their favour in a lower court and in Namibia's Court of Appeal. The state ignored both judgments, and after the second evicted Barabaig pastoralists, burned their houses, and ordered them to leave the area (IWGIA 2020: 174).

In many cases, states recognize international law principles relating to Indigenous rights—for example, by endorsing the United Nations Declaration on the Rights of Indigenous Peoples (UNDRIP)—but assert that these principles are irrelevant by denying the existence of Indigenous peoples in their territories. In other cases, states that recognize the principle of Indigenous free and prior informed consent (IFPIC) establish 'front' Indigenous organizations that are not representative and use their endorsement to claim that proposed projects have been granted IFPIC.

Even states that fully recognize and embrace their Indigenous populations do not always ensure that the behaviour of state agents is consistent with their legal frameworks. Bolivia, for example, has a majority Indigenous population and in November 2007 it became the first country to adopt the UNDRIP as domestic law. A new Hydrocarbon Law enacted in 2005 included rights for Indigenous people to prior consultation, compensation, and indemnity payments. However, Bolivian state agencies have favoured Indigenous representative organizations that are less critical of extraction activities, and have repressed or excluded more critical ones (see Gajardo (2021: 174) for a discussion of the same phenomenon in Chile). According to Schilling-Vacaflor and Eichler (2017: 1457), there is in Bolivia a 'dramatic disconnect' between the 'symbolic-political accomplishments of recognizing indigenous rights on the one hand and the continuing political-economic assimilation and exploitation of indigenous peoples and territories on the other' (see also Andreucci and Radhuber 2015).

A major issue that emerges from many of the IWGIA's country profiles is the failure of states to allow Indigenous peoples to exercise self-government and control their own affairs. In many countries, government agencies insist on taking decisions that affect Indigenous livelihoods and well-being without any reference to them (IWGIA 2020, 2021).

The picture provided by the IWGIA profiles is not entirely negative. Some states are undertaking genuine efforts to include Indigenous peoples in decision-making bodies. In 2015 the Democratic Republic of the Congo amended its Constitution to recognize its Indigenous peoples, and in 2019 issued decrees regarding special measures to improve their access to education and social services. It created a new Department for the Promotion of Indigenous Peoples with offices in 11 of the country's regions.

While few states adopt policies that are unequivocally positive for Indigenous peoples, a very wide range of approaches and outcomes occurs with varying implications for Indigenous peoples. An important focus of the case studies will be to examine the factors shaping state policies and the extent to which those policies, and their impact, are influenced by the agency and responses of affected Indigenous peoples.

Conclusion

Neither the history of the state's relations with Indigenous populations, nor contemporary state policies towards Indigenous peoples, nor theories of the state give grounds for optimism regarding the likelihood that the state would support Indigenous interests where these come into conflict with the mining industry.

Until recently, states with significant Indigenous populations excluded them from employment in state agencies, paid little heed to their welfare, and were primarily driven by a determination to make resources available for non-Indigenous economic activity and to prevent Indigenous peoples disturbing the enjoyment of their privileged position by non-Indigenous populations. In recent decades, some countries have allocated more resources to state agencies with responsibility for Indigenous peoples, who have begun to be employed in the bureaucracy and who occasionally win political office. However, Indigenous peoples continue to occupy a marginal position within the apparatus of the state, and the policies of many states are overtly hostile to their interests.

While theories of the state diverge in their understanding of the state's autonomy from societal interests and of the specific interests that shape the state's priorities, most would predict that Indigenous interests would not figure prominently in those priorities. This is particularly so where Indigenous interests conflict with those of the mining industry. The latter is much more likely to attract favourable treatment by the state, whether because of its position as a component of the dominant mode of production, because it shares in the privileged position of business, because it possesses the financial resources to win contests in the pluralist arena, or because the revenues it can generate for the state and the boost it can give to economic activity help meet the goals of 'state managers'.

Only a few glimmers of hope of favourable state action emerge from the review of state theories. Pluralism admits of the possibility that alliances which include Indigenous peoples may at least periodically achieve policy success, while policy community theory admits of the same possibility if Indigenous peoples can negotiate an 'insider' role for themselves, alongside sympathetic elements of the state and industry, in communities that shape policies relevant to Indigenous interests. Constructivist theories suggest that interaction between multiple states and international and non-governmental organizations may lead states to act on international norms favouring Indigenous peoples.

The case studies will be used to assess the impact of states on relations between Indigenous peoples and the mining industry in the contemporary period, and to test the validity and explanatory power of alternative theories of the state.

PART III

STRATEGIES, COSTS, AND OPPORTUNITIES

8

Indigenous Engagement

Negotiation and Agreements

Introduction

One response open to Indigenous peoples in dealing with the extractive industries is the negotiation of agreements with companies wishing to exploit minerals. Unknown until the late 1970s, negotiated agreements are increasingly common across all regions of the world, resulting from both their spread within countries that have in the past seen agreements negotiated only in limited contexts, and their occurrence in countries that have not historically experienced them. For instance, agreements are now negotiated for virtually all projects that might potentially affect Indigenous lands in Australia. Fewer than 20 existed in 1990; hundreds exist today. A similar trend is evident in North America, with the World Bank estimating that some 150 had been negotiated in Canada by 2010. A decade ago agreements were virtually unknown in Africa, South America, central Asia, south-east Asia, and the former Soviet Union, but are now regularly negotiated in these regions (for a detailed discussion of numbers and trends in agreements, see O'Faircheallaigh 2013b; see also Schilling-Vacaflor and Eichler 2017; Stammler and Ivanova 2016).

I discuss the reasons for the growing use of agreements in the next section. Agreements involve diverse actors and emerge from a wide range of processes, which I discuss in the following section, after which I outline the forms agreements can take and the purposes they can serve. Negotiated agreements generate considerable controversy in the research literature. Some analysts emphasize their capacity to allow Indigenous peoples to share in the benefits of mineral development while avoiding or minimizing its negative effects. Others argue that agreements allow the continued marginalization of Indigenous peoples and exploitation of their land, while giving the false impression that Indigenous interests are being accommodated. I offer a preliminary assessment of these contending perspectives, and consider them again in later chapters in reviewing the experience of Indigenous peoples in the case study countries. Contracts between mining companies and Indigenous peoples will have little impact, positive or negative, if they are not put into effect, and I outline some issues and problems in the implementation of agreements. I conclude with a discussion of Indigenous women and agreement making.

Indigenous Peoples and Mining. Ciaran O'Faircheallaigh, Oxford University Press. © Ciaran O'Faircheallaigh (2023).
DOI: 10.1093/oso/9780192894564.003.0008

Factors driving agreement making

The growing national and international recognition of Indigenous rights has been an important factor driving the increase in use of negotiated agreements. The emergence of agreement making in Canada and Australia in the late 1970s coincided with the initial judicial and legislative recognition of inherent Indigenous rights in land. The rapid expansion in numbers of agreements in Australia from the 1990s followed the Australian High Court's recognition in its 1992 *Mabo* judgment of Indigenous ownership of land prior to European settlement, which in turn led to enactment of national legislation that provides many Indigenous people with the opportunity to negotiate agreements (Harvey and Nish 2005). International recognition of Indigenous rights—for instance, through the adoption of ILO C169 by countries in South America and the United Nations' adoption of its Declaration on the Rights of Indigenous Peoples helps place Indigenous people in a stronger position to insist that companies negotiate with them about developments on their ancestral lands (Sawyer and Gomez, 2012; and see Chapter 4).

Another important factor is the growing capacity of Indigenous communities to mobilize for action, with modern modes of travel, information gathering, and communication crucial in this regard. These allow community members to communicate among themselves, a key issue where they are widely scattered. They also allow communities and local groups to obtain information about companies and projects, including information about agreements negotiated by a project developer in other situations, and to communicate with other communities affected by similar projects and with supportive national and international non-government organizations (NGOs). For example, Conservation International, a major environmental NGO based in Washington, DC, has facilitated lateral flows of information on negotiation skills and the content of agreements between its Indigenous partners in the Global South. It funded a meeting of some 50 representatives of its partner organizations in Washington in 2017 to discuss these matters and has organized regional negotiation training workshops in the Philippines, Kenya, and Guyana (Conservation International 2022; and see Chapter 13). All of this both increases the ability of communities to insist that developers enter negotiations and conclude agreements, and their capacity to disrupt projects if companies are unwilling to negotiate or to enter agreements that communities find acceptable (Coumans 2008; Katona 2002; McAteer et al. 2008; Rio Tinto 2016: 16). In some cases, democratization, decolonization, and the fragmentation of former federations have provided new opportunities for local action and local engagement with miners, with South Africa and Mongolia being cases in point.

Transnational corporations are under increasing scrutiny in their home countries and in countries where they invest, and under growing pressure to demonstrate that they have a 'social licence to operate' from affected communities (Coumans, 2008; Harvey and Nish 2005). Negotiated agreements represent a concrete and transparent mechanism that companies can use to defend themselves against criticism and to demonstrate their 'corporate social responsibility credentials'. Finally, high-profile cases that have resulted in violent upheavals or extended litigation, often in the domestic jurisdictions of mining and oil companies, serve as reminders to all concerned of the pitfalls of *not* developing robust and durable mechanisms to support company–community engagement (Brereton et al. 2011; McAteer et al. 2008; Sawyer and Gomez 2012).

One of the most damaging and potentially disruptive aspects of large-scale extractive industry is that its benefits tend to accrue at a national level, while its social and environmental costs occur mostly at a local and regional level (Le Clerc and Keeling 2015; Ritsema et al. 2015: 158–60). The inequities this creates lie behind some of the most serious conflicts that have erupted around large mines and threatened their survival, as epitomized by the Panguna copper project, discussed in Chapter 9. Concern around the spatial inequities associated with mining and the conflicts they generate has led to an interest in agreements as a mechanism for both decentralizing the distribution of benefits and helping to minimize the costs of extractive activity for affected communities. Indigenous agreements can help achieve the former by maximizing local employment and business development opportunities and by directing a revenue stream to local communities in the form of negotiated royalties. Agreements can help mitigate negative effects of mining where they contain measures that provide additional protection of environmental and cultural heritage values beyond that provided in legislation (O'Faircheallaigh and Corbett 2005; O'Faircheallaigh 2008).

Agreements can also help to address the finite nature of mining projects and the fact that, once mining ends, there may be significant adverse effects on economies and communities dependent on the incomes mining generates. To help address this problem at a national level, some mineral-producing states establish sovereign wealth funds which invest a portion of revenues from mining in long-term investment funds, creating a capital base that can generate an alternative and sustainable source of income when mining ends (Yi-chong and Bahgat 2010). Where Indigenous mining agreements generate substantial revenues and a portion are invested in what are effectively 'local-level' wealth funds, the income they generate can help moderate the negative economic and social consequences of mine closure (for a detailed discussion, see O'Faircheallaigh 2010a, and Chapter 15).

Negotiated agreements: parties and processes

Typically, the parties to an agreement are a mining company wishing to undertake exploration or develop a project, and an organization that represents an Indigenous community and/or a group of Indigenous landowners who will be affected by a project. It is rare for the state to be a party, except where a single project is so large that it has national economic implications, or where a development is regional in scale and involves several individual projects. An example of the second is a proposed liquefied natural gas 'Precinct' in Australia's north-west Kimberley region. This would be a central location for processing gas from multiple offshore fields operated by the world's largest oil companies, and involving investment of tens of billions of dollars. The government of Western Australia acted as proponent for the Precinct, and is a party to the agreements to establish it, along with the lead private investor and the Aboriginal traditional owners of the precinct site (O'Faircheallaigh 2015).

The corporate entity signing an agreement will typically be the local subsidiary of a national or international firm established to undertake exploration or to construct and operate a mine. The Indigenous party is usually an incorporated organization rather than a group of Indigenous individuals, given the need to ensure that the contracting entity has an enduring legal existence in order to guarantee ongoing compliance with obligations under an agreement. However, it is not unusual for individual Indigenous people to sign a contract to signify their support for the agreement and for the activity or project involved. Agreements may be signed by an Indigenous government, where such exists; by the elected council of an affected community; or by an organization that represents the Indigenous owners of land on which mining activity will occur. Where mining projects are large and, along with their infrastructure, affect extensive areas, there may be multiple Indigenous signatories. For example, the Western Cape Communities Coexistence (WCCC) Agreement that covers Rio Tinto's Weipa bauxite mine in north Queensland includes four Aboriginal community councils and 11 Aboriginal landowning groups.

All agreements are generated through a process of interaction between negotiation parties and their representatives, but the nature and duration of the processes involved vary enormously. At one end of the spectrum, they may consist of a few brief meetings between company officials and an Indigenous leader or leaders, and the immediate signing of an agreement. At the other end, they may involve major exercises to disseminate information on a proposed project and agreement to affected Indigenous people, possibly through a community-controlled impact assessment (see Chapter 10). Multiple negotiation sessions may occur over several years, with outcomes reported regularly to community members. The WCCC Agreement referred to above took five years to negotiate and involved scores of negotiation sessions and community meetings. Signing of an agreement may be preceded by formal authorization procedures involving plebiscites or large community meetings.

A key issue on the Indigenous side is the organizational and spatial level from which participation in negotiation processes occurs. This may involve participation only by representatives of a single landowning group or community directly affected by a project. Alternatively, it may also involve a peak organization that represents several communities: for example, the Consejo de Pueblos Atacameños, which represented 18 Atacameño communities in negotiating the lithium mining agreement discussed in Chapter 12. In Australia, regional land councils that represent multiple landowning groups, rather than discrete Indigenous communities or settlements, are often included in negotiating teams, alongside Aboriginal traditional owners for the area affected by a proposed project (see Chapters 10 and 16).

The personnel involved in negotiating agreements will also vary. On the company side, they will typically involve company employees, and legal advisers who may be in-house or from external law firms. The seniority of the company personnel will generally depend on the size of the company (see Chapter 6). If the company is small, most negotiations may be conducted by its chief executive officer. If it is a major multinational company, it is unlikely that its chief executive will ever be in the negotiating room, though they will approve any substantial agreement before the company signs it. On the Indigenous side, negotiations may be conducted by one or two leaders acting alone; by a leadership team or a negotiating committee advised by legal and financial advisers; or by a large group of Indigenous landowners, again supported by expert advice. I have been involved in several negotiations where all senior members of a landowning group, numbering up to 60 people, participated directly in negotiations. In such cases, much of the talking with company representatives may be done by a small number of Indigenous leaders and advisers, but all participants will be involved in, for instance, discussing negotiating strategies and positions, and in considering company proposals. Where negotiations are not held in the language of the Indigenous people, a translator may be involved to ensure that all understand the discussions.

The form and content of negotiated agreements

The legal context in which agreements are negotiated and their content can vary significantly, but they typically share three elements: an expression of Indigenous consent and support for exploration or mining activities; measures designed to allow Indigenous people to share in the economic benefits generated by these activities; and provisions designed to avoid or minimize their potentially negative effects on Indigenous lands and livelihoods.

Agreements are negotiated in one of three broad legal contexts. The first is where development cannot proceed without the consent of Indigenous governments or landowners, and agreements constitute the vehicle for providing this consent, if it is forthcoming. This situation can be created where legislation explicitly requires Indigenous consent, as occurs on Aboriginal freehold land in Australia's Northern Territory under provisions of the Aboriginal Land Rights (Northern Territory) Act (1976). It can also occur where ownership of subsurface minerals is vested in Indigenous landowners, giving them power to determine whether or not they can be extracted. Alternatively, legislation may require that mining companies must negotiate with and seek the consent of Indigenous landowners, but that the state may allow mining to proceed in the absence of Indigenous consent. Finally, corporations may wish to negotiate agreements that embody the consent and support of Indigenous landowners and/or affected communities for mining projects in the absence of a legal requirement to do so.

In terms of scope and form, some agreements deal with only one phase of mining-related activity—for instance, exploration—over a limited and defined period of time, while others address the entire life cycle of a mining project, which may last for decades. Agreements may be brief and written in plain language. They may be several hundred pages, include multiple schedules and attachments, and use complex language and numerous terms that require definition.

As regards content, agreements may focus heavily on one dimension of project benefits or impacts: for instance, on generating Indigenous employment opportunities or on protecting Indigenous cultural heritage from the effects of mining. Others deal with a wide range of issues and impacts, including Indigenous employment, training, and business development; royalty and other payments; Indigenous equity in the project; management of the environmental impacts of mining; protection of Indigenous cultural heritage; recognition of Indigenous rights in land and landowner access to mining leases; use of mine infrastructure such as roads, ports, and company medical facilities; mine closure and post-closure land use; agreement implementation and review; and protection of Indigenous rights in the event of a takeover of the original project developer by another company. It is possible to see an evolution in the content of agreements in jurisdictions where they have been negotiated over extended periods of time. For example, early agreements in Australia and Canada dealt only with employment of local residents or local business contracts whereas now agreements address many of the issues just listed (Kennett 1999: 38; ERM 2010; O'Faircheallaigh 2016; and see Chapter 12 for a similar evolution in agreements negotiated by Atacama peoples in Chile). Another change occurring over time is that where early agreements dealt only with the mining project itself, agreements are also now being negotiated for project infrastructure such as railways, pipelines, roads, and ports. For example, an Aboriginal group on the central Queensland coast has negotiated a payment for every tonne of coal exported from a port on its land, while Rio Tinto now negotiates agreements with landowning groups in Australia's Pilbara region whose land is traversed by the company's railways.

Another change in agreements noticeable over time in jurisdictions with a history of agreement making involves efforts to define precisely the benefits that miners undertake to deliver and to include mechanisms that help ensure that promised benefits actually materialize. For example, in relation to employment and training, in the past agreements typically contained general statements of aspirations or goals: for instance, committing developers to 'to maximize Aboriginal employment' or access by local businesses to contracts. This approach made it virtually impossible to assess a mining company's effort in the absence of any specific measures of 'success'. Recent agreements are more likely to nominate targets for local employment at different stages of project life, require specific commitments of resources in dollars or staff to local training and employment programmes, and specify penalties for the project operator if targets are not met, or require them to provide an alternative source of benefits: for example, additional payments to an education fund for local Indigenous people. Similarly, commitments to generate local business opportunities may be accompanied by a quantitative preference for local firms tendering for contracts, or a commitment to spend a specified minimum amount on contracts with local businesses.

Contending perspectives on agreement making

From one perspective, agreements constitute an opportunity to change in fundamental ways the historical pattern of relations between Indigenous peoples and mining, ending the exploitation of Indigenous land, resources, and peoples, allowing them to share in the wealth taken from their land, and giving them a degree of control over development. Agreements can be seen as allowing communities to hold mining companies accountable for the impacts of their operations. Negotiation processes can educate companies about the reality of those impacts and about the values and priorities of the Indigenous peoples on whose land they operate, to 'see land and communities differently' (Rio Tinto 2016: 18). Agreements can facilitate communication, resolve misunderstandings, and help avoid conflict that can be mutually destructive (Rio Tinto 2016: 16–19).

It is argued that not only do agreements change relations in the extractive industries, they also provide a basis on which Indigenous people can change their position for the better within the dominant society. For example, Australian Aboriginal scholar Marcia Langton has argued that because of the employment, business development opportunities, and revenue streams generated by agreements with mining companies, Australia's Aboriginal peoples have been able to take advantage of the resources boom of the 2000s. They have been able to participate in the mainstream economy in a way that had never occurred before, heralding a 'quiet revolution' in their economic opportunities and their economic and social status (Langton 2012; see also Doohan 2008; Harvey and Nish 2005).

A very different perspective is offered by researchers who propose that negotiated agreements are instruments of neo-liberal governance designed to maintain and protect corporate and state power and to continue the marginalization of Indigenous peoples.[1] The neo-liberal perspective is present in much Canadian academic writing on negotiated agreements. Its key argument is that negotiation of agreements directly between industry and Indigenous peoples has allowed the state to withdraw from its role of regulating relations between the two, exacerbating an imbalance in political and economic resources favouring industry and leaving Indigenous peoples vulnerable to exploitation. Partly as a result, Aboriginal communities 'enter the discussion over a mining project with limited knowledge, capacity and resources, placing them in a position of inferiority in terms of negotiation power' (St Laurent and Le Billon 2015: 597; see also Szablowski 2010: 125). In this way, agreements continue the state's historical role as an ally of the mining industry, and they represent a new form of

---

[1] The following section summarises a more extensive outline and critique of this literature (O'Faircheallaigh 2021)

colonization by promoting resource extraction on Indigenous lands and restricting the control of Indigenous communities over their territories. Agreements give the appearance that Indigenous peoples are exercising autonomy and free will, but in reality they subject them to webs of corporate power (Cameron and Levitan 2014: 33; St-Laurent and Le Billon 2015: 599; Scobie and Rodgers 2019).

Another aspect of this critique of agreements is the claim that confidentiality provisions, said to characterize most agreements, allow Aboriginal elite collusion with developers, stifle community opposition to exploitative agreements, prevent Indigenous communities from learning from the experience of others, and mean that they come to the bargaining table without access to critical information (Caine and Krogman 2010: 85; Scott 2020: 276). Agreement negotiations are said to be dominated by lawyers and Aboriginal elites, and to offer little opportunity for community involvement, further reducing transparency and accountability (Papillon and Rodon 2017: 220; St-Laurent and Le Billon 2015: 596). As a result, agreements 'do not appear to encourage widespread involvement of Aboriginal people ... to think and act toward their own social and economic development' (Caine and Krogman 2010: 89). Criticism is also directed at the supposedly widespread use of 'gag order' or non-compliance clauses that prohibit Aboriginal groups from undertaking any action to delay a development which is the subject of an agreement. Such provisions are seen to curb democratic rights to lodge objections if new information comes to light as a project proceeds.

Another criticism is that agreements focus almost exclusively on generating economic benefits from mining, ignoring or discounting cultural and environmental impacts and precluding alternative development trajectories that would prioritize Aboriginal cultural and environmental values. The focus on economic matters means that Indigenous peoples are unable to use agreements to advance matters of critical interest to them, including language retention, transmission of Indigenous knowledge, and time on and connection with the land (Caine and Krogman 2010: 81, 87).

Agreements are essentially seen as a technology used by corporations and the state to ensure the development of mining projects by maintaining their negotiating power and limiting the capacity for Aboriginal people to pursue their interests. There is rarely any sense in this literature that agreements might be utilized in a proactive way by Aboriginal peoples to pursue their own interests (Caine and Krogman 2010; Cameron and Levitan 2014; Galbraith et al. 2007; Howlett and Lawrence 2019; Papillon and Rodon 2017; Scott 2020; St-Laurent and Le Billon 2015).

The critique of agreements as an instrument of neo-liberal governance is based not on detailed empirical analysis of agreements but on theoretical arguments regarding the nature of the modern liberal state and its relations to the two key actors involved in negotiated agreements: corporations and Indigenous peoples. As Scobie and Rogers (2019: 238) state, '*Our analytic framework* reveals how the consultation process provides the Proponent with the power to prescribe the terms of the relationships between the company and the community' (my emphasis). On a factual level, some of the critique's assertions are open to question. As noted in discussing agreement-making processes, far from being 'dominated by lawyers and Aboriginal elites', negotiations for some agreements involve extensive community consultation and participation over extended periods of time (see Gibson and O'Faircheallaigh 2015; Innu Nation Task Force on Mining Activities 1996). On the issue of confidentiality, while agreements may not be available to the wider public, it is in fact uncommon in Australia and Canada for restrictions to be placed on the access of Aboriginal community members to information on negotiations and agreements. While it may have been the case that early agreements in Canada were dominated by economic matters, as indicated above this is now far from being the case.

There are also issues with the underlying assumptions or arguments of the critique. The assumption that the state has simply withdrawn from governance of extractive industries does not accord with recent scholarship in the field, which indicates that reality is more complex and nuanced. As Bainton and Skrzypek (2021: 6) conclude on the basis of case studies in Australia, Papua New Guinea, and New Caledonia, 'states may be absent in some ways and present in others, at different moments in time, and for different sections of society' (see also Everingham et al. 2021, and Chapter 7). In terms of the argument that agreement outcomes are inevitably detrimental to Indigenous people because of their weak bargaining position, it is certainly possible to identify extractive industry agreements that appear to offer few benefits to their Indigenous signatories. For instance, Schilling-Vacaflor and Eichler (2017: 1451) describe a hastily negotiated agreement in Bolivia which involved only a one-off compensation payment for a seismic exploration programme, a payment which the Indigenous people involved quickly realized was inadequate and which resulted in dissent within the community. Yakovleva (2011) shows that agreements negotiated with Evenki landowners for a gas pipeline in eastern Siberia were concluded without input from the wider Evenki community or supportive NGOs. The project developer did not provide detailed information on the route and timing for pipeline construction or on the natural resources that would be affected. The agreements provided only for one-off compensation payments at a flat rate that bore no relationship to the impact of the pipeline on individual landowners. Compensation related only to disturbance during construction, and none was paid for ongoing effects including the impact of infrastructure on reindeer migration and the negative effects of hunting by outsiders on game and wild foods. As one head of a tribal commune confided in Yakovleva: 'We did not do it right, it seems. Now they will tell us, here is your signature … you gave us your consent. Indeed, we put our signatures. Now, it's unlikely we can contest the agreement' (Yakovleva 2011: 714).

However, at the same time as Evenki communities in eastern Siberia were giving their consent to a pipeline in return for minimal one-off compensation, Indigenous landowners in another part of Russia, Shakalin Island, were benefiting from substantial annual payments negotiated in a tripartite agreement between oil companies, the Sakhalin regional government, and the Regional Council representing Indigenous people. Indigenous representatives controlled the allocation of funds and used them to support social development and traditional activities including hunting, fishing, and foraging (Tysiachniouk et al. 2018: 145). This picture of variable outcomes is supported by Stammler and Ivanova's analysis of three agreements in Arctic and sub-Arctic Russia, which led them to 'show how in one nation state with supposedly identically centrally organised legal fields, the relations among different resource users can take entirely different shapes' (2016: 69).

The conclusion that outcomes from negotiations between Indigenous peoples and mining companies are highly variable is supported by the most systematic empirical analysis of negotiated agreements conducted to date, my study of 45 agreements between mining companies and Aboriginal peoples across all of Australia's major mining regions (O'Faircheallaigh 2016). This found that 25 per cent of agreements represented strongly positive outcomes for their Aboriginal signatories, offering only limited consent for clearly defined mining activities and offering substantial economic benefits, a major role in environmental management, protection of cultural heritage additional to that offered by legislation, and maintenance of pre-existing legal rights (for example, to object to regulatory conditions proposed by government). At the other extreme, a similar proportion of agreements offered much broader consent for mining, minimal financial benefits, no role in environmental or cultural heritage management for Indigenous signatories, and restrictions on their exercise of rights under environmental impact assessment and other relevant legislation. The remaining 50 per cent of agreements were spread across the spectrum between these two poles (O'Faircheallaigh 2016: 66–96).

Two factors were especially important in explaining this variability in outcomes. The first involves the use of robust mechanisms for community participation in preparations for and conduct of negotiations. The conduct of community-controlled impact assessments or other comprehensive community engagement strategies appears essential to success in negotiation of agreements. These strategies help to identify community priorities for negotiations, and provide an opportunity to identify and address conflicting community interests in relation to proposed projects. In turn, this helps create two of the essential prerequisites for success in any negotiation: clarity of objectives and unity of purpose. Robust community engagement provides a third such prerequisite. By providing opportunities for community political mobilization, it creates a foundation on which to pursue alternative or complementary courses of action—for instance, protests or media campaigns—if negotiations are failing to yield the outcomes desired by a community. This is a critical consideration given that experience in Australia and Canada shows that the ability to maintain a capacity to act outside the 'negotiation room' is critical to success in negotiations (O'Faircheallaigh 2010b, 2016).

The second factor involves *regional* Aboriginal political organization. Where Aboriginal landowner groups are linked to strong regional political organizations, they are able to gain access to financial and technical resources to support negotiations, including by negotiating with developers and the state; they can make credible threats of direct political action where company or state negotiators prove recalcitrant; and they can develop a strategic approach to using environmental impact legislation, administrative law, and mining law. They can also develop regional strategies to build positive precedents from one agreement to the next. Even where Indigenous legal rights are limited, regional political organization can provide a basis on which positive outcomes can be achieved in negotiations (O'Faircheallaigh 2016).

A fundamental problem with the critique of agreements as instruments of neo-liberal governance is that while it could explain the less positive agreements discussed above, it cannot explain the strongly positive ones. If bargaining power were so comprehensively arraigned against Aboriginal peoples, it would not be possible for some Indigenous groups to achieve strongly positive outcomes.

Another issue with the critique is that it considers agreements as discrete, stand-alone phenomena, ignoring the possibility that Indigenous peoples may use agreements as part of broader strategies to achieve control over extractive activity and secure a share of its benefits, strategies that also involve selective engagement with the state. That this possibility must be considered is illustrated by Wanvik and Caine's (2017) analysis of the way in which Metis communities in Canada acted as 'strategic pragmatists' and deployed a range of approaches, including negotiation of five agreements, to engage creatively and proactively with extractive industry developments on their traditional territories. It is also illustrated by Bebbington and Scurrah's (2013) discussion of the way Indigenous communities in the Rio Corrientes region of the Peruvian Amazon used an agreement negotiated with the oil company, Pluspetrol, and the Peruvian government to address long-standing grievances regarding oil extraction.

The oil extraction activities of the Occidental Petroleum Company (OPC), which started in the mid-1970s, and of Pluspetrol, which acquired OPC's leases in 2000, had devastating environmental impacts on the region, polluting waterways, destroying agricultural land, and causing serious food shortages and health problems among the Indigenous population. Petroleum extraction failed to generate any significant benefits for affected communities, with revenues flowing to the companies, the central Peruvian state, and external providers of goods, services, and labour. These outcomes reflected the complete absence of the Peruvian state in its roles as environmental regulator, provider of health services, and supporter of local economic development, limited recognition of Indigenous rights in land and resources in Peru, and the unwillingness of the petroleum companies to undertake any serious engagement with Indigenous communities. The latter, supported by their regional peak organization, the Federation of Native Communities of Rio Corrientos (FECONACO), pursued a range of strategies designed to address the impacts of oil extraction and the lack of corporate and state engagement. These included political lobbying at regional and national levels, public protests, alliance formation with local and international NGOs, work conducted with researchers to document the impacts of oil extraction, and legal action against OPC in US courts. Failing to achieve the desired response, on 10 October 2006, community members and FECONACO occupied Pluspetrol's installations and stopped oil production. In the aftermath of this action, the national government and Pluspetrol signed an accord with community leaders and FECONACO on 22–3 October 2006. This agreement provided for company action to reduce future environmental impacts; funding for a comprehensive health plan for the region and construction of a new hospital; preparation of a regional development plan; provision of temporary food aid and of a potable water system; and joint environmental monitoring by government authorities and FECONACO (Bebbington and Scurrah 2013: 183–4).

Bebbington and Scurrah (2013: 179–86) document the important part played in these events by Peru's Human Rights Ombudsman's Office. This recently created state agency put pressure on other state actors to release information on the health and environmental impacts of oil extraction. It helped further document these impacts and provided technical and funding support to the communities and FECONACO. The Ombudsman personally intervened with Peru's president to secure his commitment to negotiate with FECONACO, after the occupation of Pluspetrol's installations. The Ombudsman's Office also played a key role in working for effective implementation of the agreement, which was dogged by a lack of state capacity, especially at the regional level, and continued inaction or hostility towards Indigenous interests by elements of the state (Bebbington and Scurrah 2013: 187; see Santoyo 2002: 37 on the role of Colombia's Ombudsperson in supporting Indigenous peoples dealing with extractive projects). According to Bebbington and Scurrah (2013, 189–92), the Ombudsman's support reflected the need for a new agency to find a high-profile case where it could establish its relevance and its credentials, and the fact that a commitment to defending human rights against state action was core to its mandate. Also relevant was that the Ombudsman's Office depends on Congress rather the presidency for funding, giving it a degree of political autonomy and legitimacy; and that its staff included lawyers with a strong personal commitment to protecting human rights.

Bebbington and Scurrah's account shows how specific state actors can align with Indigenous interests in opposition to dominant state policies that privilege extractive companies (for a similar analysis in relation to Colombia, see Santoyo 2002). Their account also highlights how Indigenous groups can use agreements as part of a wider strategy to address the environmental impacts of extraction and its failure to create local economic benefits, and to demand that the state recognize Indigenous rights and end its 'absence' by playing its role as environmental regulator and provider of services to its citizens. As Bebbington and Scurrah (2013: 187–8) note:

> the struggle to control and remedy the impacts of oil extraction on indigenous communities is part and parcel of the struggle of indigenous movements ... to bring particular sorts of state practices into their territories, particularly practices of regulation and social service provision. This has involved steady, cumulative processes of organization and alliance building, moments of direct action, sustained periods of negotiation, and joint initiatives with those parts of the state that have been ... supportive of indigenous peoples' rights.

A final point emerging from Bebbington and Scurrah's account is the key role of the Indigenous regional peak organization, FECONACO, which was centrally involved in devising and implementing each element of the Indigenous strategy. This supports my own finding regarding the critical role of regional land organizations in Australia in securing positive outcomes for individual landowning groups.

I return to the issue of negotiated agreements in several of the case studies, which provide further evidence to address the question of whether agreements constitute a basis for transforming relations between the mining industry and Indigenous people, or whether they serve to reinforce existing disparities of power between them.

Implementation of agreements

My first experience working as a negotiator was for a small Aboriginal community of 900 people in far north Queensland, which was negotiating with Mitsubishi Corporation, then the world's biggest company, regarding its application for an additional mining lease to allow expansion of an existing silica sand mine. It was a difficult negotiation that involved costs for the community, including having to watch some of its elders being subject to aggressive cross examination in court when the community had to take legal action to try and prevent grant of the mining licence in the absence of an agreement. The community viewed the agreement it secured as strongly positive. It had one of the highest royalty rates achieved by any Indigenous community to that time, provisions securing community access to mining leases for hunting and fishing, greatly enhanced environmental protection provisions, and stronger employment and training provisions, including measures designed specifically to increase female employment.

Five years after the agreement was signed, I visited the community again on another project, and was devastated to discover that many of these hard-won provisions had not been put into effect. This experience led me to undertake a research project on implementation of agreements in Australia and Canada. The title of one of my papers (O'Faircheallaigh 2002a) encapsulated my findings: 'Implementation: The Forgotten Dimension of Agreement Making'. I discovered that most agreements had no specific provisions designed to ensure that the promises made in the document would actually be put into practice. For example, an agreement might include a commitment to achieve Aboriginal employment of 35 per cent, but no funds were earmarked for advertising campaigns to alert potential recruits to the available jobs, to meet recruitment costs, to pay for trainers, or to create a work environment likely to support the retention of workers who were recruited. Other fundamental issues emerged, including lack of awareness of agreements and commitment to their goals because of high turnover among company staff; the tendency of senior decision-makers on the company and Indigenous sides to focus their attention elsewhere once an agreement was signed; and the absence of monitoring mechanisms to track performance against agreement goals. Many communities lacked the capacity and resources to take effective remedial action, including legal action, when implementation failures were discovered, and there was an absence of mechanisms to allow agreements to evolve over time as circumstances changed. Underlying many of these is a failure to develop robust and enduring relationships between companies and communities once agreements have been signed (O'Faircheallaigh 2002a; Everingham et al. 2021).

In countries with a tradition of agreement making, recognition of these issues has led to inclusion of specific measures in agreements designed to ensure and enhance their implementation, including dedicated, full-time roles for implementation officers; allocation of implementation budgets, including to augment Indigenous organizational capacity; provision for regular reviews of outcomes; and a requirement for senior decision-makers to meet at least annually to assess progress on implementation (see, for example, Limerick et al. 2012; O'Faircheallaigh 2020). However, in countries where agreement making is emerging, the failure to make specific provision for implementation is a major problem, as illustrated by a March 2020 agreement between the Canadian mining company Hudbay and the Indigenous-dominated Province of Chumbivilcas, Peru. The agreement contains broad goals in relation to local employment and business development, 'the care and preservation of the environment', and the promotion and preservation of cultural heritage. It provides for the establishment of a Management Committee for the 'execution, management and evaluation' of measures under the agreement. However, no funds are allocated for the operation of the Management Committee, and no funds or personnel are allocated to ensure implementation of the broad measures contemplated in the agreement. No provision is made for monitoring of outcomes or for review of the agreement if they are not achieved.[2] Based on experience elsewhere, the prospects for achieving the agreement's goals are not bright.

Indigenous women and agreement making

The overwhelming impression from the academic literature and the publications of NGOs is that Indigenous women are excluded from negotiation of agreements and that this helps explain why they are often excluded from the benefits of mining while continuing to experience its economic, social, and environmental costs (for a summary, see O'Faircheallaigh 2013a: 1794–5). As noted in Chapter 4 and as I argued in a 2013 article 'Women's Absence, Women's Power' (O'Faircheallaigh 2013a), the view of Indigenous women as excluded reflects too heavy an emphasis on the direct participation of women in negotiations with mining company personnel, and a failure to recognize that power in agreement making can be exercised in other ways. The content of agreements and their eventual outcomes, including their impacts on Indigenous women, are also shaped by the establishment of community priorities and negotiation agendas, the ongoing bargaining that inevitably continues after an agreement is signed, and the organizational structures established as a result of negotiated agreements. In these areas, Indigenous women often play critical roles and exercise substantial power (O'Faircheallaigh 2013a). I did not argue that women are not excluded from negotiations in some contexts. Rather I cautioned against assuming

---

[2] 'Convenio Marco Para El Desarrollo Sostenible De La Provincia de Chumbivilcas Entre La Empressa Hudbay Peru Sac Y La Provincia De Chumbivilcas', March 2020.

that Indigenous women are passive recipients of the 'impacts' of mining, or are lacking agency in the face of large-scale resource development. I return to these themes in later chapters.

Conclusion

Negotiated agreements have become a central feature of relations between Indigenous peoples and extractive industry in settler mining nations, and their geographical range is steadily expanding. While they vary widely in content and focus, their essential purpose is similar. They seek to gain the support of Indigenous groups for mining; offer them a share in the wealth it generates; and promise more effective management of the negative impacts historically associated with mineral exploitation on Indigenous lands.

The literature is polarized on the significance of negotiated agreements. Some analysts see them as transforming relations between industry and Indigenous peoples, and helping to create a foundation for Indigenous social and economic development and for a more equitable place for Indigenous peoples in the dominant society. Others see agreements as part of a neo-liberal armoury which allows the state to absent itself, secures the consent of Indigenous people to mining, but does so on a basis that leaves existing exploitative relationships unchanged because of the fundamental inequalities in bargaining power that exist between Indigenous peoples and capitalist enterprise operating with tacit state support.

The case studies presented later in the book offer an opportunity to broaden the examination of agreements outcomes discussed here and further examine the validity of contending perspectives on the meaning and significance of negotiated agreements. They also allow further consideration of the reasons for the wide variability in outcomes which is so evident from empirical analysis of agreements.

9

Indigenous Opposition

Resistance and Refusal

Introduction

The second broad response available to Indigenous peoples, when faced with existing or proposed mining projects, involves a range of actions designed to stop mining entirely, or to change the legal and economic framework within which it occurs. These actions include litigation, public protests, media campaigns designed to influence political outcomes, efforts to mobilize company shareholders to push for change in company policies, and violence. They are much wider than, though they incorporate, the notion of 'social protest', defined as 'performative events in the unfolding of social dramas' (Hanna et al. 2015: 218) or as actions that 'take place outside of normal political channels' (Wilkes 2006: 514). What the various forms of resistance have in common is that they can be initiated unilaterally by Indigenous people, whereas 'engagement', including negotiation of agreements, requires the participation of at least one other party. 'Refusal' can be thought of as a radical or fundamental form of resistance that precludes any engagement regarding extractive activity, regardless of what conditions or protections might be applied to it.

The motivations that drive Indigenous resistance include an in-principle opposition to mining; an effort to attract attention to, and end, negative environmental or social impacts; dissatisfaction with inequitable distribution of costs and benefits from mining; or a desire to shift the parameters within which engagement about mining occurs, by achieving or expanding recognition of Indigenous rights. This last point highlights the fact that resistance and negotiation of agreements are not mutually exclusive. They can be combined as part of an overall strategy to change the allocation of costs and benefits from mining.

The next section looks in more detail at Indigenous motivation for engaging in resistance, after which I discuss the issue of Indigenous women's participation in resistance and refusal. I then discuss three quite different cases of Indigenous resistance. The first involves opposition by the Mirrar people in Australia's Northern Territory to Jabiluka, a proposed uranium mine. The second provides a brief history of the Panguna copper mine in the Bougainville province of Papua New Guinea, where opposition of customary landowners to an established mine led to widespread violence and to its permanent closure. The third is an example of combining resistance and negotiation, and involves the use of litigation, occupation of mine sites,

Indigenous Peoples and Mining. Ciaran O'Faircheallaigh, Oxford University Press. © Ciaran O'Faircheallaigh (2023).
DOI: 10.1093/oso/9780192894564.003.0009

and media campaigns by the Innu and Inuit peoples to bring about major changes in government policy. This in turn allowed negotiation of agreements much more favourable to Indigenous interests for the Voisey's Bay nickel project, located in the Canadian province of Newfoundland and Labrador. I then turn to examine more closely a range of specific 'resistance tactics' employed by Indigenous peoples.

It is important to recognize the complexity and variability involved in the politics of Indigenous resistance and refusal, and in its outcomes. A key issue here is that Indigenous peoples or 'communities' are often not united in their commitment to a strategy of resistance. At the same time as some members of a community may wish to resist, others may want to negotiate and so accommodate mining (Brake 2016). Similarly, individual communities may be protesting against projects that have the support of regional Indigenous governments, reflecting the former's greater concern with specific, local-level environmental or social impacts (Cecco 2021). It is also important to stress that resistance is not always successful, either in stopping a mine or in achieving greater recognition of Indigenous rights so as to make negotiation an acceptable alternative. Indeed, those who resist may not expect their resistance to be successful, but rather may feel that they have no other choice.

Why resist?

There are several reasons why Indigenous peoples or communities might choose a 'path of resistance'. These include a philosophical or 'in principle' opposition to a proposed activity such as construction of a mine, associated with a belief that there are no impact mitigation strategies or benefit-sharing arrangements that could make mining acceptable. Its impact is seen as *inevitably* destructive and as threatening a people's core cultural values and material interests, and in some cases threatening its very existence. In this situation, there is no point in engaging in negotiations or other efforts at impact mitigation. The fact that resistance may prove futile is no reason not to attempt it, as it is the only course of action available unless a people is to compromise its Indigenous identity and possibly its continued survival. The Mirrar people's opposition to the Jabiluka uranium mine, discussed in detail below, provides a case of resistance based on philosophical opposition to mining.

Resistance may emerge when Indigenous communities discover that projects fail to generate expected benefits or create negative impacts that were not anticipated. Expected employment opportunities may not eventuate: for instance, because local Indigenous people may lack the requisite skills or because outsiders are recruited due to racism among mining company staff. Market conditions may mean that project revenues and so benefits to local communities fail to materialize. Negative environmental impacts may eventuate that were not anticipated in environmental impact studies conducted prior to mining. The likelihood of such outcomes is increased by the tendency of project developers and governments to exaggerate the likely benefits of mining, and downplay potential negative impacts, to make it appear attractive and so mobilize Indigenous support and dispel opposition. Dissatisfaction may also arise because of unequal distribution of benefits among Indigenous people: for instance, because elites appropriate a large share or because women or young people are excluded from distributions. This was a significant factor in the Bougainville conflict. More fundamentally, Indigenous populations may have expectations regarding the ability of mining to deliver outcomes that they associate with 'modernity' or 'development' but which projects are simply unable to produce. A number of studies of proposed or existing mines in Papua New Guinea, for instance, have highlighted the disappointment and subsequent resistance that has accompanied the failure of mining to deliver *enough* of the life-changing 'development' that affected peoples had expected (Jacka 2015: 1–2).

Resistance may also emerge where the companies and governments which control the decision-making systems that shape the course of mineral development are unresponsive to the interests of Indigenous peoples, but are expected to become more responsive when faced with resistance. Indigenous people may be entirely ignored by decision-makers, a circumstance which prevailed across the globe until the last few decades and which still occurs in much of the Global South (see Chapters 3 and 5). In this situation, resistance may be necessary to assert the very existence of Indigenous peoples and interests. Alternatively, corporate policies or regulatory regimes may allow only 'consultation' which affords no real power to Indigenous people, in which case protest may be designed to effect a realignment of political power, as when Indigenous people insist that their consent be obtained before governments approve mining projects.

Indigenous women and resistance

Some authors argue that women are especially active in Indigenous resistance and refusal. One perspective suggests this is because Indigenous women have particularly strong spiritual and cultural links with the natural world and as a result are intrinsically opposed to mining because of its negative environments impacts (MacLean Lane 2018). This view has been criticized for essentializing and homogenizing Indigenous women (Großmann et al. 2017: 19). A somewhat different argument, mentioned in Chapter 5, is that the impacts of mining are gendered, with Indigenous women bearing a disproportionate share of the negative effects of mining on the environment, on community, and on families, and being largely excluded from the economic benefits mining can create. Indigenous women are likely to be especially active in refusing and resisting mining because their experience of it is, on balance, more negative than that of men (Glynn and Maimunah 2021; Großmann et al 2017; Morales 2018: 61–2).

Because of their active role in resistance, women can be more susceptible to the repressive activities of states, corporations and their private security forces, and local supporters of mining projects. According to Deonandan and Bell (2019), repression of women is multifaceted and includes use of misinformation to discredit them; mobilization of social norms that deny women a legitimate role in public affairs; intimidation and harassment; criminalization of protest; arbitrary detention and torture; sexual violence; attacks on the families of women involved in resistance; and murder (see also Glynn and Maimunah 2021; Simons and Handl 2019; Torrado 2022). Deonandan and Bell (2019: 40–1) report that Indigenous women in Guatemala have been prominent in protests, local referenda on mining, and court cases; and that anti-mining activists are subjected to harassment, threats, intimidation, and assassinations. Reflecting endemic corruption and a culture of impunity in Guatemala, perpetrators are very rarely brought to justice (see also MacLean Lane 2018).

The literature suggests that resistance to mining can also strengthen solidarity among Indigenous women and help build their resilience. Glynn and Maimunah (2021) say that women in Indonesia who were reluctant to engage in open protest because, for example, their partners were mineworkers, provided behind-the-scenes support for other women who were actively opposed to mining. This support built understanding and solidarity between the two groups. Torrado reports that in Colombia, Indigenous women opposed to mining who have been subject to systematic repression and violence because of their resistance have 'reaffirm[ed] their leadership, demands, identity, culture and connection with the territory' in overcoming the multiple challenges they face, and that Indigenous women leaders have 'managed to overcome silencing practices while strengthening their mobilization power' (Torrado 2022: 43; see also Jenkins 2017; Landén and Fotaki 2018).

Jabiluka: successful resistance

The Jabiluka uranium project is located on the traditional lands of the Mirrar people, physically within but legally excised from the World Heritage listed Kakadu National Park in Australia's Northern Territory. Jabiluka is one of the largest undeveloped uranium deposits in the world, estimated to contain uranium worth in excess of US$10 billion. It is located near the Ranger uranium mine, also on the traditional lands of the Mirrar, which had been in production since 1981. The establishment of the Ranger mine had been opposed by the Mirrar because of its perceived threat to their land, their livelihoods, and their culture. However, the Australian government approved its development after a commission of inquiry had determined that the opposition of Aboriginal people should not outweigh what it regarded as major national economic benefits associated with Ranger's development. Ranger has been highly profitable and has been subject to extensive environmental regulation, but questions have been raised regarding the environmental impacts of water releases from the mine site. There is also substantial evidence that its social impacts on Aboriginal people have been strongly negative (Katona 2002; Supervising Scientist 1997). This was certainly the view of the Mirrar, a small group comprising only 26 adult members and led by Yvonne Margarula, the daughter of the senior traditional owner who had opposed the Ranger project. In her view, because of its social, cultural, and environmental impact uranium mining was incompatible with the survival of the Mirrar as a people:

> All the Mirrar are together; we are united against any more uranium mining on Mirrar country. No amount of money, no amount of political pressure, no back-room deals, no bribery or blackmail will make us change our mined. We cannot change the [Aboriginal] law and the law is that we protect our sacred sites. (Margarula cited in Environment News 2005; see also Katona 2002)

In 1997 Australia's federal government granted the owners of the Jabiluka project, North Ltd, approval to proceed with development. The Mirrar engaged in a major public campaign to garner national and international support for their opposition to the mine through the media, films about the impact of Ranger and the Mirrar's reasons for opposing Jabiluka, and a website. They created alliances with national and international non-government organizations (NGOs) and organized a national speaking tour and 'national Day of Action' rallies in major cities and country towns. The Mirrar also made representations to international bodies such as the European Parliament, the United Nations Permanent Forum on Indigenous Peoples, and the United Nations Educational, Scientific and Cultural Organization (UNESCO). In June 1998, Margarula went to a UNESCO meeting in Paris, to describe the cultural and social impacts of the Ranger mine and outline the Mirrar's fear that they would lose their identity if Jabiluka proceeded. In October 1998, a UNESCO World Heritage Mission visited Australia to determine the extent of the alleged danger to Kakadu's World Heritage values, including its cultural values, and reported that there were 'significant ascertained and potential threats' (Trebeck 2007: 555).

The Mirrar also launched high-profile legal cases in Australia's federal courts which, while unsuccessful, drew extensive media attention to the Mirrar and their cause, and engaged in shareholder activism against North Ltd and its major shareholders. A 'North Ethical Shareholders' group was established, and used to demand an extraordinary general meeting to discuss Indigenous rights and environmental concerns. Campaigners lobbied individual shareholders in North, including universities, churches, and insurance companies, and a significant number of North Ltd shares were divested as a result. In 1999 the Mirrar and their allies organized a four-day blockade of North Ltd's company headquarters in Melbourne (Katona 2002; Trebeck 2007).

North Ltd persisted in its plans to develop Jabiluka, and commenced construction in June 1998. Margarula and the Mirrar took direct action in response. They organized a series of blockades of the Jabiluka site, disrupting construction activity. Over a period of eight months, an estimated 5,000 people converged on Jabiluka from Australia and overseas, restricting the access of the mining company and government authorities to the mine site. Some 500 people, including Margarula, were arrested during the blockade. Construction activity was impeded with road blockades, forcing

North to fly workers and construction materials into the site and adding significantly to construction costs.

In August 2000, Rio Tinto took over North Ltd, primarily because of its iron ore interests, and as a result became the owner of Jabiluka. The Mirrar continued their campaign. Rio Tinto faced the same economic obstacles as had North Ltd. In addition, as one of the world's largest and highest-profile mining companies and long the subject of critical scrutiny by civil society (Moody 1992), the danger to its reputation posed by the activities of the Mirrar and their allies was significant. In 2005 Rio Tinto signed a legally binding agreement with the Mirrar stating that Rio would secure the written consent of the Mirrar prior to any future development of uranium deposits at Jabiluka. As Margarula noted, 'Jabiluka will never be mined unless the Mirrar give approval … the decision is ours alone for the first time' (cited in Environment News 2005). The Australian government actively sought to nullify the Mirrar's domestic and international efforts to stop Jabiluka, devoting substantial time and resources to lobbying the World Heritage Committee not to place Kakadu on its 'in-danger' list, and establishing a taskforce of 40 officials to advocate Jabiluka's development. But for the Mirrar the position of the Australian government was not the critical factor, because only Rio Tinto could make the decision *to develop* Jabiluka. If the Mirrar could prevail on Rio Tinto not to develop the mine without their consent, as they did through their campaign of resistance, their goal could be achieved regardless of the position of the Australian government (O'Faircheallaigh 2012a).

The Bougainville copper mine: negative impacts and disappointed expectations

The Bougainville copper mine provides a dramatic example of resistance and violence that were driven by negative impacts of mining and unequal distribution of its benefits. The factors involved in the Bougainville conflict are complex and difficult to summarize in a brief discussion. Regan (1998, 2017) offers a detailed analysis. The Bougainville copper/gold deposit was discovered in 1966 by geologists employed the Melbourne-based mining company Conzinc Rio Tinto of Australia Ltd (CRA), at Panguna in the central mountains of the island of Bougainville, then part of the Australian colony of Papua and New Guinea. Exploration work met early resistance from landowners concerned about damage to sacred springs and to land and tree crops. In 1967 the Australian colonial administration, anxious to establish local revenue sources as independence approached, signed the Bougainville Copper Agreement (BCA) with CRA Ltd (later Rio Tinto) to allow development of Panguna. Construction began in 1969, and in one of several episodes of landowner resistance to the mine, Australian riot police used batons to disperse protests by women villagers whose land was being resumed for construction of a port and mine town on the coast. Efforts by Bougainville's member of Papua New Guinea's Legislative Assembly to win a small share of royalties for landowners was rejected by the Australian administration, on the grounds that all of the revenue would be needed by the newly independent Papua New Guinea (PNG) government.

The Panguna mine commenced production in April 1972. It was then one of the largest copper mines in the world and proved so profitable that it returned Rio Tinto its investment in just 2.5 years. PNG achieved self-government in 1972 and independence in 1975. In 1974 the PNG government renegotiated the BCA, resulting in a dramatic increase in PNG's revenue from the mine. None of this additional revenue was directed to Bougainville. Growing dissatisfaction in Bougainville led to moves to secede from PNG on the eve of the country's independence. In 1976, as part of a resolution to this threat, PNG agreed to constitutional establishment of provincial government and that Bougainville's newly established North Solomons provincial government would receive royalties from Panguna. However, at just 1.25 per cent of the mine's revenue, royalty payments could do little to change the distribution of benefits between the national treasury and Bougainville.

Australia's colonial administration had approved the disposal of tailings, the waste product after copper and gold is extracted from crushed rock, into the Panguna river, from where they inundated a coastal plain and eventually flowed to the sea. Massive environmental damage occurred, including the complete elimination of all life forms from the Panguna river and its tributaries. The scale of these impacts came as a shock to Bougainvilleans, who had no previous experience of large-scale mining. Adding to the negative effects on the environment and livelihoods, the limited benefits which reached Bougainville were inequitably distributed. While some clan leaders did allocate payments they received equitably and recognized obligations to extended kin and those with secondary interests in land, others did not: for instance, favouring their immediate families and excluding younger clan members. A further source of frustration, particularly for younger, well-educated Bougainvilleans, was that their career opportunities at Panguna were limited, with highly paid skilled jobs flowing mainly to expatriates and people from elsewhere in PNG. The large number of people migrating to Bougainville to take advantage of potential economic opportunities added to local resentments (Regan 2017).

In late 1988, an armed group led by young Bougainville men, including company employees and landowners, known as the Bougainville Revolutionary Army (BRA), attacked the Panguna mine, destroying electricity pylons carrying power from the coast and stealing or destroying vehicles and equipment. After violence escalated in early 1989, the mine was closed. It now appears clear that the BRA's intention was not to shut the mine permanently, but rather to force the PNG government and the mine's owners to negotiate a major redistribution of benefits from the project and so achieve a more equitable outcome for Bougainville. However, the PNG government, heavily reliant on Panguna for its revenues, responded with a heavy-handed show of force, initially by police mobile squads and from April 1989 by PNG's army. Indiscriminate violence by members of the security forces led to a major escalation in the conflict, resulting in a declaration of independence by the BRA and intense armed conflict that led to heavy casualties among BRA fighters, PNG security forces, and civilians. In the face of determined resistance by the BRA, the PNG government withdrew in

March 1990 and enforced an embargo, including medical supplies, on Bougainville. PNG defence forces gradually returned in subsequent years at the invitation of local groups opposed to the BRA and to secession, resulting in a protracted civil war in Bougainville that was finally ended by a Peace Accord in 2001.

Rio Tinto was forced to walk away from a US$1.4 billion investment, large remaining ore reserves, and a highly profitable mine. The cost in lives and human suffering will never be accurately documented, as there was no external monitoring of much of the conflict. Thousands of lives were lost, Bougainville's physical and social infrastructure was largely destroyed, and the impacts are intergenerational: for instance, because many of those who were children during the conflict suffered serious trauma and missed out on more than a decade of schooling. The Panguna mine remains closed to this day.

The Bougainville case shows how a failure by political authorities and mining companies to allow affected landowners to participate in decisions about mineral exploration, establishment of mines, and distribution of benefits can have hugely negative consequences over a long time frame. It also illustrates how, once violence is used, it can escalate quickly, sharply, and in a way unintended by those who initiate it. As noted above, it is now clear that the BRA did not intend to close Panguna, but rather to use armed rebellion to 'change the terms of the bargain' with PNG and the mine's owner (Regan 2017). However, when PNG's security forces reacted to resistance with violence, the situation escalated dramatically and beyond the control of the participants. The pattern evident in Bougainville—negative impacts of mining, unequal distribution of its benefits, resistance by affected people, repression by state authorities, and escalation of violence—is evident in many other contexts (see, for example, Human Rights Watch 2009; New Internationalist 2009).

Voisey's Bay: combining resistance and engagement

The Voisey's Bay nickel deposit, one of the biggest in the world, was discovered in 1994 by a small company called Voisey's Bay Nickel Company (VBNC). It is located where the traditional lands of the Innu and Labrador Inuit peoples overlap on the north coast of Labrador, in the province of Newfoundland and Labrador. In August 1996, Inco Ltd, one of the world's leading nickel producers, paid C$4.3 billion for VBNC. It hoped that the mine would commence production in 1998, processing 15,000–20,000 tonnes of ore a day to produce nickel and copper concentrates.

Both the Innu and Inuit had filed comprehensive land claims over their traditional territories in 1977, but by the time Voisey's Bay was discovered neither claim was close to being finalized. The Inuit and Innu were represented by the Labrador Inuit Association (LIA) and the Innu Nation respectively, well-established organizations originally set up in the early 1970s. As the land claims of the Innu and Inuit were not settled, under Canadian law there was no obligation on VBNC to seek their consent to the development of Voisey's Bay. However, both the Innu Nation and the LIA wrote to VBNC in 1994 informing the company that it would require their consent before proceeding with the project. VBNC promised the Innu and Inuit that the company would keep them informed about progress at Voisey's Bay, but in fact it failed to do so when exploration activity intensified in the following year. The Innu Nation issued VBNC with an eviction notice, and in February 1995 more than 100 Innu occupied VBNC's exploration camp and put a stop to exploration work, action that attracted the attention of Canada's national media (Innes 2001).

The Innu and Inuit took the position that there should be no development at Voisey's Bay until land claim negotiations with the provincial and Canadian governments were settled and until impact and benefit agreements (IBAs) were finalized with Inco, providing for them to consent to the project and to share in project benefits, and ensuring that negative project impacts were minimized (Lowe 1998: 58). Inco and Newfoundland rejected this position, arguing that development of the project could proceed in advance of land claim settlements (VBNC 1997). Newfoundland was committed to developing Voisey's Bay and to securing the jobs and revenues it could generate as quickly as possible. The province, which historically had high rates of unemployment, had been dealt a serious blow by the closure of the cod fishery in 1992.

While Newfoundland might assert the principle that mineral development should proceed in advance of the settlement of land claims, the political reality was, as the Innu had clearly demonstrated, that the cooperation of the Aboriginal groups was essential to facilitate timely development of Voisey's Bay. Consequently, Newfoundland and Canada agreed to 'fast track' land claims negotiations with the LIA and the Innu. Government also responded to Innu and Inuit demands that they should be centrally involved in the environmental assessment of Voisey's Bay (Gibson 2006: 9–10).

In the meantime, Inco was coming under increasing pressure from market commentators to demonstrate that a return on its large investment in Voisey's Bay would quickly eventuate, requiring it to speed up project development. In May 1997, VBNC announced its intention to construct a 12-kilometre road, an airstrip, and a camp facility that it described as 'advanced exploration infrastructure'. If the work was indeed related solely to exploration, it would require only provincial approval and would not need to be considered as part of the project environmental review process. The Innu and Inuit believed that in fact the infrastructure would be utilized in mining and they sought a court order to prevent Newfoundland from proceeding with a provincial review. The trial court found in favour of the province and in August 1997 Newfoundland issued permits to VBNC to proceed with the work. Before work could begin, more than 250 Innu and Inuit protested the court's decision by occupying VBNC's construction site and shutting down work. While the protest was under way, the Innu Nation and the LIA were appealing the trial court's decision. In September 1997, the Court of Appeal found the permits invalid and ruled that the company must go through a full environmental review process before developing the infrastructure (Lowe 1998: 72–5, 96–9).

By this stage, NGOs and non-Indigenous community groups were mobilizing in support of the Innu and Inuit, and a number of them formed the Voisey's Bay/Innu Rights Coalition in January 1997. The Coalition included supporters from the Anglican Church, the Toronto Catholic Workers' Movement, the Canadian Environmental Defence Fund, and the Voice of Women for Peace. In April 1997, the Coalition attended Inco's annual shareholders' meeting in Toronto, forming a picket outside and distributing leaflets to increase shareholder awareness of Innu and Inuit claims to Voisey's Bay and their concerns about Inco's project (Lowe 1998: 70, 124). Such support was important in increasing media coverage and public awareness of Innu/Inuit perspectives on Voisey's Bay and of Innu/Inuit protests and legal actions and the factors underlying them.

The Voisey's Bay Panel conducted hearings and received submissions during 1997. The Panel released its report on 1 April 1999. It included 107 recommendations related to a wide range of environmental, social, economic and cultural issues. These included that Canada and Newfoundland should issue no project authorizations until LIA and the Innu Nation had each concluded IBAs with VBNC. In effect, the Panel found the project should not proceed without the consent of the Innu and Inuit.

In August 1999 both Newfoundland and Canada indicated that they would not accept the Panel recommendations on the requirement to conclude IBAs in advance of project approvals and would release VBNC from the environmental assessment process. On 5 August, Newfoundland issued the Voisey's Bay Nickel Company Limited Mine and Mill Undertaking Order, permitting VBNC to proceed with the project. On 2 September 1999, the Innu Nation initiated legal action in the Federal Court of Canada, seeking a declaration that Canada had erred in releasing the project from the environmental assessment process prior to finalization of land claims and IBAs (Innu Nation 1999).

By the end of 1999, a major disagreement had emerged between Newfoundland and Inco, in relation to Newfoundland's determination that ore from Voisey's Bay should be processed within the province. In early 2001 and after a change in Newfoundland's political leadership, negotiations between Inco and Newfoundland resumed. By this time, Newfoundland had reached a decision that had critical implications for the Innu and Inuit. Project approval would not be forthcoming without the consent of the Innu and Inuit, granted through negotiation of legally binding IBAs. This position was formalized in stand-alone land claims agreements completed in 2002, under which Newfoundland undertook not to grant any land title in the Voisey's Bay area to any person without the consent of the Inuit and Innu (Canada, Newfoundland, and the LIA 2002; Newfoundland and the Innu Nation 2002).

During June–September 2002, IBAs were concluded between the Innu and Inuit and VBNC; an environmental management agreement was concluded between the two Aboriginal groups, Canada, and Newfoundland; and a project development agreement was signed between Newfoundland, Inco, and VBNC. Highlighting the extent of control achieved by the Inuit and Innu, the initial capacity of Voisey's Bay would only be 6,000 tonnes a day as they had proposed to the Environmental Review Panel, rather than the 20,000 tonnes a day planned by VBNC. This would help to minimize environmental impacts and substantially extend mine life, thus increasing the capacity of the Innu and Inuit to share in the economic opportunities created by mining. The Innu and Inuit would be involved in all government decisions on environmental approvals and conditions, and the IBAs contain some of the most beneficial financial compensation and Indigenous employment and business development provisions negotiated in any agreement between developers and Indigenous peoples in Canada (Gibson 2006; O'Faircheallaigh 2016).

The Innu and Inuit had used protest and resistance, including litigation, occupation of the mine site, and mobilization of support from civil society allies, not to stop the Voisey's Bay project but to change the legal and political framework within which approval of the project was considered. They used these tactics, in combination with their participation in the environmental impact assessment process, to prevail on Newfoundland to acknowledge that their consent was required before the Voisey's Bay project could proceed. This, in turn, allowed them to negotiate agreements that shaped the scale of the project and significantly changed the allocation of its benefits and costs in their favour.

The Voisey's Bay case shows that 'engagement' and 'resistance' are not mutually exclusive alternatives, and indeed that there can be an iterative relationship between 'dialogue' and 'resistance' (Anguelovski 2011; see also Sánchez-Vázquez and Leifsen 2019).

Resistance tactics

This section looks more closely at a range of specific 'resistance tactics', considering their potential advantages and pitfalls from an Indigenous perspective. Just as 'resistance' and 'engagement' should not be regarded as mutually exclusive, these tactics may well be combined and indeed the efficacy of any approach may be increased where it is used in combination with others. However, this is not inevitably the case. For example, use of violence may undermine the impact of media campaigns or reduce opportunities to build alliances with civil society.

Shareholder activism

Shareholder activism targets the shareholders of mining companies to try and get them to put pressure on a company's management to abandon projects or change the way in which it engages with Indigenous peoples affected by its operations. It may involve protests outside company annual general meetings (AGMs), as undertaken, for example, by the Mirrar at North Ltd's AGMs. Indigenous groups or their allies may buy shares in a company, which allows them admittance to AGMs and other corporate events and provides an opportunity to ask questions or read statements. Shareholder activism may also involve direct lobbying of directors and shareholders by Indigenous representatives, or campaigns where the public is encouraged to write letters to company office holders. For example, the Jidi Jidi people of Western Australia encouraged their supporters to write to the managing directors of two mining companies that had refused to enter heritage agreements to protect sites of cultural and spiritual importance to the Jidi Jidi before undertaking exploration on their lands. Another approach, also used by the Mirrar, is to try and persuade socially conscious investors such as churches, universities, and ethical investment funds to exercise pressure on company managers who are failing to respect Indigenous rights or interests.

Success of this tactic is variable. McAteer et al. (2008) document two cases involving the same industry sector, the same region of the Amazon, and similar networks of Indigenous supporters, but where one company proved responsive to shareholder activism and the other ignored it entirely. Outcomes appear to be related to existing company policies, the significance of the project to the company, how many projects it is developing, whether the company sees that it will create a dangerous precedent elsewhere if it responds to pressure in one case, and the ownership structure of the company (McAteer et al. 2008). In relation to the last point, a company where a large proportion of shares is held by one individual or institutional investor may be much less open to pressure than one where ownership is widely dispersed across a large number of individual or small investors. The impact of other factors may be difficult to gauge at a general level and require analysis of specific contexts. For instance, if a company is developing only one major project, it may be unwilling to make concessions as it cannot recoup any benefits it forgoes from other projects. On the other hand, it may be less concerned about creating precedents that might affect its other projects and so be more willing to accommodate Indigenous interests.

Media campaigns

Media campaigns undertaken by Indigenous peoples and their allies are designed to create public pressure on government or company decision-makers to change their approach in dealing with Indigenous rights and interests. In some cases, the intention may be to undertake a high-profile, dramatic action to attract media attention and bring an issue to the public's attention. For example, Innu people in Labrador attracted widespread publicity when they locked a Canadian government minister, who was visiting the site of a dam they opposed, out of his media demountable and broadcast from it themselves, telling the whole of Canada their reasons for opposing the dam. Alternatively, media campaigns may have to be maintained over extended periods of time, as occurred with Jabiluka, if they are to have an impact on government or company policies or on major project decisions. Long-term campaigns are also required because it is rarely possible immediately to secure the attention of journalists and media outlets when Indigenous people need publicity. It takes time to build relations and credibility with journalists and media editors, and to persuade them that it is worth allocating 'space' to an issue in a crowded news agenda. It also takes time to make an impression on public opinion and for public sentiment on an issue to be translated into political pressure on companies and governments. The need to maintain long-term media campaigns creates substantial problems for Indigenous groups, which lack financial resources and often live in places which are distant from media centres and that have limited communication infrastructure and are expensive and time consuming for journalists to visit. Their limited ability to engage the media is one reason why Indigenous peoples form alliances with urban-based support organizations, which are often better placed to maintain sustained publicity campaigns (see next section). Changes in media and communication technologies have helped improve Indigenous access to media and directly to the public (Hanna et al. 2015). Posting of photographs of damage to Indigenous territories and sacred sites to social media, for instance, allows Indigenous peoples and their allies to generate an immediate groundswell of public opinion and do so on a national or global basis. The destruction of the Juukan Gorge rock shelters by Rio Tinto Iron Ore in May 2021 led within weeks to an extensive social media campaign, online petitions, and extensive coverage in the national and international media (BBC News 2020; GetUp! 2021). This news coverage and public pressure resulted in turn in a federal parliamentary inquiry in Australia and an internal inquiry by Rio Tinto, and contributed to a restructure of the company's internal governance, and the resignation of Rio Tinto's Chief Executive Officer and Chairman (Parliament of Australia 2020; Toscano 2021).

Networks and alliances

Indigenous peoples affected by mining are often few in number and lack financial resources, and they seek to enhance their political influence by developing networks and alliances with sympathetic groups. This can help Indigenous groups gain access to additional funds, give them contacts with journalists and editors, and help maintain their media profiles over time. It can also swell their numbers for protests, petitions, and social media campaigns, and provide them with avenues to contact and try and directly influence decision-makers. On this last point, Indigenous people living in remote areas often have no experience of gaining access to corporate boardrooms or houses of parliament, and their allies in church, trade union, or other civil society organizations may be able to provide valuable help in this regard. Universities can also be important allies, providing Indigenous peoples access to the technical expertise they need to interpret complex company and regulatory documents, undertake their own assessments of mining's environmental and other impacts, and participate effectively in impact assessment processes (Devlin and Yap 2008; Keenan et al. 2002).

Alliance building also brings risks. Allies may lose interest over time as other issues demand their attention, leaving Indigenous peoples without support at critical junctures. Civil society organizations may have underlying agendas different from those of Indigenous peoples, which may lead them to abandon or even attack their former Indigenous allies. This is a particular issue with environmental groups. They may support Indigenous communities as long as they oppose mining, but may abandon them if communities decide to engage with mining companies and governments to change the terms on which a project might proceed, rather than to oppose it (O'Faircheallaigh 2011). Such changes in position by environmental groups are especially destructive where they then form alliances with minority Indigenous elements to oppose projects, creating serious divisions that can take years to heal (O'Neill 2019).

Public protests

Public protests serve a range of functions for Indigenous peoples. They can create public awareness both directly through their visibility and by attracting media coverage. They provide a focus for seeking the involvement of other groups, widening the Indigenous community's support base and helping to cement alliances. They can create practical difficulties for companies and governments, blocking access to their offices and work sites, and so helping to put Indigenous issues 'on their radar'. In the case of companies, protests can impose significant financial cost where they disrupt exploration or construction activity, as occurred with the Innu and Inuit in Labrador and the Mirrar at Jabiluka. The responses of police and the courts to protest action can greatly increase its visibility and extend its impact over time. A protest may only last hours, but if protesters are arrested and prosecuted, media coverage can extend over weeks and even months, and can provide a focus for mobilizing support from potential allies. In December 2007, six leaders of the Aboriginal community of Kitchenuhmaykoosib Inninuwug in northern Ontario, Canada, were charged with contempt of court after they violated an injunction and protested against platinum exploration on their traditional lands. They were sentenced to six months' jail in February 2008. Their trial and their subsequent and successful court action in the Ontario Court of Appeal in May 2008 attracted extensive media attention, and a large number of non-Indigenous landowners and retirees from the area of the proposed mine attended the Appeal Court to support the defendants (Ghuman 2008). The legal system's response to a brief protest resulted in media coverage over a period of six months. Media coverage and the public's response to it helps explain, in turn, the Ontario government's highly unusual action in paying the mining company involved to surrender its platinum exploration tenements (Environmental Justice Atlas 2021).

Litigation

Court action can rarely stop mining directly or entirely, because legal regimes, as noted in Chapter 7, are generally based on the assumption that it is in the public interest for mining to proceed. Litigation can be used to cause delay and so impose costs on developers, as the Innu and Inuit did at Voisey's Bay. It can also be used to obtain rulings that part or all of a regulatory process was not undertaken in compliance with relevant law, which not only causes delay but may mean that the regulatory process, when implemented correctly, affords greater recognition to Indigenous rights and interests. In 1998, the Canadian province of British Columbia approved the Tulsequah Chief project which involved the reopening of an old metals mine on the traditional lands of the Tlingit First Nation. The Tlingit were concerned that road construction and pollution associated with the mine would damage land critical for hunting, fishing, and gathering food. Following project approval, the Tlingit initiated a judicial review of the government's decision, arguing that the environmental assessment for the project had failed to consider whether the project contributed to sustainability, as required under British Columbia's Environmental Assessment Act. The Supreme Court of British Columbia found in favour of the Tlingit, revoked the mine's approval, and ordered a revised environmental review that would address whether the project was a sustainable development, in the sense that it would protect Tlingit environmental, economic, and social interests (Keenan et al. 2002: 6). Where litigation is sustained over a period, it may help persuade government that it needs to adopt a fundamentally different approach, as occurred with Newfoundland in its decision that Voisey's Bay should not proceed without the consent of the Innu and Inuit.

Court action need not involve major legal issues or relate explicitly to recognition of Indigenous rights to have a significant impact. One Aboriginal land council in Western Australia obtained a court injunction to halt development of a multi-billion dollar liquefied natural gas project when it discovered that the company involved had failed to obtain the correct permit to clear 200 square metres of vegetation to construct a communication tower. The company concerned had refused to engage constructively with traditional owners, but then adopted a more positive approach, having incurred substantial costs as a result of delays caused by the court injunction.

Legal challenges do have a downside. They require access to skilled legal advisers if they are to be appropriately framed and have a reasonable chance of success. Legal processes are expensive and, if prolonged, can create a heavy drain on Indigenous resources. They do not allow for compromise and, however well prepared court cases are, their outcome is never predictable. If an Indigenous group is on the losing side, it may be considerably worse off as a result of litigation. Finally, legal disputes can poison relations with project developers or government agencies, reducing the chances of a negotiated outcome that meets Indigenous needs.

Violence

Violence is usually a last resort for Indigenous peoples, pursued when the other forms of resistance have failed to achieve recognition of their interests or change in the behaviour of corporations or the state. Violence can involve destruction of property, which can be very effective in attracting attention to an Indigenous cause, but may also result in hardening of attitudes by companies and governments. Violence directed against people, or that unintentionally affects people, raises serious issues. One involves the moral question of whether killing or seriously injuring people is ever justified. Violence against mining companies or state personnel or property almost inevitably invites retaliation and repression by the state. This in turn can impose heavy costs on Indigenous people. Their property may be destroyed, or they may be imprisoned, suffer violence from security forces, or lose their lives. They may incur these costs even if they were not involved in initiating violence. Perhaps most importantly, once violence starts, its escalation can be very difficult or impossible to control, and its consequences extend far beyond what might have been envisaged by those who initiate it. This reality is illustrated all too clearly by the Bougainville case.

Conclusion

Indigenous peoples engage in resistance and refusal from a variety of motives, ranging from an absolute determination to stop mining, to a desire to change the entire framework within which mines are approved and managed, to a need to resolve grievances in relation to a particular regulatory process or mining project. The literature suggests that Indigenous women are often at the forefront of resistance. Depending on their motives, Indigenous peoples may use the same instruments or tactics in pursuit of different goals, and their reasons for utilizing specific approaches can change over time, depending for example on their success in reforming legal and policy frameworks, and the issues raised by successive mining projects or proposals.

Each of the instruments reviewed here has strengths and weaknesses that can vary with the context in which they are applied, and an ability to understand these strengths and weaknesses, the way in which various forms of activism interact, and how 'resistance' and 'dialogue' can be effectively combined is critical in allowing Indigenous peoples to defend and promote their interests effectively. This is not to suggest that the effects of adopting particular forms of resistance are predictable. They cannot be predicted, given that they all generate responses by companies and governments that Indigenous peoples cannot control. This is truest in relation to the use of violence, whose consequences can escalate dramatically and unpredictably and to deadly effect. The case studies offer an opportunity for a deeper analysis of the dynamic of resistance, of the interaction between its different forms, and of the way in which resistance can interact with engagement.

10

Managing the Negative Impacts of Mining on Indigenous Lands and Peoples

Introduction

Mining and mine infrastructure such as roads, ports, and townships can have environmental, social, cultural, and economic impacts on Indigenous peoples that are profoundly negative. These are summarized in the next section. I then discuss the practice of environmental impact assessment (EIA), the primary regulatory instrument used across the globe in attempts to limit the negative environmental impacts of mining. EIA systems are increasingly intended also to address economic, cultural, and social impacts. 'Conventional' or state-administered EIA has not been effective in addressing negative impacts on Indigenous people, and the following section reviews an alternative approach, community-controlled impact assessment. I then turn to legislative measures designed to address the impacts of mining on Indigenous culture and cultural heritage, while the final section considers impacts associated with mine closure and the long-term 'legacy impacts' that mines often leave behind after extraction of minerals has ended.

It makes little sense within an Indigenous world view to treat environmental, economic, social, and cultural impacts of mining separately, as these aspects of life are inextricably interwoven. However, responses to these impacts do occur separately within mainstream legislation and policy, and within agreements, so it is difficult to structure an analysis of those responses in any other way.

The negative effects of extractive industry

Mining can destroy or pollute land and waters on which Indigenous peoples rely for their livelihoods, including through catastrophic occurrences such as the collapse of tailings dams, release of toxic chemicals such as cyanide into rivers or lakes, and ruptures of pipelines. Mining can deplete wildlife resources because of its environmental impacts, because mining and related activity causes wildlife to leave an area, or through the hunting and fishing activity of mine workers and mine town residents (Westman et al. 2020; Yakovleva 2011). Mining can have serious cultural

Indigenous Peoples and Mining. Ciaran O'Faircheallaigh, Oxford University Press. © Ciaran O'Faircheallaigh (2023).
DOI: 10.1093/oso/9780192894564.003.0010

impacts, altering familiar landscapes and destroying or damaging sites of cultural and spiritual significance. It can restrict the access of Indigenous peoples to their territories, preventing cultural activities and the transmission of cultural knowledge between generations (Parliament of the Commonwealth of Australia 2020). An influx of outsiders associated with mining can swamp Indigenous populations and result in discrimination against them and marginalization of their languages, cultural practices, and governing institutions. Bainton and Jackson (2020: 373) say that inward migration of people seeking economic opportunities is 'one of the most profound disruptions' affecting communities adjacent to mining projects.

Negative social impacts can also occur through the introduction or greater availability of alcohol and drugs, and a related increase in family violence and child abuse; family tensions when a parent or parents are absent for rotational or fly-in, fly-out employment at a mine site; and competition from non-Indigenous people for access to education, health services, and housing (Brubacher and Associates, 2002; Holden et al. 2011; Nightingale et al. 2017). A brain-drain of skilled people from communities to mining projects that pay higher wages can weaken the capacity of Indigenous enterprises and service delivery agencies. Growing inequality both between Indigenous and non-Indigenous populations and within Indigenous communities can cause deep-seated problems. Inequality among Indigenous people can occur through differential access to jobs or business opportunities, or to compensation payments made by mining companies, and its effects can undermine core social values and structures. Bainton and Macintyre (2013) describe how some landowners on Lihir Island in Papua New Guinea gained preferential access to business contracts and royalties generated by gold mining, and the profound effects of this inequality on established social norms and practices. 'Over time there has been a persistent tension between the ethics of distribution and reciprocity and the accumulative practices of the new elite ... which has dramatically restructured clans, dissolved corporate solidarity, and transformed "everyday" and ceremonial exchange practices' (2013: 147–8; see also Golub 2014: 151–5). More broadly, the advent of mining can contribute to the growth of individualism and a loss of commitment to community-driven initiatives and community well-being. Richardson et al. (2019) report that among Indigenous communities in Fiji well-being has traditionally been defined as a communal good, achieved by cooperation and working together. They found that advent of large-scale mining and tourism provided tangible resources to support development, but 'at the same time it can undermine the collective foundation of achieving well-being for the whole' (2019: 21). A community leader in northern Ontario reported a direct and immediate link between mining agreement payments and the growth of individualism:

One thing I noticed when it came time for money, everybody created their own impact agreements. I want to benefit. I want to benefit. Not once did these communities think, 'How can we benefit the community?' Not individuals, membership, but communities. And I think that's what was lost at the beginning of these impact agreements. 'How can we benefit our communities?' (cited in Dylan et al. 2013: 72–3)

Inequality and social tensions can be created or exacerbated by the deliberate actions of corporations and state agencies that engage only with sections of a community that favour mining, and target resources and economic opportunities to them. Santoyo (2002) describes how an oil company in Colombia ignored Wayu Indigenous systems and processes of consultation, participation, and negotiation, dealing only with representatives of one clan. This generated serious internal tensions that resulted in armed conflict between clans, leading to many deaths. 'The company ignored the social fabric, the territorial aspect and the traditional modes of representation, and broke all the balances of the Wayu culture' (Santoya 2002: 65–7; see also Dylan et al. 2013: 72; Schilling-Vacaflor and Eichler 2017). Finally, the very process of identifying the people who will be regarded as 'landowners' for a project site may itself be divisive. In cultures in which membership of individual landowning groups and boundaries between groups were previously more fluid and inclusive, a desire to secure mine benefits by narrowly defining group membership or by excluding neighbours will likely result in social conflict (see, for instance, Levitus 2009).

As discussed in Chapter 4, another dimension of social impact involves effects on gender relations in Indigenous communities. These can be altered because women are more severely affected than men by mining impacts; because mining companies and state agencies privilege men in their dealings with Indigenous communities; or because men have better access to mine-related employment and business opportunities.

The focus of this chapter is on the negative effects of mining and their management. This does not mean that there is an absence of social benefits that arise from mining, associated with the economic opportunities the industry creates (see Chapter 11).

Environmental impact assessment

All states have passed legislation that is at least ostensibly designed to protect the environment against the negative effects of industrial activity, and in nearly all jurisdictions EIA comprises the key legislative instrument used to address the impacts of extractive projects on the environment (Morrison-Saunders 2018). EIA involves 'the process of identifying, predicting, evaluating and mitigating the biophysical, social, and other relevant effects of development proposals prior to major decisions being taken and commitments made' (IAIA 1999). Assessment, approval, and impact management processes vary from country to country, but most display common features. The project proponent prepares an assessment of a project's expected impacts and proposes measures to mitigate these. The 'technical' work of compiling an assessment is often conducted by specialist consulting firms employed and paid by the proponent. A government statutory board or a minister with relevant portfolio responsibilities will, on the basis of the proponent's impact assessment and in some cases comments on it lodged by interested parties, determine whether or not a project should be allowed to proceed; and if it is to proceed, what conditions, if any, will be attached to it (on Peru, for example, see Li 2015: 222–9; on Suriname, Weitzner 2008; on China, Ren 2013; on India, Bedi 2008).

A high proportion of projects are approved by state decision-makers based on their consideration of proponent impact assessments (Morrison-Saunders 2018: 66). For example, by 2009 only one mining project had ever been held up at the impact assessment stage in Peru, and the reasons given in this case involved the financial capability of the proponent, not the expected environmental impact of the mine (Li 2009). While a few high-profile EIAs have attracted much attention because they led to projects being denied approval or being substantially modified (Berger 1977; Devlin and Yap 2008), these represent only a tiny fraction of all impact assessments. They attract attention precisely because they are rare.

This structural bias towards approval of projects has several implications for Indigenous peoples. An important one is that to facilitate project approval EIAs systematically understate the potential costs associated with projects and overestimate project benefits (Kløcker Larsen et al. 2022: 7–8; Kuipers et al. 2006: 193). It is not uncommon for impacts on Indigenous peoples to be downplayed or indeed for Indigenous peoples to be ignored (Weitzner 2008; Yakovleva 2011). A 2011 internal review by the World Bank found that many impact assessments of projects the Bank funded in Indigenous territories made no mention of negative impacts on Indigenous peoples, and in particular failed to consider the long-term impacts that projects could have on their livelihoods, social organization, and cultural integrity (World Bank 2011: 21).

One mechanism commonly used to limit identification of negative impacts is to define the 'impact zone' for a project narrowly: for instance, by considering only the immediate vicinity of the project, or by ignoring indirect social impacts such as those resulting from in-migration of unemployed individuals hoping to find work on a project (Goodland 2009; KLC 2010a). A related issue is that EIAs tend only to identify impacts that proponents are confident they can manage, or at least can convincingly promise to manage (Li 2009: 218).

Another result of proponent and regulator control is a tendency to limit participation by affected communities, to avoid the risk that they may raise major issues about a project's expected impact or demand rigorous and expensive impact management measures. Mechanisms for limiting public participation take many forms, including restricting public access to EIA documents by only making them available in capital cities and not translating them into local languages, and writing EIA documents in highly technical language that lay people find difficult to understand. Unrealistic time frames may be set for public input, limited or no funds may be provided to support public participation, and opportunities for Indigenous input may be limited to public meetings where Indigenous people, and especially Indigenous women, may be reluctant to speak out regarding sensitive cultural and social issues (Gibson

2017; Kuntz 2012; Li 2009; Schilling-Vacaflor and Eichler 2017; Weitzner 2008). Yakovleva (2011: 713–15) describes how the participation of Evenki communities in eastern Siberia in EIA processes was limited by failing to provide prior notification of public hearings, holding hearings in urban centres rather in affected communities, and failing to provide transport for Evenki people to attend them. Underlying these specific problems is the fact that Indigenous communities can rarely come close to matching the resources available to the proponents and the state, placing them at a serious disadvantage. One specific consequence is that processes for Indigenous consultation, where they do occur, are usually funded by proponents, allowing them substantial control over the extent and form of public participation in EIA (Devlin and Yap 2008; Rodríguez-Garavito 2011: 298).

Methodologies used in EIA field studies can also reduce participation by failing to identify affected Indigenous groups or incorporate their knowledge (Kløcker Larsen et al. 2022: 8–9; Tsuji et al. 2011). Even where Indigenous people do participate and their knowledge and perspectives are made available within EIA processes, there is no guarantee that proponents, consultants, or regulators will pay any attention to them, or assign them appropriate weight in relation to their own 'scientific' studies (O'Faircheallaigh 2007; Weitzner 2008). This is despite the fact that Indigenous ecological knowledge based on experience is more reliable than the predictive modelling typically used by EIA consultants (Peletz et al. 2020: 419). This raises a wider, and fundamental, problem with community participation in statutory EIA. Ultimately, there is no certainty that it will have any impact on the decisions that proponents and regulators make about the approval or management of large mining projects (Gibson et al. 2018: 10). There is also the risk that Indigenous participation will be used by mining companies and the state to imply, wrongly, Indigenous endorsement of EIA outcomes.

In recent years, formal EIA guidelines issued by some regulatory authorities refer to cultural and social as well as environmental impacts (Queensland 2018). However, EIA is still overwhelmingly focused on the physical environment and EIA consultants rarely possess the skills to analyse complex social issues of vital importance to Indigenous peoples (Kløcker Larsen et al. 2022: 8). EIA also tends to ignore the cumulative impacts that can result if multiple projects are occurring on an Indigenous territory at the same time (Butler et al. 2021).

A final issue involves the underlying values that underpin EIA systems. The dominant narratives around large-scale industrial development emphasize its importance as a source of employment and economic growth, devalue nature, and equate development with the 'general interest', making it difficult to oppose project approval and resulting in negative impacts being ignored. For example, Devlin and Yap (2008: 22) show how proponents of the Pilar Dam in Brazil equated the project with 'modernization and progress', arguing that it would attract industries and employment to the region and result in provision of technical support to local farmers, and on this basis suggesting the project was a 'fait accompli'.

Community-controlled impact assessment

In response to these fundamental problems with conventional or regulatory EIA, in the early 1990s Aboriginal organizations and communities in the Cape York region of north Queensland pioneered a new approach which involved undertaking their own community-based economic, social, and cultural impact assessments, referred to here as Indigenous controlled impact assessment (ICIA). Similar approaches have been adopted in other regions of Australia and by some First Nations in Canada and New Zealand (Faauia et al. 2017; Gibson 2017; Gibson et al. 2018; KLC 2010a).

Given that they are driven by communities, there is no standard model, or best practice model, for ICIAs, but they tend to display the following features. They are overseen by an Aboriginal community body, based on terms of reference developed and endorsed by the community, and conducted by a team comprised of impact assessment (IA) specialists selected by the community and local researchers and informants (referred to here as the Indigenous IA Team). The role of IA specialists is to advise on appropriate approaches and methodologies for ICIA; provide training for local employees; help secure and manage funding for the process; advise on the technical requirements of 'mainstream' IA processes, where ICIA is to be integrated with these (see below); and assist in the drafting of ICIA reports.

Information requirements are established in an iterative manner as the Indigenous IA Team interacts with community members. This contrasts with most conventional IA processes where information provision is usually carried out on a 'one shot' basis through presentation by the proponents of a standard 'information kit' to affected communities (Woodside Energy Ltd 2007). In ICIA information is communicated in a form that best facilitates its transmission and comprehension: for example, visually, using storytelling, and in local languages. The approach to consultation is driven by the community, and may, for example, occur in clan- or gender-based groups, on location at the site of planned projects, and according to schedules dictated by the requirement for effective engagement. Another advantage of ICIA is that it can incorporate specific measures to facilitate participation by Indigenous women. Kuntz (2012) documents the necessity for such measures if impact assessment is to benefit from the rich ecological, social, and cultural knowledge held by women, and in some cases only by women. This knowledge can greatly increase the reliability and thoroughness of assessments regarding the likely impact of proposed projects.

Consultation will usually occur in multiple phases, with each 'round' leading to new questions and requests for further information, and with community understandings of and attitudes to development gradually becoming clear. Consultation often becomes a forum not only for providing information and documenting community views, but also for consensus building within a community. Groups that may be differently affected (for example, men and women, young and old, those interested in wage employment and those focused on subsistence production) become aware of each other's views, and consider how these might be accommodated within a 'community position' on a project (Howitt 2001: 345–6; O'Faircheallaigh 1999).

The Indigenous IA Team prepares draft reports which document likely impacts as understood by the community, appropriate strategies for dealing with these and for maximizing benefits, and community attitudes towards a proposed project (which may be complex and varied). The team seeks feedback on the draft reports, typically in small-group and later in community-wide meetings, and where necessary then amends the reports before they are finalized and endorsed by the community's governing body.

In some cases, ICIAs are conducted independently of government EIA processes, and then used as a basis for community decisions either to oppose projects in principle, or to negotiate legally binding agreements with developers and governments regarding the terms on which projects will be supported. In other cases, the Indigenous groups involved negotiate an arrangement with regulators whereby the Indigenous component of an EIA is 'extracted' from the government project approval process, is conducted by the community, and the community's ICIA report is then 'inserted' into the regulatory process as a part of the proponent's EIA.

An example of a recent ICIA is that conducted in relation to a proposed US$35 billion liquefied natural gas (LNG) precinct to process offshore natural gas near Broome in the Kimberley region in the north of Western Australia (WA). This ICIA was undertaken in 2009–10 as part of a joint federal–state government strategic assessment of the LNG project. The terms of reference for the strategic assessment agreed by the two governments included a requirement that it address the potential impacts of the proposed LNG precinct on Indigenous people. The Kimberley Land Council (KLC), which represents all Aboriginal landowning groups in the region, negotiated with the WA state government that the KLC would take responsibility for addressing the 'Indigenous impacts' component of the strategic assessment. It did so through a comprehensive 'Indigenous impacts assessment' that included economic, social, cultural, archaeological, and ethno-biological studies and reports.

The studies were overseen by a Traditional Owner Task Force (TOTF), comprised of senior representatives of each landowning group affected by the proposed LNG project. Decisions about which groups and which areas of land should be included in the ICIA were made entirely by Aboriginal people and their representative organization. The TOTF approved terms of reference for each component study, and created a Community IA Team comprised of specialist consultants working with knowledgeable elders, and with younger Aboriginal people employed as researchers and field workers. The Community IA Team undertook consultation on the basis preferred by Aboriginal people, and included formal community meetings; separate meetings with individual landowning groups 'on country'; separate meetings for men and women; informal meetings with teenagers at sporting venues and barbecues; and dialogue with senior high school students in their classrooms. All draft reports were reviewed by the TOTF and amended if necessary. The six volumes of the *Indigenous Impacts Report* constituted one component of the overall EIA submitted to the WA and federal Ministers for the Environment, and which formed the basis on which they would decide whether or not to approve the project. Each volume contained recommendations for conditions that should be attached to any approval of the project.

The *Indigenous Impacts Report* also helped frame agreements negotiated by the KLC and Aboriginal traditional owners with the lead commercial proponent for the Kimberley LNG project and the state of WA, signed in June 2011 (O'Faircheallaigh 2013c).

The critical advantage of ICIA is that it affords a central place to Indigenous community interests and understandings, and so addresses many of the concerns regarding regulatory, proponent-driven EIA outlined in the previous section. Terms of reference are created by the community, which thus controls the definition of 'impacts' and the 'impact zone', and so the basis on which the IA is conducted. ICIA is based on community understandings of project impacts, and insights into how they can be effectively managed. It recognizes the legitimacy and power of Indigenous knowledge, including women's knowledge, and Indigenous authority to manage resources that affect their livelihoods (Peletz et al. 2020). It uses appropriate methodologies and channels to communicate information and establish community attitudes towards proposed projects; and assists in developing the research and communication skills of local people working on IA teams. It can also play a critical role in resolving or managing community conflicts over development, as it identifies the range of groups and interests within a community in relation to a project, and provides a forum within which these can be accommodated.

The extent of the difference between ICIA and conventional IA can be illustrated by comparing the *Indigenous Impacts Report* for the Kimberley LNG project, discussed above, and the relevant components of the IA prepared for the proposed Pluto LNG project in the Pilbara region of WA (Woodside Energy Ltd 2007). This comparison is especially useful as the projects are similar in both scale and purpose (processing of offshore natural gas); are in close geographical proximity; were assessed within a few years of each other and under the same state and federal legislation; and had the same lead proponent, Woodside Energy Ltd. The major difference is that the Indigenous impact assessment work for the Pluto project was carried out by the proponent and its consultants, while that for the Kimberley LNG project was conducted by Aboriginal people and their organizations.

Woodside's IA report, which deals with both Indigenous and non-Indigenous economic, social, and cultural impacts, is just 31 pages. It states that Indigenous 'community members and individuals' were consulted, but no information is provided on how many people were involved or how they were consulted. Most of the potential impacts predicted for Indigenous people are positive—in particular, creation of training, employment, and business development opportunities. The Woodside IA does recognize the possibility that the project might result in 'Disturbance of heritage sites *within* project footprint' (emphasis added), to which the proposed management response is 'Ensure appropriate controls are put in place for exclusion zones' (Woodside Energy Ltd 2007: 21, 25). This is the only reference to impacts on Indigenous cultural heritage. The focus on sites within the project footprint ignores the reality that site damage could occur much more widely as a result of a predicted increase in the non-Indigenous population living in the region, and that in Aboriginal culture, sites in one area are almost inevitably linked to sites elsewhere and to cultural practices associated with such clusters of sites. These realities are at the heart of the KLC's analysis of heritage and cultural impacts in the *Indigenous Impacts Report* for the Kimberley LNG project, which extends to three volumes and a total of over 350 pages and, following Aboriginal understandings, adopts a *regional* approach to the identification and management of LNG project impacts.

More broadly, the KLC *Indigenous Impacts Report* comprises six volumes and some 750 pages, an indication of the breadth and depth of its analysis. It deals with a wide range of cultural, environmental, social, and economic impacts and issues, ranging for example from the LNG project's potential effect on social inequality; to the risk that project shipping might introduce exotic marine species and threaten the Aboriginal subsistence base; to the pressure on health and education services from the large project workforce; to the risk that Aboriginal people would fail to obtain employment unless education and housing services were greatly improved. The report identifies over 100 specific recommendations for the effective management of the many potential impacts it identifies (KLC 2010b). The contrast between proponent-controlled and community-controlled IA is very clear.

While ICIA has considerable potential to help effectively manage the negative impacts of mining, its application in practice is at the moment severely limited, for several reasons. There is no legal requirement for it to be undertaken in any jurisdiction, and so its application is patchy. Substantial resources are required to conduct ICIA, especially for large-scale environmental studies, given the heavy emphasis on intensive and iterative community participation. There is the added challenge of trying to ensure that action is taken to address impacts identified through ICIA, especially where projects operate for decades. One approach that can help address this last issue is the integration of ICIA with negotiation of Indigenous–industry agreements of the sort discussed in Chapter 9. Several Aboriginal groups have used ICIAs to help set the agenda for negotiations, with agreement provisions linked to addressing impacts or potential impacts identified in ICIAs. For instance, the Indigenous IA for the Browse LNG project documented widespread concern among Aboriginal people about the effects of drawing on aquifers for the large quantities of water required in processing of gas. It recommended that Aboriginal traditional owners should have an ability to shape decisions about the project's water use and alternative water sources. The agreements for the project require the operator to stop using water from aquifers and instead construct a desalination plant if traditional owners believe that damage to aquifers is happening or is about to happen (State of Western Australia et al. 2011: schedule 8, clause 8).

Protecting Indigenous cultural heritage

Indigenous cultural heritage can be seen as having three dimensions. The first involves material manifestations of Indigenous occupation during earlier periods of time, including burial sites, middens created by discarded shells and other food debris, rock and cave paintings, and scatters of stone tools. The second involves places, sites, areas, or landscapes that are of cultural or spiritual significance to living Indigenous people. They may be important for a variety of reasons. They may be associated with the actions of mythological beings during the period when today's world was created and when laws that govern people's interactions with the land and each other were established. They may be important because they are breeding grounds for key food species, are associated with initiation, mortuary, or other ceremonies, or because they are the location of important historical events. The third involves Indigenous cultural knowledge, including language, economic production, and rules for social interaction—knowledge that is applied every day and in its use transmitted from generation to generation. For many Indigenous peoples, the distinction between these three categories of 'cultural heritage' is artificial. They see the land and the sea, all of the sites they contain, and the knowledge and laws associated with land and with sites, as interrelated components of a single entity that must be protected as a whole, and also see themselves as intimately linked with earlier generations who have used the land and later generations who will use it in the future (Butler et al. 2021; Carmichael et al. 1994; O'Faircheallaigh 2008; Rose 1996).

As noted above, mining can have negative and dramatic impacts on these three dimensions of Indigenous cultural heritage. There is no typical legislative response aimed at managing these impacts, in contrast to the widespread use of EIA to manage the effects of mining on the physical environment. What is common across the globe is that national or sub-national cultural heritage legislation is universally ineffective in protecting Indigenous cultural heritage. In many cases, especially in the Global South, states fail even to recognize the existence of distinct Indigenous cultural heritage or Indigenous ownership of cultural heritage, let alone give Indigenous peoples a role in managing their heritage. In Chile, for instance, Atacameño people have seen many areas of significance, including sacred springs, damaged by lithium and copper mining. Like other Indigenous peoples in Chile, the Atacameños are not granted any legal rights over places or remains of significance to them. Cultural heritage is regarded as state property, and decisions about whether such places can be disturbed are made by state-appointed archaeologists. Atacameño people have mounted campaigns since the early 1990s to gain control of their cultural heritage, to date without success, and their declared desire that burial sites of their ancestors should remain untouched and undisturbed have at times been ignored by archaeologists (Kalazich 2015: 50–1). The end result of an absence of state recognition and protective action is that 'The unruly development of projects by transnational corporations continuously disregard[s] indigenous spiritual sites and [deprives] indigenous communities of their natural heritage' (Xanthaki 2017: 1).

In other jurisdictions, including Australia, Canada, and the United States, legislation exists whose stated intent is to protect Indigenous cultural heritage, but which in reality often operates to ensure that Indigenous heritage can be damaged or destroyed if it is perceived to impede development. A case in point is WA's Aboriginal Heritage Act (1972). While the purpose of the Act is stated to be the 'preservation' of 'places and objects customarily used by or traditional to the original inhabitants of Australia or their descendants', section 18 allows the relevant government minister to consent to a landowner using a place designated for protection under the Act for another purpose, even where this results in damage to or destruction of the place. This provision is routinely used by companies to damage or destroy Aboriginal cultural heritage to make way for mining. Hundreds of sites have been destroyed, for example, in the Pilbara iron ore region of WA. The Eastern Guruma people, who have seven iron ore mines and three railway lines on their land, estimate that 434 of their heritage sites have been destroyed, while a further 285 are very close to current mining (Allam and Wahlquist 2020).

The use of the Aboriginal Heritage Act to allow destruction of sites was dramatically illustrated in May 2020 when Rio Tinto Iron Ore destroyed two rock shelters, believed to have been occupied by Aboriginal people as long as 46,000 years ago, at Juukan Gorge on the lands of the Puutu Kunti Kurrama and Pinikura (PKKP) peoples. The destruction of Juukan Gorge caused international outrage because of its unique status as a site of such antiquity, evidence it contained of continued human habitation during the last ice age, and the discovery of a coil of human hair over 8,000 years old, sharing DNA with living PKKP people (Allam and Wahlquist 2020; Parliament of the Commonwealth of Australia 2020). However, the key point to note is that the destruction of sites is routine, both in WA and other jurisdictions. For instance, in 2020 the New South Wales government approved all 86 applications by landowners to impact registered Aboriginal heritage sites. In British Columbia, described by Ziff and Hope (2008: 184) as having 'the most ambitious' Aboriginal heritage legislation in Canada, the relevant government minister can, after consultation with its First Nation custodians, exempt a cultural heritage site from protection to allow for development to occur (BC Heritage Conservation Act (1996), section 12). This situation reflects the fact that most national and sub-national legislation is 'legislation by the non-Indigenous community for the non-Indigenous community that creates a superficial veneer of protection for Indigenous interests' (Ritter 2003: 208).

Given the weakness of legislation, two other possible sources of protection for Indigenous cultural heritage gain added significance: company policies and agreements negotiated between Indigenous peoples and mining companies. In 2021 the author and his colleagues, Ginger Gibson and David Percy, examined the Indigenous cultural heritage policies and Indigenous peoples policies of 27 of the world's largest mining and metals companies, which constitute the membership of the International Council on Mining and Metals (ICMM), by reviewing company websites and corporate social responsibility documentation.[1] Only three of the 27 companies published an Indigenous cultural heritage policy. Half had Indigenous peoples policies that mentioned cultural heritage, but these policies displayed features that raise serious concerns about their likely efficacy. None offered any indication of engagement with Indigenous communities as part of policy development or review.

---

[1] We conducted this research in February 2021 as input for a webinar series on Protecting Indigenous Cultural Heritage developed for ICMM member companies in the wake of the destruction of the Juukan Gorge rock shelters. The webinars were not public and the results of the research have not previously been published.

Many referenced government legislation as the basis for policy, but as noted, legislation is ineffective in protecting cultural heritage. Only four of the policies indicated how their implementation would be resourced. Lines of authority for implementation were not mentioned in any policy, and none discussed mechanisms for auditing policy success or failure. Eight did refer to grievance mechanisms that Indigenous people can use where they believe that policy has failed to protect cultural heritage, but little detail was provided about how such mechanisms might operate. In sum, there is little indication that, as of 2021, mining company policies are likely to be effective in protecting Indigenous cultural heritage.

Provisions of negotiated agreements related to cultural heritage protection were examined as part of the wider study of Australian agreements discussed in detail in Chapter 9. This study developed numerical criteria for assessing agreements in terms of the *level of protection* offered to cultural heritage (from a complete lack of protection to unqualified protection); and the *means of protection* (for example, resources, stop work procedures, and capacity-building initiatives) provided to achieve the desired level of protection (for details, see O'Faircheallaigh 2016: 72–4). In terms of level of protection, only one in ten agreements contained an unqualified commitment to avoid damage to Indigenous cultural heritage. In terms of means of protection, only 7 per cent of agreements fell in the upper third of the scoring range. These outcomes reflect the fact that state legislative and policy regimes governing negotiations put Aboriginal people in a weak bargaining position. Only where they can counter this weakness through political mobilization are Aboriginal groups able to use agreement making as a way of effectively protecting their interests. Currently, only a minority of groups are in this position (O'Faircheallaigh 2016). As a result, while negotiation of agreements has the potential to ensure protection of Indigenous cultural heritage, that potential is in many cases not yet being realized.

Mine 'closure' and the continuing legacy of mining

Mine closure tends to be defined by governments and the mining industry as a finite, well-defined process that begins as the operational stage of a mine is ending or has ended, involves the decommissioning of a mine and rehabilitation of a mine site, and ends when mining lease ownership is relinquished by the mine operator and responsibility for land management is accepted by the next land user (see, for example, Australian Government 2006: 1). Such a definition belies the enormous complexity of economic, environmental, social, and cultural issues that arise for Indigenous communities when corporations, capital, and resources exit from large-scale resource projects. It can also be criticized for assuming, wrongly, that mine 'closure' is an event, or an outcome. In reality, mines are never fully closed. Their physical impacts extend far beyond the operational life of the mine by way of environmental pollution, or the risk of pollution, that may last decades, centuries, or even thousands of years. Mines cannot simply be 'closed' and the physical landscape restored and rehabilitated to a functioning ecosystem, as indicated by the fact that there are few examples of successfully restored mine sites (O'Faircheallaigh and Lawrence 2019: 67). Systemic challenges arise, for example, in establishing long-term and stable flora and fauna restoration on remediated mine sites; stabilizing landforms (i.e. preventing erosion); and preventing contaminants (such as heavy metals and chemicals in mine tailings) from entering local water systems (Cristescu et al. 2013; Gould 2011; Le Clerc and Keeling 2015).

Mining legacies relate not only to the physical environment, but also to economic, social, and cultural impacts (see O'Faircheallaigh and Lawrence 2019 for a detailed discussion of these impacts). Industry and government discussions around mine closure presume that once a mine closes, and the (mining) dust settles, the social and cultural impacts of the operations will also settle and disappear. Yet as Scott Midgley argues, drawing on the work of geographers and environmental historians, 'mining communities, memories, and legacies persist long after mining activity formally ends' (Midgley 2015: 294; see also Keeling and Sandlos 2015). Indigenous communities are commonly left to deal with the various legacies of mining after companies have left and the attention of governments has moved elsewhere. This is especially so, given that up to 75 per cent of mine closures are unplanned or premature (Lebre et al. 2021: 3) and that there is a growing trend in the mining industry for major companies to use abandonment, asset transfers, and indefinite care and maintenance arrangements to avoid incurring the costs of orderly and environmentally responsible closure. Placing mines on an indefinite 'care and maintenance' basis is a vivid illustration of the reality that, even in terms of narrow legislative definitions, mines 'never close'. Companies can cease operations, leave an individual on site as a 'caretaker', claim that it may be viable to reopen the mine at some point in the future, and defer indefinitely any spending on rehabilitation and closure (Lebre et al. 2021; O'Faircheallaigh and Lawrence 2019).

A key contextual factor in any discussion of mine rehabilitation and closure is recognition that the large majority of corporate resources, community engagement, and governmental regulation are focused on what might be termed the 'front end' of the mine life cycle. This encompasses exploration, or the search for potentially viable mineral resources; feasibility and approval, which involves establishing whether a project is economically and technically feasible and can achieve government approval; mine construction; and operations, or extracting the minerals. The remaining stages, or the 'back end' of the mine life cycle, involve decommissioning, closure, post-closure, and relinquishment. These remain the poor cousins of the industry, which receive few corporate resources and little government regulation. Indeed, it is only in recent years that governments have begun to require mining companies to start planning for closure early in the mine life cycle or to make financial provision for the costs involved in mine closure (O'Faircheallaigh and Lawrence 2019). Further, the attention of government and industry is very much focused on the technical and physical aspects of closure, rather than on its social and cultural effects (Monosky and Keeling 2021).

Indigenous people, unlike companies and governments, are tied to the land and unable to escape the impacts that ensue or occur after mining ends. Given this fact, it is crucial that Indigenous peoples have a major involvement in regulatory systems being established to deal with mine closure, and more generally in decisions about how closure should occur, including the nature of post-mining landforms and the extent to which ongoing impacts are acceptable. An analysis of relevant regulatory regimes across a number of countries fails to show any evidence that affected Indigenous peoples are being included in decision making. Closure is managed solely by mine operators and regulatory agencies. This applies even in situations where there is statutory recognition of Indigenous rights in land (Bond and Kelly 2021; Monosky and Keeling 2021; O'Faircheallaigh and Lawrence 2019).

Could negotiated agreements offer an alternative means by which Indigenous peoples can influence mine closure planning and closure outcomes? An analysis of 50 agreements negotiated across Australia's major mining regions over the period from the early 1980s to 2015 shows that many negotiated agreements fail to address issues around mine closure in any depth or detail. Sixty per cent of the 50 agreements make no reference at all to closure, except by stating that benefits payable to the Aboriginal parties will be suspended or terminated if and when production is suspended or a project is closed. A further 20 per cent of agreements contain broad commitments to comply with environmental legislation or to consult with Aboriginal people in relation to environmental management or to lodging of environmental applications. Either type of commitment might relate to mine closure, but there is no specific indication that they will or should do so. Only seven of the 50 agreements address closure in a direct and substantive sense. These require Aboriginal consent before a project operator can submit a closure plan to the environmental regulator and/or include in the agreement specific conditions that will apply to closure, relating for instance to recontouring of disturbed areas, treatment of open cut voids, or standards to which land must be rehabilitated (O'Faircheallaigh and Lawrence 2019). In summary, agreements may have the potential to allow Indigenous peoples some say in relation to mine planning, but this potential is not currently being realized in Australia. Given that agreement making is unusually prevalent and well established in Australia, it seems safe to assume that the same conclusion would apply to other jurisdictions.

Conclusion

Mining can have substantial and negative cultural, social, and environmental impacts on Indigenous peoples, impacts that can continue long after mineral extraction has ended. Mitigating those impacts would not, it must be stressed, constitute a benefit for Indigenous peoples. Rather, it would constitute a reduction in loss and so possibly contribute to a balance of costs and benefits less heavily weighted against them or possibly weighted in their favour. Globally, the current legislative and policy regimes for mitigating or avoiding negative impacts is ineffective. Statutory EIA regimes often exclude Indigenous peoples and their interests, and they are particularly poor in dealing with social and cultural impacts and with the effects of mine closure. Legislation dealing with cultural heritage fails completely to address mining's impact. Either it does not even recognize the existence of Indigenous cultural heritage and so does not contemplate dealing with impacts on it, or it purports to protect Indigenous cultural heritage but in effect establishes systems to ensure that mining companies can destroy cultural heritage with impunity where they believe it constitutes a barrier to their profitable extraction of minerals.

There are signs of change in what would otherwise be a bleak picture indeed. The international outcry that followed Rio Tinto's destruction of the Juukan Gorge rock shelters in May 2020 had no parallel in earlier decades when destruction of sites of comparable significance to Indigenous people gained little international attention. What is also significant about Juukan Gorge is that loss of cultural heritage, which usually only has an impact on its Indigenous owners, had serious consequences for the mining company involved. After an internal inquiry into the destruction of Juukan Gorge, Rio Tinto initially proposed only to reduce the annual bonuses of a small number of managers directly involved. After sustained pressure from Aboriginal people in the Pilbara, through social media on a global scale, and from ethical investor groups in London and elsewhere, Rio Tinto sacked three of its most senior managers, including its Chief Executive Officer. The company's Chairman and the director who conducted the internal review subsequently resigned.

Another sign of change is the growing use of ICIA to allow Indigenous peoples to make their own assessments of mining's likely effects and their own recommendations to minimize them, and to increase the attention paid to Indigenous impacts in regulatory EIA. A small number of agreements are adding substantially to the protection offered to Indigenous cultural heritage and, as agreement making becomes more widespread and Indigenous negotiating capacity improves, this source of protection will become more important. Agreements could also allow Indigenous people to have some input into decisions regarding mine closure.

Despite these signs of change, however, the situation today is that the mining industry, governments, and non-Indigenous society as a whole are failing to ensure that negative impacts of mining on Indigenous peoples are avoided or substantially mitigated.

11
Maximizing Mining's Economic Potential for Indigenous Peoples

Introduction

Many Indigenous communities experience average cash incomes and rates of formal employment much lower than those of non-Indigenous populations in the countries where they live. Their economic disadvantage may not be as great as figures on cash incomes and formal employment suggest, given their access to hunting, fishing, and other food production opportunities not available to the mainstream. However, many Indigenous peoples are keen to increase their access to market incomes, which are often seen not only as providing a basis for improving quality of life, but as indispensable to the maintenance of subsistence food production and of the social and cultural systems within which it occurs. In 2009 a senior Aboriginal woman expressed to me her belief that if formal employment opportunities did not soon become available to young people in her community, culture would be lost within a generation as they would leave to seek opportunities elsewhere. Such views are not unusual, though they are certainly not universal, and indeed some Indigenous groups are simply not interested in working in the mining economy. This is especially so where Indigenous economies remain intact. Even in these cases, Indigenous peoples may welcome the opportunity to gain an additional source of income from revenue flows generated by royalty and other payments from mining projects.

Economic opportunities associated with mining fall into three main categories: direct employment in mining and associated logistical activity; establishment or expansion of businesses to sell goods and services to mining companies and to residents of mining towns; and revenue flows generated by mining for affected Indigenous communities. The opportunities created by each and the challenges associated with them are examined in turn.

Employment in mining

Modern mining projects generate relatively little employment relative to the scale of investment involved. However, in absolute terms and relative to the size of adjacent Indigenous communities, the hundreds and sometimes thousands of jobs that large projects create can be very significant, particularly if rates of formal employment are

Indigenous Peoples and Mining. Ciaran O'Faircheallaigh, Oxford University Press. © Ciaran O'Faircheallaigh (2023).
DOI: 10.1093/oso/9780192894564.003.0011

low (Dylan et al. 2013). In addition, wages in mining tend to be well above those in other economic sectors, and so mining employment may be highly valued even if alternative opportunities are available. Occupational categories range from unskilled work as labourers or cleaning staff; to semi-skilled jobs as truck drivers and plant operators; to skilled manual roles in plant maintenance and repair (for instance, electricians or mechanics); to professional roles in geology, engineering, industrial chemistry, environmental sciences, and community relations; and to supervisory and managerial positions.

In many parts of the world there has been a fundamental change in the location of mine workforces since the 1980s. There has been a move away from the previous practice of building new towns close to remote mine sites, to systems where workers live in established regional centres or capital cities and fly into mine sites for work rosters: for example, two weeks 'on' and one week 'off'. They live in single-person accommodation during their stays at a mine. Automation has been another important trend affecting the mining workforce, leading to a reduction in less skilled roles such as labouring and truck driving and, relatively speaking, to an increase in skilled positions. Automation has added to the tendency for workers to live away from mine sites for part or all of the time, as it has made it possible, for instance, to use integrated remote operations centres hundreds of kilometres away to control mining and transport operations (Holcombe and Kemp 2018).

A final point about mining employment, noted in Chapter 5, is its historical dominance by men. This has only been challenged recently, though it is far from being reversed, as companies make efforts to increase recruitment and retention of women. Indigenous women workers and potential workers face continuing challenges including racism and sexual harassment in the workplace; lack of access to permanent, skilled employment and absence of women in leadership roles at mine sites; an absence of affordable childcare and flexible workplace arrangements; and criticism and violence from family and community members (IWIMRA 2019; Lahiri-Dutt 2008; PIWC 2016). Male dominance is reinforced in some cases by Indigenous cultural values that militate against women working outside their homes or their communities, or more generally participating in public life (Bainton 2010: 131–7; Esteves 2008: 134).

In the twentieth century, Indigenous people often failed to gain substantial employment in mining projects located on their ancestral lands, with jobs, especially skilled roles, taken mainly by non-Indigenous people, often recruited from outside the region (Cousins and Nieuwenhuysen 1984; Green 2013). A major obstacle to Indigenous employment arose from racism or stereotyping among mining companies and their non-Indigenous employees, leading to assumptions that Indigenous people would not be capable of, or interested in, industrial employment. Exclusion of Indigenous people from formal education and their inability to speak the language used on mine sites meant they often found it hard to compete for mining jobs, especially in professional and managerial roles. Some Indigenous people found the working and social environment of mine sites alien and onerous, or the demands of regular wage employment incompatible with continued participation in traditional economic and cultural activities and fulfilment of social obligations. Use of job advertisement and staff selection processes designed for the mainstream could mean that Indigenous people were not aware of, or were at a disadvantage in applying for, job opportunities. Even where companies were formally committed to increasing Indigenous employment, managers often tended to prioritize the demands of production and cost containment over Indigenous employment and training in allocating financial and other resources, including their own time. State authorities frequently showed little interest in providing regulatory or financial support to increase Indigenous employment (Green 2013; Haley and Fisher 2014; O'Faircheallaigh 2002b, 2006).

Within these broad generalizations, the experience of individual Indigenous peoples varied depending on a range of factors. These included the degree of cost, difficulty, and political acceptability associated with recruiting non-Indigenous staff; the specific histories and cultural values of specific Indigenous groups; and company policies and practices on Indigenous recruitment, training, and employment. In relation to the last factor, O'Faircheallaigh (2002b: 70–136) showed that quite different employment outcomes for Aboriginal people occurred in the same region and industry sector because of the willingness or otherwise of mining companies to devote resources to Aboriginal training and employment, and to vary standard employee rosters in ways that accommodated work patterns preferred by Aboriginal people. More broadly, Indigenous employment could be virtually non-existent in situations where alternative labour sources were easily accessible and where dominant social norms supported racist attitudes to Indigenous people. Indigenous people might comprise a significant part of the workforce where the opposite pattern prevailed. Local economic conditions also had an impact. Indigenous people in Chile's arid Atacama region took up employment in copper and lithium mining when reduction in water availability and militarization of Chile's border with Argentina undermined the viability of long-range pastoral activity and seasonal work in Argentina, on which they had previously relied (see Chapter 12).

Despite the persistence of substantial barriers to their participation and their continued concentration in lower-skilled positions (Schott et al. forthcoming; Stokes et al. 2019), there has been a broad tendency for the Indigenous share of employment in mines in Indigenous territories to increase in recent decades. This tendency has been most pronounced in jurisdictions, such as Australia and Canada, where the historical record of Indigenous employment had been especially poor (Holcombe and Kemp 2020; Rescan 2012; Schott et al. forthcoming). For example, the number of Indigenous people employed by Rio Tinto Iron Ore (RTIO) rose from 47 in 2011 to 1,108 in 2014. RTIO cut its total workforce after 2014 as iron ore prices fell, but Indigenous employment fell less sharply than overall employment (Tulele 2020: 135). Given that the average wage in Australian mining exceeds A$120,000 per annum, adding 1,000 Indigenous employees to its workforce would have added A$120 million to the incomes of Aboriginal workers and families in the Pilbara region. Factors facilitating increased Indigenous employment include legislation to outlaw racial discrimination in the workplace; improved Indigenous access to formal education;

corporate social responsibility policies that create incentives for mine managers to expand Indigenous employment; and negotiation of agreements between mining companies and Indigenous peoples (see Chapter 8). Relevant agreement provisions include targets for Indigenous employment and sanctions for failure to achieve them; Indigenous recruitment, training, retention, and career development initiatives; scholarships to fund Indigenous students completing high school and attending university; and measures to recognize Indigenous cultural and social values—for instance, through provision of hunting leave. They also involve initiatives to make the workplace more conducive to Indigenous retention and advancement (for example, cross-cultural training for non-Indigenous staff supervising Indigenous employees); to facilitate family and community support for Indigenous workers; and specifically to encourage recruitment of Indigenous women (O'Faircheallaigh 2016).

Especially given the high wages paid in the mining industry, growing employment has the potential to improve substantially the living standards and social well-being of Indigenous workers and their families (Barker 2006). Mine employment also has the potential to help address social problems including substance abuse and youth suicide, the latter a serious problem in many Indigenous communities—problems that can be associated with low incomes and lack of economic opportunities and hope (Ritsema et al. 2015: 159–60). A resident of one First Nation in northern Ontario expressed it in this way:

> When we don't have much hope, we grope for things … we find sometimes the things that we look for to make us happy don't make us happy—drugs, alcohol, those kinds of things, bootlegging, drug dealing. I want to make money; I'll deal that type of thing, and it becomes a vicious cycle … so what I think we need to do is to get people back to work and make a clean living … and that in itself will bring self-worth back to people. (cited in Dylan et al. 2013: 68)

One drawback associated with mining employment is that it can be unreliable. Reflecting volatility in mineral markets, mines can close temporarily or permanently with little notice. This can be highly problematic for Indigenous workers, particularly given that mines are often located in areas where few alternative wage-earning opportunities exist. It is especially problematic when workers have incurred debts— for example, to purchase a house—which they are no longer able to service, and where wage employment has led to a loss of capacity to produce food from the land. The relationship between mining employment and the ability to spend time on the land in cultural and food production activities is complex. On the one hand, full-time employment does reduce the time available for such activities. On the other, rostered fly-in, fly-out systems mean that workers still have extended periods of time in their home communities. In addition, wage income can increase their capacity to buy the vehicles, boats, skidoos, and fuel that have become increasingly essential for land-based activities, given that Indigenous people are increasingly living in larger centres that may be distant from their traditional lands (Brubacher and Associates 2002; O'Faircheallaigh 1995; Saxinger forthcoming; Southcott and Natcher 2018).

Supplying goods and services

Another potential source of income for Indigenous people is to establish or expand businesses to supply goods and services to mining projects. While complex mining equipment and machinery and specialized items such as tyre trucks are likely to be bought from major industrial centres, Indigenous businesses may be able to win contracts in areas including earth moving, construction, fuel supply, air, road and sea transport, catering, cleaning, and environmental monitoring and rehabilitation. Indigenous businesses create incomes not just by generating profits but also by employing Indigenous workers, a significant potential benefit given that Indigenous businesses tend to employ a higher proportion of Indigenous employees than do non-Indigenous contractors or in-house mining company operations supplying the same items (O'Faircheallaigh and Langton 2008: 30). Indigenous businesses can also generate significant non-financial benefits by conducting their activities in a way that is consistent with Indigenous values: for instance, by working to protect the subsistence economy, focusing on creating long-term careers for their Indigenous workers, and prioritizing youth employment (Lasley 2019). Many also channel profits into social programmes and development of community infrastructure (Anderson et al. 2006).

As with direct employment in mining, Indigenous people have in the past faced significant challenges in gaining access to contracts with mining projects. This reflects some of the same factors, such as prejudice against Indigenous businesses and consequent doubts about their ability to operate reliably and efficiently, and the difficulty faced by Indigenous people in gaining access to education. It also reflects the problems Indigenous businesses face in breaking into markets typically supplied by large national or international firms with established track records and benefiting from economies of scale (Belayneh et al. 2018; Pearson and Helms 2013). Indigenous participation in contracting has increased substantially in recent years, and some notable successes have been achieved, particularly where multiple mines located in the same region create their own economies of scale. Examples are diamond mines in Canada's Northwest Territories and iron ore mines in the Pilbara region of Western Australia (Langton 2013; Tlicho Investment Corporation 2015). For example, it is estimated that in 2014 the diamond mines in Canada's Northwest Territories spent C\$248 million with Aboriginal businesses and that the cumulative value of contracts with those businesses reached C\$4.8 billion in that year (NWT & Nunavut Chamber of Mines 2015: 2, 8). The construction of the Victor diamond mine in northern Ontario generated C\$167 million in contracts for Aboriginal businesses (Dylan et al. 2013).

Negotiated agreements can also play a significant role in facilitating Indigenous access to contracting opportunities. Clauses that are helpful in this regard include commitments by mining companies to award contracts to a minimum level to Indigenous businesses; to bypass or simplify complex and expensive tendering processes for Indigenous contractors; and to assist Indigenous businesses in raising finance—for example, by providing them with letters of intent to purchase goods and services.

They also include a requirement for major contractors to provide subcontracts to Indigenous businesses; granting of a 'price tolerance' to Indigenous businesses so that small price differentials do not result in them losing contracts to non-Indigenous firms; and support for the creation of joint ventures with established non-Indigenous suppliers to help Indigenous businesses build their skills and capacity. In Canada, an additional important factor in the success of Indigenous businesses has been the ability of Aboriginal groups to combine together to win large contracts that would be beyond the capacity of any one of them: for instance, the contract to maintain the ice roads used to transport supplies to the Northwest Territory diamond mines during winter.

The potential of Indigenous businesses linked to mining to generate sustainable benefits is significantly increased when the skills and capacities developed to supply one mine can be used in supplying other projects and other industry sectors, helping to defray the risks associated with volatility in the mining industry and promising a continued life when a particular mine ends. Catering, environmental services, construction, and transport are examples of activities with considerable potential in this regard. However, the remote location of many mines and resultant high transport costs and absence of other markets constitute substantial barriers to achieving sustainability. The tendency in some contexts to regard access to business opportunities as a form of compensation for the impacts of mining can also create a significant obstacle (Bainton and Macintyre 2013; Batise 2016). Bainton and his colleagues have shown how in Papua New Guinea, for instance, contracts are regarded by both affected landowners and mining companies as one way in which landowners are compensated, and companies win acceptance for their operations. The result is that businesses trying to diversify by moving into areas away from their place of origin face strong hostility because they are seen as encroaching on the rights of local landowners to monopolize contracts. This view of business contracts as an entitlement rather than as payment for the efficient provision of goods and services can also undermine the competitiveness of landowner businesses and result in their demise (Bainton and Jackson 2020; Bainton and Macintyre 2013).

Provision of goods and services to residents of mine towns can offer additional economic opportunities. This can involve sale of fresh and cooked food and of personal services such as vehicle maintenance and entertainment. Activities of this sort can be especially important in the Global South where informal economies can quickly expand to take advantage of available opportunities. For example, Bainton and Jackson (2020: 371) cite evidence that informal economic activities employ considerably larger numbers of people in Papua New Guinea than employment associated with mining companies or the formal businesses that supply them. Informal business activity may also be more readily accessible to women, and so help mitigate gender inequality in the distribution of benefits from mining (Esteves 2008; Mahy 2008).

Revenues from mining

The third way in which mining can generate economic opportunities for Indigenous peoples is through monetary payments made to Indigenous organizations or communities. These occur most commonly through agreements negotiated with mine operators, and more rarely through allocation by the state of a proportion of its mineral tax revenues to local or regional governments (Browne and Robertson 2009; Söderholm and Svahn 2015: 84–5, 87). Conceptually, there are two rationales for such monetary payments (Bainton and Jackson 2020: 368). The first is to compensate communities for costs they incur because of mining. Those costs can be economic—for instance, loss of land used for food production—or they can arise from social disruption or negative effects on cultural or environmental values. The intention behind this rationale is that communities are *no worse off* because of mining. The second category is in addition to payments meant to ensure against loss, and is intended to leave an affected community *better off* as a result of mining: that is, with a 'net benefit'. These two categories are not dealt with through separate payments under negotiated agreements or state allocations. Rather, a single set of payments is designed to cover both. The fact that affected communities are intended to receive a net benefit, and not just be compensated for costs, is clearly indicated by the use of payments related to project revenues or profits (see next section). If the intention was only to compensate for loss, then the amount of that loss could be estimated and addressed through fixed payments spread over the life of the mine.

Reflecting the fact that payments usually result from negotiated agreements, their scale and form vary greatly across the Indigenous world, reflecting factors discussed in Chapter 8 in regard to agreements. In some cases, Indigenous peoples receive no payments at all; in others, they may receive only a single modest payment at the start of mine life; in yet others, they receive annual royalty payments in the tens of millions of dollars and may also own equity in a project, entitling them to a share of dividends.

Revenues are fungible and can in principle be channelled to uses that are a priority for Indigenous people and which may not, unlike for example wage employment in mining, require acceptance of social and cultural norms of the dominant society. In the Canadian and Australian north, mining revenues have been used to support the establishment or re-establishment of settlements on ancestral lands; the maintenance of subsistence food production and related cultural activities; transmission of Indigenous languages and cultural knowledge; and Indigenous management of lands and resources (Gibson MacDonald et al. 2014: 68–73; Southcott and Natcher 2018). For example, one First Nation receiving revenues from De Beers Victor diamond mine in northern Ontario has used a large part of its income to support 'harvesters' funding' for community members engaged in trapping, hunting, and fishing (Dylan et al. 2013: 78).

Revenues can also have other, less positive effects: for instance, if they are used to support socially destructive behaviour such as excessive alcohol consumption;

if their availability discourages traditional economic activity; or if they are distributed inequitably, causing social conflict and enmity (Golub 2014: 151–4; O'Faircheallaigh 2002b: 153–79; York 1990: 88–106). As a result, a question arises as to whether revenues do in fact constitute an economic opportunity, a question encapsulated in the concept of the 'resource curse', discussed below. The specific ways in which mining payments are extracted from projects, and the way in which they are used, have a major bearing on this question (O'Faircheallaigh 2018). The variety of forms in which payments occur is discussed in the next section, after which I review several ways in which these payments can be used and consider three specific issues related to the impact of mining revenues: their tendency to be unstable, their finite nature, and the economic and social dynamic they create in recipient communities.

The form of monetary payments

Payments occur in multiple and diverse forms. A useful way to categorize them is to relate them to key economic components of an extractive industry project, the points at which financial benefits may be extracted from it by an Indigenous community, and the calculations that determine the amounts involved. This is done in Table 11.1. A key point to note is that there can be considerable difference in the degree of certainty regarding whether specific forms of payments will materialize, with certainty declining as one moves down through the table. This reflects the fact that more unpredictable variables (in particular, mineral prices and production costs) affect payments, and that an expanding body of stakeholders other than the project investor and the affected community (company workers, suppliers of goods and services, government, lenders) have priority in gaining access to the revenue stream from the project. Uncertainty and the order in which actors gain access to project revenues are inextricably linked. To the extent that a community has priority over other actors in gaining access to revenues, uncertainty as to whether it will receive benefits declines. The main points at which a community can extract benefits and the form they take are discussed separately and their implications for communities and investors are explored.

Pre-production payments and rental payments

Before production begins, payments may be made in return for the community providing its consent for a project—for instance, by signing an agreement with the investor—or as the project achieves specified milestones, such as grant of a mining lease or commencement of production. Such payments typically take the form of fixed monetary amounts, which can vary substantially depending on the size of the project and the bargaining power of the parties. In Australia, for example, they have varied in the last decade from as little as A$50,000 for smaller mining projects to more than A$10 million for a proposed multi-billion dollar liquefied natural gas (LNG) project.

Table 11.1 Points in project economic structure where payments can be extracted

	Item	Form of payment	Comment	
Pre-production and rental payments	Payment, e.g., for signing agreement; annual payment for useof land	Set amounts, one-off or continuing (rental)		MORE CERTAIN
Operating mine, economic components				
A	Volume of production	$ per tonne		
B	Unit price		Highly uncertain and variable	
$C = A \times B$	Revenue	% of revenue		
D	Operating costs, including interest payments		Some uncertainty	
$E = C - D$	Gross profit	% of gross profit		
F	State taxation			
$G = E - F$	Net profit	% of net profit		
H	Loan repayments			
I	Profit retained in business		Variable, may be specified, e.g., in joint ventures	
$J = G - H - I$	Dividends to shareholders	Dividends on community equity in project		LESS CERTAIN

No or little risk or uncertainty is attached to such payments for the communities involved, as they occur even if the project fails to commence operations, a very real possibility in the extractive sector. Indeed, it is not at all unusual for projects to be cancelled or indefinitely delayed after a community has signed a benefits agreement. Large extractive firms typically have a number of potential projects under assessment at any time, and may decide not to proceed with a specific project because detailed feasibility studies show that another is more profitable. Firms, especially smaller ones, may fail to raise the capital required for project construction because of falling demand for the commodity involved, or may find environmental or other conditions imposed by regulators too onerous. Alternatively, decades may pass as a succession of owners assess a potential project but do not develop it. For example, the Aurukun bauxite deposit in far north Queensland was discovered by Pechiney in the 1970s, and has since been taken over by a succession of owners including Chalco (the Chinese state aluminium company) and Glencore. It is still undeveloped.

It is especially important for communities to obtain some benefit regardless of whether development proceeds because they incur significant costs in dealing with proposed projects. These include the human and financial resources committed to negotiate an agreement and more generally to dealing with project proponents and government agencies; the negative cultural and environmental impacts of exploration activity; and the divisive social effects of proposed projects, with different community members often taking conflicting views of a proposed development. The proposed Browse LNG project in northern Western Australia is a case a point. This caused serious internal conflict in the local Aboriginal community, exacerbated by the involvement of environmental groups opposed to the project, conflict which persists even though the project did not proceed for commercial reasons (O'Neill 2019).

For a project developer, pre-production payments constitute a cost incurred at a time when a project has yet to generate an income stream and, especially for smaller firms that may not have a revenue stream from other projects, may constitute a substantial burden. This acts as a significant constraint on the scale of benefit a community may be able to extract through pre-production payments. Yet given the reality that impacts start as soon as a potential project is announced, and that many proposed projects do not proceed, there is a strong argument for communities to receive substantial pre-production payments.

Like pre-production payments, rental payments are for fixed amounts, but they are paid annually as long as a company holds a mining lease. They are made regardless of whether production occurs, and may be paid after mining ceases permanently where a company must continue to hold a lease until its rehabilitation and closure obligations are complete. Rental payments reflect the fact that even if mining is not occurring, a group's land is being occupied by a mine and is usually not available for alternative uses. Rents also have a high degree of certainty because they involve fixed amounts that do not vary over the terms of a mining lease.

Output-based charges

The next point at which benefits can flow occurs as minerals are extracted and these benefits are based on a fixed payment (usually adjusted for inflation) for each unit of production ('A' in Table 11.1): for example, $1 for each tonne of bauxite produced. The only source of uncertainty here is whether and at what level production occurs. The (relative) predictability of output-based fixed payments has the advantage that it facilitates community planning, as long-term commitments can be made to developing infrastructure and services with a reasonable level of confidence that a steady income stream will be available to support them, given that payments do not fall even if mineral prices decline. If no payments are made, this is because no production is occurring, which in turn means that impacts on land and people are likely to be much less than if mining was taking place.

The disadvantage of this approach is that while payments may adjust with changes in the local consumer price index (CPI), the community does not benefit if commodity prices rise more rapidly than CPI. For example, several Indigenous communities with output-based royalties received no additional benefits when mining company profits soared with the boom in commodity prices in the 2000s.

Revenue-based payments

Revenue ('C' in Table 11.1) is the product of the volume of production ('A') and the unit price received by the company ('B'). Given that mineral prices can be unstable even over short periods of time, revenue can vary considerably. Falling mineral prices usually reflect a fall in demand, which may result in cuts to the volume of minerals produced, further reducing revenue. Similarly, output may rise as prices increase. Community benefits extracted at this point take the form of a percentage of revenue.

Revenue-based payments have the benefit that community income increases as the value of resources extracted from its territory rises, but of course if prices fall, so does community income. The risks involved are well illustrated by the experience of the Gagudju Association, which received revenue-based royalties from the Ranger uranium mine in Australia's Northern Territory. After a sharp decline in uranium prices and consequent cuts in Ranger's output in the early 1990s, the Association's income fell by 50 per cent in one year. Gagudju had raised bank loans to finance investments in tourism based on its projected royalty income, and when this collapsed it could not service its loans and was forced to sell its flagship hotel at a significant loss.

Another important issue that arises in relation to revenue-based royalties is whether the prices a mine charges for the minerals it produces reflect the full, 'open market' value of the mineral concerned or alternatively, where minerals are traded between subsidiaries of a single corporation, whether prices are determined by the corporation so as to minimize its overall tax liabilities ('transfer pricing'). For example, the author estimated that product from one mine in Australia appeared to be priced at only 40 per cent of its market value when it was sold to another subsidiary of the same corporation located in a different country. In this situation, communities are deprived of a significant proportion of the value of resources extracted from their territories.

Transfer pricing is a particular problem where mineral products are highly differentiated and where market transparency is low. Transparency is high for metals such as gold and copper which are sold in forms that are physically consistent (for example, gold bars that are 99.5 per cent pure), on markets with numerous buyers and sellers. It is possible to establish, literally in an instant, the 'open market' price for gold, and this can be used as a reference to ensure that the price obtained by any individual gold mine reflects the full value of the mineral extracted. The situation is very different for some other commodities—for instance, bauxite and silica sand—whose physical characteristics can vary markedly from mine to mine and which are typically traded under confidential contracts between buyers and sellers. This combination of circumstances makes it very difficult to establish a reliable 'reference point' for sales from a project, and so whether a community royalty based on revenue yields a benefit commensurate with the wealth extracted from community lands.

Royalties on profits

Gross profit ('E' in Table 11.1) is what remains after deduction of operating costs and interest payments from revenue, while net profit' ('G' in Table 11.1) is what remains after the state has imposed tax on gross profits. Income derived by communities by charging a percentage royalty on gross or net profits tends to be more volatile and unpredictable than a revenue-based royalty because operating costs may change, as may interest rates and government tax rates. There is also the possibility that operating costs and interest payments may be manipulated in the same way as mineral prices. Two mechanisms used in this manner are for the parent company to charge above-market interest rates on loans it provides to the operating subsidiary, or to charge management fees that are excessive given the management services the parent provides. Both appeared to have affected the original agreement between the north Queensland Aboriginal community of Hope Vale and Mitsubishi Corporation, which operated a silica sand mine on the community's land. This led the community to change from a profit- to a revenue-based royalty when its agreement with Mitsubishi was renegotiated in the 1990s (Holden and O'Faircheallaigh 1995).

Equity and dividends

Communities can obtain access to benefits by taking an ownership stake (equity) in the project concerned or in the company which operates it. This can occur either through the purchase of shares from the project owner or on the stock market, or through negotiation of 'carried equity' where the company building the project funds the community's share of development costs and retrieves the amount involved from project revenues when (and if) these eventuate. Dividends ('J' in Table 11.1) constitute the income flow to shareholders after portions of net profit ('G') have been used to repay the capital component of any project loans ('H') and/or retained in the business ('I') to provide working capital and to build up reserves in anticipation of future capital needs or as a cushion against difficult trading conditions.

Dividends constitute the least certain of all forms of community benefit because they constitute, in effect, the 'last call' on project revenues (see Table 11.1). Care must be taken in how an equity arrangement is structured. For example, joint venture arrangements with the project developer may be organized so as to allow the latter to siphon off profits through management fees or interest charged on 'carried equity' until such time as it is repaid from revenues. However, where a project involves a significant degree of risk, which reduces the 'cost of entry' to the project for the original investors, and generates high profits, dividends can generate very substantial returns. These result both from the income stream paid to shareholders and from the possibility of selling a portion of the community's equity at a capital gain once the project's profitability has been established.

Focusing community payments at the top end of Table 11.1 reduces the uncertainty and variability of income, but has a number of drawbacks. Investors will rarely be prepared to make substantial payments before a project's profitability has been established, and so pre-production payments are likely to be modest relative to the value of resources that will be extracted. Royalties based on the volume of production do not allow a community to share in the benefits of rising prices or in the wealth that a profitable project generates for investors. Revenue-based and profit-based royalties do adjust upwards in response to higher prices, and project equity, in particular, allows a community to share in above-average profits. However, these sources of benefits are unpredictable and uncertain, and prices and profits may be subject to manipulation where purchase of inputs and sale of minerals occur within a single corporation that operates across national boundaries.

To try and address this dilemma, in recent years communities have increasingly sought to combine elements from throughout Table 11.1. One agreement currently under negotiation in north Australia illustrates this point. It provides for pre-production payments of several hundred thousand dollars; for the community to receive a share of the state government's royalty income, which is based on a fixed payment per tonne; for a royalty calculated as a percentage of revenue; and for the community to receive 'carried' equity in the project of 12.5 per cent.

Time horizons, risk, and uncertainty

The revenue-raising mechanism or mix of mechanisms that best suits an individual community will depend in part on its time horizons (O'Faircheallaigh and Gibson 2012). For example, an Indigenous community that is in urgent need of resources to develop basic governing structures to support its engagement with the non-Indigenous world may place a premium on getting pre-production or output-based payments that are certain and arrive early in project life. This community may feel that the benefits potentially available from revenue- or profit-based royalties are unlikely to be realized, and that such payments may prove divisive, if the community does not first have in place robust governance structures to ensure accountability, transparency, and effective financial management. Similarly, if a community is faced with an urgent need—for instance, for funds to address an imminent health crisis—then relying on a dividend flow that may take many years to eventuate is not advisable. On the other hand, it may make sense for a community already receiving income from an operating mine, which is due to close after a decade, to forgo immediate or short-term income from pre-production or output-based payments from a new mine in return for substantial revenue- or profit-based royalties that will take some years to eventuate. Its ability to reduce a developer's tax burden in the early years of project life may allow it to negotiate a substantial share of revenue and profits in later years.

A community's risk profile is also important in choosing revenue-raising mechanisms. This will be affected by the way in which revenue from an agreement will be used and the variety of alternative revenue sources available to it. For example, a community that will rely on income from a mining project to pay for basic services in areas such as health, housing, and education, and has few alternative sources of income, may be highly risk averse and focus on benefits in the top part of Table 11.1. This is especially so where maintenance of funding over several years (for instance, for a scholarship programme to help at-risk youth stay at school) is essential to the success of a programme. On the other hand, a community that has a diverse range of reliable income sources to meet its basic needs—for instance, an existing mine as well as long-term agreements with government for funding of education and health services—may choose to focus on the less certain sources of income in the bottom half of Table 11.1, which, if they eventuate, will yield a large return.

In addition, communities must take into account the uncertainty that often surrounds the impacts that will arise from mining when they negotiate financial provisions. The use of output-based payments can help address this uncertainty because the scale of impacts tends to be related to the level of production, and as production and impacts increase, so do payments. However, environmental impacts, for instance, may continue even if a mine is producing at low levels or is inactive. The use of rental payments which are made even if a mine is not producing can be helpful in dealing with this possibility.

Uses of monetary benefits

Payments from mining projects can be allocated by Indigenous people and communities in four general ways: to fund payments to individual community members in cash or in kind (for example, in vehicles, snowmobiles, white goods, funeral services); to pay for social or community services such as public transport, health, education, housing, or cultural revitalization; to fund business development initiatives; or to finance long-term investment. The distinction between the last two is that 'business development' involves support for individual community members or organizations to establish businesses in local or regional markets in order to create immediate economic opportunities; long-term investment is focused on maximizing returns to a capital fund designed to generate an income after mining ends.

Individual payments

Indigenous people can face serious economic challenges in meeting living costs and in dealing with periodic financial demands such as school fees or funeral costs. Inability to meet these demands can involve high personal and social costs, especially when they occur, as in the case of funerals, at a time when people are already facing personal trauma. Some communities distribute cash payments to members and leave it to them to decide how to spend money. Others may establish a fund and contribute a set amount towards the costs of education or of funerals and other events.

Based on research on individual 'dividends' paid from oil revenues to Indigenous people in Alaska, Berman (2018) found that payments have a significant effect in raising incomes above the poverty line, especially for older people who received higher payments. The final impact of individual payments depends not just on their level but on how they are spent. Their use to pay children's school fees, for example, benefits not only the children and families involved but also a community as a whole by adding to its human capital. Use of payments to purchase large quantities of alcohol can, in contrast, involve serious costs for individuals, families, and communities. Regardless of their use, the cost of administering individual payments can be high relative to the benefits received. In most cases, there is little lasting impact from individual payments. Indigenous people have frequently commented to me that where they consume a large proportion of revenues, 'there is nothing to show for mining'.

Community projects

An alternative approach is to allocate revenues to community services such as health or education, or to physical infrastructure such as housing or roads. Two factors are important in determining the impact of such allocations. The first is whether provision is made for ongoing funding of services or maintenance of infrastructure. If this does not occur, funds invested in establishing services or building infrastructure may be lost. A second issue involves the response of government to Indigenous community initiatives in this area. If government service providers respond by cutting their own allocation to these same services, which has been shown to occur in some cases, there may be no net benefit from application of funds in this way. Alternatively, if the community's commitment of its own funds can be used to leverage additional investment by government, the net gain can substantially exceed the allocation from community benefits (O'Faircheallaigh 2004).

Investment in business development

Some Indigenous groups use mining revenues to purchase established businesses or to provide capital to start new businesses. Investment in local or regional business development can involve significant risks, because of the small markets, high cost structures, and limited opportunities that characterize remote regions, and because there may be pressures to draw resources from businesses to meet immediate cultural and financial needs of business managers and their kin. The economic track record of local businesses established using mining revenue is consequently mixed. For instance, the Gagudju Association in Australia's Northern Territory bought a motel that was run down but located close to a national park experiencing rapidly growing tourist numbers, and built the motel into a thriving and highly profitable enterprise. A neighbouring Aboriginal association bought a barge, a service station, and a small airline, all of which failed despite injection of substantial funds in efforts to make them viable. The airline failed in part because company directors commandeered aeroplanes to take them to football matches in neighbouring communities (O'Faircheallaigh 2002b: 166–7). Purchasing a local business is not always based only on an economic calculus. For example, the Gagudju Association's purchase of the motel was partly motivated by a desire to control its sales of alcohol, an approach adopted by other Indigenous groups. Social benefits gained in this way must be weighed against the opportunity costs involved, especially if a business becomes an ongoing drain on a group's finances.

Long-term investment in capital funds

Mining is a finite activity and monetary payments must inevitably end. This can create major problems for communities that have become reliant on mineral revenue, especially where it has been directed to provision of essential services or provides replacement income where mining has adversely affected production of food and other essentials. In addition, it raises the question of intergenerational equity. Future generations will continue to experience the consequences of mining due to its irreversible impacts on landscapes and places of cultural and spiritual significance, and, in many cases, its long-lasting environmental effects. In addition, their inheritance has been depleted through the removal of valuable minerals. If all income from projects is consumed by the current generations, their children and grandchildren will pay part of the costs arising from mining projects but will not share in the financial benefits.

To help address these issues, several Indigenous communities have established long-term investment funds. Revenue from mining is invested, usually in a portfolio of assets including national and international share and property markets, and income is reinvested in the fund while mining lasts to help build its capital. Once mining ends, income from the fund is used to help replace the mining payments that are no longer available. Long-term investment funds require a sufficiently large flow of payments to meet immediate needs and leave a surplus to invest; governance structures that can ensure the fund is maintained over time, including by managing demands for higher levels of immediate consumption; and high-quality investment advice to ensure that the fund is managed prudently so that its capital is preserved, but at the same time grows over time (see O'Faircheallaigh 2010a for a detailed discussion of these and other issues associated with long-term investment funds).

Tensions and dilemmas in managing mining payments

Mining payments to Indigenous communities have the potential to cause significant internal conflict and dissension, and to result in social or cultural harm, an issue raised in Chapter 10 in discussing the negative impacts of mining. Conflict can arise because funds are stolen or misused by people trusted with their stewardship, or are monopolized by powerful individuals or families (Cross 2020; Knowles 2021). Where entitlement to benefits is defined based on membership of a clan or other Indigenous entity, conflict can arise between those seeking recognition and those who are already recognized and do not want to see their incomes reduced as the pool of beneficiaries is expanded (Richardson et al. 2019: 21). Social tensions can arise because of inequality or perceived inequality in the distribution of benefits across family or clan groups, or across different categories of affected people: for instance, those close to a mine and those more distant from it (Bainton and Macintyre 2013; Richardson et al. 2019). A key issue here is whether allocation of payments is aligned with the distribution of rights and interests in land used by a mining project and/or with the distribution of project impacts. For example, an equal distribution of payments across a number of landowning clans, or allocation of funds to an 'umbrella' organization covering multiple clans sharing social and cultural bonds, may be regarded as inequitable and cause conflict if some groups have more direct and substantial interests than others in the area being mined, or are more heavily impacted by mining (Levitus 2009). In northern Chile, for example, equal distribution of payments from lithium mining between 18 Atacameño communities has caused tensions because some communities are close to the mine and experience major impacts, including from its use of water from aquifers, while other communities are distant from the mine and suffer no such impacts or experience only minor effects.

Another source of tension involves the allocation of payments and of power to make decisions on their use across different organizational and spatial scales. Especially where regional authorities or peak organizations play a key role in nego-tiating agreements and approving projects, allocation of a portion of payments to them can cause tension with local communities or specific landowning groups. This has occurred in Canada's Nunavut Territory, for instance, where regional Inuit associations play the key role in negotiations with mining companies and in allo-cating payments they negotiate. Some local Inuit communities directly affected by mining argue that this situation has resulted in an allocation of resources which unfairly favours the region. Some of the Inuit who govern regional organizations are drawn from these same communities, but their focus on regional issues and priori-ties may conflict, or be seen to conflict, with the interests of their local communities (Bell 2021; Ritsema et al. 2015: 166–9).

Communities also face difficult choices regarding what proportion of revenues to allocate to immediate needs and to long-term investment. There are strong arguments for spending the bulk of revenues immediately, given that most Indigenous commu-nities have urgent needs for employment opportunities and for health, education, youth, and housing services. Yet, as discussed above, it is also important to invest money for when mining ends and to ensure that future generations receive some benefit from exploitation of non-renewable resources and its impact on their coun-try. There is no 'right' resolution to this quandary, and it is one that communities tend to revisit again and again.

The ability of Indigenous communities to find ways of managing these tensions and dilemmas tends to be stronger when decisions regarding distribution of money and institutional arrangements for managing it are negotiated before substantial payments commence, and where these arrangements afford a high degree of trans-parency regarding the basis on which, and the way in which, decisions on allocating and managing payments are made. It is considerably easier for a community carefully to consider alternative uses for mining revenue and to achieve consensus on this issue when the arrival of money is still some time in the future. In the absence of arrange-ments for its management, the arrival of large amounts of money tends to result in a scramble to gain access to it, in which politically powerful individuals and families are at an advantage. The result may be internal community tensions which can take a long time to heal. Lack of transparency can generate similar outcomes, as it can lead to rumour and misinformation about what is occurring, even when there is no underlying problem in the way in which payments are being used (O'Faircheallaigh 2012b: 52–4).

Mining payments: curse or opportunity?

What of the overall impact of mining payments on Indigenous peoples? It appears counterintuitive to suggest that the revenues flowing to Indigenous peoples and communities from mining on their traditional lands could be anything other than advantageous, given their relative economic disadvantage and their need for resources to promote their social and cultural well-being. However, in the non-Indigenous context there has been considerable debate regarding the effects of mineral revenues on economic and social development. Much of the relevant literature, often based on the concept of a 'resource curse', is pessimistic regarding the likelihood that such revenues encourage broad-based economic and social development. Some of the reasons for this pessimism relate to factors that operate at a national, macroeconomic scale (for example, the impact of mineral export revenue on currency exchange rates and so on the competitiveness of other industries), and are not relevant to the impact of revenue flows on individual Indigenous communities. The literature also discusses 'microeconomic' and behavioural responses to revenue flows at the individual, institutional, and community level, and these could certainly be relevant. They include the possibility that when mineral prices and revenues are high, political leaders may be under pressure to increase spending and embark on major capital projects, and when prices decline it may be hard to rein in spending to match the available revenue. Access to mining revenues may diminish the incentives to save to fund investment, by creating the impression that current and future wealth will be generated by mining. Another factor is the supposed tendency of mining revenues to encourage 'rent seeking', a preoccupation with appropriating existing resource revenues for immediate consumption, rather than engaging in productive activities that can generate additional economic and social benefits.

Yet analysis of the empirical evidence regarding the role of mineral revenues in national development suggests that there is no inevitability that resource revenues will have negative implications for development, that the impact of mining and mineral revenues varies from case to case, and that these variations depend, critically, on the policy and institutional settings that apply in particular cases (Brunnschweiler and Bulte 2008; Collier and Venables 2011; Harris et al. 2020; Siakwah 2017; Sovacool 2010). They also depend on the quality of leadership in recipient communities and polities, an issue rarely discussed in the literature. In fact, leaders can play a critical role: for example, by raising people's horizons beyond the short-term, individual benefits represented by rent seeking, and in developing the organizational capacity to use mineral revenues productively (O'Faircheallaigh 2018: 104; Ritsema et al. 2015: 162).

Conclusion

For much of the twentieth century, Indigenous peoples across the globe had few opportunities to share in the economic opportunities created by large-scale mining. This started to change in the 1980s and 1990s, and in many parts of the world growing numbers of Indigenous people are now finding jobs in mining. Indigenous participation in business opportunities associated with mining is also growing, and more affected Indigenous communities are receiving payments to compensate them for the impacts of mining and allow them to share in the wealth it generates. There is much diversity within this general picture, even within individual countries and between projects in the same country. This partly reflects differences in company policies and in the history and skill levels of local workforces, but it also reflects wide variation in the negotiating power of Indigenous peoples.

Indigenous groups also vary in their ability to make the most of the opportunities that are available, especially evident in relation to mining payments. This is a complex area with payments occurring in many different forms, each with different implications in terms of risk and uncertainty for Indigenous peoples. Considerable technical skill and strategic capacity is required to extract and manage revenues successfully from mining projects, and Indigenous groups vary considerably in their possession of or access to both. For example, as noted above, it is very important for Indigenous recipients to understand their own risk profiles and match these to different forms of payments or, more likely, to combinations of different forms. Not all Indigenous peoples have the capacity to do so, let alone the leverage to negotiate the optimal combination of payment types at the levels needed to meet community needs.

While the trend to greater Indigenous participation in economic opportunity is clear, the ultimate consequences of this trend are a matter for debate both within Indigenous communities and in the research literature. This is illustrated, for example, by the question of whether mining payments constitute a 'resource curse' or a unique opportunity to foster economic and social development, and of whether industrial employment is compatible with traditional Indigenous modes of production and cultural activities. The case studies will provide an opportunity to explore these debates further.

PART IV

CASE STUDIES

12
Chile

Indigenous Strategies of Resistance and Engagement

Introduction

Chile occupies a long, narrow strip of land between the Andes to the east and the Pacific Ocean to the west, stretching from Peru in the north to Antarctica in the south. Chile is the world's largest copper producer, and its output of the metal is more than twice that of the second largest producer, Peru. The copper industry was developed by US capital during the late nineteenth and early twentieth centuries, nationalized by the Allende government in 1971, and partially privatized by the Pinochet regime after 1974. Chile is the world's second largest producer of lithium, extracted through solar evaporation of brine pools in the Salar de Atacama salt flat in the north of the country. While the Chilean state has consistently supported large-scale mineral development regardless of the political complexion of governments (Urkidi 2010: 220), development has not proceeded unopposed in recent years. For instance, Barrick Gold Ltd abandoned its Pascua Lama gold project in 2020 due to opposition from Indigenous, community, and environmental groups, after the company had invested several billion dollars in developing the mine.

The Republic of Chile is a unitary state which declared independence from Spain in 1818. Authoritarian regimes dominated its political system in the nineteenth century. Democratization proceeded during the twentieth century, and a period of political polarization occurred in the 1960s and 1970s, highlighted by the election of Socialist President Salvador Allende in 1970 and his removal and assassination in a 1973 coup d'état which instituted a right-wing military dictatorship led by Augusto Pinochet. The Pinochet regime, which lasted until 1990, pursued a vigorous program of neo-liberal economic reform including widespread privatization and deregulation, measures largely left in place after Chile's return to democracy (Babidge and Belfrage 2017). Privatization placed many of Chile's resources within the realm of the free market. Water, for example, was regarded 'as a good whose use becomes an appropriable right' (Cavallo 2013: 234), and Chile's Water Code (1981) allowed powerful corporate entities to accumulate rights in much of Chile's water resources. Chile's neo-liberal economic policies attracted large amounts of foreign investment. For instance, between 1990 and 2001, nine of the world's 25 biggest investments in mining were made in Chile (Urkidi and Walter 2011: 683).

Indigenous Peoples and Mining. Ciaran O'Faircheallaigh, Oxford University Press. © Ciaran O'Faircheallaigh (2023).
DOI: 10.1093/oso/9780192894564.003.0012

In the 2017 census, nearly 2.2 million people or 12.8 per cent of Chile's population of 17 million identified as Indigenous. The Mapuche, who live in Chile's southern regions, are by far the most numerous at almost 1.8 million. A substantial number of smaller peoples account for the balance, with the Yagán people, for instance, numbering only 1,600 people (IWGIA 2021). Recognition of Indigenous rights in Chile has been slow and uneven. The state tends to define Indigenous recognition based on possession of common cultural characteristics rather than on possession of rights in territory or resources, and at the same time fails to recognize Indigenous ownership of Indigenous cultural heritage (Kalazich 2015; Quinteros 2020: 9). Yet progress has been made, as indicated by Chile's recognition of the International Labour Organization (ILO) Convention 169 (see below), and by the fact that the Constituent Assembly elected in 2021 to oversee the reform of Chile's constitution included reserved seats for Indigenous peoples.

The following section traces key points in the evolution of relations between Indigenous peoples, the Chilean state, and the mining industry. Two case studies follow which allow detailed analysis of different facets of those relations in contemporary Chile. The first focuses on Pascua Lama, and considers why and how Indigenous peoples and their allies were able to stop a major multinational company from developing what would have become one of the world's largest gold mines. The second traces engagement of Atacameño peoples with the copper and lithium industries in northern Chile, including through a detailed analysis of an agreement negotiated in 2016 between Rockwood, a wholly owned subsidiary of Albemarle Corporation, one of the world's largest lithium producers, and 18 Atacameño communities represented by the Council of Atacamanian Peoples (Consejo de Pueblos Atacameños, or CPA). In combination, the case studies allow us to further examine issues involved in strategies of engagement and resistance, discussed in Chapters 8 and 9.

Chile and Indigenous peoples

As occurred elsewhere in South America, the Spanish conquest brought death and dispossession to Chile's Indigenous peoples, but also revealed their determination to retain their lands and cultures. The Mapuche, for example, successfully resisted the invaders for a century, leading the Spanish to sign a peace treaty with them in 1641. The peace did not last as the Spanish renewed their attacks on Mapuche people and resources, attacks which were continued by the Chilean state after Chile declared independence from Spain in 1818. These culminated in a 'pacification' campaign by the Chilean army, beginning in 1861 and ending with the military defeat of the Mapuche in 1880. This defeat was followed by confiscation of all Mapuche lands by the Chilean state, the removal of Mapuche to reserves, and allocation of less than 7 per cent of their ancestral lands to the Mapuche by a commission for 'Indigenous peoples' resettlement'. Even these limited lands continued to be a target for exploitation by non-Indigenous private and state agencies, exploitation resisted by the

Mapuche over many years through direct action, litigation, and, in more recent decades, through the creation of alliances with academics and Chilean and international non-government organizations (NGOs) and appeals to international legal fora. This pattern of dispossession, allocation of lands to non-Indigenous settlers, and continued Indigenous resistance and assertion of rights to territory and resources occurred throughout Chile (Aylwin 1999; Gajardo 2018; Johnston and Garcia-Downing 2004; Kalazich 2015; Mariqueo 2004).

Measures to improve the status of Chile's Indigenous peoples were enacted by the government of Salvador Allende (1970–3), which passed an Indigenous law recognizing distinct Indigenous cultures and began to restore Indigenous communal lands. These measures were reversed after Allende was deposed, and the military regime set out to destroy Indigenous communities as separate entities: for example, by segmenting communal lands and permitting their sale to individuals, and prohibiting communal forms of land use. Many Indigenous leaders were murdered, imprisoned, or exiled (Mariqueo 2004; Rodriguez and Carruthers 2008).

In the late 1980s, Indigenous organizations began negotiating with the political parties that were to assume power after the restoration of democracy in 1990 to gain legal and constitutional recognition as distinct peoples, and in 1993 the Chilean government enacted the 'Law on Protection, Promotion and Development of Indigenous Peoples' or the 'Indigenous Law' (*Ley Indigena* 19.253). The law recognized several of Chile's Indigenous peoples for the first time; acknowledged and sought to protect Indigenous cultures and languages; offered protection to current Indigenous lands; and created a fund to allow the acquisition or transfer of land and water rights to Indigenous communities. The law also created a development fund to help finance initiatives to improve living conditions in Indigenous communities; and established a National Corporation for Indigenous Development (CONADI), which included Indigenous representation, as the state body responsible for implementing the new legislation. CONADI's Executive Council would consist of eight elected Indigenous representatives, eight non-Indigenous representatives (comprising government ministers and three presidential appointees), and a national director appointed by the president (Aylwin 1999; Rodriguez and Carruthers 2008).

The Indigenous Law provided a process for certification of individual Indigenous identity, which in turn is a prerequisite for establishing 'Indigenous organizations' and accessing measures designed to benefit Indigenous peoples, such as scholarship funds (Gajardo 2021: 178–9). Certification must be applied for by individuals, and applications are determined by CONADI on administrative criteria set out in the Indigenous Law. This system means that many Indigenous people may not be 'certified' as such because they have not submitted applications, and that some Indigenous people may be denied certification because they are deemed by CONADI not to meet the criteria, despite having always self-identified as Indigenous and being recognized as such by their communities and by other state authorities (Wiebe 2015: 6).

Indigenous organizations can be either Indigenous communities, being peoples who share an Indigenous ethnicity and share one of a number of features, including possessing or having possessed Indigenous lands in common or coming from the same ancient village; or Indigenous associations, voluntary groups of at least 25 people with Indigenous certification that work for a common interest and objective, but do not meet the criteria for recognition as an Indigenous community. As Gajardo (2021: 175) notes, 'in Chile, so-called "indigenous communities" are organizations created by the Indigenous Law and shaped by the state's bureaucratic logic ... [they respond] to the need to comply with the state's criteria of indigeneity'. This approach turns on its head that used in Australia, for instance, in recognizing Indigenous rights. There Indigenous people must show that they existed as a community (as a 'society', to coin the legal terminology) *before* the imposition of colonial law to achieve recognition in contemporary Australian law.

The Indigenous Law does not recognize collective Indigenous status or territorial rights, or create a legal regime governing interactions between Indigenous peoples and extractive industry in the way which occurs, for example, under Australia's Native Title Act or under the Philippines' Indigenous Peoples Rights Act. The Indigenous Law does recognize Indigenous areas of territorial interest through the concept of Indigenous Development Areas (IDAs) which constitute a focus for creating benefits for Indigenous people and for governing these lands. IDAs include territories in which Indigenous ethnic groups have lived ancestrally, or which have a high density of Indigenous population, or which contain Indigenous community lands.

CONADI was intended to support a collaborative approach between the state and Indigenous peoples in working to address Chile's history of dispossession and marginalization. However, as the 1990s progressed and Chile pursued a strategy of thoroughgoing neo-liberal economic and social reform and promotion of mega-projects in forestry, hydroelectricity, fish farming, and mining, state authorities undermined the original intention of the Indigenous Law and promoted the interests of foreign capital over those of Chile's Indigenous peoples (Gajardo 2018, 2021). CONADI was starved of the funds it needed to restore Indigenous land and water rights, it was pressured to give priority to the state's economic agenda in decisions about which land transfers to fund, and the state engaged in increasingly repressive activity in response to efforts by the Mapuche and other groups to resist renewed confiscation and despoilation of their land and resources. State agencies acted to marginalize and criminalize movements claiming Indigenous land rights and hindering the development of extractive projects; security forces were used to break up Indigenous protests; government agencies fomented internal divisions among Indigenous groups; and Indigenous leaders who continued to resist were charged with terrorism offences, jailed, and subjected to violence including beatings and extrajudicial killings. In summary:

> When indigenous demands ran counter to industrial and development interests, state agencies and policies perpetuated the Pinochet-era pattern of siding with the private companies against the expressed interests of Indigenous communities. In the eyes of Mapuche and other Indian leaders, the promise of democratic co-participation deteriorated into a cruel fraud. (Rodriguez and Carruthers 2008: 7; see also Gajardo 2014, 2018, 2021; Mariqueo 2004)

Reflecting the ebb and flow that characterizes moves towards recognition of Indigenous rights, in September 2008 Chile took a significant positive step in ratifying ILO C169, the Indigenous and Tribal Peoples Convention 1989, after a proposal to adopt ILO C169 had earlier been rejected by the Chilean Senate several times. As noted in Chapter 4, ILO C169 requires signatory states to recognize the right of Indigenous peoples to decide their own priorities for the development of lands they occupy or use; and to allow them to participate in the formulation, implementation, and evaluation of plans for national and regional development which may affect them directly. ILO C169 also requires states to 'take measures, in cooperation with the peoples concerned, to protect and preserve the environment of the territories they inhabit' (Article 7). States must consult with Indigenous peoples regarding proposed developments on Indigenous lands, though this does not extend to a requirement for governments to seek the consent of affected Indigenous peoples, except in the cases where their relocation is considered necessary. The continued contestation regarding Indigenous rights is indicated by the fact that conservative politicians and elements of the extractive industry mounted a campaign in 2019 for Chile to withdraw from ILO C169 when this became a possibility under Article 39 of the Convention, which allows a signatory to 'renunciate' the Convention once a decade has elapsed since ratification. It is also indicated by the fact that Chile, even though the Indigenous Law explicitly seeks to protect Indigenous cultures and languages, has failed to take any steps to recognize Indigenous ownership of Indigenous cultural heritage or to support Indigenous peoples in ensuring its protection. As Kalazich (2015: 45) notes, Indigenous peoples in Chile are not granted any explicit rights over places or remains of significance to them, and more generally are subject to a hierarchy that places 'the archaeological above the Indigenous'.

Continued resistance to recognition of Indigenous rights and interests is due in part to deep-seated racism that permeates parts of Chilean society (and of South America generally: Hale 2004). Racism persists even though Indigeneity can now be used by some Indigenous Chileans as leverage to negotiate access to social and economic opportunities (Gajardo 2021). Racism shapes the response to Indigenous peoples of many business and government leaders, government officials, and non-Indigenous Chileans (Richards 2013). This racism manifests itself in continuing assumptions regarding the inferiority of Indigenous peoples, and in a failure to afford them protection and opportunities available to other Chileans (IWGIA 2021; Quinteros 2020). For example, in August 2020 Mapuche people taking part in a peaceful public protest in Curacautín were abused and beaten by a non-Indigenous mob in the presence of police officers who not only made no attempt to prevent the violence, but arrested a number of Mapuche people, who were charged the next day for crimes of public disorder. As a Mapuche leader noted: 'The government made no effort to lay responsibility at the feet of anyone other than the Mapuche for these violent acts, making it clear that we are facing a structural racism that is embedded not only in the police but which is supported and justified by the central authority itself' (IWGIA 2021: 353–4).

Racism can also manifest itself in a continued refusal even to accept that Indigenous peoples exist as a distinct category in Chile. In June 2019, I gave an address on recognition of Indigenous rights in Australia and Canada to a Santiago meeting of one of Chile's major business organizations, the Chilean Institute of Rational Business Administration. The editor of Chile's leading conservative newspaper thanked me for my talk, but stated that it lacked relevance to Chile because the concept of distinct Indigenous rights made no sense given that 'all Chileans are Indigenous, as we are all descended from unions between the Spanish conquistadores and Indigenous women'.

Pascua Lama

In August 1994, the Toronto-based Barrick Gold Ltd bought another Canadian company, LAC, that had been exploring the mining potential of an area that straddles the Andes on the border between Chile and Argentina, in the headwaters of the Huasco valley in the county of Alto del Carmen. The valley is a narrow strip of fertile land in an area that is otherwise arid and mountainous. In the years that followed, Barrick drilled hundreds of exploration holes and delineated one of the largest reserves of gold, silver, and copper in the world, holding an estimated 15.4 million ounces of gold, 675 million ounces of silver, and 250,000 tonnes of copper. Barrick planned an open-pit mine that would affect three glaciers and involve creation of huge waste dumps. Pascua Lama would produce 800,000 to 850,000 ounces of gold and 35 million ounces of silver per year in the first five years of its 25-year life, making it one of the world's largest gold mines.

Pascua Lama is located in the territory of the Diaguita Indigenous people. As occurred elsewhere in Chile, the Diaguta were decimated by violence, dispossession, and disease after the Spanish conquest. They were considered to have been rendered extinct by the Chilean state, and by anthropologists (Gajardo 2018). In reality, the Diaguita have continued to occupy their traditional territories, earning their livelihood through subsistence agriculture and pastoralism and, in recent decades, through commercial production of vegetables and grapes. In 1903 a large group of Diaguita families established the Huascoaltino Diaguita Agricultural Community ('the Agricultural Community') under Chile's law of agricultural communities, because at the time no form of ethnic or cultural organization was recognized by the state. The Agricultural Community obtained a private title to some 380,000 hectares, and it now comprises some 260 families. Gajardo (2018: 98) describes the Agricultural Community and its territory as follows:

the Community's territory has traditionally been inhabited by families of predominantly indigenous ancestry and its history stretches back to the early days of colonization ... the contemporary physical boundaries specified on the title deed ... correspond to those of the former *Pueblo de Indios du Guasco Alto*, a territory in which cultural practices, family names and toponymic elements of the societies which occupied this territory prior to the arrival of the Europeans have been preserved to this day.

It was not until 2006, when the Chilean government afforded official recognition to the Diaguita as an Indigenous people, that members of the Agricultural Community could claim Indigenous status in the eyes of the state. This status was only available to individuals through personal certification as 'Indigenous'. In 2006 the Agricultural Community was denied designation as an 'Indigenous community' under the Indigenous Law because it was already registered as an 'agricultural community' under a different law (Gajardo 2018: 98; see also Wiebe 2015: 10).

The Agricultural Community opposed Pascua Lama from the beginning, fearing its environmental effects and in particular its potential impacts on the region's scarce water resources and especially on glaciers which fed the community's water supply, including the Huasco river. The Chilean state strongly supported the project as part of its economic strategy of promoting large-scale extractive industry, and the regional branch of Chile's National Environmental Commission (CONAMA) granted the project an initial environmental approval in 2001 and environmental approval for a revised project plan in 2006. The latter was subject to numerous conditions, including a requirement that mining activity in Pascua Lama would not cause any retreat, displacement, or destruction of the three glaciers that fell within the project area; and that the company build a canal system to divert glacial runoff, groundwater, and precipitation around the open pit and slag heaps, keeping the water free of any natural acidity in the rock (Cavallo 2013: 241; Vel 2014). The Chilean government granted final project approval in the same year, and Barrick planned to open the mine at the end of a three-year construction period.

Barrick's plans were generating wider opposition among agricultural, environmental, and civil society groups in the region, a number of which coordinated protest, media, and communication activities through the Coalition for Water of Huasco. The Coalition brought together farmers, business owners, Indigenous and non-Indigenous people, immigrants, the Catholic Church, and environmental groups, which became increasingly active in protests in Alto del Carmen, including blocking roads to the mine site, and in the regional capital, Vallenar. The aim of local opponents was to have Barrick's environmental licence revoked and so stop the Pascua Lama project (Haslam 2018: 170). The Coalition formed alliances with national environmental NGOs based in Santiago, with groups opposed to the Argentinian portion of the project, and with international environmental groups, especially in the company's home country Canada, where protests were organized to coincide with Barrick's annual general meetings (AGMs) (Urkidi 2010; Wiebe 2015). As Li (2017) shows, the project's potential impact on glaciers constitutes an iconic issue which focused national and global attention on Pascua Lama. Barrick's original environmental impact assessment had ignored the glaciers. A revised assessment which proposed mining under them and in some cases breaking up the ice and moving it to other glaciers served to focus criticism further on Pascua Lama and helped raise what had largely been a local and regional conflict into a national and international one (Haslam 2018: 164; Ostrow 2015; Urkidi 2010).

In December 2009, the Agricultural Community filed a complaint with the Inter-American Commission on Human Rights (IACHR), arguing that the Chilean government had violated their rights by approving the Pascua Lama project, including by failing to consult with them prior to the approval, denying them access to water and to their lands and resources, and depriving them of their livelihoods. The IACHR admitted the complaint in 2010. This complaint was not finalized over the coming decade, but its existence signalled the intention of the Agricultural Community to bring Pascua Lama to the intention of an international audience. The complaint to the IACHR was just one of many legal avenues pursued by the community, which by 2015 had 10 complaints in process before state administrative bodies, and national and international courts (Vel 2014; Wiebe 2015).

Not all Diaguita were opposed to Barrick. From the early 2000s, the company developed a corporate social responsibility (CSR) programme which sought to create local benefits through provision of social infrastructure and support for cultural activities. Barrick funded a new secondary school, school buses, and uniforms, and established grants for local economic development and social projects. After Chile recognized the Diaguita as Indigenous in 2006, these efforts focused on new Diaguita associations or communities established pursuant to the Indigenous Law. Both Barrick and CONADI assisted individuals to register as Diaguita, and CONADI facilitated the speedy registration of Diaguita 'communities' which these individuals then set up. Barrick channelled substantial funding through these same 'communities', focused especially on 'revival' of traditional Diaguita culture and cultural practices. The company paid anthropologists to document 'traditional' cultural practices, and funded workshops for local residents including traditional weaving, ceramic production, and use of herbal medicines. Barrick's support for Diaguita culture focused on 'non-political' aspects and avoided issues such as Indigenous self-determination and territorial and natural resource rights (Gajardo 2018).

Some 17 Diaguita 'communities' were formed pursuant to the Indigenous Law, and a number expressed support for Barrick, attacked the Agricultural Community for opposing Pascua Lama, and questioned the Agricultural Community's status as a Diaguita Indigenous organization. Wiebe (2015) and Gajardo (2018) show that Barrick's support for Diaguita cultural practices and organizations was part of a deliberate strategy to undermine the Agricultural Community and foster internal division. Wiebe (2015: 10) quotes a senior Barrick manager who stated that the 'the strategy and objective of Barrick is to support this political process in an effort to solidify a social base of support within the ethnic group for the implementation and operation of the Pascua Lama Project'. According to Gajardo (2021), the internal divisions that emerged among the Diaguita had a gender dimension, in that the leadership of the Agricultural Community was predominantly male and many of the leaders and beneficiaries of the new 'communities' were women.

Barrick began to formalize some of its CSR initiatives through negotiating agreements. In one of these, concluded in 2006, the company committed to pay the Junta de Vigilancia, the organization that manages water allocation in the Huasco valley, US$3 million per year for 20 years. In return, the association agreed not to oppose the mining project and to take any concerns over the project directly to the company, not to the environmental assessment process that was then under way. Only large agricultural producers, who dominate the Junta, were included in the agreement, with smaller farmers only hearing about it after it was signed (Nolen 2014; Wiebe 2015).

Despite its efforts to shore up support for Pascua Lama, Barrick continued to face growing opposition locally, nationally, and abroad. An indication of the last was Barrick's difficulties in securing finance for the project. In 2010, the company applied for loans for the project from public financial agencies in Canada (Export Development Canada) and the United States (Export-Import Bank). In 2011, the company's negotiations with both organizations for subsidized credit loans were cancelled. In July 2012, Barrick announced a further, year-long delay and revealed large cost overruns for the project of between 50 and 60 per cent, bringing the total expected cost of the project to $8 billion, in contrast to initial estimates in 2001 of $950 million.

In 2009, the Operational Control Committee (a governmental supervisory body), after inspecting Barrick's operations, found that the company had failed to comply with several of the conditions attached to its 2006 environmental approval, extracting water from a non-authorized point, conducting operations in a way that generated excessive dust that was accumulating on glaciers, and altering the free flow of water of the Estrecho river, and so threatening the water resources of the Huasco river basin. In January 2010, the Chilean authorities sanctioned and fined the company for these breaches (Cavallo 2013: 241–2).

At this time Chile, as part of its efforts to gain membership of the Organisation for Economic Cooperation and Development (OECD), substantially increased its legal and administrative infrastructure for regulating its mining industry. It created a Ministry of the Environment, amended environmental legislation to enable more effective monitoring of mining company operations, and established a new environmental regulator, La Superintendencia del Medio Ambiente, or Superintendency of the Environment (SMA), with greater powers and human and technical resources at its disposal. The SMA became operational in November 2012 (O'Neill 2014; Ostrow 2015).

In January 2013, the SMA brought several charges against Barrick in relation to breaches of its environmental permit. Barrick admitted a number of these, including that a water diversion channel had collapsed, leading to Barrick site managers deciding to let natural runoff water flow through the mining site, in direct contravention of its permit conditions. The SMA then suspended Barrick's environmental approval and required the company to undertake a number of environmental mitigation measures. In April 2013, in response to legal action initiated by local Diaguita communities opposed to Pascua Lama, the Court of Appeal of Copiapo upheld SMA's temporary suspension of Barrick's operations, except those aimed at preventing further environmental damages. In the following month, the SMA imposed a US$16 million fine on Barrick because of its infringements (O'Neill 2014). The

Diaguita communities appealed the Court's decision to Chile's Supreme Court, arguing that Barrick's environmental licence should be permanently withdrawn. In September 2013, the Supreme Court declined to withdraw the permit, but upheld the temporary closure of Pascua Lama until the completion of environmental mitigation measures required by the SMA. In October 2013, Barrick Gold announced that because of political and social opposition it was suspending operations and dismissed 1,500 employees.

Barrick had not given up on building local support for Pascua Lama. In May 2014, the company signed a Memorandum of Understanding (MoU) with 15 Diaguita communities, providing for exchange of technical and environmental information about the project, for which Barrick committed to provide financial and material resources to support its analysis. However, the MoU quickly attracted controversy, with accusations that the way in which it was developed lacked transparency, that it was signed by people who were not Diaguita leaders, that some signatories were paid for their support, and that consultation with the wider Diaguita community was lacking. Further tensions arose because allocation of payments under the MoU lacked transparency. The controversy surrounding the MoU further deepened opposition to Barrick's plans (Wiebe 2015: 11–13).

By 2014 Barrick was embroiled in extensive litigation with Chilean regulators and opponents of Pascua Lama (see Protestbarrick.net 2015 for details). On the day of Barrick Gold's AGM in April 2014, yet another legal action was initiated, when Montreal-based law firm Trudel & Johnston filed a suit on behalf of shareholders against Barrick and four of its directors and senior officers. This suit alleged that between 2009 and 2013, Barrick had failed to provide timely disclosure of material changes and made several misrepresentations regarding the progress, cost, and feasibility of Pascua Lama (Mining Watch Canada 2014). Barrick settled this suit for $140 million in 2016. In October 2017, it also settled another arbitration case brought by associations in the Huasco valley, after Barrick halted payments under agreements with them, for $20 million. In December 2014, the Chilean Supreme Court declined to consider Barrick's appeal of the Environmental Court decision regarding the sanctions imposed by the SMA in May 2013. By this point Barrick had written off more than $6 billion against its investment in Pascua Lama (Barrick Gold Corporation 2015: 40).

Community representatives continued to send complaints to the SMA, supported by the results of their own environmental monitoring, regarding alleged ongoing violation of environmental conditions by Barrick. The communities contested SMA's 2013 actions before Chile's Second Environmental Tribunal as failing to sanction the company adequately (Haslam 2018: 174). The Court required the SMA to reopen the sanctioning process, and in January 2018 the SMA ordered the 'total and definitive closure' of the Pascua Lama project because of findings of ongoing environmental infringements against Barrick, numbering 33 in total. The company appealed the decision to Chile's most senior environmental court, the First Environment Court. On 17 September 2020, the Court dismissed the company's appeal, and confirmed three of the five main charges against Barrick outlined in the SMA's original ruling.

These charges were that Barrick had failed properly to monitor glaciers surrounding the project; adversely affected the water quality of the nearby Estrecho river; and used an unauthorized methodology for calculating water quality levels. The Court also imposed a US$9.7 million fine on the Canadian mining company. Given that Barrick had no further legal avenue of appeal, the company accepted the inevitable and on the following day announced it was abandoning development of Pascua Lama (Barrick Gold Corporation 2020).

Summary

What explains the ability of Diaguita Indigenous peoples and their allies to stop a large mining project that offered significant economic benefits to Chile?

The strength and persistence of Diaguita resistance was a key factor. Urkidi argues that this opposition arose, in part, because Pascua Lama endangered one of the few aspects of their Indigenous identity that they had been able to maintain: subsistence farming and extensive shepherding. In his view, the Diaguita community 'sees mining as the last step in the colonization process that has destroyed their cultural identity' (2010: 224). Nolen notes that another key element in Diaguita resistance was that while the opportunities offered by a major mine were not unwelcome, Diaguita already had viable livelihoods and were not desperate for jobs or incomes from mining. Rather, mining was seen as a threat to those livelihoods, as explained by the Town Administrator of Alto del Carmen: 'the people don't want to work in mining, they work their land ... They're not interested in the mining company offering them big salaries. Because if you change their way of life and their environment, what are they going to offer their children and their grandchildren?' (cited in Nolen 2014).

The organizational, financial, and human resources associated with a large land base and a long-established communal organization, the Agricultural Community, were critical in allowing Diaguita opposition to mining to be converted into effective legal and other strategies. This was especially important in the early years of the conflict over Pascua Lama, before the project was opposed by national and international NGOs, which later supported Diaguita. That support was essential in allowing resistance to Pascua Lama to be maintained over two decades and to be mobilized at national and global scales, and it was generated to an important extent by the use of Pascua Lama's impact on glaciers as a talisman and focal point to generate media coverage, and public and NGO support.

The attitudes and actions of state agencies were also important. CONADI supported Barrick's efforts to register Diaguita as 'Indigenous' and to establish 'Indigenous associations' supportive of Pascua Lama, and CONAMA did facilitate the initial environmental approvals for the project. On the other hand, the newly established SMA pursued Barrick over environmental infringements, fined the company, and ultimately terminated Pascua Lama. The SMA and Indigenous and community opponents of the project were able to make effective use of Chile's judicial system, which showed no hesitation in supporting action against Barrick by Chile's environmental regulators. The actions and independence of the courts reflected the fact that the rule of law was by now well established in Chile.

The wider political context must also be considered. Chile ratified ILO C169 in 2009, and the Chilean government was keen to establish that this was not merely a symbolic act but signalled a determination by the state to depart from its discriminatory practices towards Chile's Indigenous peoples. Chile's desire to gain admittance to the OECD was another part of the broader context, as it led to the establishment of a stronger, better resourced, and more autonomous regulatory regime. Also significant was that Michelle Bachelet, the presidential candidate for the centre-left coalition (Concertación), sought to bolster her campaign in 2005 by promising to protect the glaciers threatened by Pascua Lama. Her election meant that Barrick could not count on the unstinting political support enjoyed by the mining industry in Chile in previous decades; that Pascua Lama was on the government's political agenda; that the actions of regulatory bodies would have political support; and that court decisions against Barrick would be endorsed by government (for examples, see Jarroud 2013; and more generally, Haslam 2018; Ostrow 2015). Another key aspect of the political context was that by 2010 the promotion of untrammelled industrial development pursued by successive Chilean governments was meeting extensive resistance from civil society and the broader public, reflected in a series of nationwide protest campaigns and resistance to major projects. For example, in 2009–10 a broadly based public campaign developed against the government's plans to allow GDF Suez, one of the world's largest power utilities, to construct a huge thermoelectric power station at Barrancones Bay, an area of great natural beauty and high environmental value on Chile's northern coastline. This resulted in intervention by Chile's President, who announced in August 2010 that the plant would not be constructed at Barrancones, followed soon after by GDF Suez's decision to abandon the project (Spoerer 2014).

Barrick's behaviour was instrumental in its own demise. The company sought to manipulate the environmental approval system—for example, by submitting applications for different parts of the project separately to avoid more rigorous assessment—and it was repeatedly negligent in complying with its environmental obligations. For example, the collapse of a diversion canal in January 2013, which helped precipitate SMA's suspension of operations at Pascua Lama, resulted from the company's failure to comply with an environmental condition requiring it to complete the canal before starting to strip overburden from the area where the open pit would be located (Nolen 2014; Ostrow 2015). The company's community engagement initiatives lacked transparency and were designed to manipulate sections of the community into supporting the project, rather than offering genuine consultation and equitable access to project benefits. Barrick's behaviour may have reflected the fact that it had grown largely through acquisition and had limited experience of developing projects alone and from the ground up, and that serious problems arose in ensuring coordination between its head office in Toronto and actions taken on the ground in Chile (Nolen 2014). It may also have resulted from a conviction that intervention by Chile's political elite would ensure, as it had in the past, that mining companies could circumvent their regulatory and community obligations and still proceed with development. That conviction was misplaced because of the determination and resourcefulness of the Duigita and their allies, the autonomy of Chile's courts and of the new environmental regulator, and changes in Chile's political environment.

Copper and lithium mining in the Salar de Atacama

The Salar de Atacama is a salt pan in the Antofogusta region of northern Chile, an area that is one of the most arid on earth. The limited water that exists originates from snowmelt from the Andes which flows into aquifers, small lagoons, and springs. Formerly part of Bolivia, the region was integrated into Chile after the Pacific War of 1879–94. It is the home of the Atacameño-Likanantay Indigenous people, whose ancestors have inhabited the area for some 6,000 years. Until the 1980s, Atacameños gained their livelihood through agriculture and large-scale, long-range pastoralism, drawing on naturally occurring waters and irrigation systems. They also engaged in seasonal labour migration in Argentina until its border with Chile was closed in the 1980s under the Pinochet regime. As a result of climate change, reduction in water availability due to mining, and the militarization of the border region, people have come to rely on subsistence agriculture and animal husbandry close to their communities, and on wage employment and small business opportunities generated by mining. According to Chile's 2017 Census, there were then 30,069 people who self-identified as belonging to the Atacameño people, representing 1.39 per cent of the national Indigenous population. In the Salar de Atacama, most Atacameños live in small communities, which also include non-Indigenous populations (see Fig. 12.1).

Given its arid climate, water is highly valued as an economic resource and is integral to Atacama culture, ritual, and spirituality. Due to climate change and the demands of a rapidly expanding mining industry, the region's water resources are under severe pressure and current water extraction rates are not sustainable, a matter of great concern to Atacameños (Babidge et al. 2019: 747). Chile's regulatory authorities, long absent from any active role in overseeing or limiting water extraction, have belatedly introduced measures to protect some waters on which communities rely (Babidge 2015: 5–9). However, in a wider regional context little has been done to ensure the sustainability of water resources, reflecting both the privatized nature of water rights, which means the state will not withdraw existing water allocations to industry, and the state's unwillingness to limit further expansion of mining activity. There are also serious gaps in understanding of water resources and water flows, and of the long-term implications of mining expansion. To some extent these gaps reflect the inherent challenges in gaining greater knowledge of water resources and flows that are largely subterranean, but also the reluctance of industry and the state to establish knowledge that might compel them to limit extractive activity (Babidge 2018; Babidge et al. 2019: 739–45).

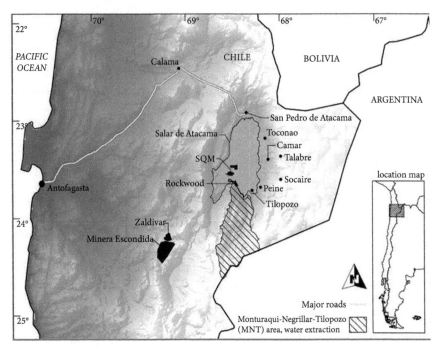

Fig. 12.1 Mining locations in the Salar de Atacama, Chile

Source: Babidge, S., 2018. 'Sustaining Ignorance: The Uncertainties of Groundwater and Its Extraction in the Salar de Atacama, Northern Chile'. *Journal of the Royal Anthropological Institute* 25: p. 87.

As elsewhere in Chile, the rights of the Atacameños as Indigenous peoples were not recognized by the Chilean state prior to introduction of the Indigenous Law in 1993. The Atacameño region was recognized as an Indigenous territory in 1997, land in the immediate vicinity of Atacameño villages was recognized as Indigenous land, and Atacameño rights in surface water lying within Indigenous community lands and actively utilized by community members could be recognized and protected. However, no recognition was or is afforded to land in the wider region in which Atacameño communities are located, including much land traditionally used for pastoralism and other forms of economic production. As noted earlier, water rights in Chile are permanently allocated by the state to private users and, similarly, minerals are deemed to belong to the state and are allocated to private companies or state corporations. No requirement exists in Chile for the negotiation of agreements between mining companies and Indigenous peoples affected by extractive operations.

Two major types of mineral extraction occur in the region. Since the early 1990s copper, and associated gold and silver, has been extracted to the south-west of the Salar by Minera Escondida Limitada (MEL), the operating subsidiary of a consortium led by the Australian-based Broken Hill Proprietary (BHP). Escondida is located 160 kilometres south-east of the port of Antofagasta, at an elevation of 3,000 metres above sea level. A second copper mine is operated adjacent to Escondida by the Chilean-based Compañía Minera Zaldivar (CMZ). These mines rely on water from aquifers in the southern Salar for processing. Lithium and potassium extraction commenced in the 1980s, and is now undertaken by Sociedad Química y Minera de Chile SA (SQM), the world's largest lithium producer, owned by Chilean and Chinese interests; and Rockwood, a wholly owned subsidiary of the US-owned Albermarle Corporation. These operations pump brine from underground in the Salar de Atacama, evaporate it in large surface ponds to increase lithium concentrate, and process the dried material into lithium products in the regional industrial centre of Antofagasta and other locations. Like copper mining, lithium extraction and processing require large quantities of fresh water.

Atacameño engagement with the mining industry

BHP's Escondida mine was located some 100 kilometres from the community of Peine, which was constituted as an 'Indigenous community' in 1997. Community residents did not obtain employment there, as they did in the growing lithium industry (see below). However, Escondida obtained a substantial part of the fresh water it used in processing from aquifers on Peine's territory, which brought the mine and the community into contact. In 1997 the two negotiated an agreement providing for MEL to provide modest support ($50,000 per annum for 15 years) for development projects in the community, one of the first such agreements negotiated in Chile. While MEL framed the agreement as part of its CSR policy, Peine saw it as a recognition of mining's impact on the community's precious water resources. MEL's willingness to negotiate an agreement may have reflected its recognition that 'the regulatory tide was turning', as indicated, for example, by Peine's recognition as an Indigenous community in the previous year (O'Faircheallaigh and Babidge forthcoming). Yet the corporate policy of MEL's international owners may also have played an independent role, as indicated by the fact that its neighbour, CMZ, which has substantial Chilean ownership, did not negotiate any agreements with Peine, despite efforts by the community over a number of years to secure one.

Three specific features of this 1997 agreement are worth noting. First, while its genesis was in BHP's use of water from Peine's territory, the agreement fails to address issues related to environmental matters generally or mining's impact on water specifically. Second, the use and administration of funds was not at Peine's discretion, but was overseen jointly by the community, MEL, and the state's Indigenous agency, CONADI. Funds were used to make small but significant additions to community infrastructure, including a water project, new teachers' accommodation at the school, and upgrading the surrounds of the swimming pool. Third, the agreement did not involve any recognition of Indigenous rights in Peine's land or water (Babidge 2013: 283–86).

By 2004 community leaders were pushing MEL for a revised agreement that would deliver greater benefits to Peine, in a context where the community was increasingly concerned about, and resistant to, MEL's efforts to gain access to additional water resources. In 2007 MEL submitted an application to extract water from Pampa Colorada, an area of high-altitude wetlands above Peine and other nearby communities. Peine, its neighbouring community Socaire and the Atacameño regional political organization, the CPA, launched a campaign of resistance against MEL's application. People marched in the streets of San Pedro de Atacama and in the regional capital Antofagasta, and flew black banners on their homes when company employees visited villages. In 2007 the regional government declined to approve MEL's water application (Babidge 2018: 88).

A new agreement between Peine and MEL was signed in 2007, shortly before rejection of MEL's application. The new agreement, which would last for 20 years, provided for a higher level of funding for projects within the context of Peine's community development plan, which emphasized the need for Peine to achieve greater control of its territory and address pressing environmental issues. Yet the revised agreement, like its predecessors, did not provide for Peine's participation in environmental management and continued to give MEL significant influence over how agreement funds could be spent. Both points are illustrated by the fact that the company refused to allow agreement funds to be used by Peine to employ independent consultants to monitor the environmental impacts of MEL's operations (Babidge 2013: 284–5). More generally, a joint Peine–MEL committee continued closely to supervise spending under the agreement, and MEL periodically demanded prompt and thorough audits of all expenditure of funds. MEL did undertake to produce annual reports on environmental sustainability, which are available online, and some were presented in person to meetings of the community by teams of company scientists (in 2010–12), but in each meeting company claims that there was a lack of evidence of negative environmental impacts from its operations were met with significant expressions of distrust from community members (O'Faircheallaigh and Babidge forthcoming).

An agreement of quite a different sort was negotiated between 18 Atacama communities, the CPA, and Rockwood, Albemarle's Chilean subsidiary, in 2016. In 1984 the Chilean Lithium Society (SCL) established what was initially a small lithium operation, expanding its output over the following decade. In 2012 SCL was renamed Rockwood Lithium, and in 2015 Rockwood was taken over by the US-based Albemarle Corporation, one of the world's leading lithium producers. The company now employs some 500 workers at its Salar de Atacama facility, many of them Atacameño people, and at its processing plant near Antofagasta. In early 2017, the company received government approval to expand its annual production of lithium salt from 26,000 tons to 82,000 over coming decades.

The CPA was created as an Indigenous association in 1994 and brings together the leaders of 18 indigenous communities of the Atacama la Grande IDA. The mission of the CPA, which employs some 20 people, is to:

Strengthen the union of indigenous communities, through the Atacameño Lickanantay historical legacy and worldview present in the territory for more than eleven thousand years. Preserve and promote the development of the culture and values of the people. As well as, the care of the environment and the permanence in the territory of the communities. (cited in SMI ICE Chile and Cuatro Vientos 2020: 33)

Some CPA communities like Peine and Socaire are close to the lithium mines, others a considerable distance from them. Beginning in 2012, the CPA started discussions with Rockwood regarding the possibility of negotiating an agreement between the communities represented by the Council. In 2014 the CPA and Rockwood signed an agreement designed to establish a framework for negotiations that would deliver benefits to the CPA communities. This agreement committed the parties to human rights and sustainable development principles that would promote the sociocultural and environmental values of the communities, and dealt with representation in, and a time frame for, negotiations. Discussions were undertaken over the next two years, with the negotiation framework being modified to allow the communities represented by the CPA to participate in negotiations and to consider proposals (SMI ICE Chile and Cuatro Vientos 2020: 22–3).

The Atacama–Rockwood agreement

The agreement was signed on 21 February 2016 between Rockwood Litio Ltda, Albemarle's wholly owned Chilean subsidiary, the CPA, and the CPA's 18 constituent communities. The agreement is to remain in force as long as the operations of the company, or of any legal successor, last in the Salar de Atacama. This is an unusually 'open' term for such agreements, which usually employ a more specific time frame tied, for example, to the duration of a mining lease. The contents of the agreement fall into two distinct categories: those that involve contractual commitments between the CPA and Rockwood; and those, mainly originating with the CPA, that are general assertions of, or record the state's acknowledgment of, Indigenous status and Indigenous rights and ownership of territories and resources ('declaratory' provisions).

Contractual commitments
The major financial provisions of the agreement are as follows (numbers in brackets refer to agreement clauses):

- An annual contribution of the equivalent of US$20,400 to the Andean Boarding School (*Internado Andino*) (5).
- In 2016 a payment of US$2,032,240 to three communities (6.6).
- If the Environmental Qualification Resolution (RCA) of the project is unfavourable and expansion of the mine does not proceed, from 2017 onwards an annual contribution of US$2,075,760 (6.7).

- If the RCA is favourable, payment in 2017 of 2.75 per cent, and from 2018 of 3 per cent, of the annual sales of lithium carbonate and potassium chloride produced from brine extracted from the company's Salt Flat Plant (6.8).
- From 2018 onwards, an annual contribution of US$76,400 to finance the granting of study scholarships (6.22).
- From 2017 onwards an annual contribution of US$30,560 each to two Atacama associations for projects or activities (6.23).

At face value, an annual payment of some US$2 million if the RCA of the project is unfavourable, and a royalty of 2.5–3 per cent of mineral sales if it is favourable, constitutes an outcome at the upper end of the scale of payments made to Indigenous peoples across the globe (O'Faircheallaigh 2016). Payments under the agreement dwarf those under Peine's agreements with MEL, with the communities' share of annual distributions amounting to some $2.5 million per annum during 2016–18, compared to $50,000 under Peine's initial agreement.

However, a more definitive assessment would require a careful analysis of Rockwood's corporate structure, and in particular whether its sales of saline products will be at 'arms length' and at market prices. If Rockwood's operations at its Salt Flat Plant are selling product to related companies at 'administered' or 'transfer' rather than market prices, there is a risk that the true value of mineral production subject to the royalty will be understated, resulting in a significant loss of revenue to Atacameño people. This is a real possibility given that in January 2015, Rockwood became a wholly owned subsidiary of Albemarle Corporation, a US-based multinational corporation. Albemarle promotes itself as maintaining 'the strongest vertical position in the industry, from raw material extraction to specialty product manufacturing' (https://www.albemarle.com/businesses/lithium). Such vertically integrated structures are often associated with transfer pricing and shifting value from one jurisdiction to another so as to minimize exposure to taxes and royalties. The requirement that the Atacama royalty is applied to Rockwood's sales revenue as reported to Chilean state authorities (6.11) is presumably meant to reduce the risk that Rockwood might understate revenues. However, it does not remove this risk, as indicated by the fact that multinational mining companies operating in other countries with substantial regulatory and oversight capacity, such as Australia, have been found to have engaged in transfer pricing and tax evasion in recent years (Ker 2015).

The agreement is unusual in the extent to which Atacameño people are required to report to Rockwood on the use of payments made under the agreement, and in providing that those payments may be suspended if there is any failure to comply with reporting requirements (6.12–6.21). It is highly desirable to have strong accountability requirements in place and to ensure that spending of payments under an agreement are aligned with a community's general planning priorities, as provided for in clauses 6.12, 6.15, and 6.16. Such probity and accountability measures are usually directed to the community and not to the mining company making the payments, as to do the latter is seen as undermining Indigenous autonomy. However, this is an area in which knowledge of the context is important. It is possible that the

Atacameño leadership was happy to have a substantial measure of 'external' account-ability to Rockwood to protect against internal pressures to use money wastefully, or in ways not aligned with community priorities.

In relation to the environment, the company's undertakings are in general very broad and at the level of principle; their relevance is often not explained; and they do not constitute specific undertakings that might be legally enforceable. For example, it is provided (7.3) that:

The parties shall also keep in mind:

- The territorial space occupied by the Indigenous Communities that make up the Council of Atacameño Peoples.
- The fragility of the ecosystems associated with the Atacama la Grande.
- The Communities' interest in safeguarding the hydrological resources.
- The spiritual and cultural value it means to the cosmology of the Lickanantay people, the territorial space of the Atacama la Grande.
- The financial initiatives underway in the Atacama la Grande.

The practical implications of 'keeping these matters in mind' is unclear, as is the rel-evance of 'financial initiatives underway' to the 'fragility of ecosystems' and 'spiritual and cultural value'. Are negative impacts on ecosystems and culture more acceptable because of the 'financial initiatives'?

Rockwood makes no specific commitments in support of such broad prin-ciples and undertakings—commitments that are frequently included in modern agreements. Such commitments might involve, for example, Atacameño participa-tion in decisions relating to certain environmental matters; company funding for Atacameño people to have access to independent technical advice; independent review of the company's environmental management system; and a requirement for the company to respond to any concerns Atacameño people might have on specific environmental issues once operations are under way. The only specific commitments Rockwood makes are to include Atacameño people in environmental monitoring and in environmental studies, but no indication is given as to what action the company must take if the monitoring and/or the studies reveal any significant environmental problems (7).

Negotiated agreements depend for their efficacy on the inclusion of specific and appropriately resourced implementation arrangements to ensure that the potential benefits they offer are actually delivered. The agreement provides for the estab-lishment of a Permanent Working Table Council, with equal representation from Rockwood and the CPA. The Council 'may address the matters dealt with in this Agreement, those relating to its implementation and application, as well as in gen-eral, all those that contribute to the better coexistence and social responsibility of the Company' (4). A number of other clauses can also contribute to effective imple-mentation, including the requirement that the parties meet at a senior level at least once a year to assess the status of the agreement (12.5); and the provision for external review of the agreement's implementation every two years (12.6). However, there is no indication of what will happen if an external review reveals any problems, whose responsibility it will be to address these, or where funding to do so will come from. It is also positive that the parties will each appoint an Agreement Coordinator (13.7), though no provision is made for funding of these positions, and there is little indication of their roles, responsibilities, powers, and lines of reporting. In this last regard, a particular omission is any reference to what should occur if the Agreement Coordinators identify implementation problems which they themselves are not able to address.

The agreement pays limited or no attention to a several matters that figure prominently in Indigenous–mining company agreements in other jurisdictions. It contains no provisions in relation to Atacameño participation in employment opportunities associated with Rockwood's operations. Such provisions are contained in nearly all modern mining company–community agreements we are familiar with, including those in the Global South. Similarly, the agreement makes virtually no mention of Atacameño participation in business opportunities, other than an indication by Rockwood of its future intention to purchase electricity from the CPA, generated through a photovoltaic plant (3.2 (v)). While the CPA asserts the obligations of the Chilean state to respect the 'spiritual and cultural values' of the Atacameño people, and while the CPA agrees to 'keep in mind … spiritual and cultural value' (7.3), there are no provisions in relation to protection of cultural, spiritual, or religious sites or areas of significance. In other Indigenous contexts, it is very common for agreements to include such protective provisions, especially where legislation is deficient in recognizing and protecting Indigenous cultural heritage. This situation certainly applies in Chile, and Atacameño people have mounted campaigns since the early 1990s to gain control of their cultural heritage, to date without success, while their declared desire that burial sites of their ancestors should remain untouched and undisturbed have at times been ignored by archaeologists (Kalazich 2015: 50–1).

Declaratory provisions

While the contractual provisions of the Atacama–Rockwood agreement are comparable to those of agreements in settler states, a substantial part of the agreement consists of what I term 'declaratory statements'—assertions of rights and interests that are directed at the Chilean state rather than at Rockwood, the signatory of the agreement. Such statements are almost entirely absent from agreements in settler states and, where present, typically take up less than a page and provide specific context for the commitments that follow: for example, stating that the mining company has lodged certain mining lease applications, or citing the court reference for a determination of native title.

These declaratory statements in the Atacama–Rockwood agreement are of four main kinds. The first are intended to establish the status of the CPA as the representative body of the 18 communities, and the legal standing and cultural legitimacy of the CPA and of the individual communities (1.3, 1.5). There is a clear statement of their standing as *Indigenous* communities whose existence predates that of the current Chilean state. The communities:

> are moral and legal successors of ancient settlements, lineages or *ayllus* of the Atacameño people, who are also the owners of community land and water in territories traditionally delimited by the same communities since pre-Hispanic times, and definitely since before the signing of the Treaty of Peace and Friendship with Bolivia in 1904 that left the old Province of Atacama under Chilean sovereignty. (1.4)

Related to this is the claim that the territory Rockwood uses for its operations is 'indigenous territory' and therefore belongs to the communities that make up the CPA (2.3). The CPA declares that it shares a 'cosmovision with other Andean and highland people', which includes beliefs regarding the spiritual and collective relationship between water, land, and people, a relationship invoked in various rituals that make it rain and reproduce community life (2.7).

A second category of statements involves establishing that the Salar de Atacama meets criteria established by legislation and by state authorities related to the area's importance to Indigenous peoples, the fragility of its ecosystems, and the need to manage development so as to protect those ecosystems. The region is deemed to meet the requirements of Chile's Indigenous Act in being designated an IDA, an area in which 'indigenous ethnic groups have lived ancestrally; High indigenous population density; Existence of lands of indigenous communities or individuals … and Dependence on natural resources for the balance of these territories, such as management of basins, rivers, banks, flora and fauna' (1.7). The agreement also notes that the Ministry of Planning and Cooperation declared the area as an IDA in 1997 (1.16). Chile's National Lithium Commission is cited in relation to the fragility of ecosystems and the potential impacts of lithium on the environment and on livelihoods, and regarding the need to manage the environmental and economic sustainability of the salt flats carefully, in part by limiting the scale of lithium extraction (1.7, 1.8). Chile's Water Code is cited on the need to place limitations on water extraction, including 'in aquifer zones that feed plains and wetlands' (1.17, 1.18).

The third category is designed to place the agreement in the context of wider ambitions held by the communities and wider challenges they will face in a time frame well beyond the likely life of a single mining project. They have signed the agreement because they want to 'take their development into their own hands', and over a time frame of a century help address issues including global warming, water scarcity, an ageing population, and the precarious situation of retired men and women (1.6).

A fourth and extensive set of provisions involve declaring the relevance and importance of national and international laws relating to the status and treatment of Indigenous peoples. These include Chile's Indigenous Act, the obligations it imposes on corporations to 'safeguard' different categories of land, resources, and property owned by Indigenous people and communities, and its specific requirement for waters on community land, 'such as rivers, canals, irrigation ditches and springs', to be 'particularly protected', and for the 'normal supply of water to the affected communities' to be guaranteed (1.14). The obligations that the Indigenous Act places on the Chilean state, which is, of course, not a party to the agreement, are highlighted (1.15): 'The services of the State administration and organizations of a territorial nature, when dealing with matters that are related to indigenous issues, must listen to and take into consideration the opinion of the indigenous organizations recognized by this law.'

ILO C169 is cited in relation to Chile's obligation 'to respect the special importance for the cultures and spiritual values of the [Indigenous] people concerned with regards their relationship with the lands and territories, or both, as the case may be, which they occupy or otherwise use, and in particular the collective aspects of that relationship' (1.19). The requirement for states that are parties to the agreement to 'respect, preserve and maintain the knowledge, innovations and practices of indigenous and local communities embodying traditional lifestyles relevant to the conservation and sustainable use of biological diversity' is noted (1.20). In summary, the CPA declares that under the Indigenous Act, ILO C169, and the United Nations Declaration on the Rights of Indigenous Peoples (UNDRIP), 'it is the duty of society in general and of the State in particular to respect, protect and promote the development of the Atacama people, their culture, families and communities ... as well as to protect, manage and add value to their lands, territories and natural resources' (2.2).

The provisions outlined so far essentially involve unilateral statements by the CPA and the Atacameño communities. There are also (much briefer) joint statements and commitments to principles by both parties. They acknowledge the fragility of the Salar de Atacama's ecosystem, its vulnerability to human intervention, the need for them to 'unite and coordinate efforts for [its] conservation', and their willingness to cooperate with each other with a view to making 'a shared contribution to the conservation and enhancement of the habitat in which they live' (1.21, 2.6). They jointly recognize the potential for ILO C169, the UNDRIP, and the Indigenous Law to 'be transformed into a tool for participation and cooperation in good faith for mutual benefit and with respect for indigenous rights', while also recognizing that obligations under ILO C169 fall primarily on the state of Chile (2.1). They state their respect for 'the sociocultural and environmental aspects of the communities that integrate the Council and, on the other hand, the natural development of the Company in the mining operation' (2.10).

The extensive nature of the declaratory statements in the Atacama–Rockwood agreement presumably arises from the fact that the CPA is seeking to use the agreement as a vehicle for asserting positions or demands or highlighting legal rights not only, or perhaps not even mainly, in relation to Rockwood, but in relation to the Chilean state.

Environmental litigation

In recent years the CPA has sought, at times in conjunction with state regulatory authorities, to use Chile's legal and judicial system to address the long-term environmental impacts of MEL's copper mining and the impact of SQM's operations. In 2018 the CPA, the Atacameños communities, and the State Defence Council filed an environmental damages lawsuit against MEL, suing the company for the negative impacts in the Punta Negra salt flats of the extraction of fresh water for its copper production operations between 1997 and 2017. This lawsuit has yet to be finalized (IWGIA 2021, 354–5).

In 2016, the SMA opened a sanctioning process against SQM, charging that it had committed a number of environmental violations, including by extracting more brine than allowed, causing damage to the ecosystem. The company risked the revocation of its environmental permit unless it presented a Compliance Plan, through which it could remedy the violations. The SMA approved the company's Compliance Plan and the sanctioning process was stopped. The CPA initiated legal proceedings against SQM and the SMA, arguing that the Compliance Plan was inadequate to reverse the environmental damage caused by SQM, and that the company's environmental permit should be revoked. In December 2019, the First Environmental Court recognized the effects of SQM's operations on the water systems of the salt flats, and ruled that the company's Compliance Programme was inadequate and that the SMA should resume the sanctioning process against SGM. On 6 July 2020, the Court gave the SMA 30 days to enforce the judgment, and 20 days later the SMA restarted the sanctioning process against the SQM.

In the meantime, both the SMA and SQM had appealed the Environment Court's decision to Chile's Supreme Court. The day before the appeal was to be heard, both the SMA and SQM withdrew their appeals, alluding to an out-of-court agreement reached with one of the claimant communities (Carrere 2020; IWGIA 2021: 354–5). The agreement, with Camar, provided for payments to the community and support for health and education programmes, and for a cooperative approach to managing environmental issues. The agreement, according to the community, 'does not in any case imply a negotiation on the rights of indigenous peoples or on the territory or on water, but rather establishes a new way for SQM and the community to work together to take care of the environment' (Carrere 2020, author's translation). SQM has also entered agreements with two other affected communities, Toconao and Talabre. The company's ability to undermine the CPA's solidarity was expected to reduce the likelihood that the SMA would revoke SQM's environmental licence. However, the CPA and Peine expressed their determination to continue with the sanctioning process against SQM, and the ultimate outcome has yet to be determined (Carrere 2020).

Summary

Copper and lithium mining operations were established in the Salar de Atacama, and extensive private water rights were allocated to mining companies in the region, before the Chilean state began to recognize the Indigenous rights of Atacameño peoples. When that recognition of rights occurred, it was limited to land and waters within the communities and, in the case of water, was restricted to water bodies or flows actively used by the communities. Recognition of rights did not extend to the land and water utilized by the mining companies, and neither did it confer on Atacameño communities any right to negotiate agreements with companies whose operations affected them. Highlighting this fact, CMZ, which produced 125,000 tonnes of copper and generated turnover of more than US$600 million in 2020, has not negotiated an agreement with any Atacameño community. SQM, the world's largest lithium producer, has only very recently negotiated limited agreements with a few communities as part of a defensive strategy against threats to its environmental licence. While Peine's leaders may deny that MEL's agreements with the community were voluntary and claim that, rather, they reflected MEL's obligations to provide benefits to help compensate for the company's impact on water resources, in a legal sense the agreements negotiated with Atacameño communities are indeed 'voluntary'.

The Atacama–Rockwood agreement represents a major change from those negotiated between MEL and Peine. The quantum of financial benefits provided is of a different order of magnitude, as is the number of Atacameño communities and people who share in those benefits. Yet there are also continuities with the earlier agreements. While the fact that environmental issues are addressed at the level of principle in the Atacama–Rockwood agreement does represent a departure, there is an absence of concrete provisions to give expression to those principles. As with the earlier agreements, there is substantial oversight of community spending by Rockwood, though there is no prohibition on the communities allocating funds to environmental monitoring or management.

A notable feature of the Atacama–Rockwood agreement is the extent to which the CPA has utilized it to assert Indigenous rights, drawing on the historical attachment of Atacameños to, and their occupation and use of, their ancestral lands and waters, and recognition of that attachment by Chilean state authorities and in international law. The emphasis given to these matters reflects the CPA's perceived need to assert rights whose recognition is recent and is still limited, as is the willingness of copper and lithium miners to share the management of mineral extraction, and its benefits, with the Atacameño communities. Recently, the CPA and the communities have begun to use litigation to insist on recognition of their right to help shape the environmental impacts of mining, and to insist that mining companies address those impacts if agreements are not effective in getting them to do so.

Conclusion

The two case studies have somewhat different implications regarding the ability of Indigenous peoples to shape the direction and impact of mining on their ancestral lands. In Pascua Lama, Diaguita people were able to exert considerable power to shape the course of mineral development, stopping, albeit after a prolonged struggle, a proposal to establish a large gold mine by one of the world's most powerful mining companies. In the second, Atacameño people have, despite sustained and ongoing efforts to do so, been unable to secure a substantial say in the conduct of mineral extraction on their ancestral lands, including in the vital area of water resources and their management. However, they have increasingly been able to use recognition of their Indigenous rights and Chile's judicial system to challenge mining company dominance. Only in the case of Rockwood have they been able to negotiate a significant share of the benefits of mining.

Several important differences exist between the two cases. One involves timing. As mentioned above, copper and lithium mining were both established prior to any recognition of Atacameños as Indigenous peoples or of Indigenous territory in the Salar. Diaguita people achieved recognition at an early stage of the struggle over Pascua Lama. Timing was also important in that Chile's desire to gain admittance to the OECD led to the establishment of new and more powerful environmental regulators and judicial mechanisms just as the conflict over Pascua Lamas was coming to a head, and Diaguita opponents of the mine were able to make highly effective use of the additional avenues this provided in their battle to stop the project. The existence of the Diaguita-established Agricultural Community and the economic resources associated with it were also significant. These provided a powerful organizational platform from which to oppose Barrick Gold, especially during the early years of the conflict before national and international NGOs became involved. The economic base associated with agricultural activity meant that there was little need for Diaguita people to take jobs in mining, and so little pressure on them to support Pascua Lama. In contrast, Atacameños had seen a significant decline in their traditional economic base and employment in lithium mining constituted a significant economic opportunity, which meant that while they were determined to protect their water and associated cultural resources, they needed mining in a way the Diaguita did not. A final point involves the ability of the forces opposed to Pascua Lama to draw on the iconic status of glaciers in mobilizing national and international support for their cause.

I am not suggesting that the Atacameño communities should be judged to have failed in their efforts to control development on their land or secure benefits from it. They are clearly playing a 'long game', as their circumstances demand, indicated for example by the establishment of the CPA with its broader base for political mobilization; by the quantum increase in the benefits offered by the Atacama–Rockwood agreement compared to the earlier MEL–Peine agreements; and by the emphasis in the Atacama–Rockwood agreement on demanding recognition of fundamental human and Indigenous rights that can provide a basis for further gains. The Atacameños are also making incremental progress in their ability to control water and its uses, as indicated for instance by their growing participation in environmental monitoring and by their increasing ability to use judicial and political avenues to influence the allocation of water resources to the mining industry. It is significant that the CPA has started to bring the situation of Atacameños to the attention of international audiences, as the Diaguita did with Pascua Lama. For example, in December 2019 the then Chairperson of the CPA spoke at the UN Climate Change Conference in Madrid. He demanded that Chile's Minister of the Environment go beyond rhetorical commitments and take action to address the massive environmental damage that the mining industry causes in northern Chile, and the industry's impact on Atacama communities through its use of scarce water, which, he added, is contributing to the destruction of glaciers. 'Really act, don't just stay within the speech, because the salt flats are drying up, the glaciers are being demolished.' He also criticized the Chilean government's calls for further investment in the lithium sector in the absence of proper environmental impact studies of the industry's existing impacts.[1]

Considerable change has occurred in relations between the mining industry and Indigenous people in the Solar de Atacama in the last two decades, and change seems likely to continue and to accelerate in coming years.

[1] See   https://www.cooperativa.cl/noticias/sociedad/medioambiente/cop25/cop25-representantes-indigenas-tomaron-la-palabra-y-emplazaron-al/2019-12-03/160011.html. I am grateful to Diego Garcia for bringing this speech to my attention and for providing a summary of its major points in English.

13

Botswana and South Africa

A Contrast in Indigenous Strategies and Outcomes

Introduction

In September 2019, I helped facilitate a negotiation training workshop for Indigenous leaders from Tanzania, Kenya, Botswana, and South Africa at the Maasai-owned Il Ngwesi wildlife lodge in northern Kenya. Engaging with the participants and listening to the case studies they presented as part of the workshop, I was struck by the distinct and formidable barriers faced by Indigenous peoples in Africa in achieving recognition of their rights and in dealing with mining and other commercial development. I was also struck by the very different narratives and outcomes described by San participants from Botswana and a leader of the Xholobeni Indigenous community, from South Africa's Eastern Cape province. The San, despite a sustained struggle over more than 20 years, have been unable to achieve a significant degree of control over government and private sector activities on their homeland in the Kalahari desert. Xholobeni, in contrast, have recently stopped a proposed mining project that they believed would threaten a major part of their ancestral estate.

This chapter seeks both to highlight what is distinctive about the African context, and to explore the reasons why, though faced with some common problems, individual Indigenous peoples can experience different outcomes. The next section offers a broad survey of the situation that Indigenous peoples in Africa have confronted in recent decades. I then present case studies dealing with government policy and histories of development for San people whose homeland is the Central Kalahari Game Reserve in Botswana, and the Xholobeni community in South Africa. I conclude by considering the wider lessons that their different histories reveal about the factors shaping Indigenous experiences with extractive industries.

Indigenous peoples in Africa

Governments in postcolonial Africa have focused on establishing and consolidating national identities, building their economies, and establishing their ability to foster sustained social and economic development. Inheriting colonies created by European powers with little regard for cultural or geographical boundaries, newly

Indigenous Peoples and Mining. Ciaran O'Faircheallaigh, Oxford University Press. © Ciaran O'Faircheallaigh (2023).
DOI: 10.1093/oso/9780192894564.003.0013

independent African states have often been composed of several tribes or nations that had no experience of working together within autonomous political systems and, in some cases, had long histories of rivalry and armed conflict. Barriers to economic development were formidable given the sparse social and physical infrastructure developed by colonial powers, and the lopsided nature of colonial economies, often geared to produce one or two primary commodities that could be exported profitably to the industrialized world. For many African governments, the very concept that their territories might contain minority populations defined as 'Indigenous peoples' was alien, threatening, and even illogical. As far as they were concerned, the critical distinction was between their national populations and non-nationals, the latter in some cases including residual populations from former colonizers and/or powerful economic interests. From this perspective, all nationals of a country were 'Indigenous' (Crawhall 2011: 17). Recognition of distinct 'Indigenous peoples' separate from the national majority, and the possibility of Indigenous territorial claims, seemed only to create a further source of tension and division in contexts where national unity was often fragile and in need of nurturing, and ultimately to threaten state sovereignty. Such anxieties were heightened by Africa's history of secessionist movements in the wake of decolonization, some of which led to bloody and costly wars (Crawhall 2011: 14).

Against this background, many African governments have opposed any suggestion that international legal regimes that recognize Indigenous interests should apply to their countries. They have also bluntly and consistently denied the existence in their territories of 'Indigenous peoples', and so rejected the need to provide recognition of distinct Indigenous cultures, languages, or rights in land, or to provide specific mechanisms for Indigenous peoples to have a say in decisions that affect their territories and resources. If 'Indigenous peoples' do not exist, it clearly makes no sense to create policies or structures that provide separately for their participation, or for them to share in the benefits of development in ways different from the population as a whole (Anaya 2010; Gilbert 2017: 660–1).

Yet 'Indigenous peoples', according to the United Nations (UN) definition of the term, clearly do exist in many African countries (ACHPR 2005; Gilbert 2017: 657–8; Hitchcock and Vinding 2004). There are peoples who were the original inhabitants of the areas in which they live, who have maintained continuity of residence over long periods of time, who are now a minority in their homelands, who are distinct culturally and socially from majority populations, and who find themselves socially and politically marginalized and exploited. Like Indigenous peoples elsewhere in the world, large parts of their territories had been taken over by in-migrating agricultural peoples who now control the state apparatus and often look down on Indigenous peoples as 'backward' and 'primitive'. The territories they continue to inhabit are generally unsuitable for commercial agriculture, including deep rainforest, deserts, and mountains (Crawhall 2011: 14–24; Hitchcock and Vinding 2004).

The situation in relation to African states and recognition of Indigenous rights is not static. A range of factors have led some states to modify their positions in recent years, at least in international fora, as indicated, for example, in the willingness of all but three of 53 African states to support the United Nations Declaration on the Rights of Indigenous Peoples (UNDRIP). This change in turn is explained by the concerns of a democratic South Africa, especially under the leadership of Nelson Mandela, to advance a broad human rights agenda; by the work of new regional human rights bodies, in particular the African Commission on Human and Peoples' Rights (ACHPR); and the growth of Indigenous transnational civil society movements, represented by, for example, the Indigenous Peoples of Africa Coordinating Committee (IPACC). IPACC is a regional Indigenous peoples' network which by 2011 had 155 member organizations in 22 African countries (Crawhall 2011). However, the position adopted by states in international fora is not necessarily reflected in their actions in domestic arenas, and it is in the latter that critical decisions affecting the rights and well-being of Indigenous peoples are made (Saugestad 2011).

Another important aspect of the African context involves the rule of law. Most African countries inherited judicial systems based on the institutions of their colonizers. Such systems are not necessarily embedded in, or supported by, national cultures and values. Court decisions may be ignored by governments, and many Indigenous peoples have experienced intimidation, rights violations, land loss, forced removals, denial of identity, travel restrictions, and in some cases incarceration and torture (Hitchcock and Holm 1993; IWGIA 2021). As Crawhall notes (2011: 32), the rule of law, established traditions of democracy, and participatory negotiated solutions to conflicts over land and resources are uncommon in Africa.

Also militating against Indigenous interests are the land tenure arrangements inherited from colonial powers, particularly those with British legal systems. European doctrines of land tenure based on agricultural usage mean that Indigenous rights in land were often denied in favour of those attributed to sedentary, colonizing peoples (European or African). Equating interest in land with its use for commercial agriculture reflects, in turn, a Eurocentric view that hunter-gatherers are at the bottom of a human hierarchy, which moves upwards through nomadic pastoralists to subsistence agriculture, commercial agriculture, and international trade and industry. This bias is maintained in modern African law, with many legal and constitutional systems failing to recognize the property rights of hunters and pastoralists, and leaving them largely excluded from citizenship and political rights (Crawhall 2011: 18; Hitchcock et al. 2011: 71; IWGIA 2021).

Botswana and the Kalahari San

Botswana gained its independence from the UK in 1966. Tswana-speaking people, comprised of eight subgroups, are politically and numerically dominant. The Tswana began to migrate into the area that is now Botswana no later than AD 1200, displacing other groups including the San, also known as the Basarwa, and previously referred to by Europeans as 'bushmen'. The British negotiated independence with the Tswana. Botswana established formal institutions on the British model, adding tribal authority structures, including a House of Chiefs which advises Parliament and the executive on issues related to Botswana's tribes. These structures privileged the eight Tswana tribes which, unlike minority groups such as the San, are guaranteed membership. In the same way, the Constitution recognizes the eight Tswana subgroups, but does not mention the San (ACHPR 2005: 47–9; Anaya 2010). Botswana's post-colonial economy has relied heavily on diamond mining, which in the early 2000s accounted for 33 per cent of the country's GDP, 65 per cent of government revenue, and 80 per cent of exports. Reflecting the industry's key economic role, very close relations have developed between Debswana, the local subsidiary of the main diamond producer, De Beers, and Botswana's political and bureaucratic elite, particularly after 1975 when the government of Botswana became a 50 per cent shareholder in Debswana (Good 2003: 17).

Along with many other African governments, Botswana has taken the position that all Botswanans are indigenous and places a high value on consolidating a single national identity over the identities of diverse groups. While it voted in favour of the UNDRIP in the UN General Assembly, it is reluctant to consider recognition of distinct Indigenous identities or to establish mechanisms through which Indigenous peoples could establish rights in land based on their collective identity and traditional patterns of occupancy and use (Anaya 2010: 8, 15; Hitchcock et al. 2011: 63; IWGIA 2020: 39). The government has allocated large areas of land to cattle ranchers and categorized most remaining state land as national parks or wildlife reserves. It has severely restricted hunting by Indigenous groups through licensing and wildlife management schemes and, after 2014, by placing a total ban on subsistence hunting and the keeping of livestock on state lands. Government policy has resulted in land dispossession of groups like the San, and no alternative lands have been set aside for them, reducing many to a state of poverty (Anaya 2010; IWGIA 2020: 40–1).

Archaeological evidence indicates that the San have lived in current-day Botswana for many thousands of years. The San population is now around 66,000, or 3 per cent of Botswana's population, and they are among Botswana's poorest people. Until the 1960s, they were a semi-nomadic people who practised a hunter-gatherer and agro-pastoralist lifestyle, moving within designated areas based on the seasons and availability of resources, such as water, game, and edible plants (Hitchcock et al. 2011: 68; Moeti and Gakelekgolele 2020). In postcolonial Botswana, the San have experienced discrimination and marginalization, being regarded by many Tswana as 'primitive', 'backward', and not deserving of inclusion in Botswana's polity. The country's Vice President, for instance, referred to them as 'stone age creatures' in an interview with the London *Guardian* in 1996 (Good 2003: 16). They have been paid very low wages for work on cattle farms, and been deprived of most of their territory, excluded from political life, shunned by many Tswana, and largely excluded from the benefits of government programs. Loss of access to land combined with government initiatives to relocate them into settled communities have resulted in a shift away from hunting and gathering towards domestic food production and wage earning (Anaya 2010; Hitchcock and Holm 1993; Hitchcock et al. 2011).

The Central Kalahari Game Reserve (CKGR) was established in 1961 by the British colonial authorities to protect wildlife resources and to provide San living in the area with land on which to continue their hunter-gatherer way of life. It is the second largest game reserve in Africa. At that time, there were approximately 3,000–4,000 San people living in the game reserve (Anaya 2010: 26). In 1986 environmentalists led by the Kalahari Conservation Society decided that the San were keeping too many domestic animals and hunting too freely in the CKGR, and lobbied for their removal. In response, and concerned about the high cost of providing services to people within the reserve, the government made plans to move the San out of the reserve. This initiative came to a temporary halt when Survival International (SI) and other human rights groups mounted a campaign to publicize the government's plans, but it was quickly resumed and led to the removal of most San from the reserve to newly established settlements outside its boundaries over the period 1986–96.

While the government claimed that relocation was voluntary, measures such as the termination of services inside the reserve, the dismantling of existing infrastructure, confiscation of livestock, harassment, ill-treatment of some residents by police and wildlife officers, and hunting prohibitions created considerable pressure on San people to relocate. The removal and resettlement had and continues to have serious social, cultural, economic, and health impacts on many of the San involved, reflected partly in high levels of alcohol abuse, family violence, and self-harm, and in a high incidence of tuberculosis and HIV/AIDS (ACHPR 2005: 52; Anaya 2010: 27; Good 2003; Hitchcock et al. 2011: 68–77; Moeti and Gakelekgolele 2020).

San women have suffered disproportionately from resettlement. Women traditionally played a key role in hunting, gathering, and pastoral activity, and experienced a substantial degree of equality and involvement in decision making. Resettlement has undermined women's economic status and involvement in community affairs. Physical removal from the CKGR and the government-imposed bans on hunting and on keeping livestock have undermined their roles as producers and providers. This situation is worsened by the Botswana government's practice of treating only men as household heads, directing any livestock compensation to men and creating obstacles for women getting certificates to access residential or arable land. Men have largely monopolized jobs on farms and in tourism, increasing their mobility and their access to wage income, and providing an opportunity to learn the national language, Setswana, or English. Language proficiency allows men, in turn, to play a dominant role in interactions with government and more generally with the external world. Women in settlements have experienced an increase in domestic and sexual violence both from within their community and from visiting males (IWGIA 2011).

In January 2002, the Botswana government shut down all services in the CKGR, closing wells on which residents relied for water and stopping all food deliveries. In late January and early February 2002, the government moved people and their possessions out of the reserve. Houses were dismantled, fruit trees uprooted, and water tanks destroyed. Livestock were loaded on trucks or scattered into the bush, and people were placed on the trucks and moved out of the reserve to two resettlement sites,

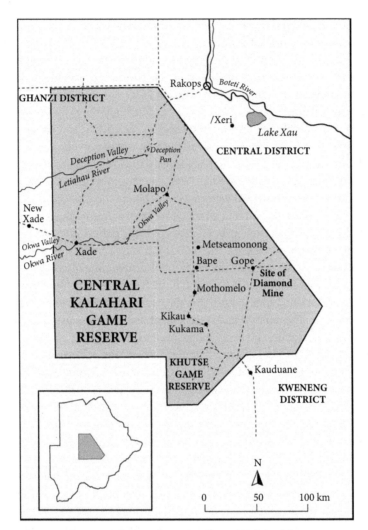

Fig. 13.1 San resettlement from the Central Kalahari Game Reserve

Source: Sapignoli, M., and Hitchcock, R.K., 2013. 'Chronology of the Central Kalahari Game Reserve: Update III, 2002–2012'. *Botswana Notes and Records* 45: p. 60.

New Xade and Kaudwane (see Fig. 13.1) (Sapignoli and Hitchcock 2013: 53). By late 2002 almost all San had left the CKGR, and the government capped the borehole that provided water to the remaining inhabitants of the reserve.

Many San believed and still believe that they were removed from the reserve because the Botswana government wanted to use it for diamond mining and for commercial wildlife tourism (Hitchcock et al. 2011: 77; Moeti and Gakelekgolele 2020). The government explicitly rejected the charge that people were relocated outside of the reserve because of diamond mining, maintaining instead that the relocation was to facilitate provision of services to the San and enable their economic and social development. Throughout 2002 government ministers continued to deny that there was any intention for mining to occur, the President telling the *Sunday Times* in November that there were 'no plans for future mining inside the reserve' (Good 2003: 38–9).

De Beers had in fact been exploring for diamonds in the CKGR since 1985, and the government had announced the location of kimberlite deposits in 2000, indicating the presence of diamonds. Exploration expanded during the period when the San were being removed, and within nine months of the removals being completed virtually the whole of the CKGR was covered by exploration licences, held by DeBeers and its subsidiaries and by BHP Billiton. One of BHP's subsidiaries received a grant of US$2 million from the International Finance Corporation to help cover the costs of aerial reconnaissance exploration (Good 2003: 39). In June 2007 it was announced that the British-based company Gem Diamonds had purchased the mining licences for sites around Gope, where De Beers had been prospecting, for US$34 million, while De Beers retained its remaining exploration licences in the reserve. Environmental impact assessments (EIAs) of the proposed Gope diamond mine were conducted in 2008, following which the government announced development approval for the mine.

During the 1990s, the San had started to organize politically. In 1993 they formed the First People of the Kalahari (FPK), the first national-level San organization in Botswana, under the leadership of Roy Sesana, one of those who was to be removed from the CKGR. The FPK received active support from local non-government organizations (NGOs), including Ditshwanelo, a human rights centre based in the capital, Gabaronne, which campaigned for greater tolerance of minorities and respect for their cultures. Local NGOs engaged both with the government in an effort to influence its policies, and with international Indigenous rights groups. One of the latter, the International Working Group on Indigenous Affairs (IWGIA), provided funding for the FPK, while others, including SI, began to raise international awareness of what was happening in the CKGR.

In February 2002, 243 San individuals who had lived in the reserve, supported by locally based NGOs and South African lawyers, filed an urgent application with the High Court of Botswana, seeking an order declaring unlawful and unconstitutional the government's refusal to issue special game licences to the San and its refusal to allow them to enter the CKGR unless they possessed such a permit. The San also sought an order declaring the termination of basic and essential services by the government unlawful and unconstitutional, and requiring the government to restore these services and their access to the lands and resources within the reserve. The High Court initially dismissed the case but it was reinstated on appeal. Litigation was put on hold in 2004 when the San ran out of funds, but was resumed when SI provided funding for a London-based barrister, Gordon Bennett, supported by local lawyers.

In the meantime, a number of San had returned to live within the CKGR. In September 2005, the government announced that they would be required to leave the reserve, which would be off limits for residential use. The Department of Wildlife and National Parks refused entry to the reserve to lawyers representing the San, contravening orders of the High Court, which had determined that lawyers should have the right to enter the reserve to confer with their clients. In September 2005, armed police and wildlife officers entered the reserve, told people living there to leave, and confiscated a radio transmitter belonging to FPK, making it impossible for communications to be maintained between San people in the reserve and those outside (Moeti and Gakelekgolele 2020: 5; Sapignoli and Hitchcock 2013: 55).

After four years of litigation in December 2006, the High Court of Botswana in the case of *Roy Sesana* v. *The Attorney General* found that 'the applicants were: (a) in possession of the land which they lawfully occupied in their settlements in the CKGR; (b) deprived of such possession by the respondent [the government of Botswana] forcibly or wrongly and without their consent'. The Court found that 'The respondent's refusal to issue special game licences to the applicants is (a) unlawful (b) unconstitutional' and that 'The respondent's refusal to allow the applicants to enter the CKGR unless they are issued with a permit is both unlawful and unconstitutional.' However, the Court also found that 'The termination with effect from 31 January 2002 by the respondent of the provision of basic and essential services to the applicants in the CKGR was neither unlawful nor unconstitutional' and that 'the respondent is not obliged to restore the provision of such services to the applicants in the CKGR' (High Court of Botswana 2006).

The High Court's decision represented a significant victory for the San in that, for the first time, they had successfully challenged the actions of Botswana in removing them from their territories. The decision also had serious limitations. As the case was taken on behalf of 263 individuals rather than as a class action, only those individuals were the subject of the Court's order. The government took the view that the order did not permit other San to return to the reserve, a position it enforced by physically preventing their return. Second, the Court's decision that Botswana was not required to restore services to San communities meant that returning residents, of whom there were an estimated 500–600 people in five communities by May 2010, lacked access to water. They also lacked access to vital education, health, and housing services. Perhaps most importantly, the High Court did not address the fundamental question of whether the San's continuous occupation and use of their territories conferred on them inherent rights in land that Botswana would be required to recognize and address in its future dealings with the San (Gilbert 2017; Saugestad 2011).

The High Court's decision may have had some broader effects in highlighting the plight of the San and the human rights issues involved in their treatment. For example, in October 2008 De Beers announced after a round of community consultations and in the wake of the High Court's decision that 'until such time as a sustainable long-term management plan for the Central Kalahari Game Reserve is agreed, we will continue to focus our exploration activities in areas outside the CKGR' (De Beers 2008). BHP Billiton also disposed of its exploration interest.

A fundamental problem for the San, in addition to its content, was that the Botswana government largely ignored the High Court's decision. For example, local hunters were not given game licences and San continued to be arrested by government game scouts and police for 'illegal hunting'. Some people from the settlements who attempted to enter the CKGR were prevented from doing so, and government authorities entered the reserve and confiscated livestock belonging to residents (Anaya 2010; Hitchcock et al. 2011).

The San were also encountering organizational problems. After the FPK was provided a large grant by an overseas NGO, one of the FPK's employees, not a San person, stole a substantial sum and continued to be employed by the FPK after the theft was discovered. This subsequently made other potential donors wary of providing funds to the organization. The tactics of SI also caused some difficulty for the San. SI did not seek to engage with the government of Botswana and adopted an aggressive campaign strategy, emphasizing the role of diamond mining in Botswana's approach to the San in the CKGR; arguing that Botswana's diamonds were tainted, constituting 'blood diamonds' or 'conflict diamonds'; and picketing the offices of De Beers and BHP Billiton in London. It also accused local NGOs of being subservient to the Botswana government. Given the critical role of diamonds in Botswana's economy, SI's linking of Botswana with 'blood diamonds' alarmed politicians and led to a hardening attitude towards the San and their allies. Government ministers attacked San leaders, accusing them of sedition and claiming that they were under the influence of, and in the pay of, foreigners (Taylor and Mokhawa 2003: 273–4, 279–80). SI's strategy also alarmed local NGO supporters of the San, keenly aware of their own vulnerability in a country whose leaders had limited understanding of, or tolerance for, a vibrant and critical civil society (Good 2003). The outcome was that local NGOs, including Ditshwanelo, reduced or ended their support for the San, who were then isolated and heavily dependent on the support of international NGOs and, in particular, of SI (Gilbert 2017; Saugestad 2011).

Given the reliance on litigation, the role of lawyers also created issues as they, rather than the community, tended to drive the legal strategy. The legal procedures being used were highly complex and laden with jargon, making it very difficult for the San, few of whom had any formal education, to maintain control. As Saugestad (2011: 44) noted, 'once the case proper started, the formalities of the legal process took control, the lawyers took centre stage, and the applicants became spectators'.

In June 2010, the FPK commenced a second case in the High Court against the government of Botswana. The San sought recognition of their right to access water, and to recommission, at their own expense, a key borehole that had been closed by the government in 2002, on land which the High Court had recognized in 2006 the San were 'in "lawful possession of"'. Again the High Court initially dismissed the applicants' request, and the San filed an appeal in September 2010 (Hitchcock et al. 2011). In January 2011, the Botswana Court of Appeals ruled on behalf of the San. However, as occurred after the High Court's 2006 decision, the San again faced an uncooperative and often hostile government which blocked their attempts to gain access to water (Gilbert 2017: 682; Simpson 2013).

By September 2014, Gem Diamonds was operating the Ghaghoo (formerly Gope) diamond mine. Botswana was continuing to grant mineral rights: for instance, issuing permits to explore for coal-bed methane to two companies in 2013. By 2017, a second mine was planned in the north-west of the reserve to extract copper and silver, and additional exploration permits were pending. In 2020, four diamond exploration companies were operating in the CKGR (IWGIA 2021: 43).

The San have continued over the last decade to push their demands for recognition of their inherent rights in land, to live in the CKGR, and to have access to water and to health, education, housing, transport, and communication services available to Botswanans. They face formidable problems in doing so, including in their organization and leadership. The FPK is effectively defunct. Its former leader and the main applicant in the 2006 High Court case, Roy Sesana, took employment with the Botswana government in 2017 when the government established a committee ostensibly to represent the San in negotiations for the establishment of a trust that would channel resources into the San communities. The government put Sesana on its payroll as the liaison person between the government and the San in relation to negotiations regarding the trust. The government also appointed a public servant as secretary of the committee and drafted a constitution for the trust without any input from the San communities. The San are unable to gain legal advice about these developments (personal communication, Smith Moeti and Galomphete Gakelekgolele, 9 September 2019). Many San, while respecting Sesana's historic role in the struggle for recognition of their rights, are concerned that Sesana is in a conflict of interest because he is on the government payroll, and they do not have confidence in his ability to promote their interests. They feel that the public servant appointed as committee secretary is similarly in a position of conflict (Moeti and Gakelekgolele 2020: 5).

Another significant problem is that since 2013 the government has prohibited the entry to Botswana of the lawyer, Gordon Bennett, who, funded by SI, played a key role in the 2006 and 2011 court cases. The San have petitioned the government to allow him to enter Botswana, without success. They are still in contact with Bennett but find it extremely difficult to develop a coherent legal strategy given their inability to engage with him in person or to find alternative sources of legal advice within Botswana (personal communication, Smith Moeti and Galomphete Gakelekgolele, 9 September 2019). Younger San leaders are seeking to mobilize community members in the reserve (now numbering around 800) and in the relocation settlements, but they continue to face fundamental problems in doing so. The San are dispersed across numerous small communities, communication systems are poor, and resources are scarce. They endure ongoing harassment including in some cases physical violence, from government officers who continue to deny the rights of San to live in the reserve and use its resources (Moeti and Gakelekgolele 2020). For instance, in March 2020 four San men were arrested for hunting in the CKGR, and by December 2020 they had still not been brought to trial (IWGIA 2021: 41).

A systemic problem for the San is that they rely heavily both for resources and for political leverage with their government on attracting the attention of international media and NGOs (Taylor and Mokhawa 2003: 274). However, that attention is fickle. The focus of NGOs and the media moves on, and when it does the San are left in an extremely vulnerable position given the hostility or indifference of the Botswana government and their paucity of domestic allies. Hitchcock and Holm's comment (1993: 315), made two decades ago, is sadly still valid today. Europeans and North Americans periodically 'discover' that the Batswana are grossly abusing and exploiting the San. This evinces a short-term response from government that usually involves establishing a committee or inquiry, but no fundamental change occurs, and as soon as the 'discovery' wanes, the San are back where they were. Illustrating this point, after international criticism of the forced removal of San from the CKGR, in 1997/8 the government established a 'Negotiating Team', including the FKP, to negotiate a land claim settlement with the San (ACHPR 2005: 63). Such a settlement has yet to be concluded (for a further, more recent example, see Gilbert 2017: 682–3).

An important consequence of the San's parlous position is that at no time during the last 40 years have they been able to engage with mining companies active in the CKGR. The San have not shared in any of the government revenue generated by exploration and mining; have had no opportunity to negotiate with companies to achieve any sort of structured participation in employment opportunities; and have had no say in managing the impacts or potential impacts of mining on their territories.

There is no mention in any of the sources reviewed for this case study of women's role in pursuing recognition of San rights in land or in dealing with mining issues. Felton and Becker (2001: 20) reported that women have been adversely affected by resettlement, including that resulting from removal of San from the CKGR, but noted that sufficient information is not available to assess that impact adequately. More broadly, they found 'San women are subject to multiple forms of marginalization. They are discriminated against as San, as women, and as San women, by their broader national societies and within their own communities' (Felton and Becker 2001: ix). The expulsion of San women from the CKGR and their relocation to settlements experiencing high rates of alcohol abuse and domestic violence can only have served to exacerbate their marginalization (Felton and Becker 2001: 20; Good 2003: 25; Hitchcock et al. 2011: 74).

South Africa, the Xholobeni community, and mineral sand mining

South Africa's population is around 59 million, of which Indigenous groups are estimated to comprise about 1 per cent. Given South Africa's apartheid past and the wholesale alienation of land that apartheid involved, democratic South Africa has placed a high priority on reversing the injustices of the past, recognizing the rights of those who lost their land and, where possible, achieving restitution for that loss. South Africa's Constitution (section 25(6)), adopted in 1996, states: 'A person or community whose tenure of land is legally insecure as a result of past racially discriminatory laws or practices is entitled, to the extent provided by an Act of Parliament, either to tenure which is legally secure or to comparable redress.' Section 211 of the Constitution recognizes the status of customary law and states that 'courts must apply customary law when that law is applicable, subject to the Constitution and any legislation that specifically deals with customary law'. South Africa's Constitutional Court has endorsed the status of customary law as follows:

> While in the past indigenous law was seen through the lense of the common law, it must now be seen as an integral part of our law … Its validity must be determined by reference not to the common law, but to the Constitution … It is clear that the Constitution acknowledges the distinctiveness and originality of indigenous law as an independent source of norms within the legal system. (High Court of South Africa 2018: 32)

In 1996, South Africa introduced the Interim Protection of Informal Land Right Act. The Act provides 'for the temporary protection of certain rights to and interests in land which are not otherwise adequately protected by law'. The protection was deemed 'temporary' because the law was seen as an interim measure that would be replaced by permanent legislation, but in the absence of the latter the legislation has been continually extended since 1996. Critically, the Act states:

> 2. (1) Subject to the provisions of … the Expropriation Act, 1975 (Act No. 63 of 1975), or any other law which provides for the expropriation of land or rights in land, no person may be deprived of any informal right to land without his or her consent.
>
> (2) Where land is held on a communal basis, a person may … be deprived of such land or right in land in accordance with the custom and usage of that community.
>
> (4) For the purposes of this section the custom and usage of a community shall be deemed to include the principle that a decision to dispose of any such right may only be taken by a majority of the holders of such rights present or represented at a meeting convened for the purpose of considering such disposal and of which they have been given sufficient notice, and in which they have had a reasonable opportunity to participate.

The Xholobeni Indigenous community is located in the Umgungundlovu coastal region of South Africa's Eastern Cape province, in an area of great natural beauty and cultural interest known as the Wild Coast. One reason for the region's high cultural value is that it is one of the few places in the world showing evidence of continuous human occupation through the last ice age. The people of Xholobeni are AmaMpondo, whose ancestors have lived in the area for several centuries, having migrated there to avoid Zulu expansion into their original homeland. The Xholobeni community consists of about 600 people, who rely mainly on production of food crops and livestock husbandry for their livelihoods.

The sands of the coastline where Xholobeni are located are rich in titanium minerals. In February 2002, Transworld Energy and Mineral Resources (TEM), a South African subsidiary of an Australian company, Mineral Resources Commodities (MRC), was awarded a prospecting permit for a coastal area 22 kilometres long and 1.5 kilometres inland from the high-water mark. It established mineral sands reserves totalling 350 million tonnes, and proposed developing an open-cut mining operation covering 855 hectares. In October 2003, TEM established a partnership with a local company, Xholobeni Empowerment Company (XolCo), as required under South African Black Empowerment law, with XolCo eventually taking a 26 per cent stake in the project. By May 2004, TEM/MRC had commenced EIA work in preparation for submitting applications for a mining lease and development approval (MRC 2005).

MRC stated in its *Annual Report 2005* that the local community was being regularly briefed on the project 'and continues to support the Company and XolCo in their efforts to secure mining rights' (MRC 2006: 5). MRC later claimed that it had always sought to engage in an open and proactive manner with the Xholobeni community (MRC 2016). The reality appears to have been otherwise, with most engagement with the public occurring outside the area, and the company at times hiding the true purpose of its activities from the local population (High Court of South Africa 2018; Zukulu 2020). The large majority of the Xholobeni community, most of whom live close to the proposed mining area, in fact opposed MRC's mine from the start, viewing it as a fundamental threat to their environment, their land, and their way of life. In July 2007, the community established the Amadiba Crisis Committee (ACC) to coordinate opposition to the project. The ACC was composed of both elders and young people, to help ensure that it would attract participation from both young and old (Zukulu 2020).

Despite the Xholobeni community's small size, it organized, with the help of several NGOs, a sophisticated campaign against the proposed mine. Its local allies included Sustaining the Wild Coast and the Alternative Information Development Centre, while the international NGO Amnesty International, concerned about the human rights implications of MRC's project, also offered support. The ACC documented, with the help of volunteers, the environmental values of the area and the potential impact of mining on these and on the livelihoods of the AmaMpondo. It highlighted the biodiversity of the area that MRC planned to mine, including the presence of 200 endemic plants. It documented the fact that the entire coastline of Xholobeni is littered with archaeological sites containing evidence of human settlement dating back tens of thousands of years, including sites of a sort that are under the sea elsewhere in the world because they were flooded when sea level rose after the last ice age. The ACC also documented the potential economic benefits of ecotourism over a much longer period than mining was expected to last (Zukulu 2020). Xholobeni's campaign against mining began to attract extensive media attention in South Africa and overseas, attention which grew further in September 2007 when the King and Queen of AmaMpondo visited the traditional court or Komkulu of Umgungundlovu, attracting a crowd of some 2,000 people.

In August 2008, South Africa's Department of Mineral Resources (DMR) awarded mining rights to MRC's subsidiary, TEM, despite the fact that the Xholobeni community was neither notified nor consulted before the licence was awarded. Xholobeni had the support of the Legal Resources Centre (LRC), an NGO that volunteered to assist it when its staff saw the story in the news, and fundraised to help meet legal costs. The community's legal team also included the law firm of Richard Spoor, who initially became involved as a pro-bono adviser to the community. Spoor was a human rights lawyer with extensive experience in dealing with mining companies. The ACC lodged an appeal with the DMR challenging the grant of the mineral licence, in response to which the Minister for Mineral Resources suspended the mining rights and MRC halted work on the project for several years (MRC 2011: 3). Long delays occurred in the DMR's processing of Xholobeni's appeal, but eventually in 2012 the department cancelled MRC's mining right. At the same time, the DMR confirmed its intention to grant MRC a replacement mining right, and in 2015 TEM lodged a further application for a mining licence and resumed impact assessment and development work. The ACC submitted a series of further objections to the grant of mining rights to TEM, including one which was joined by the King of AmaMpondo.

Sinegugu Zukulu, a Xholobeni community leader, explains that the AmaMpondo, despite being affected by colonial rule and apartheid, have maintained their autonomous governance structures. These are based on a hierarchy of sub-headmen and sub-headwomen, headmen and headwomen, the chief, and finally the king or queen. This system can come into conflict with South Africa's electoral democracy in relation to projects such as MRC's:

> The community on the ground expects their decisions to be respected by government while government on the other hand expects people to listen to government aspirations, as they are ostensibly undertaken for the public benefit. People claim to own the land through their traditional system and as such expect to have the final say on how their land should be used. These different ways of making decisions normally lead to conflicts between government and community when there are different views about proposed development projects. (Zukulu 2020)

By 2008 a number of community members, including the chief of the Xholobeni community, who had previously opposed the project, had begun to agitate in favour of mining. It later transpired that TEM had given this individual a four-wheel-drive vehicle and other financial benefits, and that he and other supporters had been appointed directors of TEM and XolCo. TEM and XolCo engaged in other questionable tactics in lobbying for approval of the mine: for instance, bussing 50 supporters to Pretoria to present the DMR offices with a petition supposedly signed by 4,000 local residents, urging DMR's Director General to approve TEM's mining rights. It transpired that many of the signatures were fraudulent, including those purported to have been provided by prominent critics of mining (Zukulu 2020).

Opponents of MRC confronted the pro-mining chief in public meetings, holding him to account for his actions in supporting the proposed mine. The community also used the traditional practice of composing songs for community gatherings, singing songs that openly challenged the government's push for mining and its divisive effects, criticized some members of the traditional leadership for not leading by example but causing conflict, and criticized the behaviour of pro-mining community leaders. Others showed their dissatisfaction with supporters of the mine by naming their dogs after them (Zukulu 2020).

Tensions escalated in Xholobeni in 2014 after a large number of community members acted to prevent MRC/TEM consultants from gaining access to the proposed mine site to undertake work for the EIA, without which TEM could not gain final approval. Supporters of the mine attacked its opponents on several occasions, and in May 2015 an interim court interdict was granted against several of the mine's supporters, 'preventing them from intimidating, victimising, threatening, assaulting members of the community and from bringing firearms to community meetings' (High Court of South Africa 2018: 9). In March 2016, an ACC leader was shot dead by unknown assailants, a killing that the mine's opponents attributed to TEM's supporters (High Court of South Africa 2018; MRC 2016; Zukulu 2020).

In July 2016, MRC announced that it had decided to sell its stake in TEM to its Black Economic Empowerment partner. It said: 'In light of the ongoing violence and threats to the peace and harmony of the local Xholobeni community, the Company accepts that the future viability of the Xholobeni Project should be managed by stakeholders and organizations exclusively owned by South Africans' (MRC 2016). However, in June 2017, the Minister for Mineral Resources placed a moratorium on granting of mining licences in the Umgungundlovu area given the extent of community disputation regarding the project. The moratorium is still in place five years later and as a result MRC's disposal of its interest has yet to occur.

In the meantime, the Xholobeni community had lodged a claim in South Africa's High Court against the DMR, asking the Court to declare that the grant of a mining licence would be invalid unless DMR complied with provisions of the Interim Protection of Informal Land Right Act (1996), which prohibits expropriation of 'land or rights in land' without the consent of the community that owned the land. Indicating the extent of opposition to the proposed mine, 68 of the 70–5 households comprising the Xholobeni community were among the applicants who lodged the claim. The DMR, several other government agencies, and TEM opposed the claim, arguing that TEM was required only to consult with the community as required by the Mineral and Petroleum Resource Development Act (2002), and that MRC had fulfilled this requirement.

Litigation lasted more than two years. Xholobeni argued that South Africa's Constitution, its interpretation by the Constitutional Court, the Interim Protection of Informal Land Right Act (1996), and developments in international law granting Indigenous communities the right of free prior and informed consent in relation to proposed mining projects, all supported its position that grant of a mineral licence to TEM would be unlawful (High Court of South Africa 2018). In November 2018, the High Court handed down a judgment in favour of Xholobeni, ruling that the DMR lacked any lawful authority to issue a mining licence to TEM and that 'in terms of the

Interim Protection of Informal Land Right Act 31 of 1996 the First Respondent [the Minister for Mineral Resources] is obliged to obtain the full and informed consent of the Applicants and the Umgungundlovu community, as the holder of the rights in land, prior to granting any mining right to the Fifth Respondent [TEM]'. Costs were awarded against the Minister for Mineral Resources and the other respondents (High Court of South Africa 2018: 39–40).

After the High Court ruled in favour of Xholobeni, the minister announced that an 'independent survey' would be held to establish community sentiment in relation to the mine and the future of mining rights (MRC 2020: 23). As Zukulu (2020) notes, the survey seems pointless given that all but a few households in the community had joined the court action against it. The minister's announcement may indicate that he and his department were reluctant to accept the High Court's (and the community's) decision, a position that Tlale (2020: 3, 13–14) believes is leading to an 'alarming' number of disputes appearing before South Africa's courts.

Women played a central role in Xholobeni opposition to mining. The First Applicant in the High Court case was Xholobeni's Headwoman, Duduzeli Belini. Women played a prominent role in the ACC and in leading confrontations with TEM and with pro-mining members of the community. For instance, in October 2007, XolCo director Zamile Qunya physically ejected ACC member Nonhle Mbuthuma from a community consultation meeting at Xholobeni High School when she questioned why the consultation was not being held at the Komkhulu, the royal house where meetings dealing with land matters should be held according to custom. In May 2015, Duduzeli Belini supported Xholobeni residents in refusing MRC/TEM consultants access to community lands to carry out environmental impact studies (Zukulu 2020).

Conclusion

At the start of this chapter, I mentioned my impression that outcomes for Indigenous peoples in Botswana and South Africa have been very different. It is now possible to explain the reasons for these very different outcomes, which will also highlight factors that influence the experience of Indigenous peoples with mining.

South Africa's apartheid past, a past not shared with Botswana or with many other African countries, has led its democratic government to attach a high priority to recognition of informal rights in land denied by the apartheid regime, and Indigenous people have benefited from this. The commitment of South Africa to recognition of Indigenous rights should not be exaggerated. For example, when an Indigenous group sought to assert their title over an area of land earlier confiscated for a diamond mine now operated by South Africa's state mining company, the government opposed the claim (unsuccessfully in the end) all the way to South Africa's Constitutional Court (Gilbert 2017). As Meyer notes (2020: 3), many Indigenous groups in South Africa have yet to gain recognition of their land rights, and the legacy of apartheid cannot be cleansed simply by scrapping its most offensive legislation.

Meyer (2020: 20) also notes the potential negative implications of South Africa's Traditional and Khoi-San Leadership Act (2019), which allows traditional leaders to consent to mining operations and sign agreements on behalf of their communities, undermining court decisions requiring the consent of these parties. The role of Xholobeni's traditional chief in seeking to approve sand mining against the opposition of his community highlights the risks involved. However, South Africa's government did enact the Interim Protection of Informal Land Right Act and its courts have acted to affirm Indigenous rights and their exercise in relation to mining projects.

No equivalent legislative or constitutional protections exist for the San. The Botswana government has refused to implement, or fully implement, High Court decisions favouring them, preventing the San from returning to their homeland, from accessing water, and from hunting game. The importance of the rule of law is highlighted by the contrast between this behaviour and events in South Africa, where the Minister for Resources immediately suspended MRC/TEM's mining rights when Xholobeni lodged objections to them, and complied with the High Court's decision that the rights not be granted without Xholobeni's consent.

Another key difference involves the economic resources and capacities of the San and Xholobeni. The latter had an independent economic base provided by a viable agricultural economy, whereas the San's hunting and gathering economy had largely been destroyed and not been replaced by any viable alternative. In addition, the San were dispersed across a number of settlements and beset by poor communication, whereas Xholobeni was a compact community where meetings could be called quickly and strategies executed. Xholobeni was also able to connect to a vibrant local NGO community, offering it access to legal and environmental advice, research services, and the media. Botswana's civil community was not as robust and faced a hostile government. The San's reliance on international NGOs created a vulnerability that was not experienced by Xholobeni and which, because of SI's aggressive tactics, alienated the San's local support and led to increased government repression. Reliance on an international NGO created a specific vulnerability as Botswana was able to isolate the San from their legal advisers. Gilbert (2017) suggests that there may also be an underlying tension between international NGOs and Indigenous groups that render the relationship inherently unstable. He argues that the San became a 'receptacle of Western imaginaries of anti-modernity and otherness as peoples' and that 'external actors will engage on the basis of their own visions and interests [which] might not always match and relate to the interests and vision of the community concerned' (Gilbert 2017: 680, 685).

A further point of contrast involves the role of women. The AmaMpondo people have a strong tradition of parallel structures of governance involving both women and men. Building on this foundation, Xholobeni has been able to draw on the skills, resourcefulness, and determination of its women, who have played a major role in the campaign against mining, including in confronting its supporters in their community and in leading litigation in the High Court. There is little evidence on the public record that San women have played an equivalent role, and resettlement has undermined their economic status and subjected them to increased violence. It cannot be assumed that women have not been influential in the background in relation to the San's public campaign, and they have been fully involved in efforts to return to the CKGR and so assert their ongoing connection to their land and their Indigenous way of life. They are setting up women's groups, starting to attend international Indigenous gatherings, and their networks are helping to build and maintain links between a San community fragmented by expulsions from the CKGR and resettlement (personal communication, Smith Moeti and Galomphete Gakelekgolele, 9 September 2019; IWGIA 2011).

The San and Xholobeni did share two things in common. The first involves dissent within their community. In Xholobeni's case, this emerged when the chief of the community and his allies began supporting RCM/TEM, and to attack community members who opposed mining. Opponents of mining applied a range of tactics to neutralize its supporters, including use of the traditional practice of song writing to confront the chief, and invoking a court injunction to try and prevent the use of violence. The latter raises again the importance of an effective legal system for Indigenous people, who can often find themselves aligned against powerful economic and political interests. In the case of the San, younger members of the community fear that a former leader of the opposition to their expulsion from the CKGR has now defected to the government. This is very much a live situation, the outcome of which has yet to be decided.

The second thing the two groups have in common is their resilience and their determination to protect their attachment to their territory and their Indigenous way of life. This has allowed Xholobeni to avert a major threat to its country and way of life. In the case of the San it has meant that, despite enormous odds and in the face of the full power of the state, they have persisted in their efforts to return to the CKGR and so maintain their connection to their ancestral territory.

14

Indigenous Rights and Mining in the Philippines

Introduction

The Philippines is composed of 7,107 islands and islets spanning 1,854 kilometres from north to south and stretching from China in the north to the Indonesian archipelago in the south. Parts of the country were settled by Muslim immigrants starting in the fourteenth century. It was colonized by Spain (1521–1898) and the United States (1902–36), and was occupied by the Japanese during the Second World War before becoming an independent country in 1946. It contains many ethno-linguistic groups, including nearly 100 distinct Indigenous peoples who account for an estimated 12 per cent of the population of around 101 million people recorded at the last census in 2015. Since the 1970s, the Philippine Indigenous peoples have been besieged by a growing number of foreign and local corporations engaged in mining, logging, and plantation agriculture, and by state projects to build roads, dams, and other infrastructure. As a result, many have withdrawn into more remote inland regions, the same regions where many Philippine mineral resources are located (Molintas 2004). Those resources are rich, particularly in gold, copper, nickel, and chromite, 19 large-scale projects were operating in the country in 2019, and the mining industry employs some 200,000 people. However, the Philippines has faced substantial barriers in fully developing its mineral resources. Some of these are political and regulatory, and are discussed in detail below. Others relate to the country's vulnerability to natural disasters including earthquakes, typhoons, volcanoes, and landslides (IWGIA 2021; PH-EITI 2019; Republic of the Philippines 2016).

Ferdinand Marcos was president and then dictator of the country from 1965 until 1986, when he was forced from power by a popular movement. Governments have since been elected democratically, and some civil rights such as freedom of religion are widely respected. The Philippines has experienced a number of armed insurgencies in recent decades, in particular by the Moro Islamic Liberation Front (MILF) and the New People's Army (NPA), the military arm of the Philippine Communist Party, which seeks to overthrow the state by means of guerrilla warfare. The state, partly in response to these threats, has developed repressive characteristics, including the extensive deployment of its armed services and paramilitary groups that they arm, train, and in some cases command. State military repression justified in the name of countering insurgency groups often extends to the non-armed civilian population, and has led to suspension of civil liberties and a situation in which the Philippine

Indigenous Peoples and Mining. Ciaran O'Faircheallaigh, Oxford University Press. © Ciaran O'Faircheallaigh (2023).
DOI: 10.1093/oso/9780192894564.003.0014

military operates with a sense of impunity and extrajudicial killings are common (Sanz 2019: 37–8). Environmental activists and Indigenous leaders are frequently the target of this state-condoned violence (see IWGIA 2021: 293–5, which documents numerous cases of violence, including extrajudicial killing, against Indigenous leaders in 2020 alone). Corruption is a serious problem, and the rule of law is widely regarded as weak, with long delays occurring in the judicial system and courts favouring elite and state interests (Hamm et al. 2013; IWGIA 2021: 290–4; Mongabay 2021; Visaya 2020).

The police, military, and paramilitaries are regularly deployed to protect the operations of mining companies, which frequently involves use of violence against Indigenous people. For example, in April 2020 regional and provincial police acted with company security personnel to dismantle barriers and arrest protestors trying to stop fuel trucks entering a gold mine operated by Oceania Gold, an Australian company whose operating licence had expired nine months previously (Visaya 2020; see also IWGIA 2021: 293–5).

The Philippines has faced and faces substantial economic challenges, including high levels of foreign debt, low growth rates, sharp income inequality, and major gaps in the provision of physical infrastructure and social services such as education, housing, and health. Its government has consistently looked to the mining industry to generate export income, employment, and revenues to help address these problems (Hamm et. al. 2013; IWGIA 2021: 296; Sanz 2019: 281). At the same time, the industry has been highly contentious because of an association with the state's repressive activities, corruption, and a history of failing to undertake environmental rehabilitation of mined sites and of causing environmental disasters. The latter include a breach in the drainage tunnel of a pit containing mine waste at Marcopper's mine on the island of Marinduque in 1996, which led to a discharge of 1.6 million cubic metres of toxic material into the Makulapnit–Boac river system. One village was buried in six feet of muddy floodwater, causing the displacement of 400 families, and twenty other villages had to be evacuated. Drinking water was contaminated and fish and freshwater shrimp stocks were decimated (Hamm et al. 2013; Tan 2006: 193–4). An indication of the controversy surrounding the industry is that on his election in 2006 President Duterte confirmed a ban on any new open-cut mines in the Philippines.

Indigenous Peoples' Rights Act (1997)

The Philippines is one of the few countries that has introduced comprehensive legislation which aims to recognize the rights of Indigenous peoples, including in their interaction with extractive industry (World Bank 2007). When Ferdinand Marcos was driven out of office, the country's Constitution was rewritten, including to incorporate recognition of the rights of Indigenous peoples. Article XII of the Constitution states: 'The State, subject to the provisions of this Constitution and national development policies and programs, shall protect the rights of indigenous cultural communities to their ancestral lands to ensure their economic, social, and cultural well-being.' The Department of Environment and Natural Resources (DENR) subsequently issued a number of directives aimed at giving practical expression to those rights. Through Administrative Order No. 2 (1993) DENR offered the possibility of Certificates of Land Claims, allowing residential or agricultural land to be claimed by individuals, families, or clans; and Certificates of Ancestral Domain Claims (CADCs) covering ancestral lands and their natural resources, which could be claimed by an entire community or tribe. The processes involved in making a claim were complex and time consuming, and assumed that underlying ownership of land would remain with the state (Molintas 2004).

A more comprehensive approach was adopted with the passage of the Indigenous Peoples' Rights Act (IPRA) in October 1997. IPRA requires the state to:

> protect the rights of ICCs/IPs [Indigenous cultural communities/Indigenous peoples] to their ancestral domains, to ensure their economic, social and cultural well being and [to] recognize the applicability of customary laws governing property rights or relations ... The State shall recognize, respect and protect the rights of ICCs/IPs to preserve and develop their cultures, traditions and institutions. It shall consider these rights in the formulation of national laws and policies. (section (s.) 1)

Central to the operation of the Act is the declaration of 'ancestral domains', which comprise:

> lands, inland waters, coastal areas, and natural resources therein, held under a claim of ownership, occupied or possessed by ICCs/IPs, by themselves or through their ancestors, communally or individually since time immemorial ... [They] shall include ... mineral and other natural resources, and lands which may no longer be exclusively occupied by ICCs/IPs but from which they traditionally had access to for their subsistence and traditional activities ... (s. 3)

Ancestral domains 'include such concepts of territories which cover not only the physical environment but the total environment including the spiritual and cultural bonds to the areas which the ICCs/IPs possess, occupy and use and to which they have claims of ownership' (s. 4). Ancestral domains constitute 'community property which belongs to all generations and therefore cannot be sold, disposed or destroyed'.

The Act provides for a process for the declaration of ancestral domains and for the issue of Certificates of Ancestral Domain Title (CADTs), 'formally recognizing the rights of possession and ownership of ICCs/IPs over their ancestral domains identified and delineated in accordance with this law' (s. 3). The declaration of an ancestral domain confers on ICCs/IPs the:

> right to develop, control and use lands and territories traditionally occupied, owned, or used; to manage and conserve natural resources within the territories and uphold the responsibilities for future generations; to benefit and share the

profits from allocation and utilization of the natural resources found therein; the right to negotiate the terms and conditions for the exploration of natural resources in the areas … (s. 7(b))

It also confers the right 'to regulate the entry of migrant settlers and organizations into the domains', the 'Right to Safe and Clean Air and Water', the 'Right to Resolve Conflict', and the right to 'self-governance and self-determination' (s. 7 (e), (f), and (h), s. 13). The state undertakes to 'ensure that the employment of any form of force or coercion against ICCs/IPs shall be dealt with by law' (s. 21).

The Act establishes a National Commission on Indigenous Peoples (NCIP) to be the primary government agency responsible for the formulation and implementation of policies, plans, and programmes to recognize, protect, and promote the rights of ICCs/IPs, including through the recognition of ancestral domains. The NCIP is an independent agency under the Office of the President and is composed of seven (7) Commissioners belonging to ICCs/IPs and appointed by the president of the Philippines from a list of recommenders submitted by authentic ICCs/IPs (s. 38, s. 40, s. 44). The NCIP also issues 'appropriate certification as a pre-condition to the grant of permit, lease, grant, or any other similar authority for the disposition, utilization, management and appropriation by any private individual, corporate entity or any government agency … on any part or portion of the ancestral domain taking into consideration the consensus approval of the ICCs/IPs concerned' (s. 44 (m)).

The Act sets out the process for delineating and declaring ancestral domains. The process may be initiated by the NCIP with the consent of the ICC/IP concerned, or through a Petition for Delineation filed with the NCIP by a majority of the members of the ICC/IP. The official delineation of ancestral domain boundaries is undertaken by the NCIP's Ancestral Domains Office, and is to be carried out with 'genuine involvement and participation by the members of the communities concerned'. The Act sets out a variety of forms of proof that ICCs/IPs may use to support their claims for ancestral domains, including testimony of elders or community members under oath, 'authentic documents' attesting to the possession or occupation of the area since time immemorial, and descriptive histories of traditional landmarks such as mountains, rivers, creeks, ridges, and hills. Based on this evidence, the Ancestral Domains Office prepares a perimeter map of the ancestral domain, complete with technical descriptions, and a description of natural features and landmarks, which is advertised to allow objections by any opposing claimants. The Ancestral Domains Office prepares a report to the NCIP, endorsing a favourable action upon a claim that is deemed to have sufficient proof, or, alternatively, requiring additional proof, or, where a claim is deemed false or fraudulent, recommending rejection of the claim. Where the NCIP accepts a claim, it issues and registered a CADT (s. 52).

An entity that is a non-member of the ICC/IP concerned may be allowed to take part in the development and utilization of the natural resources of an ancestral domain 'for a period of not exceeding twenty-five (25) years renewable for not more than twenty-five (25) years: Provided, that a formal and written agreement is entered into with the ICCs/IPs concerned or that the community, pursuant to its own decision making process, has agreed to allow such operation' (s. 57). All governmental agencies are 'strictly enjoined from issuing, renewing, or granting any concession, license or lease, or entering into any production-sharing agreement' without the NCIP's approval, which approval is not to be provided 'without the free and prior informed and written consent of ICCs/IPs concerned' (s. 59). Free and prior informed consent means 'the consensus of all members of the ICCs/IPs to be determined in accordance with their respective customary laws and practices, free from any external manipulation, interference coercion, and obtained after fully disclosing the intent and scope of the activity, in a language and process understandable to the community' (s. 3).

Importantly, all claims by ICCs/IPs for recognition of rights in land are subject to existing property rights: 'Property rights within the ancestral domains already existing and/or vested upon passage of this Act, shall be recognized and respected' (s. 56).

Liberalization of mining legislation

In the years immediately prior to passage of the IPRA, the Philippine government, as part of a structural adjustment programme negotiated with the World Bank and the International Monetary Fund, had substantially liberalized legislation governing mining in order to attract greater investment, and especially foreign investment, into the industry. These changes were given effect through the Philippine Mining Act (1995) (henceforth the Mining Act), developed with substantial input from the mining industry as well as the World Bank (Caruso et al 2003: 56). The Mining Act, which remains in force today, stated that 'Mineral resources are owned by the State and the exploration, development, utilization, and processing thereof shall be under its full control and supervision' (chapter II). The Act included highly favourable tax treatment for the industry (chapter XVI); rights to water and timber on lands containing mineral resources and easement rights to lands adjacent to those containing mineral resources (chapter XII); and guarantees of the right of repatriation of the entire profits of the investment as well as freedom from expropriation (s. 94). The Act created a new type of production agreement, the Financial or Technical Assistance Agreement (FTAA), that can last for up to 25 years, is approved by the president of the Philippines, and allows 100 per cent foreign ownership of the mineral concession, an option not previously available to foreign investors (chapter VI). The Mining Act was favourably received by the international mining industry, and the number of foreign mining companies represented in the Philippines increased by 400 per cent between 1994 and 1996 (Holden et al. 2011: 146).

There was obvious room for conflict between the IPRA and the Mining Act. The State's claim to own minerals and have 'full control and supervision of their development' is in tension with the *IPRA*'s statement that Indigenous Peoples have 'the right to negotiate the terms and conditions for the exploration of natural resources' in ancestral domains, and the requirement for Indigenous free prior and informed consent (IFPIC) in relation to grant of any 'concession, license or lease, or entering into any production-sharing agreement' in those domains. The Philippine government's *Rules and Regulations* implementing the IPRA highlighted the potential impact of the requirement for IFPIC, stating that 'The ICCs/IPs shall, within their communities, determine for themselves policies, development programs, projects and plans to meet their identified priority needs and concerns. The ICCs/IPs *shall have the right to accept or reject a certain development intervention in their particular communities*' (emphasis added: part III, s. 3).

More broadly, the extensive rights afforded Indigenous peoples appear at odds with the priority and privileges offered foreign mining companies: for instance, in relation to use of timber, water, and lands adjacent to their mining concessions. In fact, the mining industry saw the IPRA as a major deterrent to investment (Holden et al. 2011: 151). In 1998 mining industry representatives sought to have the IPRA declared unconstitutional by the Philippine Supreme Court on the basis that it contravened article XII (s. 2) of the 1987 Constitution, which gives the Philippine state the property rights to all natural resources. The challenge failed, but lobbying of the NCIP by the mining industry did result in a weakening of the IFPIC provisions of IPRA through amendments to the Act's *Rules and Regulations* via the National Commission on Indigenous Peoples Administrative Order No. 1998–3 (World Bank 2007: 11). This order exempts all leases, licences, contracts, and other forms of concession within ancestral domains prior to 1998 from the coverage of IPRA's provisions on IFPIC, including large numbers of leases that mining companies applied for after the Mining Act was passed in 1995; it declares that all written agreements with and/or resolutions by Indigenous peoples communities prior to 1998 shall be considered as constituting the IFPIC required by IPRA; and it shortens the period for the processing by the NCIP of certification of Indigenous consent applications.

The following two case studies allow for an analysis of how the IPRA has operated in practice and how tensions between the IPRA and the interests of the mining industry have been resolved. The first involves a Canadian mining company, Toronto Ventures, Incorporated (TVI), which operated a profitable and highly contentious copper/gold mine on Indigenous land in the decade to 2014. The second involves the Tampakan copper/gold project, which a number of companies have sought unsuccessfully to develop in the face of Indigenous opposition, but which, in May 2021, was yet again proposed for development.

The Subanon and Toronto Ventures Incorporated

The Subanon are an Indigenous people whose territory lies in the Siocon area of the Zamboanga Peninsula in the far west of Mindanao. They constitute about 10 per cent of Siocon's population, with the remainder comprising Christians and Muslims. The Subanon avoided integration with colonists in part by moving inland from coastal areas, where they continue to live by farming, hunting, and fishing. They maintain their Indigenous religious beliefs, which include the association of specific places with creation stories. Of particular importance to Subanon living in the Canatuan area is Mount Canatuan, which they wished to remain untouched. It is believed to be where the Subanon leader Apu Manglang made a covenant with the Apu Sanag, an immortal being, to protect Apu Manglang's people, in return for which Apu Manglang promised to treat the mountain as sacred and protect it. Mount Canatuan is also where the Subanon perform the *boklog*, their highest ritual for Thanksgiving, every seven years (Rights and Democracy 2007: 40; Sanz 2007: 110–12).

Each Subanon local territory is headed by a *timuay* (also spelt *timuoy* or *timouy*), or traditional leader, supported by a *soliling*, who provides the *timuay* administrative support. Only Subanon who belong to the *timuay* or *soliling* lineage, which is established mainly on a patrilineal basis, can legitimately fill these posts. Major disputes may be settled by a gathering of *timuay* from several local territories known as a Gukom, the supreme decision-making body of traditional leaders of the seven rivers that flow through the Canatuan area (Rights and Democracy 2007: 44; Rovillos and Tauli-Corpuz 2012).

From the 1970s, the territory of the Subanon was threatened by timber companies and by growing numbers of settlers and small-scale gold miners from elsewhere in Mindanao. Partly for this reason, under the leadership of Timuay Boy Anoy, the Subanon sought to take advantage of the opportunities being provided under Philippine law to gain formal recognition of their territorial rights. In 1993 members of the Subanon living in Canatuan applied for a CADC as permitted by DENR's Directive 1993/02, but this was not awarded until 1997, in part because the process to gain a title to land is complex and expensive, in part because a group of pro-mining Subanon, assisted by TVI, filed a competing CADC application. The CADC awarded in 1997 was converted into a CADT in June 2003 under the provisions of the IPRA. Long delays in processing applications for recognition of Indigenous rights also reflected the government's failure to provide adequate resources to the NCIP and other agencies to implement their mandates on the ground, to such an extent that NCIP officers regularly had to rely on mining companies for transport (World Bank 2007: 33, 37–9).

In 1990 a small-scale miner, Ramon Bosque, applied for a prospecting permit for a large area included Mount Canatuan. After teaming with a Philippine gold-mining firm, Benguet Corporation, Bosque was granted the prospecting permit. Together they applied for a Mineral Production Sharing Agreement (MPSA) in 1992. In 1994, TVI signed an agreement with Bosque and Benguet for an option to explore the area and to purchase the MPSA, which was still making its way through the government approval process. The Philippine government approved the MPSA in 1996, and in 1997 it was assigned to TVI. Under the MPSA, which had a 25-year term, the company was obliged to protect the environment, assist in the development of local communities, respect local rights, customs, and traditions, and pay a royalty equivalent to 1 per cent of the market value of minerals from the mine to Indigenous people who had a valid ancestral domain claim (Rights and Democracy 2007: 41).

TVI began operations in 2002 by processing waste dumps left from small-scale miners, and from 2004 it operated a profitable gold/copper open-cut mine at Mount Canatuan, employing some 600 people. The local Subanon, led by Timuay Anoy and his *soliling* Onsino Mato, were strongly opposed to TVI's operation because of its negative environmental impacts on land and water, and because they believed, correctly as it transpired, that it would result in the destruction of Mount Canatuan. The Subanon were supported in their opposition by farmers and fishers downstream from the mine, by a large majority of local government councillors in the area, and by the Catholic Church (Christian Aid and PIPlinks 2004; Sanz 2007, 2019). The Subanon sought an injunction to stop TVI, but long delays in the courts combined with their limited resources to pursue litigation negated their efforts in this regard. With the assistance of local and international non-government organizations (NGOs), the Subanon sought to pursue their opposition to TVI in international fora. They made representations to the United Nations Working Group on Indigenous Affairs in July 2001 and appeared before a Canadian Parliamentary Committee investigating the overseas activities of Canadian mining companies in March 2005.

The Subanon argued that under the provisions of the Mining Act (1995) and the IPRA, TVI was required to obtain their informed consent before undertaking any mining activity, and that the company had failed to do so. The company argued that because its MPSA was granted in 1996, the year before the Subanon CADC was accepted, s. 56 of the IPRA applied, which stated that 'Property rights within the ancestral domains already existing and/or vested upon passage of this Act, shall be recognized and respected.' In TVI's view this exempted the company from the need to obtain the consent of the Subanon (Christian Aid/PIPlinks 2004: 31). The NCIP supported the company's position (Alternative Law Group Inc. et al. 2009: iii).

From 1994 to 2001, TVI tried unsuccessfully to secure the endorsement of the recognized Subanon leaders, including Timuay Anoy. It then attacked the legitimacy of Anoy and Mato as Subanon leaders, claiming that they were motivated by self-interest because they held interests in small-scale mines that would be displaced by TVI's operations (Christian Aid/PIPlinks 2004: 40). TVI sought the consent of certain other Subanon people who were supportive of its operations, through the Siocon Subanon Association, Inc. (SSAI). The SSAI was established by Anoy and other leaders in 1991 as an officially registered organization because their traditional forms of leadership were not recognized by the Philippine state. Like Anoy, the SSAI had consistently and strongly opposed the entry of mining operations into their lands (Sanz 2007: 116). In November 2001, supporters of TVI convened a meeting of the SSAI board at the Sicon town centre, Zamboanga, without the knowledge or sanction of Anoy or Mato, who was Secretary of the SSAI. The TVI supporters pressed the meeting to pass a vote supporting the company's operations. The traditional leaders who were present opposed what they saw as a culturally unacceptable process and withdrew from the meeting. A new set of SSAI officers who supported the mine, some of whom were employed by TVI, was elected. The company recognized the new group, and subsequently signed a Memorandum of Agreement under which the 1 per cent royalty payable to Indigenous landowners was allocated to SSAI. Anoy and Mato challenged the SSAI elections. They argued that not all the current officers had been informed of the election, and that the new head of the SSAI was not of *timuay* lineage (Christian Aid/PIPlinks 2004; Rovillos and Tauli-Corpuz 2012: 143–7; Sanz 2007: 119–20).

The NCIP appointed a 'Council of Elders' to resolve the dispute among the Subanon. Anoy and his supporters objected, on the basis that many Council members were not residents of the area, that some were TVI employees, and that the NCIP had appointed the head of the pro-mining SSAI faction as chair of the Council. In September 2002, the NCIP convened a meeting of the Council in the presence of the Subanon community in Canatuan. That meeting passed a resolution opposing TVI's operations. The NCIP then organized a second meeting of the Council some weeks later in Zamboanga City, a day's travel from Canatuan, which was asked to again consider whether TVI's operations should be supported. After several Council members who objected to the community's decision being contested left the meeting, the Council voted to support TVI (Sanz 2007: 120–1).

Anoy then requested the Gukom of the seven rivers, the Subanon's supreme judicial body, to meet and consider the legitimacy of the Council of Elders. The Gukom summoned TVI to attend its meeting but the company ignored the summons and the Gukom's process. The Gukom rejected the Council of Elders' legitimacy on the basis that 21 of the 30 members were not of *timuay* lineage, that some were not even from the Canatuan area, and that there was no precedent in the Subanon traditional culture for having such a Council. The Gukom declared that these new structures were illegitimate under Subanon customary law and instructed the NCIP to declare agreements between them and TVI null and void. The Gukom imposed sanctions and penalties on the members of the Council, and communicated its findings to the NCIP in August 2004. The Gukom's statement included the following:

> Jose 'Boy' Anoy is the present Timuay of Canataun ... Undeniably the Anoy family in Siocon are the legitimate traditional leaders in Siocon ... the Council of Elders organised and constituted in gross violations of Subanon customs, traditions and practices is declared abolished. Furthermore, all acts entered into by said group of persons be declared NULL AND VOID ...There was not FREE PRIOR and INFORMED CONSENT of the Subanon residents of Canatuan and there was a failure to first ascertain the legal status of the traditional leaders. (cited in Christian Aid/PIPlinks 2004: 35; capitals in original)

The NCIP refused to accept the Gukom's instruction and insisted on treating the support of SSAI and the Council of Elders as constituting free prior and informed consent by the Subanon for TVI's operations (Alternative Law Group Inc. et al. 2009: 45, 50; Rights and Democracy 2007: 45; Sanz 2007: 122–4).

The World Bank later reported that members of the Council of Elders were offered PhP5,000 (US$90) to support the pro-TVI resolution at the meeting in Zamboanga in October 2002, and that the Council of Elders was paid PhP6,000 ($105) a month by TVI as an honorarium for attending meetings. However, the only people who attended Council of Elder meetings once payments were offered were pro-TVI members, because in Subanon culture taking money implies acceptance of and an obligation towards the giver (World Bank 2007: 54).

Another contentious aspect of TVI's operations involved its use of security forces. Canatuan is located in a region with a history of conflict between the Philippine army and the MILF and other armed groups. TVI's installations and personnel were attacked on several occasions, leading to fatalities among company staff and local residents. TVI established a security force made up of private security guards and members of the Special Civilian Armed Force Geographical Active Auxiliary, which were recruited, trained, and armed by the Philippine army and were under its command, but whose salaries were paid by the company. TVI also entered into agreements with elements of the Philippine police and army to provide security. Ostensibly the role of these forces was to protect TVI's mine and the surrounding population from the MILF. However, they were also used to repress Subanon opposition to TVI's operations and to forcibly evict small-scale miners from TVI's leases. For example, in September 1999, members of the Philippine National Police Mobile Group violently dispersed a human barricade formed by Subanon attempting to prevent the company from bringing drilling equipment onto their territory. A criminal suit filed against the police was dismissed by the courts (Rights and Democracy 2007, 47–8; see Sanz 2019 for other examples). The use of Philippine state security to repress opposition to mining conformed to a pattern common elsewhere in the Philippines (Christian Aid and PIPlinks 2004; Hamm et al. 2013).

In early 2009, as TVI was planning the closure of its mine at Mount Canatuan, a reconciliation was affected both among the Subanon who were previously in conflict over mining and between the Subanon and TVI. At a ceremony that brought together all the Subanon and followed a series of preliminary meetings and reconciliation events, Timuay Anoy was conferred with the title of Chieftain of the Seven Rivers of the Zamboanga Peninsula. His position was recognized and endorsed by all the members of the Council of Elders and by TVI's President and the NCIP's Regional Director, who attended the ceremony. The Subanon made gifts of traditional *timuay* clothing to senior TVI officials, which they wore during the ceremony (TVI Resources Development Inc. 2009). Two years later, TVI publicly admitted its fault in not recognizing Timuay Anoy as Subanon's leader and performed a mandatory cleansing ritual or *Boklug* at the company's expense and organized by the Gukom. A TVI manager stated that 'This is our atonement for desecrating the sacred Mt. Canatuan. It's an atonement for our sins.' The Subanon's Chief Elder explained that the ceremony was TVI's 'spiritual cleansing ritual and act of offering reconciliation to the people of Canatuan and our ancestors after they admitted the violations of Subanon customs and traditions that resulted to destructions in the ancestral domain and chaos of the community in Canatuan' (cited in PIPlinks 2011).

The actions of Anoy and other traditional leaders in reconciling with TVI and its supporters after resolutely opposing the company over many years, and just months after filing a complaint against the Philippines in the United Nations Committee for the Elimination of Racial Discrimination (CERD), surprised commentators and some of the Subanon's NGO allies (PIPlinks 2011; Sanz 2019: 385). Sanz, who had a long-term working and personal relationship with Anoy and other leaders, reports that three factors shaped their decision to pursue reconciliation (Sanz 2019: 390–6). First, TVI was applying for other mining interests in the region, as were other companies. Anoy and his colleagues felt that it was imperative to secure recognition from TVI and the NCIP as the legitimate leaders of the Subanon to ensure that mining companies and government agencies engaged with them in relation to future development in their territory (see also Alternative Law Group et al. 2009, 42). As one leader noted: 'If we are not going to do that (negotiate with TVI), the rest of the 8,000 hectares (of the Subanos ancestral domain in Canatuan) will be mined. Boy [Anoy] can now defend his ancestral domain' (cited in Sanz 2019: 393).

Second, the leaders felt it was essential to heal internal conflict among the Subanon if they were to have any chance of exercising control over externally driven development. The desire to pursue economic benefits offered by mining were leading some Subanon to abandon their traditional leadership, whose ongoing opposition to mining would further undermine their authority. Third, the leaders felt that the NGOs which had supported the Subanon in opposing TVI had provided the Subanon with no help in securing alternative development opportunities, and had no interest in doing so. As one *timuay* explained to Sanz (2019: 391–2):

> Although the NGOs have helped us in terms of campaigning against mining, they did little in addressing ... the economic hardship among the Subanos in Canatuan ... We expected that while we campaign against mining, the NGOs will also look after people who were displaced. They did not address that. While they are spending millions for the campaign against mining, they did not look after [our] livelihood. Now they criticized [Anoy], who is now recognized as Canatuan's traditional leader because he made an agreement with TVI. They (the NGOs) all criticized us.

Against this background the leaders felt it was imperative for the Subanon to engage with the mining industry to secure much-needed economic opportunities.

The experience of the Subanon shows clearly that the passage of legislation purporting to protect Indigenous rights is no guarantee that those rights will be protected in practice. Delays in registering the Subanon's interests in land, due in part to TVI's support for a rival claim, combined with the slowness and cost of the court system and the Subanon's lack of financial resources created serious constraints for them. TVI's access to state security forces meant that the ability of the Subanon to use direct action to halt the company's operations was limited. TVI refused to accept Subanon opposition to its mining of Mount Canatuan, and applied divisive tactics, financial inducements, and force to undermine the requirement for IFPIC, which is at the heart of the IPRA. Perhaps most significantly, the NCIP, designated by the IPRA as the primary government agency responsible for protecting and promoting the rights of Indigenous peoples, consistently supported the pro-mining faction of the Subanon, acted to undermine the Subanon's traditional leadership, and refused to accept the judgment of the Gukom that TVI's supporters lacked legitimate authority and could not provide Subanon consent to TVI's operations. The NCIP's activities were a major reason for the Subanon lodging a complaint with CERD against the Philippines government, which, as one *timuay* explained, was directed 'against the violations of the Philippine Government to our rights, customs and traditions' (cited in PIPlinks 2011).

Tampakan

Tampakan is regarded as the largest undeveloped copper and gold deposit in southeast Asia and the western Pacific, with reserves of 2.9 billion tonnes grading on average 0.6 per cent copper and 0.2g/t gold. It could support annual output of 375,000 tonnes of copper and 360,000 ounces of gold, which would make it one of the world's largest copper mines. It is located on the territory of the B'laan Indigenous peoples in a mountainous region in the east of Mindanao, 65 kilometres north of General Santos City and straddling the provinces of South Cotabato, Sultan Kudarat, Sarangani, and Davao del Sur. The Tampakan orebody was first discovered by the Australian company Western Mining Corporation (WMC) in the early 1990s. Its development would cover an area of about 10,000 hectares, and would require the creation of a large open pit with an area of 500 hectares and a depth of 785 metres, clearing of some 5,000 hectares of forest, and construction of a power plant, waste rock storage facility, tailings dam, a 100-kilometre underground pipeline from the mine to the coast, and a port. It would directly affect 11 B'laan communities and some 5,000 people would have to be resettled to make way for the mine. It would employ about 7,200 workers during construction and 1,800 workers during operations (Hamm et al. 2013; SMI 2011).

Thirty years after its discovery, Tampakan has yet to be developed. Attempts to do so continue, and the long history of the project is revealing in terms of relations between mining companies, Indigenous peoples, and the state.

The B'laan, like many Indigenous peoples in the Philippines, have been forced into increasingly remote regions and higher altitudes by pressure from successive waves of non-Indigenous settlers. Traditionally, swidden farmers engaged in shifting cultivation across an extensive territory, they have been forced to adopt a sedentary lifestyle as they have lost land to forestry companies and been encircled by immigrant farmers from elsewhere in the Philippines. The B'laan continue to rely heavily on a subsistence economy, which includes upland farming of rice and corn, and hunting, gathering, and fishing. Traditionally, headmen referred to as *Bong To* and *Bong Fulong*, the latter title given to especially knowledgeable and wise leaders, play the key role in B'laan governance. Where headmen felt they could not decide upon an issue on their own, they would call a community meeting. There was no intermediate structure between the *Bong To* and the community. In recent decades, state agencies have created 'tribal councils' as a vehicle through which the state seeks to organize its relations with the B'laan, creating internal tensions where tribal council leaders are not *Bong To* or *Bong Fulong* (Davis 1998; DINTEG and KALUHHAMIN 2015: 5).

Once WMC had established the scale of the Tampakan deposit, it signed an FTAA with the Philippine government in March 1995, covering an area of some 99,000 hectares. The company undertook a concerted effort to engage with the B'laan and obtain their consent to develop the project. It invested substantially in community development activities, including health facilities, mobile clinics, education facil-ities, and agricultural advice. It also engaged in extensive consultation activities, and provided ethnographic and archaeological teams over a period of three years to support the B'laan in applying to the Philippine government for certificates of ancestral domain claims. As WMC noted at the time, it was in the company's interest to 'clarify the status of the land and establish, as far as is possible, any underlying titles' (Davis 1998: 240). By 1998 a number of these applications had been accepted. Given a history of broken promises by timber companies, farmers, and the state, the B'laan demanded written agreements with WMC in relation to Tampakan (Davis 1998: 239). WMC negotiated agreements with the B'laan and also with three affected municipalities, which included a commitment to pay a royalty on gross project rev-enues of 1 per cent to the municipalities, in addition to the 1 per cent royalty payable to the B'laan under the Mining Act (1995). Under the agreement with the B'laans of the Folu Bato ancestral domain, the B'laans gave their consent to WMC to explore the area for copper and gold deposits, allowed company personnel, contractors, vehicles, and equipment access to the land, and undertook not to prevent the company from carrying out activities permitted under its FTAA. The B'laans would receive a range of benefits including the 1 per cent royalty, a community quota for employment, finan-cial assistance to students, and emergency medical assistance (World Bank 2007: 47).

Despite the signing of this agreement, attitudes among the B'laan towards the com-pany and the project were divided. Some supported WMC on the basis that the project would bring much-needed education, health, and transport service to the region which the Philippine government was unable to unwilling to provide, and that WMC could provide them with valuable support in developing their communi-ties and in resisting further incursions by non-Indigenous settlers. One senior B'laan man expressed this position thus:

We, the leaders of Bong Mal, need help to explain our situation to the government. We are very poor and cannot afford even the salt we need in our diet. But, we do not have any advocates. We would like WMC to stay in our area and be our advocate. Talk to the government and help us. (cited in Davis 1998: 242)

Others were concerned at WMC's practice of engaging with tribal councils rather than the traditional B'laan leadership, and that the project, especially because of the extent of forest clearing required and the need to resettle thousands of people, threatened their connection to their land and its sacred places, and their continued existence. B'laan and other groups outside the immediate project area were also concerned about the impact of the project on watersheds, downstream water quality, irrigation systems, and fishponds (Hamm et al. 2013: 28). WMC attributed opposition to the project to civil society groups and environmental activists, and to non-Indigenous squatters resentful of WMC's support for formal recognition of B'laan title to their territory (Davis 1998: 240–1). However, it is clear that some B'laan were indeed strongly opposed to WMC's operations and regarded B'laan leaders who supported WMC as having betrayed their responsibilities to defend B'laan territories and interests, or as having been tricked into signing agreements they did not understand (Caruso et al 2003: 59–60). Opponents of the mine began attacking WMC property and employees, and took refuge in the most remote B'laan communities when the police and military responded. The NPA was already active in the Tampakan area, and some B'laan reportedly joined its ranks because of their opposition to WMC and the Philippine government (DINTEG and KALUHHAMIN 2015: 8, 15; Hamm et al. 2013: 21, 53).

In 1997, a church-based tribal association, La Bugal-B'laan, sued the DENR for violating the 1987 Philippine Constitution by awarding the Tampakan orebody to a foreign firm, WMC, with 100 per cent equity. Seven years later in February 2004, the Philippine Supreme Court ruled in favour of the La Bugal-B'laan. The Court's decision would not come into effect until the expiration of a specified time period for lodging a motion for reconsideration. The Philippine government and mining interests quickly filed a motion, and in December 2004 the Supreme Court reversed its decision after extensive lobbying by mining industry interests and government officials, including the President, congressmen, senators, and department secretaries (Tan 2006: 195). Tan (2006) in a detailed analysis of the Court's second decision noted that it is 'remarkable' the extent to which the majority judges endorsed the government's arguments on foreign investments and on the need for community interests to be sacrificed in pursuit of economic growth. 'Far from seeking a balance between the interests of developers and affected communities ... the Court swung the pendulum in the favour of the pro-mining lobby ... there was little attempt at reconciliation; the Court adopted a simple all-or-nothing utilitarian stance, suggesting that those who stand in the path of the collective good must simply give way' (Tan 2006: 202).

In the meantime, WMC had transferred its rights to explore and develop the Tampakan orebody to another corporation, Sagittarius Mines, Inc. (SMI). SMI had a complex ownership structure comprising Class A shares, the owners of which control the project, and Class B shares, which constitute a non-controlling interest. The majority of Class A shares were held by a Swiss-based multinational mining company, Xstrata, which in turn merged with a British/Swiss mining and commodity trading company, Glencore, in 2013. The remaining Class A shares were held by an Australia-based firm, Indophil Resources, in which Glencore and Philippine businesses and politicians held interests. Class B shares in SMI were held by the Philippine-owned Tampakan group of companies.

SMI expanded exploration activities in the proposed project area, increased infrastructure development, and worked to obtain the environmental and other approvals required for the project to proceed, including a certificate of IFPIC from the B'laan. Between 2009 and 2012, the company sought stakeholder input for the proposed mine plan and its environmental impact assessment (EIA), through a series of small, private consultation meetings and larger public meetings. In June 2011, the company presented its EIA to stakeholders, and planned to commence production in 2016 (SMI 2011). By 2012, SMI's workforce counted 377 employees, while an additional 946 contractors were commissioned. Nearly half of employees were drawn from the surrounding region and 53 were members of the B'laan communities. SMI expanded its scholarship programme, supporting 24,963 students between 2008 and 2011 (Hamm et al. 2013: 43, 50).

SMI's employment and community engagement activities, especially in the field of education, won support among some B'laan people and other residents of the region (Hamm et al 2013: 50). However, SMI incurred criticism for focusing its engagement too heavily on tribal councils rather than on the traditional tribal leader system and community members more generally (Hamm et al. 2013: 35–6). More broadly, as the company's plans became clearer, opposition to the Tampakan project grew not only among sections of the B'laan, but also among civil society groups, including the Catholic Church and environmental NGOs, both concerned about the environmental and social impacts of large-scale mining generally and especially of open-cut mining. One indication of this opposition was when the government of South Cotabato in 2010 passed an Environment Code banning open-pit mining in the province. In January 2012, the DENR denied the company's application for an Environmental Clearance Certificate (ECC), citing the South Cotabato Environment Code prohibiting open-pit mining. SMI appealed this decision, and after President Acquino issued an executive order requiring local governments to align their local ordinances with national policies, SMI's ECC was issued subject to a number of conditions, including attainment of IFPIC from affected Indigenous communities.

Local resistance continued to escalate and became increasingly violent. In 2008, the NPA twice blew up SMI's diamond drill rigs and attacked and burned its base camp. A special Civilian Armed Auxiliary commanded by the military, later called Task Force KITACO, was created by the 10th Infantry Division that was providing security to SMI. The company provided a salary supplement for each member of the 60-man Task Force and made an annual contribution to the KITACO Secretariat (DINTEG and KALUHHAMIN 2015: 9; Hamm et al. 2013: 27). By 2011, a number of B'laan had openly joined the armed resistance to SMI. In February of that year, a group of B'laan led by Daguil Capion formally declared armed resistance (*pangayaw*) against SMI and the government, and in June and July they launched ambushes against government troops. SMI suffered attacks on its staff and contractors, resulting in three fatalities. Philippine troops and auxiliaries were active in repressing resistance to SMI's activities (Hamm et al. 2013: 26; Sarmiento 2012). In October

2012, Daguil Capion's wife and his two children were killed by soldiers searching for Capion. Capion's younger brother, Kitari, was killed by troops in January 2013, and another B'laan leader, Datu Anting Freay, and his 16-year-old son were killed by members of Task Force KITACO and Philippine troops in August 2013 (DINTEG and KALUHHAMIN 2015, 10; Franciscans International 2014). Criminal charges were laid against an army colonel and a number of soldiers for the murder of Capion's family, but were dismissed in August 2013 by Davao del Sur's provincial prosecutor because evidences filed were 'circumstantial and insufficient to establish probable cause of murder'. On 18 March 2015, the Department of Justice ruled that 13 soldiers involved should be charged with murder (DINTEG and KALUHHAMIN 2015: 21, 22). As far as I can establish, this case did not go to trial.

Despite armed repression, resistance to SMI's project continued unabated. In January 2014, B'laan leaders lobbied NCIP to make a declaration that Tampakan did not have IFPIC, and B'laan and other community leaders and church groups collected petitions against SMI's project. One B'laan leader stated: 'Our community does not want the NCIP to conduct FPIC for mining in our land because this will only cause more problems and troubles. There are a lot of casualties and violations done against our people. How much more if we allow them to enter our territory?' (cited in BankTrack 2016). In December 2014, thousands of people barricaded the national highway in Digos City demanding the withdrawal of Glencore-SMI from the region and that troops leave B'laan communities (BankTrack 2016).

In June 2015, Glencore sold its stake in Tampakan, having earlier disposed of its subsidiary's holding in Indophil Resources. The Tampakan project was now controlled by Philippine interests, including Alsons Prime Investments Corporation, whose owners include a number of prominent politicians and business leaders.

In June 2016, the Mines and Geosciences Bureau issued an executive order granting SMI a 12-year extension to its FTAA, four years before it was due to expire. The extension was not made public until January 2020. The 2016 election of Duterte as president seemed to bode ill for SMI as his electoral platform included a nationwide ban on open-cut mining. The fate of the project appeared to be sealed in February 2017 when Duterte's Environment Secretary, Gina Lopez, cancelled SMI's ECC. However, in May 2019 the ECC was restored by the Office of the President. By July 2020, the DENR was waiting for SMI to submit the remaining regulatory requirements, including the certification on IFPIC from the NCIP. The Catholic Diocese of Marbel and allied groups stated their intention to reinvigorate their campaign against Tampakan due to concerns regarding the plight of the Indigenous peoples and the environment. The Bishop of Marbel stated that: 'Regardless of different cultures and beliefs, we are making a loud statement … that the Tampakan project will not be allowed to proceed' (cited in Sarmiento 2020).

SMI received a further setback in October 2020 when a Philippine court dismissed a request by pro-mining groups for an injunction against the South Cotabato province's ban on open-cut mining. However, on 23 April 2021, President Duterte issued Executive Order 130, lifting a national moratorium on open-cut mining that had been in place for nine years. The decision was regarded as likely to lead to the resurrection of SMI's project (Calderon 2021). The 30-year battle over Tampakan appears to be far from over.

Conclusion

The Philippines is unusual in recognizing Indigenous rights in its Constitution and in legislation, and in enshrining the principle of IFPIC in law. Both projects examined in this chapter faced overwhelming or substantial Indigenous opposition, expressed for example in legal action taken against projects or their proponents, in direct action such as protests, petitions, and blockades, and especially in the case of Tampakan, in violence. Yet despite the legal protection of Indigenous rights, TVI was able to conduct mining on Subanon territory for over a decade, while the Tampakan project, despite 30 years of opposition from B'laan people and their allies, has still not been definitively halted.

A major factor explaining this outcome is the support of state agencies for mining. This is evident in the role of the security forces in supporting exploration and mining, and in suppressing Indigenous opposition to it. State support is also evident in the role of the NCIP, whose reason for existing is to give effect to Indigenous rights, in undermining legitimate Subanon leadership and supporting pro-mining individuals who lacked support among the Subanon, an approach by no means confined to this particular case (Balana 2011; Christian Aid and PIPlinks 2004: 13; Wetzlmaier 2012). Indeed, in 2011 a senior NCIP official admitted that the process of acquiring consent from tribal communities in connection to mining permits 'has been marred with irregularities and rampant violations of the Indigenous People's Rights Act of 1997' (cited in Caliguid 2011). State support is especially obvious in the Supreme Court's reversal of its finding that the grant of a FTAA to WMC was illegal, under pressure from the mining industry and politicians.

The state's support for mining reflected both the severity of the economic challenges facing the Philippines and the conviction of politicians that mining offered one of the few available hopes of overcoming these challenges. It also reflected the close personal links between politicians, senior military leaders and the mining industry. For example, President Duterte's Finance Secretary, Carlos Dominguez, was previously a mining company executive, resigning just two weeks before Duterte's inauguration, and Dominguez's brother Paul is a former president of SMI, developer of Tampakan. Paul is closely linked to the Alcantras family, major shareholder in Alsons Consolidated Resources, which took over Glencore's share in SMI (Calderon 2021). TVI's security group was headed by a former army colonel (Sanz 2019: 116), and after his retirement General Alexander Yapching operated an armed security service providing protection for mining companies, including some that were operating illegally on Indigenous lands (Philippine Daily Inquirer 2011). The form of state support for mining reflects broader aspects of Philippine politics and society. The use of security forces reflects in part an unstable political context characterized by violent communist and Islamic movements designed to overthrow the state and, linked to this, the frequent involvement of security forces and state-sponsored militias in human rights abuses, including extrajudicial killings.

It was not the case that state agencies always supported mining interests. As noted earlier, the courts upheld the legitimacy of South Cotabato's ban on open-cut mining, and in 2020 the Court of Appeals denied a petition by the Australian company Oceana Gold to allow mining operations to resume after a lower court had supported a decision by the provincial governor to close Oceana's mine when its FTAA expired (Abagado 2020). However, the weight of state institutions is overwhelmingly aligned with the mining industry and against Indigenous peoples when the two are in conflict.

Another important factor shaping outcomes is the support of some Indigenous people for mining. Faced with an absence of state-funded services and economic opportunities, community engagement programmes such as those mounted by WMC and SMI at Tampakan persuaded some Indigenous leaders that it was advisable to support mining. TVI, WMC, and SMI were all able to negotiate agreements that had the support of a section of the Indigenous community. This undermines the ability of Indigenous peoples to maintain a united front in their dealings with mining companies and the state. Where companies are willing to manipulate such divisions to gain some form of approval for their operations, as occurred most obviously in the case of TVI, then divisions within Indigenous communities are further sharpened.

The Philippines also highlights the agency and persistence of Indigenous peoples, supported in many cases by the Catholic Church, which occupies a powerful position in Philippine society, and by civil society groups, which have remained very active despite the repressive activities of the state. The B'laan, notwithstanding 30 years of company persuasion and state repression, have with their allies consistently sought to prevent development of Tampakan. So far they have succeeded. The Subanon's traditional leadership used a wide variety of local, national, and international fora to oppose TVI's operations and then, in the face of a situation stacked heavily against them, used an agreement with TVI during the final stages of its operations to win widespread recognition of their legitimacy from both company and state. Faced with the prospect of further exploration and mining on their territory, they adopted a strategic approach and sought to improve their negotiating position for the long haul. As Sanz notes (2019: 300), the Subanon case highlights the fact that Indigenous responses to mining involve 'a dynamic process with everchanging consequences as actors improvise and strategize in response to the actions of other actors'.

The experience of Indigenous peoples in the Philippines is mirrored in other parts of Asia. In the immediate postcolonial period, states generally resisted recognition of Indigenous rights, but in recent decades there has been a growing willingness to afford formal recognition in policy and law (see IWGIA 2021 for examples from Malaysia, Bangladesh, India, and Cambodia). However, in these and other cases there has been a failure to translate formal recognition into more positive outcomes for Indigenous peoples on the ground. Government repression of civil society and Indigenous groups, limits on press freedom, and use of security forces to protect mines and suppress opposition to mining, including through extrajudicial killings, is also common across the region (APWLD 2009; IWGIA 2021: 208, 221–2, 257–9, 272–4). However, as in the Philippines, Indigenous peoples continue to assert their rights strongly, and insist on controlling mining in their territories (IWGIA 2021).

15

Australia and Canada

A Test for Indigenous Engagement Strategies

Introduction

Australia and Canada are major mineral producers whose economies rely heavily on exports of natural resources. By the end of the nineteenth century, European immigrants had settled virtually all lands suitable for commercial agriculture in both countries, destroying the foundations of autonomous Indigenous economies, except in geographically remote and climatically extreme regions. Australia and Canada are federal, Westminster-style constitutional democracies and in recent decades both have, though in different ways, recognized the existence of inherent Indigenous rights in land. That recognition has been uneven across space and time, and this, combined with the different pace and extent of colonial settlement in different regions, has resulted in a patchwork of institutional and political arrangements governing relations between Indigenous peoples and mining.

This chapter analyses the recent experience of Indigenous peoples in Australia and Canada with mining, seeking to establish broad patterns rather than to focus in detail on individual mining projects, of which there are 350 in Australia alone, many of them on Indigenous territories (Geoscience Australia 2022; Hunter et al. 2015: 517). It provides a brief summary of settlement history in both countries, discusses how recognition of Indigenous rights has developed, and outlines the nature of relations between Indigenous peoples and the mining industry. On this last point, both countries are now characterized by an almost universal adoption of negotiated agreements as the primary mechanism for governing those relations. This raises two issues. First, what shapes the content of these agreements in terms of permitting Indigenous peoples to share in the benefits of mining, and in allowing them to influence its impact on their traditional territories? Second, what effect do agreements, and the presence of mining activities more generally, have on the well-being of Indigenous communities in mining regions?

A key finding is that there is wide diversity in the content of agreements and in outcomes from mining, with significant implications for Indigenous livelihoods and well-being. I seek to explain this diversity and consider its wider implications. In relation to agreements, an important explanatory factor is that in most cases Indigenous people do not have a right under Australian or Canadian law to prevent mining and so cannot insist that mining must generate substantial benefits, and that

Indigenous Peoples and Mining. Ciaran O'Faircheallaigh, Oxford University Press. © Ciaran O'Faircheallaigh (2023).
DOI: 10.1093/oso/9780192894564.003.0015

its costs must be contained, if it is go ahead. Legal regimes in both countries create *opportunities* for negotiations to generate such positive outcomes, but realization of these opportunities depends on the institutional arrangements that apply in specific cases, and on the organizational and political capacity of individual First Peoples to insist that preconditions be met before mining occurs. These factors are highly variable, explaining the diverse outcomes from agreements. In relation to the final impact of mining on Indigenous well-being, an additional variable comes into play, involving the specific ways in which revenues from mining are managed and used by Indigenous communities. Here also there is diversity, illustrated by reviewing three cases where royalties generated by mining have had different consequences for recipient communities. The chapter finishes with a discussion of strategies being pursued by Indigenous peoples in both countries to gain greater control over mining, given their lack of legal powers to decide whether or not it should proceed.

The wide range of outcomes evident in Australia and Canada affords a valuable opportunity to gain insights into the factors shaping the impacts of mining on Indigenous peoples and territories.

Indigenous peoples and settler histories in Australia and Canada

In 2016, the most recent date for which census data are available, an estimated 798,400 people, or 3.3 per cent of Australia's population, identified as Aboriginal or Torres Strait Islander, Australia's two Indigenous peoples (AIHW 2022). Some 4.9 per cent of Canada's population, or 1.7 million people, identify as First Nation or 'North American Indian', Métis, or Inuit (Statistics Canada 2018).

British settlement in Australia commenced in 1788, and over the following century much of the continent was appropriated from its original owners. Virtually no land remained under Aboriginal ownership in Victoria, New South Wales, the southern portions of Queensland, South Australia, and Western Australia. The Aboriginal population was decimated (Butlin 1993: 139, 229), reflecting the impact of introduced diseases, warfare (including state-sanctioned massacres), competition from settlers for land and water, and the profound impact of dispossession on the social structures of Aboriginal peoples. In regions of Australia remote from major urban centres and unsuited to Western agriculture, Aboriginal people were generally left in possession of their traditional lands. However, no legal recognition was afforded to their interests in land. While such areas might be classified as 'Aboriginal reserves', their reserve status could be revoked at any time at the discretion of government and the land made available to miners or pastoralists (see Chapter 3).

European settlement of Canada commenced in the early seventeenth century, and during the next 200 years focused primarily on the extraction of natural resources including furs, fish, and timber. Particularly in the fur industry, First Peoples undertook much of the required labour, and the extent and intensity of European settlement was therefore limited. From the early nineteenth century, large-scale agricultural development increased, particularly in Ontario, Quebec, and the Prairie provinces of central Canada. The European population expanded greatly and as this occurred the First Peoples of Canada experienced patterns of colonial impact similar to those experienced in Australia: large-scale dispossession in regions suitable for Western agriculture; precipitous decline in populations; and the weakening and in some cases destruction of First Peoples' social and governing structures (Alfred 2009).

There were two fundamental differences between the colonial contexts in Australia and Canada. The first was the key role initially played by Canadian First Peoples in allowing economic exploitation to occur, which had no equivalent in Australia, where furbearing animals were absent and where the animals hunted by Aboriginal people competed directly with the sheep and cattle of the colonizers. The second key difference was that while Australia had but one colonial power and no adjacent colonies of any significance, Canada had two colonial powers in Britain and France and had America as its neighbour, which made First Peoples valuable allies for the warring colonizers. In combination, these two factors resulted in recognition of First Peoples' political and economic rights in ways that have no precedent in Australia. Two specific aspects warrant mention. The first was the Royal Proclamation of 1763. This established a process for obtaining First Peoples' lands by negotiation and treaty, and stated that until that process had occurred the 'Nations or Tribes of Indians' were to remain unmolested in their use of land and under the protection of the Crown. Only the Crown, not private individuals, could acquire land from Indians. The second was that the British Crown, and subsequently Canada, signed treaties with numerous First Nations in eastern and central Canada, though treaty making had come to an end by the time that Canada came to engage in a systematic way with First Peoples in much of British Columbia (BC) and the far north (Russell 2005: 40–2).

Despite these differences, by the mid-twentieth century the position and status of First Peoples in both countries were similar. Their Indigenous economies had been largely destroyed by the impact of white settlement, and they had been subject to racist and discriminatory government policies, denial of civil and political rights, and government interference in personal and family life, including the removal of children. This experience left First Peoples politically and economically marginalized (for a detailed discussion, see Althaus and O'Faircheallaigh 2019). While civil and political rights were gradually restored in the 1960s and 1970s, the legacy of the colonial impact continues today, and is reflected in social and economic disadvantage relative to mainstream populations. In both countries, on average Indigenous incomes are substantially lower and unemployment substantially higher than national averages; levels of formal education are relatively low; and access to physical services such as housing, sewage, and clean water is poor. Health status also tends to be poor, as indicated, for example, by high infant mortality rates and low life expectancy. In both countries, Indigenous people are hugely overrepresented in the criminal justice system (AIHW 2022; Government of Canada 2013; Health Council of Canada 2013). On the other hand, in both countries, Indigenous populations are youthful and growing rapidly; connections to land and to culture and kin continue to offer powerful sources of resilience and vitality (AIHW 2022; Watego 2021); and, as discussed in the next section, after long and arduous battles, important victories have been achieved in winning state recognition of inherent Indigenous rights in land and resources.

Recognition of inherent Indigenous rights in land

Australia

For nearly 200 years after the arrival of Europeans, no recognition was afforded to the rights of Aboriginal and Torres Strait Islander peoples in their traditional lands. From the mid-1960s, Aboriginal and Torres Strait Islander peoples began to push for legal recognition of their status as landowners. In 1976, this pressure had its first tangible result when the federal government introduced the Aboriginal Land Rights (Northern Territory) Act (1976) (henceforth the Land Rights Act). The Land Rights Act allows Aboriginal people in the Northern Territory to claim ownership of their traditional lands and, where they are successful, to determine whether mineral exploration and development should occur on their land. Major changes occurred in 1992 because of the Australian High Court's decision in the *Mabo* case. The Court agreed with litigants from the island of Mer in the Torres Strait that their inherent rights in land were not extinguished by the imposition of colonial rule. Those rights could survive, if they had not been extinguished by valid government grants of interest to third parties and as long as the people involved had maintained their connection with their traditional lands. The Court's decision did not threaten existing non-Indigenous interests in land, including mining interests, but it did set aside the fundamental assumption of land law in Australia, that inherent Aboriginal and Torres Strait Islander interests in land were extinguished as Britain established its colonial rule.

The Australian government responded to the *Mabo* decision by introducing federal legislation, the Native Title Act (1993). This validated existing titles in land, but also created a process through which Aboriginal and Torres Strait Islander peoples could claim land in which native title survived. It created what is called the 'Right to Negotiate', which provides groups that have won recognition of their native title or registered native title claims with an opportunity to negotiate about the terms of any mineral development with the company involved and with the state government that proposes to issue the relevant mining tenements. Unlike the Land Rights Act, the Native Title Act does not confer on landowners a veto over exploration or mining, but rather gives them a limited opportunity to sit down and negotiate with developers. If agreement is not reached, developers can apply to a government tribunal, the National Native Title Tribunal (NNTT), for permission to proceed in any case, which is granted in almost every case. To avoid this situation, Aboriginal landowners may sign agreements even where they are unhappy with their terms, as the alternative is that the project proceeds and they receive none of its benefits and have no opportunity to negotiate measures to mitigate its impacts (for a full discussion, see O'Faircheallaigh 2016).

Canada

First Nations that signed treaties continued to occupy and use (small) portions of their traditional territories. However, reserves were held in trust on behalf of band (group) members by Canada, which exercised substantial control over land use and over time allowed large areas of reserve land to be alienated and/or used for commercial purposes. The Canadian government's view has been that native title is extinguished in areas subject to treaties, a view rejected by many affected First Nations people. As in Australia, Canada's legal system did not recognize the existence of any *inherent* First Peoples' rights in land. This changed in 1973 when Canada's Supreme Court, in the *Calder* case, recognized that such rights did exist at the time of European settlement, and could continue to exist under certain circumstances. In 1982 a change to Canada's Constitution entrenched 'existing Aboriginal and treaty rights' in the following terms:

35. (1) The existing aboriginal and treaty rights of the aboriginal peoples of Canada are hereby recognized and affirmed.
    (2) In this Act, 'aboriginal peoples of Canada' includes the Indian, Inuit and Métis peoples of Canada.
    (3) For greater certainty, in subsection (1) 'treaty rights' includes rights that now exist by way of land claims agreements or may be so acquired.

The Constitution does not define these rights, and subsequent attempts to define them in negotiations involving Canada, the provinces, and First Peoples failed (Abale 1999: 449–50).

In the area of land and native title, it has been left to the Supreme Court to do so. In a series of decisions including *Delgamuuk, Sparrow, Haida Nation,* and *Mikisew Cree First Nation,* the Court has both helped define the content of First Peoples' rights, which importantly are deemed to confer the right to a share of mineral and other resources extracted from the land, and laid down substantial requirements for government to consult with First Peoples and in some cases to accommodate their interests before granting any rights in their traditional lands to third parties (AANDC 2014; Gibson and O'Faircheallaigh 2015: 29–32).

As noted earlier, treaty making ceased in the late 1920s and left large areas of northern Canada and BC without treaties. After the *Calder* case, the Canadian government began to negotiate a series of land claim settlements or 'modern treaties', designed in part to address issues of Indigenous rights and resource development. While land claim settlements have evolved over time and differ significantly in their specific provisions, their basic structure is similar. First Peoples are granted surface and sub-surface rights to a portion of their traditional lands, typically around communities and in areas of critical importance for key food species, and resource development cannot occur in these areas without their consent. They also hold surface rights to somewhat larger areas, and potential developers of resources in these areas will have to negotiate access before developing them. Several settlements have an explicit requirement for negotiation of impacts and benefits agreements (IBAs), while others, by conferring surface rights, establish such a requirement *de facto*. Finally, native title rights will be extinguished over the remainder of the group's traditional lands, though First Peoples typically retain rights to hunt and fish and to be involved with government in the management of wildlife (Gibson and O'Faircheallaigh 2015: 32–3; Usher 1997). Reflecting the history of treaty making in Canada, land claim settlements also involve the creation of Aboriginal governments which have jurisdiction over nominated areas including land management, education, culture, and criminal justice. There is no equivalent in Australia. Negotiation of land claims is time consuming, in part because of the reluctance of many First Peoples to accept extinguishment of native title rights over large parts of their traditional lands.

The dominance and impact of agreement making

A striking characteristic of relations between Indigenous peoples and the mining industry in Australia and Canada is the central role played by negotiated agreements. By way of illustration, there were over 400 active agreements in effect between First Peoples and mining companies in Canada in 2020 (Natural Resources Canada 2020). In both countries, agreements are now in effect a prerequisite for all major mining projects on land which has been recognized as Indigenous, or which is or may be subject to claim by its Indigenous owners. The reason for their prevalence is somewhat different in each country. In Australia, the key driver is the passage of the Native Title Act and the 'Right to Negotiate' it confers on native title holders or claimants. As of January 2022, 63 per cent of Australia's land area is the subject of a native title determination or is subject to a native title claim, and the proportion of land in these categories is much higher in Australia's major mining regions (NNTT 2022). There is, of course, no requirement for native title holders or claimants to engage in negotiations, nor any certainty that if they do negotiate they will achieve an acceptable agreement. However, if they fail to negotiate, the NNTT will usually allow the project to proceed in any case, creating a strong motivation for them to do so. In addition to the Native Title Act, the Northern Territory's Land Rights Act and Queensland's Mineral Resources Act (1989) also require negotiation of an agreement before development proceeds. This means that virtually all new projects trigger an *opportunity* for Aboriginal landowners to negotiate with the developer.

In Canada, many land claim settlements contain a requirement for negotiation of IBAs or land access requirements that trigger negotiations. A more general influence arises from the decisions of the Supreme Court regarding the Crown's duty to consult with First Peoples, and in some cases to accommodate their interests, before granting rights in land to commercial entities, including mining companies. While the Crown cannot transfer the duty to consult to mining companies, it can delegate procedural aspects to them. In other words, the negotiation of an agreement between a mining company and a First People can be taken as evidence that it has been consulted and that its interests are being taken into account (Gibson and O'Faircheallaigh 2015: 30).

In both countries, increased recognition of Indigenous rights and the growing political mobilization of Indigenous peoples and organizations have led some mining companies and government entities to negotiate agreements even where there is no legal requirement to do so. For multinational mining companies, the growing international recognition of Indigenous rights may also be a factor.

In terms of the content of negotiated agreements in Australia and Canada, all agreements include the provision of some form of consent for the mining company's operations, and this, of course, is a key reason for their negotiation from the perspective of industry. Virtually all agreements have a strong emphasis on generating employment and business development opportunities for their Indigenous signatories. This is not surprising given the fact that Indigenous peoples in both countries experience serious disadvantage in terms of their access to incomes and employment. There is considerable variation in provisions in this area. At one end of the spectrum, some agreements contain only general commitments by project operators to 'make best endeavours' to create employment or business opportunities for Indigenous signatories. At the other end, extensive and specific provisions may be included which establish goals and time frames in terms of the percentage of employees who should be Indigenous or of contracts that should be awarded to Indigenous businesses; provide for remedial action or alternative benefits if these goals are not achieved; and include measures to make the workplace conducive to Indigenous recruitment, retention, and advancement. These measures may include initiatives to combat racism in the workplace, arrangements for Indigenous mentoring, and special leave arrangements to facilitate maintenance of Indigenous cultural practices. All agreements include some form of financial payment, though here also there is great variation, a point I return to shortly.

Most agreements seek to supplement existing legislative provisions to achieve greater protection from negative environmental and cultural impacts. In Australia, provisions designed to protect places of cultural and spiritual significance tend be especially extensive, reflecting the inadequacy of legislation in this regard and the ubiquity of places of contemporary cultural and spiritual significance in many landscapes affected by mining (O'Faircheallaigh 2008).

Another general feature of agreements in both countries is that the state is usually not a party, with agreements involving only the project developer and First Peoples. There are exceptions, usually where projects are very large and have wider implications for regional development (for examples, see O'Faircheallaigh 2015, 2016). This does not mean that the state is 'absent'. State actors including legislatures and courts play a key role in creating the legal frameworks within which negotiations occur, and their decisions regarding provision of negotiation funding for Indigenous communities, or regarding whether or not to apply discretionary powers to acquire land compulsorily for mining projects, can have a major influence on negotiation outcomes.

As noted in Chapter 9, my 2016 study of 45 Australian agreements indicates that outcomes from negotiations between the mining industry and First Peoples in Australia have been highly variable (O'Faircheallaigh 2016). Similar findings have been documented through case studies of negotiations in Australia and Canada (O'Faircheallaigh 2016), and through analysis of the implementation provisions of some 60 agreements in both countries (O'Faircheallaigh 2002a); in relation to liq-uefied natural gas (LNG) projects in Australia (O'Neill 2016); and in research by Canadian scholars on agreement outcomes in Canada (see, for instance, Bradshaw et al. 2016; Craik et al. 2017; St-Laurent and Le Billon 2015: 599).

The extent of the variability in outcomes can be illustrated by a comparison of two pairs of agreements concluded within similar time frames in Australia and Canada. The first comparison involves agreements negotiated in the early 2010s for development of LNG projects in the Kimberley region of Western Australia and in central Queensland. The LNG projects planned for both regions were similar in scale, constituting massive industrial projects requiring investment of billions of dollars and potentially creating significant environmental and cultural impacts: for example, through numerous shipping movements, their demand for large quantities of water, and their large construction workforces (KLC 2010a; O'Faircheallaigh 2015; O'Neill 2016).

In the Kimberley region, a series of agreements signed in 2011 with the state of Western Australia and the lead project proponent, Woodside Energy Ltd (WEL), offered affected Aboriginal landowners and communities, and their regional repre-sentative organization, the Kimberley Land Council (KLC), extensive economic ben-efits and a major role in project management of a proposed Browse LNG 'Precinct'. This Precinct would constitute a single location for processing all gas piped ashore from the Browse gas field off the Kimberley coast. Agreement provisions include:

- A A$1.5 billion economic benefits package, including annual payments by WEL linked to project scale, and substantial additional and ongoing state government investments in community services and economic development initiatives.
- Extensive funding for agreement implementation and monitoring of environ-mental impacts, including government funding for an environmental compli-ance officer to be employed on site for the whole of project life, which could exceed 40 years.
- Prohibition of any further processing of offshore gas, and of any industrial projects using gas as a feedstock, along the Kimberley coast.
- Protection of Aboriginal rights to object to, and seek judicial review of, pro-posed conditions for grant of project titles for the LNG Precinct.
- Protective mechanisms for Aboriginal cultural heritage in addition to those provided by legislation.

- A right for Aboriginal traditional owners unilaterally to require the developer to build a desalination plant if they fear adverse impacts from use of water from a major aquifer (O'Faircheallaigh 2015; State of Western Australia et al. 2011).

At exactly the same time as the Browse LNG agreements were signed at Kimberley, agreements were signed between oil and gas companies and Aboriginal traditional owners in relation to a number of proposed LNG projects in central Queensland. The outcomes of negotiations in this latter case were starkly different. For instance, these agreements:

- Have limited financial benefits. In some cases, these consist only of one-off payments on signing of agreements with no ongoing benefits. In others, fixed annual payments are made only during the first 10 years of projects that can have operational lives greater than 40 years. A number of these agreements contain total financial benefits smaller than the amount the KLC received to consult with traditional owners in preparation for negotiations in relation to the Browse LNG project.
- Contain no dedicated implementation funding.
- Provide no role for traditional owners in environmental management.
- Have no review clauses that might allow changes to what are highly disadvantageous agreements the future.
- Constrain the rights of Aboriginal people to object to or criticize projects. For instance, under one agreement the Aboriginal signatories state that they 'will not … question or challenge, or commence any claim, proceeding or action to question or challenge, the validity of (and also will not make any formal or informal objection or adverse public comment in relation to) … the [LNG] Project'.[1]

Similarly, highly variable outcomes can be observed in Canada. For instance, as in the Kimberley LNG case, Innu and Inuit peoples in Labrador, in the province of Newfoundland and Labrador, negotiated agreements for the Voisey's Bay nickel project which contain substantial financial and other economic benefits, and afford them a key role in project design and in environmental management. The agreements:

- Include royalty payments linked to the value of production on a scale similar to those paid to provincial government, with a further upside when nickel prices are high.
- Require that the project be developed on a scale much smaller than that desired by the project developer (6,000 tonnes per day (tpd) versus 20,000 tpd).

---

[1] Unlike the Browse LNG agreements, the agreements for central Queensland LNG developments are not published. This summary is based on a review of six agreements related to several projects, which were provided to the author on a confidential basis. My discussions with Aboriginal traditional owners in the region and published literature (e.g. O'Neill 2016) suggest the agreements reviewed are typical of those signed in central Queensland in recent years.

- Set limits on routes for shipping through sea ice and on the annual duration of shipping.
- Require Innu or Inuit environmental monitors to be on site 365 days a year.
- Give Innu and Inuit a role in the grant of environmental permits for the project.
- Include extensive and detailed provisions to encourage Aboriginal employment, including specific provisions on employment of Innu and Inuit women (O'Faircheallaigh 2016: 190–2).

At the same time, agreements were negotiated for diamond mines in Canada's Northwest Territories that:

- Lack royalty payments, providing only for fixed dollar payments that would not rise if output increased.
- Have no provision for Aboriginal involvement in environmental management.
- Limit the exercise of the existing legal rights of Aboriginal signatories, for example, to object to project approval or proposed environmental conditions. One agreement requires that the Aboriginal signatories 'shall not engage in any unreasonable action that could either delay or stop the project'.
- Contain only vague commitments by mining companies on Aboriginal employment and training—for instance, in terms of undertakings to 'use best endeavours' to maximize employment (O'Faircheallaigh 2016: 162–4).

What explains these variable outcomes? As noted in Chapter 8, neo-liberal governance theory could explain the less positive outcomes discussed above, but it cannot explain the variability in outcomes. If bargaining power were so comprehensively arraigned against Indigenous peoples, it would not be possible for agreements of the sort negotiated for the Voisey's Bay and Kimberley LNG projects to be concluded, especially as these agreements reflect a shift in power over fundamental issues such as project scale and choices regarding project infrastructure.

In both Australia and Canada, many agreements that are weak from an Indigenous perspective do occur under legal regimes that offer limited recognition to Indigenous rights in land. The Queensland LNG agreements were negotiated under the Native Title Act (1993) which, as discussed earlier, places Aboriginal landowners under considerable pressure to conclude agreements even if they are unhappy with the terms. Similarly, in Canada the agreements for the Northwest Territory diamond mines were concluded in a context where comprehensive land claims had yet to be settled and the consent of Aboriginal landowners was not required for development to proceed (O'Faircheallaigh 2016: 152–3). However, the legal context does not in itself offer an adequate explanation, because the strongly positive outcomes discussed earlier were achieved in the same legal context as the weaker ones (the Kimberley LNG project also under the Native Title Act, Voisey's Bay also in a situation where land claims had not been settled). More broadly, my comparative analysis of 45 agreements in Australia revealed that some of the strongest from an Aboriginal perspective were negotiated under the Native Title Act, or in a context where development approval was already in place—in other words, where Aboriginal landowners had no legal basis on which to insist that negotiations even occur (O'Faircheallaigh 2016: Chapter 5).

The same two factors identified in Chapter 8 in explaining negotiation outcomes in Australia apply in Canada. The first involves community participation in preparations for and conduct of negotiations, which help to identify community priorities for negotiations and provide an opportunity to identify and address conflicting community interests in relation to proposed projects. This in turn helps achieve clarity of objectives and unity of purpose, and provides opportunities for community political mobilization if negotiations are failing to yield the outcomes desired by a community. The Innu and Inuit, for example, engaged in direct action to stop work on the Voisey's Bay project on a number of occasions when the developer or the Newfoundland government was refusing to engage seriously in negotiations; challenged unfavourable decisions by Newfoundland and Canada in the courts; and developed political alliances with church groups and trade unions to put pressure on Inco to agree to Innu and Inuit demands (see Chapter 9).

The second factor involves regional Aboriginal political organization, which provides greater access to financial and technical resources to support negotiations, makes credible threats of direct political action, and increases capacity to use multiple legislative avenues to increase bargaining leverage. This is very evident in the negotiation of the Kimberley LNG and Voisey's Bay agreements, based on the role of the KLC in the former case and the Innu Nation and the Labrador Inuit Association in the latter (for details, see O'Faircheallaigh 2015; and O'Faircheallaigh 2016, which provides further examples of the critical role played by Aboriginal regional organizations).

Another noticeable feature of the Kimberley LNG and Voisey's Bay agreements has been the very active involvement of Indigenous women. The Inuit lead negotiator for the Inuit Voisey's Bay agreement was a woman, as were the implementation officers appointed to ensure the Innu and Inuit agreements were properly implemented. In both cases, women made a major contribution to community consultations and environmental impact assessments (EIAs), by organizing and participating in community meetings, making EIA submissions, and working on teams conducting community impact assessments. Their skills and extensive networks were vital in making sure that consultations could be conducted effectively and often within tight time constraints (Cox and Mills 2015; KLC 2010c; O'Faircheallaigh 2013a).

Mining and Indigenous well-being: the impact of revenues

It is also important to consider the ultimate impact of mining on Indigenous well-being in Australia and Canada. While this impact is mediated by the content of agreements, it is not determined by them, as illustrated by the case of mineral revenues. Here final outcomes are decided not just by the quantum of payments provided for in an agreement, but also by how the revenues involved are managed and used. As discussed in Chapter 10, in the non-Indigenous context there has been considerable debate regarding the effects of mineral revenues on economic and social development. Much of the relevant literature, often based on the concept of a 'resource curse', is pessimistic regarding the likelihood that such revenues encourage broad-based economic and social development.

There are certainly cases where large revenue flows to Indigenous communities from mining projects appear to have had limited impact on the long-term economic and social well-being of recipients. One such case involves Groote Eylandt, in Australia's Northern Territory, where Anindilyakwa people and organizations affected by one of the world's largest manganese mines, established by BHP and now operated by its spin-off company South 32, have received hundreds of millions of dollars in royalties over the decades since 1970. This revenue flow, despite amounting to a significant annual income per capita for Groote Eylandt's 1,700 Anindilyakwa residents, has not transformed their lives (Laurie 2021). Its limited impact reflects several factors. One involves the fact that large sums have been allocated to the provision of services that could properly be considered the responsibility of the state, including youth welfare, health, early childhood literacy, education and training, housing for the elderly, sewage services, road maintenance, and addressing substance misuse (ALC 2015; GEBIE 2015). The rationale for allocating funds to such areas is, presumably, that in their absence government would fail to fulfil its funding responsibilities and Anindilyakwa people would suffer as a result. The counter-argument is that the availability of royalty income to fund services allows government to evade its responsibilities, creating a major opportunity cost in that the royalty funds committed here could have been used to promote the well-being of Anindilyakwa people in other ways, and to compensate for the social and economic impacts of manganese mining (for a detailed discussion of these issues, see O'Faircheallaigh 2004).

Another issue is that over the decades a substantial proportion of income has been allocated to individuals, and that these amounts have largely been devoted to immediate personal consumption, including on vehicles, alcohol, and drugs (ALC 2015; Turner 1996). The practice of allocating royalties in this way was established very early in the life of the Groote Eylandt mine (Altman 1983: 114–15), and it is difficult to stop individual distributions once they have become established. The potential long-term benefit of royalty income has also been reduced by the tendency, evident over many decades, of recipient organizations to hold large sums in cash, term deposits, and bonds. In mid-2015 two of the three organizations involved between them held some $90 million in bank deposits and cash investments. In comparison, investments in shares and property were less than $10 million (GEAT 2015; GEBIE 2015). The propensity to hold a high proportion of assets appears to constitute a substantial opportunity cost in terms of the higher returns that could be achieved through a more diverse investment portfolio. Investments have been made in local business development, but these have generally not been successful and in some cases have incurred large losses. For example, Groote Eylandt and Bickerton Island Enterprises (GEBIE) invested substantially in a tourist accommodation facility on Groote Eylandt, but this lost A$4.7 million in 2013/14 and $3.7 million in 2014/15. The value of the facility, originally carried by GEBIE at A$28 million, declined to A$2 million in 2015 (GEBIE 2015: 27).

A specific problem that occurred after royalties increased rapidly in 2008–9 due to steeply rising mineral prices was fraudulent and corrupt activity by several officers of one of the royalty recipient organizations, the Groote Eylandt Aboriginal Trust (GEAT). This resulted in the loss of millions of dollars, and ended with the conviction for fraud, and imprisonment, of GEAT's Public Officer (ABC 2015a, 2015b; Supreme Court of the Northern Territory 2014; Wild 2014). The fact that community members were not aware of warnings from GEAT's auditors that irregularities were occurring meant that fraud continued for longer than might otherwise have been the case (GEAT 2010, 2011).

Mining royalties have not failed entirely to generate benefits for Groote Eylandt residents. Funds have been directed into a wide range of cultural activities, and in recent years education has become a significant focus for recipient organizations, offering the promise of long-term benefits for the young people involved and their community (ALC 2015; Laurie 2021). In addition, the substantial cash surpluses accumulated by recipient organizations could still provide the basis for an investment strategy that will ensure an ongoing income after mining ends, which is expected to happen within a decade. However, given the scale of the revenues generated by manganese mining, which I estimate at some $55 million per annum during 2013–15, the positive impact seems very limited.

There are cases in Australia and Canada where much more positive outcomes have been and are being generated by mining revenues. During a decade and a half in the 1980s and 1990s, the Gagudju Association, recipients of royalties from the Ranger mine, also in Australia's Northern Territory, used its revenue to build successful tourism and other businesses; leverage additional funding from government for health and education services; establish trust funds for children of Association members; and secure technical advice to support their joint management of Kakadu, the National Park surrounding the Ranger mine (O'Faircheallaigh 2002b).

A contemporary example involves the experience of the Ely Bauxite Mine Aboriginal Trust, which receives royalties from one of Rio Tinto's leases in western Cape York. Until 2017, revenue under this agreement was limited to some $800,000 per annum, which provided little scope for any major development initiatives and was only sufficient to cover the Trust's administrative costs and small per capita payments of about $600 per annum to its Aboriginal beneficiaries, a practice initiated soon after the Ely agreement was concluded in 1997. In late 2017, Rio Tinto informed the Trust that due to changes in its mine plan, bauxite production (and so royalty income) would jump by a factor of 10, but that mining would end in 2027. The Trust's directors, all traditional owners for the mine lease area, set about devising a strategy to ensure that some benefits could continue to flow after mining ended, and that in the interim significant benefits would be greeted for the three Aboriginal communities that are beneficiaries of the Trust. The strategy involved allocated about 40 per cent of annual income to a long-term investment fund, designed to create a capital base that could generate an ongoing income after 2027. The criteria for this fund solely involved profit maximization, and professional investment advice was secured on a competitive basis to help achieve the highest possible return, and to ensure that the Trust's affairs were conducted in a tax-effective manner. A further 25 per cent of income was allocated for 'community projects', to be allocated based on applications from community organizations and designed to create broad benefits for community members and to avoid duplicating basic services that government should provide. Funding already available under the Ely agreement to encourage business development would be supplemented, as a second part of the strategy to make sure that benefits could continue to flow after mining ended, while existing payments to individuals would be maintained. This strategy was discussed and endorsed after two rounds of community meetings during 2018.

Directors decided the Trust should discontinue individual payments in 2019 after Rio Tinto revised its forecast of future royalty payments downward due to declining world demand and prices for bauxite, which, along with a rapid rise in the number of beneficiaries claiming the payments, would make it impossible to maintain the Trust's other initiatives. The proposal to discontinue payments was also discussed in community meetings and, despite opposition from some recipients, was strongly endorsed because of support for the strategy of maintaining long-term investment and community benefits.

The Ely Trust's investment strategy has been successful to date, with almost A$20 million now held in the long-term investment fund and forecasts indicating that this amount will rise to $40 million by 2027. In 2020–1 the Trust allocated $1.5 million to community projects. Some of these involve items that government will not provide under any circumstances. An example involved purchase of a hearse for the beneficiary community of Mapoon, where the need to hire a hearse from the regional centre of Weipa had imposed considerable cost and stress on grieving families. Another involved the allocation of funds to purchase a second dialysis chair for the Weipa hospital. In this case the government, using a standard funding formula, had built a dialysis facility which it will maintain and staff on an ongoing basis. By funding an additional dialysis chair, the Trust was able, at marginal cost, to increase the capacity of the dialysis facility and reduce the need for patients to travel for treatment away from their families and their homelands.

Another positive example is provided by the Benefits and Legacy Fund operated by the Qikiqtani Inuit Association (QIA), a regional representative body for Inuit communities in Canada's Nunavut Territory, and which receives income from revenue-sharing arrangements with the Nunavut government and from agreements with mining companies in QIA's territory (QIA 2021). The Fund was established in 2016 when the QIA adopted a Revenue Policy that aimed to establish clear and transparent goals and reporting regarding how money was invested and used. In an approach like that of the Ely Trust, the QIA established a Legacy Fund to invest money for the future and a Benefits Fund that delivers programmes for Inuit beneficiaries.

Legacy Fund money is not used for daily operations, but is invested to provide opportunities for the future. The Benefits Fund currently allocates projects to cultural activities, including land-based hunting and youth education programmes and craft activities; daycare and early childhood programmes and subsides; and an Opportunities Fund which provides support for capital projects and entrepreneurial activities. During 2020–1 the Benefits and Legacy Fund allocated just over C$1 million to the Benefits Fund, and as of 31 March 2021, the Legacy Fund had a balance of C$81 million. As with the Ely Trust's investment fund, the Legacy Fund is allocated to a portfolio of investments designed to preserve the capital of the Fund, while generating long-term average annual returns that will allow its value to grow significantly over time (QIA 2021).

How can we explain the very different outcomes from revenue summarized above? To some extent the answer lies in the earlier discussion (see Chapter 10) regarding alternative uses for revenues. In particular, allocation of large sums to individual payments in situations where there is a tendency to dissipate them quickly on consumption substantially reduces the prospects of achieving sustainable benefits. Allocation of funds to services that government might otherwise provide reduces the possibility of achieving net benefits. However, these points raise another question: why is it that some groups allocate revenues in sub-optimal ways, whereas others avoid this pitfall? After all, the Ely Trust succeeded in reversing the long-established practice of making payments to individuals, and the Gagudju Association succeeded in allocating revenues in a way that led government to increase, rather than reduce, its commitment to service provision.

As suggested in the literature (see Chapter 10), governance is a key factor, with accountability and transparency being especially important. The Board of the Ely Trust, for example, made extensive use of community meetings to tell beneficiaries about its planned strategies and to win support: for instance, for the decision to reallocate individual payments to community projects and long-term investment. The QIA uses annual reports on the Benefits and Legacy Fund that are written in Inuit as well as English, and which make extensive use of graphics and photographs to report to its members on its allocation of community funds and on the composition of its investment portfolio (QIA 2020, 2021). The Gagudju Association convened general meetings of its members every year to present information on how funds would be allocated in the next year (O'Faircheallaigh 2002b: 198). Another factor is the capacity to undertake and implement strategic planning, to clearly demarcate priorities both across time (current benefits versus building a future capital base), and across alternative uses for funds, as for example in the QIA's prioritization of cultural activities and childcare, or the Ely Trust's support for dialysis services. The capacity to obtain and effectively deploy expert financial advice is also important. Both the QIA and the Ely Trust have shown an ability to use such expertise in developing strategies that avoid high-risk investment and so preserve their capital, but at the same time develop a diversified portfolio of shares and property that allows them to build a capital base that will be sufficient to maintain an income after mining ends. In contrast, the Groote Eylandt trusts appear to have lost out by pursuing investments in local businesses that had a high level of risk, and at the same time foregoing opportunities to build their capital base by holding a large proportion of their assets in cash.

I noted in reviewing the general literature on the resource curse that insufficient attention has been paid to the role of leadership. Its importance is evident in the examples discussed here. Leadership may be difficult to define, but its presence or absence is very evident. For instance, leadership by the Ely Trust directors was critical in responding effectively to the changed circumstances created by Rio Tinto's revision of its mining plans. Lack of leadership has been equally evident and influential in the dissipation of funds and cultural capital experienced by the GEAT in 2008–12.

Changing the rules of the game: barriers and responses

While Australia and Canada now afford some recognition to the rights and interests of Indigenous peoples, the political environment in both countries remains strongly disposed towards promotion of extractive industry, often at the expense of Indigenous interests. It is significant that the fundamental shifts in recognition of Indigenous rights in land have come via the courts (the Canadian Supreme Court's *Calder* decision and the Australian High Court's *Mabo* decision), not because of political decisions. Australia and Canada were two of only four countries that voted against the United Nations General Assembly resolution that adopted the UN Declaration on the Rights of Indigenous Peoples (UNDRIP). (The other two opposing votes also came from settler states, New Zealand and the United States.) While Australia and Canada have since formally endorsed UNDRIP, federal and sub-national state authorities in both countries have not accepted the principle of Indigenous free prior and informed consent (IFPIC) which is integral to UNDRIP, and they regularly act in ways inconsistent with it. Australia's entire native title regime is inconsistent with IFPIC, given that the Commonwealth government can approve mining projects, and regularly does do, where the company concerned has failed to achieve the consent of affected Aboriginal landowners. Since the introduction of the Native Title Act, the NNTT has approved the grant of over 130 mining leases where Aboriginal consent was absent. In Canada, oil sands projects in Alberta, discussed below, have been approved in the face of sustained opposition from affected First Nations. In both jurisdictions, sub-national levels of government, more dependent than their federal counterparts on royalties and economic activity generated by mining, have been especially strong in their support for extractive industry, and have been correspondingly weak in their protection of Indigenous rights (Baker and Westman 2018: 146; O'Neill 2016; Parlee 2015: 430).

The parlous position of some First Peoples and the extent of state support for extractive industry is well illustrated by Canada's oil sands industry, based in Alberta. The industry is located on the traditional territories of Dene and Cree First Nations, which were the subject of Treaty 8, signed in 1899. First Nations retained only about 5 per cent of their territories, but were guaranteed continued access to the remainder to support a livelihood based on hunting and trapping, subject to the government 'taking up' land from time to time for purposes such as mining (Parlee 2015; Westman 2013).

The oil sands industry constitutes one of the largest energy production facilities in the world, based on oil reserves second only to Saudi Arabia. It produced 3 million barrels of oil a day in 2020, and helped to make Canada the world's fourth-largest oil producer and the top exporter of crude oil to the United States. It involves extraction of oil from shale rocks, requiring mining of huge quantities of material from open pits which is then heated up and treated with chemicals to allow extraction of oil. Alternatively, where removal of rock is not physically or economically feasible, in situ extraction occurs, making use of heating, pumping, and pipeline networks to liquefy and extract bitumen underground beneath expanses of boreal forest that become scarred with roads, pipelines, and hundreds of drill holes (Parlee 2015). The industry, which began in the 1960s, now involves scores of large mining and processing operations covering an area larger that New York City and generating enormous quantities of contaminated waste that must be stored in above-ground ponds, giving rise to the world's largest open-pit mines and tailings ponds. Less than 1 per cent of disturbed areas have been rehabilitated. The industry consumes huge amounts of water; restricts the access of First Nations to their land and resources; contaminates lakes, waterways, and wildlife and other food resources; and creates significant health issues for residents of the region. Some First Nations are now surrounded by oil sands projects and their continued existence is under threat (Baker and Westman 2018; Kuznets 2021; Westman 2013; Westman et al. 2020).

EIAs of proposed projects, undertaken by proponents, often provide very limited opportunity for consultations with affected First Nations; ignore Indigenous interests, knowledge and world views; exaggerate project benefits, and downplay negative effects; and treat each project in isolation, ignoring cumulative impacts which are especially significant in a region already heavily affected by development and experiencing numerous new projects (Baker and Westman 2018; Westman et al. 2020). The sheer scale and speed of development creates enormous challenges for First Nations seeking to participate in regulatory processes. As George Poitras, a former chief of the Mikisew Cree First Nation, stated:

If you are trying, as a First Nation or as an environmental NGO, trying to keep pace with the development, trying to intervene or review the different applications that come before the province for every one of these projects, it's a nightmare, trying to keep up. The pace of the development is unfathomable. It's actually hard to think about. (cited in Baker and Westman 2018: 149)

Despite opposing the approval of proposed projects on numerous occasions in EIAs and taking legal action to try and stop them proceeding (Kuznets 2021), First Peoples have been unable to slow the growth of an industry which threatens their continued existence, in the face of the determination of Alberta and of Canada's federal government to allow its continued expansion. This determination has, for instance, led governments to approve new mines despite expressions of concern about project impacts and the process for assessing them by prestigious independent commentators, including the Royal Society of Canada, Canada's foremost scholarly society (Baker and Westman 2018: 149). First Nations have been able to negotiate agreements with some proponents providing for Aboriginal employment and business development initiatives, and some of these have yielded significant benefits (Milke and Kaplan 2020). However, they have constituted rear-guard actions to try and extract some benefit from a situation over which First Nations have little or no control (Kuznets 2021).

How have Indigenous peoples in Australia and Canada responded to situations in which they do not have a legal capacity to stop projects to which they are opposed in principle, or for which they are unable to negotiate acceptable development conditions? One approach is to use protest and political opposition to try and stop individual projects, an approach that, as outlined in Chapter 9, was successful in allowing the Mirrar people to stop development of the Jabiluka uranium project. The obstacles Indigenous peoples face in seeking to stop projects they oppose must be recognized. Mounting a campaign of the sort undertaken by the Mirrar is expensive. The Mirrar had substantial funding at their disposal provided, ironically, by royalties from the existing Ranger uranium mine. Mirrar people were united throughout the campaign in their opposition to Jabiluka, an important element in their success. In many situations, divisions exist within Indigenous groups between those determined to oppose a project and those willing to allow a project to proceed on terms that allow them to achieve substantial economic benefits and effective harm mitigation (Brake 2016; Milke and Kaplan 2020; O'Neill 2019). Given the number of mining projects being developed in Australia and Canada at any one time, it is difficult to attract media and public attention to any one project, unless it has qualities that mark it as especially controversial or iconic. In this regard, the Mirrar were assisted by the fact that Jabiluka involved uranium, mining of which has been highly contentious in Australia; was located within Kakadu, a national park with iconic status in Australia and recognized by the United Nations Educational, Scientific and Cultural Organization for its global significance; and was on Aboriginal land recognized as being of the highest cultural value. Finally, by 2005 Jabiluka was owned by Rio Tinto, a high-profile multinational corporation conscious of its public reputation, and for which Jabiluka was not a 'core' asset, both of which could help explain its willingness to bow to pressure not to proceed with the mine.

Another approach pursued by First Peoples in both countries is to establish policy and regulatory regimes to govern mining on their territories which *do* require their consent before development can proceed, and to seek compliance from industry and the state with these regimes. Papillon and Rodon (2019) discuss two cases in Canada where First Peoples have attempted to implement this approach. One involves the Cree people of James Bay in Quebec, where nine communities have established a central political organization, the Grand Council of the Cree. The Grand Council has established a Cree Mineral Policy, which states that the Cree 'support and promote the development of mineral resources in the James Bay region of Northern Quebec

[and] … recognize the increased economic and social opportunity offered by the mining sector, subject to ensuring that their unique social and environmental regime is adhered to'. However, all developments must conform with the underlying principle that 'no mining development will occur within Eeyou Istchee [Cree territory] unless there are agreements with our communities' (Grand Council of the Cree 2010: 1, 3). As Papillon and Rodon note (2019: 331), the Cree Mineral Policy has no legal force under Canadian law, but rather relies on the political and mobilization capacity of the Grand Council to influence corporate and state actors to comply with it. They discuss two situations where the policy was applied. In one, the Cree provided their consent, after community consultations, for a gold-mining project by signing an IBA. In the second, a proposed uranium mine, consultations revealed strong community opposition to the project and as a result the Grand Council refused to enter negotiations for an IBA with the proponent. In 2013 the government of Quebec announced a moratorium on uranium mining and rejected the project, citing the absence of Cree consent in explaining its decision (Papillon and Rodon 2019: 332–3).

Papillon and Rodon's other example of a First People attempting to introduce a regulatory regime involves the Squamish Nation (SN), which incorporates nine coastal communities in British Columbia. The SN joined other First Nations and environmental groups in successfully challenging federal approval for the Trans Mountain pipeline, which would have carried gas from Alberta for processing on the BC coast, on the basis that consultation processes undertaken by the federal government were unconstitutional. At the same time, the SN approved another pipeline terminal project proposed by Woodfibre Natural Gas (WNG). In this case, the SN initiated its own impact assessment process and negotiated with the project proponent to fund the process. In 2014, WNG committed in a legally binding agreement to respect the outcome of this process, thus complying with the SN's policy that developments on its territory must be subject to IFPIC. The SN impact assessment resolved that the project could proceed subject to 25 conditions and mitigation measures. These were accepted by the proponent and an IBA for the project was signed in 2018. The SN was not successful in its efforts to gain recognition for its assessment and approval process from BC and Canadian regulatory authorities, though the BC minister did refer to the SN process and the proponent's undertaking to comply with the 25 conditions in explaining his reasons for approving the project (Papillon and Rodon 2019: 325–9).

An example of a similar approach in Australia involves the Browse LNG project mentioned earlier in discussing agreement outcomes. In this case, the regional Aboriginal land organization, the KLC, took the view that LNG development should only proceed with the consent of traditional owners. The government of Western Australia initially supported this position, indicating that development would only proceed 'with the consent and substantial economic participation' of affected Aboriginal people. The initial phases of a site selection process for the proposed LNG Precinct that would process gas from several offshore fields was based on this principle, and several traditional owner groups were permitted to withdraw proposed sites from the selection process. After a change of government in 2008, the conservative Liberal Party premier rejected the requirement for Indigenous consent, nominated the state government's preferred site for the Precinct and required negotiation of an agreement for the project to proceed. However, the new government did not seek to revisit the earlier decision by some traditional owner groups to withdraw potential locations from the site selection process (KLC 2010d).

Conclusion

In Australia and Canada, Indigenous peoples faced large-scale dispossession and economic and social marginalization as their lands were occupied by European immigrants and as their civil and political rights were crushed by settler states. Since the 1970s their ability to reassert those rights and to benefit from the legal systems of constitutional liberal democracies have allowed many of them to achieve, in a variety of ways, at least limited recognition of their inherent rights to land and the ability to negotiate terms for mineral development on their territories. In the absence, in most cases, of a right to halt mineral development, First Peoples have had to rely on their capacity to supplement limited legal rights with organizational and political capacity in seeking to negotiate agreements that allow them to share substantially in the benefits of mining and to mitigate its negative effects. However, organizational and political capacities are uneven and the inevitable result of a reliance on negotiated agreements is that different First Peoples experience very uneven outcomes from mining on their land. Application of leadership, communication, organizational, and financial skills is required to translate the potential benefits of agreements into improvements in well-being for Indigenous communities, as emerges clearly from the discussion of mining royalties. Access to those skills is also uneven, however, adding further to the diversity of outcomes that is so notable in Australia and Canada.

The significance of the gains achievable through negotiation of agreements should not be underestimated. The Innu and Inuit in Labrador and the Aboriginal traditional owners in the Kimberley, for instance, have been able to shape the design and management of projects in ways that deeply affect their impact on Indigenous territories, and to substantially alter the distribution of project benefits in their favour. The problem is that the legal and regulatory regimes in Australia and Canada fail to *ensure* that such outcomes will eventuate.

This situation reflects the reality that state agencies in both countries have been determined to promote the continued growth of extractive industry even at the expense of Indigenous interests. Given that in most situations Indigenous peoples have no legal right to stop mining, this inevitably means that mining may proceed in ways that are highly detrimental to them. This reality is highlighted at a systemic level by the repeated action of Australia's NNTT in approving mining leases against the opposition of Aboriginal traditional owners, and at a more specific level by the severely negative impacts experienced by First Nations in Alberta from oil sands development. In some circumstances, First Peoples may be able to mobilize politically to overturn state approvals, though the case of Jabiluka suggests that the conditions for success of this strategy will rarely occur. Jabiluka also suggests that it may be easier to influence decision-makers in corporations than their state counterparts. First Peoples are also seeking to establish their own regulatory systems that do require consent before mining can proceed. Examples from Canada suggest that here also it may be easier to secure the compliance of corporations, anxious to avoid costly project delays and disruptions, than of state regulators.

16
Not Just Mining

Cumulative Impacts and Sami Reindeer Herders
in Sweden

Introduction

The Sami (also spelt Saami) are an Indigenous people whose ancestral territories,
referred to as Sapmi, span northern Finland, Norway, and Sweden, and the Kola
Peninsula in Russia. Sami territories are facing growing encroachment not just from
exploration and mining but also from wind farms, pipelines, roads, and tourism, and
at the same time the Sami are dealing with the impacts of climate change. These factors, in combination, are threatening the viability of Sami reindeer herding. This
chapter focuses on the experience of Sami reindeer herders in Sweden, which is
Europe's largest mineral producer, and which has experienced a rapid growth in mineral exploration and development in the last two decades. Virtually all large-scale
mining occurs on Sami territories (Lawrence and Åhrén 2016). An analysis of the
Sami experience brings into sharp focus the way in which cumulative impacts from
mining in combination with other development activities affect Indigenous livelihoods. While my focus is on Sweden, similar issues arise across Sapmi (Johnsen 2016;
Nygaard 2016).

The next section provides a brief overview of the Sami as a people and of reindeer
herding as a way of life. I then review the policies of the Swedish state in relation
to recognition of Sami rights, and to development of Sweden's mineral resources.
The following section outlines how exploration and mining activity can affect reindeer, and the viability of reindeer herding. Historically, Sami, in the face of overwhelming state support for mining, have had little capacity to stop, or to benefit from,
industrial development on their territories. The final section uses case studies of two
mining projects that are currently stalled by Sami opposition to assess whether this
situation is changing.

The Sami and reindeer herding in Sweden

Sweden's census does not record ethnicity and the number of Sami is not
known with any certainty, with 20,000 being a common estimate, of whom some

Indigenous Peoples and Mining. Ciaran O'Faircheallaigh, Oxford University Press. © Ciaran O'Faircheallaigh (2023).
DOI: 10.1093/oso/9780192894564.003.0016

15–20 per cent are thought to be directly involved in reindeer herding. Reindeer herders rely on the land for other resources including game and fish, and some engage in wage employment to supplement their earnings from herding. For many Sami people not engaged in the industry, including those living in urban areas, reindeer herding and the cultural practices surrounding it constitute an important part of their identity, as does their continuing connection to land, resources, and cultural sites (Persson and Öhman 2014: 116–17).

Sami people have lived in areas that now constitute northern Sweden 'since time immemorial' and, according to the archaeological evidence, for several thousand years. They relied on hunting, fishing, and gathering, and kept reindeer for domestic consumption and as pack animals. A shift towards large-scale pastoral activity based on reindeer took place gradually from the 1600s, and involved following herds of animals on a seasonal cycle that typically involved spending summers on mountain pastures and winters in wooded areas near the coast. Current national boundaries were not fully established until the mid-nineteenth century, and movement was dictated purely by the requirement to access suitable pastures throughout the annual cycle. Land not only provided livelihoods, but also contained significant sites and areas that were central to cultural, social, and religious life (Laevas Sami Village 2012).

Reindeer require access to land and resources on a very large scale, which means that Sami reindeer herders face unique challenges in maintaining their livelihoods at a time of widespread industrial development. Reindeer migrate over long distances, mostly at their own initiative and in their own time. They consume a wide variety of plants, including lichens and herbs, depending on location and season, and the land they utilize covers about 50 per cent of Sweden's area. Reindeer also require access to specific types of pasture in each season as well as undisturbed calving grounds and unblocked migration routes and resting areas in between seasonal pastures (Lawrence and Åhrén 2016). Reindeer are not domesticated, will follow certain routes on their own initiative, and will choose to avoid sources of noise and human activity such as mines, wind farms, roads, or tourism centres, with this 'impact zone' being 15 kilometres in some cases and even more depending on local conditions (Fohringer et al. 2021; Kløcker Larsen et al. 2022). Females are especially sensitive during the calving season. Both reindeer and Sami herders have an intimate connection with specific areas of pasture, migration routes, and calving grounds. Thus while a community's total pasture area may be large, a small area of land can be of vital importance to the viability of reindeer herding because it is particularly rich in pasture or lies on a migration route, or because reindeer depend on the pasture in a particular resting area, if only for a few days (Åhrén 2004: 103; Lawrence and Kløcker Larsen 2019: 32–41). Åhrén (2004: 69–70) describes reindeer herding as follows:

> ... the reindeer are free, mobile and independent ... the reindeer will neither wait for, nor are dependent on, the reindeer herder. The reindeer herder must negotiate and compromise with the animal ... It is not only the Saami people that have an inseparable connection to its traditional land; the reindeer's connection to the

land implies that a Saami community would change its grazing areas and migration paths only after serious consideration and for compelling reasons.

Sami customary law recognizes the rights of individuals to use specific areas of land, but ownership of land, waters, and natural resources is vested in the collective. As Åhrén notes (2004, 71), 'The Saami people have never understood land as constituting a form of bartered goods. The value of land is … based on the fact that the individual and his or her family and descendants could live off the land for generations.'

It is possible to feed reindeer with substitutes for plant material, such as pellets, and to intervene in migration: for example, trucking reindeer from one area to another or using helicopters to direct them. However, this can result in a deterioration in the condition of reindeer and in their survival during winter, and imposes additional work on herders. In the longer term, the viability of reindeer herding and the Sami cultural and social practices associated with it depend on reindeer having continuous access to suitable pastures and the ability to move freely between them on a seasonal cycle. It is enactment of traditional practices and the use of associated concepts and narratives as an integral part of travelling with reindeer on the land that is at the heart of culture and of its renewal and transmission (Lawrence and Åhrén 2016; Lawrence and Kløcker Larsen 2019; Osterlin and Raitio 2020).

Since the nineteenth century, reindeer herders have been organized into communities known as *sameby*, which are units of both economic production and governance. There are currently 51 *sameby* in Sweden, each with a defined territory which typically comprises an elongated strip reaching from the Baltic coast westwards to the mountains bordering Norway (see Fig. 16.1). *Sameby* represent a hybrid of colonial attempts to govern reindeer herding, combined with Sami social and cultural practices. Each community is governed by a council, and typically consists of a number of winter groups or *siida*, which comprise one or several herding families connected through family ties and traditional use of their lands. Only Sami can engage in reindeer husbandry in Sweden, and reindeer herding is regulated by the Reindeer Herding Act (1971), discussed further below (Herrmann et al. 2014; Kløcker Larsen et al. 2018; Sehlin MacNeil 2015: 12).

Reindeer herding constitutes a major economic activity, with turnover estimated at about US$43 million in 2019 (OECD 2019: 13), and with demand and prices for reindeer meat increasing in recent years. Other parts of the animals are used to make implements, clothing, and decoration. The access of reindeer herders to an economic base and their residence in a country with a comprehensive social welfare system has meant that Sami people in Sweden have not experienced the same level of social and economic disadvantage endured by Indigenous peoples in many other countries. Yet as discussed in the next section, the Swedish state has consistently refused to recognize Sami ownership of their traditional territories. Sami have suffered from discrimination and racism, being regarded as backward and inferior to agricultural and industrial society, being denied educational and other opportunities available to non-Indigenous Swedes, and, more generally, suffering the political marginalization

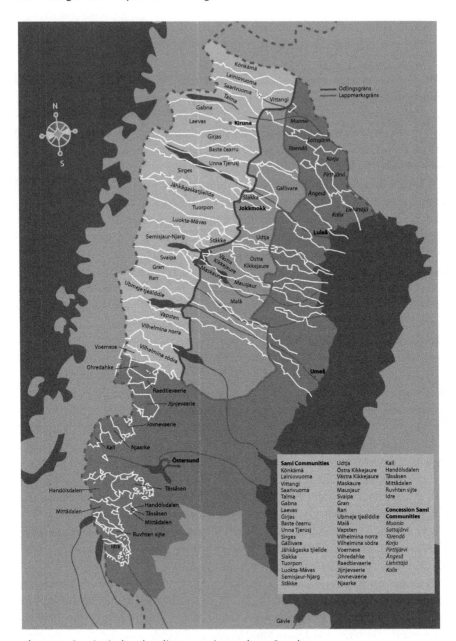

Odlingsgräns
Lappmarksgräns

Sami Communities
Könkämä
Lainiovuoma
Vittangi
Saarivuoma
Talma
Gabna
Laevas
Girjas
Baste čearru
Unna Tjerusj
Sirges
Gällivare
Jåhkågaska tjiellde
Slakka
Tuorpon
Luokta-Mávas
Semisjaur-Njarg
Ståkke

Udtja
Östra Kikkejaure
Västra Kikkejaure
Maskaure
Mausjaur
Svaipa
Gran
Ran
Ubmeje tjeälddie
Malå
Vapsten
Vilhelmina norra
Vilhelmina södra
Voernese
Ohredahke
Raedtievaerie
Jijnjevaerie
Jovnevaerie
Njaarke

Kall
Handölsdalen
Tåssåsen
Mittådalen
Ruvhten sijte
Idre

Concession Sami Communities
Muonio
Sattajärvi
Tärendö
Korju
Pirttijärvi
Ångeså
Liehittäjä
Kalix

Fig. 16.1 Sami reindeer herding areas in northern Sweden

Source: OECD, 2019. *Linking the Indigenous Sami People with Regional Development in Sweden*. Paris: OECD Publishing, https://doi.org/10.1787/9,789,264,310,544-en, p. 32.

associated with their position as a small minority (Lantto and Mörkenstam 2015: 137–9; Sehlin MacNeil 2015).

In an effort to counter their political marginalization, in 1950 the Sami established a national organization, the National Union of the Swedish Sami (SSR). The SSR aimed to represent all Sami people in Sweden, but in order to bolster its organizational strength it sought to base itself on the reindeer-herding districts and devoted considerable attention to policy and legal issues affecting reindeer herders. In the following decades, the SSR maintained a consistent critique of Swedish government policies towards reindeer herding and towards Sami in general, including by lobbying and undertaking court action to seek recognition of Sami rights in land. It sought to situate Sweden's treatment of Sami people in the international debate on the rights of Indigenous peoples; developed links with Sami people in other states; and pushed for the establishment of a Sami parliament (Lantto and Mörkenstam 2015: 143–6). The SSR has also supported Sami herding communities in their dealings with the state and mining companies, helping them to deal with environmental impact assessment (EIA) processes, to run campaigns in the media and with ethical investors, attending company annual general meetings, and assisting in negotiating agreements to mitigate project impacts where communities have felt this was the only option available to them. SSR has been constrained by a lack of resources, and has not been able to meet or fully meet all the requests for support it receives (personal communication, Rebecca Lawrence, 11 January 2022).

In 1993 a Sami parliament, the Sametinget, was established by legislation, and it has acted as an additional focal point for articulating both Sami political demands and the interests of reindeer herders (Lantto and Mörkenstam 2015). However, the Sametinget's impact is limited by the fact that it does not have independent sources of revenue; does not exercise responsibility or powers in relation to dealing with non-Sami interests operating on Sami territories; and did not acquire key powers exercised by other government agencies in relation to Sami, including the power of Country Administrative Boards (CABs), the local embodiment of the Swedish state, to set reindeer quotas. In addition, the Samitinget is part of the Swedish state administrative apparatus as well as being a representative body, generating significant tensions between the Swedish government and the Samitinget regarding the latter's roles and priorities (Lantto and Mörkenstam 2015: 148–54; Lawrence and Mörkenstam 2016).

The Swedish state, Sami rights, and mineral development

Until the eighteenth century, Sami people who lived in what is now Sweden enjoyed a high degree of autonomy. They paid taxes to the Crown reflecting the fact that they were recognized as landowners by state authorities, and were otherwise left to organize their economic, land management, cultural, and social affairs as they deemed fit, including by dealing with legal matters in their own courts (Åhrén 2004: 73–7). This situation changed as the modern Swedish state firmly established its presence in the north and no longer required the Sami to act as footholds of the state and demonstrate its sovereignty, and as the state began to direct its attention to exploiting the land and resources of the country's north. The state's aim became to regulate reindeer herding so that it did not interfere with the fostering of non-Indigenous settlement and agriculture, and in the longer term to assimilate Sami into Swedish mainstream society. In pursuing these aims, local state officials often ignored the legal protections that Sami should have enjoyed and refused to act when Sami highlighted breaches of their rights by state agencies constructing infrastructure or by the growing non-Sami population (Össbo and Lantto 2011: 331). The state enrolled the support of Christian missionaries, who discouraged or prohibited Sami cultural and religious practices, and destroyed cultural artefacts such as ceremonial drums (Ojala and Nordin 2015: 11–13).

In support of its policies, the Swedish state mobilized views of cultural hierarchy that regarded Sami culture as inferior and incapable of contributing to a developed society, and regarded Sami legal and social institutions as historical anomalies that should be replaced by Sweden's modern administrative structures. Critically, the state's position was that the inferior Sami nomadic way of life did not result in legal rights to land, with only permanent utilization of specific land area, such as agriculture, justifying title to land (Åhrén 2004: 73–4; Lawrence and Åhrén 2016; Ojala and Nordin 2015: 11). As Åhrén notes (2004: 81–2), 'being a nomadic, "barbaric" people, the Saami were now deemed to have no legal rights to lands, waters, and natural resources'. The Reindeer Grazing Act (1886) referred to grazing 'privileges' and declared the Sami people's traditional land the property of the Crown. Sweden subsequently gave away substantial parts of the Sami people's traditional land to non-Sami settlers as if no Sami population existed in the areas (Åhrén 2004: 89, 92; Persson et al. 2017: 22).

In the latter part of the twentieth century, the Swedish state afforded greater formal recognition to Sami culture and to the Sami as an Indigenous people. Sami were acknowledged as Indigenous by the Swedish parliament in 1977; the Sami language was declared an official minority language in 2000; and the Sami were recognized as a people in the international law sense by the Swedish government in 2006. On 1 January 2011, the Swedish Constitution was amended to recognize Sami as a people rather than a minority group, and the Constitution (chapter 1, article 2) states that 'The opportunities of the Sami people and ethnic, linguistic and religious minorities to preserve and develop a cultural and social life of their own shall be promoted'. Sweden's law on national minorities (Law 724, 2009, sections 4 and 5) sets out the more specific state duty to actively promote conditions necessary for the Sami to maintain and develop their culture and requires administrative authorities to give them the opportunity 'to influence issues that concern them'.

However, the Swedish state has consistently and stubbornly refused to acknowledge that legislative and constitutional recognition of Sami people confers on them any ownership of or control over territories that they have occupied and used since time immemorial and that they continue to use today, including any right to regulate activities undertaken by non-Indigenous interests (Åhrén 2004: 93, 107; CERD 2020; Lawrence and Mörkenstam 2016: 114). This is despite the Swedish state's positioning of Sweden internationally as a champion of human rights, including Indigenous rights, in part by affirming its commitment to the principles underlying the United

Nations Declaration on Indigenous People (UNDRIP) in 2014 (UNHRC 2016: 16), and despite the fact that Sweden has been subject to sustained international criticism for its failure to fulfil its human rights obligations in the domestic sphere (CERD 2020; Lawrence and Åhrén 2016; Raitio et al. 2020: 5; UNHRC 2011, 2016). The state insists that the Sami have only a right to make use of land and resources for reindeer herding and subsistence fishing and hunting, subject to state regulation and to the needs of other existing or potential users of land. This position makes it difficult for the Sami to exclude other activities from land they need, or to use recognition of their property rights to negotiate with developers to access land in a way that ensures the sustainability of reindeer herding.

The Swedish state's position is highlighted by its interpretation of free prior and informed consent (FPIC) which is central to the UNDRIP, including to article 32(2) which requires application of FPIC to projects affecting Indigenous lands, 'particularly in connection with the development ... of mineral ... resources'. Sweden takes the view that this article 'shall be interpreted as a guarantee that indigenous peoples must be consulted, not as giving a right of veto', and should only apply to 'such lands or territories that are formally owned by indigenous peoples' (cited in Doyle 2015: 163). Sweden, of course, does not consider that Sami territories are 'formally owned' by Sami people. On 26 January 2022, the Swedish parliament passed a bill setting out the state's duty to consult with Sami people on matters that include 'land use, enterprise issues, reindeer husbandry, fishing, hunting, predator animals, mines, wind power, forestry issues, cultural issues, place names, and biodiversity on reindeer grazing grounds'. However, the new law does not signal a departure from Sweden's position on FPIC, as it contemplates only a duty to consult, and allows the government to end consultations if it determines that consensus cannot be reached. The duty to consult does not apply in pressing cases when a delay is associated with 'a risk of considerable inconvenience' or when 'it is clear that the consultation is not needed or when the consultation is manifestly inappropriate' (Library of Congress 2022).

Several authors have argued that Sweden's failure to apply human rights principles in the domestic sphere has its origin in the country's refusal to engage with its colonial past and to recognize that its activities on Sami lands in northern Sweden constitute a 'colonial present'. According to this view, colonies are defined as territories geographically distant from the imperial centre, and so Sweden's behaviour towards Sami cannot be compared with the activities of colonial powers such as Britain and France (Lawrence and Åhrén 2016; Overud 2019; Sehlin MacNeil 2017: 5).

Consistent with its general approach to Sami rights, Sweden has always closely regulated not only reindeer herding but also the ability of Sami to utilize other resources such as game and fish, aiming to ensure that reindeer herding does not compete with land use by non-Sami people, including agriculture and forestry. Since the introduction of the Reindeer Herding Act (1971), the state has determined, for instance, the boundaries of reindeer-herding communities and the number of reindeer that Sami people can have (Lawrence and Kløcker Larsen 2019: 29–31).

These regulations are stringently enforced by the state, to the extent of requiring rein-deer to be slaughtered when the state considers their numbers to be excessive. The state insists that its agencies, and only its agencies, have the right to grant licences for the taking of game and fish, and that Sami people have neither the right to use these resources as they see fit, nor the right to regulate their use by non-Sami peo-ple. As the non-Sami resident population of the north, and visitation and tourism from southern Sweden have increased, the inability of Sami to regulate hunting and fishing has become more and more detrimental to their livelihoods and cultural prac-tices. The extent of Sweden's regulation of the economic practices of Sami has few contemporary parallels across the Indigenous world.

While Swedish authorities acknowledge their obligations to support the Sami in practising reindeer herding and associated cultural practices, they consistently act on the assumption that reindeer herding is not incompatible with alternative forms of land use, including forestry, renewable energy, and mining, a claim also espoused by the mining industry (Sehlin MacNeil 2015: 8). Linked to this position is a perspective on reindeer herding which sees it as an industry rather than a way of life. If social and cultural aspects of reindeer herding are ignored, it is easier to argue that it is not incompatible with industrial activity. It also justifies treating the Sami as one land user among many, and the failure to recognize their unique position as rights holders and as a people whose cultural and social identity is inextricably linked to reindeer herding (Kløcker Larsen and Raitio 2019: 15–16).

Viewing reindeer herding solely as an 'industry' also provides a rationale for the position of the state and of private commercial interests that mitigation of negative impacts only requires substitution of some alternative economic input: for instance, cash to buy food pellets or to transport reindeer in trucks. This means that the Swedish state denies that there is any need for it to limit other economic activities to protect Sami livelihoods (CERD 2020; Kløcker Larsen et al. 2017). One concrete manifestation of this approach is that the state has never set areas aside exclusively for reindeer herding (Raitio et al. 2020: 4). As Kløcker Larsen and Raitio note:

> the notion of co-existence is evoked by politicians and developers alike to prop-agate what is effectively a myth that Sami reindeer herding is inherently and endlessly 'adaptable', and hence not significantly impacted by developments, i.e. it can 'co-exist' with rapidly expanding mining, hydropower and wind power oper-ations on Sami traditional lands. (Kløcker Larsen and Raitio 2019: 15; see also Lawrence and Kløcker Larsen 2017: 1171)

These attitudes flow through, in turn, to regulatory decisions regarding grants of per-mits for mining and other industrial activity. There is often a failure to recognize potential negative cultural and social impacts of proposed resource developments and that state agencies inevitably make trade-offs between the rights of the Sami and commercial interests. This in turn makes it difficult for Sami to appeal licensing decisions (Kløcker Larsen and Raitio 2019: 15; UNHRC 2016: 13).

Historically, such appeals have been almost universally unsuccessful, including one case in which a permit was awarded to a forestry company to log Sami pasture areas even though the land involved comprised only 1 per cent of the company's holdings (Åhrén 2004: 104; Össbo and Lantto 2011). The state frequently cites the 'national interest' to justify rejection of Sami appeals, arguing that the economic benefit to Sweden of a proposed activity outweighs any negative impact on Sami (GOS 2013: 17). For example, a decision by a lower authority to grant the concession for the Rönnbäck nickel mine on Vapsten community lands was upheld by the government in August 2013, arguing that restrictions on constitutionally protected Sami reindeer husbandry rights were permitted on the basis that they were in the public interest, in this case represented by the substantial economic gain expected to be generated by the mine. The government also argued that even if mining did hamper reindeer herding in the area of the mining project, this did not prevent the Sami community from undertaking reindeer herding elsewhere (Koivurova et al. 2015: 23–4; UNHRC 2016: 13). This constitutes one example of what has been a consistent state policy that mining is always in the public interest and that permitting the demands of reindeer herding to restrict mining would never be in the public interest. For example, between 2004 and 2012 the Mining Inspectorate approved 38 applications for mining concessions, and declined none (Anshelm and Haikola 2018: 570). By 2015 there was not a single case in which the Land and Environment Court had not allowed a mining project to proceed (CERD 2020: 8).

Sami reindeer-herding communities have mounted several court cases, until recently with limited successes, arguing that they have established property rights through traditional use, and inviting the courts to reject the state view that the ability to engage in reindeer herding is a 'privilege' rather than the exercise of a property right (Lawrence and Åhrén 2016). One important recent gain for Sami involved a decision by Sweden's Supreme Court in 2020 that a Sami community does have the right to grant licences for hunting and fishing on its territory, and that this right is not shared with the Swedish state. This in effect gives the community the ability to regulate the use of game and fish. This decision is being contested by the Swedish government and has resulted in considerable public backlash against the Sami community concerned (Ruin 2021).

Sweden's mineral policy and mining regulatory system

Sweden's policy towards mineral exploration and development constitutes another important element of the state's approach to Sami rights. Sweden has a long history as a major producer of silver, copper, and particularly of iron ore, of which it has been for over a century, and still is, western Europe's largest producer. As noted earlier, the overwhelming majority of Sweden's mineral production occurs on traditional Sami lands. Until the 1990s, the mining industry was dominated by Swedish firms, some of them state-owned, and did not experience significant growth. In the last two decades, the state has encouraged investment by foreign firms and maintained an extremely favourable investment climate, including relieving the industry of the obligation to pay state royalties, generosity almost unheard of in a global context (Persson et al. 2017: 23). This policy approach has resulted in a rapid growth in mineral exploration and the discovery of several significant orebodies, a number of which have been approved for development or are being considered for approval.

In 2013 the Swedish government released the 'Minerals Strategy: For Sustainable Use of Sweden's Mineral Resources that Creates Growth throughout the Country' (hereafter 'the Strategy') (GOS 2013). The central goal of the Strategy is to increase the mining industry's competitiveness and so strengthen Sweden's position as the EU's leading mining and mineral nation, while at the same time ensuring that 'Sweden's mineral assets are to be exploited in a long-term sustainable way, with consideration shown for ecological, social and cultural dimensions' (GOS 2013: 4).

The Strategy includes or foreshadows a wide range of measures to pursue expansion of the industry, which it predicts could result in an increase in the number of operating mines from 16 to 30 in 2020 and 50 by 2030. The planned measures include ensuring an adequate supply of skilled labour; attracting more investment, domestic and foreign; increasing the 'efficiency' of, and shortening the time involved in, environmental assessment and planning processes; making mining towns more attractive to potential residents; and encouraging investment in science and innovation relevant to the industry. The basis on which mining growth will 'show consideration' for 'ecological, social and cultural dimensions' is much less clear. In relation to Sami reindeer herding, the Strategy states:

> Reindeer husbandry is a basic prerequisite of Sami culture, which is also protected in Sweden's Instrument of Government … Key reindeer herding areas are also exposed to a number of other activities in addition to mining operations, including wind and water power and infrastructure such as roads and railways, which can make reindeer husbandry more difficult in these areas. The cumulative consequences of other interests in the local environment can also make it difficult for reindeer herders to use alternative grazing areas. (GOS 2013: 26)

However, the Strategy does not suggest that recognition of Sami interests should constrain mineral development. Rather, the proposed solution to any potential conflict between the two, repeated at numerous points in the Strategy, is to promote 'coordination and dialogue among the industries and activities that lay claim to the same land' (GOS 2013: 26; see also GOS 2013: 20, 29, 31). The goal is to promote 'dialogue between actors in the regions affected by the mining industry's expansion … identifying possible obstacles and needs that arise as a result of the substantial expansion of the mining industry; and proposing measures to overcome and meet these obstacles and needs' (GOS 2013: 31; the word 'dialogue' occurs 37 times in the 50-page strategy). Thus, the Strategy articulates very clearly the assumption that underlies Sweden's policy on mining and reindeer herding, that the two are compatible, and that 'good dialogue … [will] avoid conflicts of interest' (GOS 2013: 22).

The effect of the Swedish government's failure to recognize Sami rights in land and resources and its consistent prioritization of mining are both reflected in, and exacerbated by, specific aspects of Sweden's system for evaluating and approving mineral projects. The general approach to evaluating potential projects is to consider each in isolation and to assume that Sami pastoral areas are free from other intrusions. Both the mining industry and regulatory authorities overlook, or downplay, the cumulative impacts of already existing mining interests and of other activities including forestry, hydroelectric and wind projects, infrastructure, and tourism (Kløcker Larsen et al. 2018; Lawrence and Åhrén 2016). There are other weaknesses in corporate impact assessment processes. These include failure to provide details of consultations conducted as part of the impact assessment (IA) process; failure to consider reindeer herding as a way of life rather than an industry, or to examine social and cultural impacts on Sami communities; and failure to identify specific *siida* that would be affected by the proposed development (Kløcker Larsen et al. 2018: 379–81). Lawrence and Kløcker Larson show (2017, 2019), in their study of Boliden's proposed Laver copper mine and its potential impacts on the Semisjaur Njarg reindeer-herding community, that the statutory EIA process does little to accommodate Sami participation, interests, or knowledge. As in other jurisdictions, EIA reports are prepared by the project proponent. The time frames involved are short, driven by project demands rather than the need to facilitate Sami participation, and negative impacts on reindeer herding are downplayed, despite evidence to the contrary. Reindeer herding is treated as a commercial exercise rather than a way of living, as indicated by Boliden's proposal that reindeer be fed almost exclusively with pellets during the winter, rather than allowing them to graze on winter pastures. The value of Sami knowledge and experience—for instance, in relation to the wider impact of a mining site on reindeer behaviour—is systematically discounted in favour of corporate perspectives.

Turning to the project approval process, Sweden's system is complex and fragmented, involving the grant of multiple approvals by several agencies at different stages of project life (Lawrence and Kløcker Larsen 2019; Raitio et al. 2020). The first step involves an exploration permit with an approved work plan, granted by the Mineral Inspectorate, which assesses any potential impact on Sami reindeer herding, prior to making grants. A draft plan must be provided to any affected reindeer-herding communities and, since 1 August 2014, the affected Sami can require that the work plan is translated into the Sami language, but there is no requirement for consultation with them. An affected community may lodge an objection to the plan or the grant, but to date no such objection has been upheld by the Mineral Inspectorate (Raitio et al. 2020: 6–7).

The second permit involves grant of an exploitation concession, also made by the Mineral Inspectorate, which is valid for 25 years. This approval indicates that the orebody involved has the potential for commercial development and that no reason exists why it should not be developed. This is not the final approval, but it is of enormous significance, for two reasons. First, it constitutes a decision by the state that mining is an acceptable and indeed preferred use for the land and resources involved, and so can proceed. The only issues that remain are the specific design of the project and the conditions that will be applied to its development. Second, an exploitation concession *must* be granted if a deposit has been found which can potentially be utilized on an economic basis, and if the location and nature of the deposit do not make it inappropriate to grant the applicant the concession (Labba 2014: 95; Raitio et al. 2020: 7). A key point to note is that while grant of an exploitation concession thus involves a judgement by state authorities that any impacts on Sami reindeer herding are insufficient to warrant denial of a permit, until 2016 a full EIA did not have to be submitted by the developer at this stage. Only a preliminary IA of the mining operation itself was required, which did not need to include associated infrastructure such as transport, power, water and waste storage facilities, or mineral-processing plants. This is different from the situation in most other jurisdictions, where a fully inclusive project IA must be conducted before governments come to a decision that mining is permissible.

There is no requirement to consult affected Sami people in relation to the grant of an exploitation concession, though companies have increasingly chosen to go beyond what is required by law and engage in consultations (Kløcker Larsen et al. 2018: 379). The EIA is reviewed by the CAB, which in turn advises the Mining Inspectorate whether it is acceptable. The mining company and affected Sami communities have the right to appeal the Mining Inspectorate's decision to government (Lawrence and Kløcker Larsen 2019).

When the exploitation concession applied for is in an area that is of national interest for the purposes of both reindeer husbandry and mineral extraction, the examining authority must determine which interest is to be given priority and ensure that the operation of whichever interest is prioritized is not obstructed by other activities. This weighing of interests does not always occur, as demonstrated by the Rönnbäcken case discussed below. Where it does occur, it is often undertaken from a purely economic perspective, and on the assumption that the jobs and revenue generated by mining will always outweigh those associated with reindeer herding (CERD 2020; Raitio et al. 2020: 10; UNHRC 2016: 13).

The third and final phase of the approval process involves grant of environmental permits by the Land and Environment Court; official expropriation of the land involved, effected by the Mineral Inspectorate; and specific sector permits for associated infrastructure, granted by the CAB. A full EIA must be undertaken before grant of an environmental permit, and this must include the proponent consulting with affected stakeholders. These include Sami reindeer herders, who are treated in the same way as any other stakeholder. EIA consultations have tended to be limited, focusing mainly on provision of information by proponents and regulators, and are adversely affected by limited understanding of Sami livelihoods and cultural practices among those undertaking the consultations (Kløcker Larsen and Raitio 2019: 12; Kløcker Larsen et al. 2017).

Sweden's project approval system provides very little opportunity for Sami reindeer herders to be involved in decisions that may have a major impact on their lives, particularly in critical decisions regarding grant of exploitation concession permits, where there is no requirement for consultation to occur. Opportunities are available to Sami to make written submissions or to lodge legal appeals at various stages of the approval process. However, making submissions or taking legal action requires a substantial commitment of time and resources, and until recently legal appeals have been unsuccessful (Kløcker Larsen and Raitio 2019; Kløcker Larsen et al. 2018). In addition, legal appeals are limited to procedural issues regarding the correct conduct of the statutory approval process (Raitio et al. 2020: 8). Sami reindeer herders have no recourse to a court that can examine whether a proposed mine infringes their property rights, regardless of the extent of or nature of predicted impacts (CERD 2020: 8; Lawrence and Åhrén 2016).

The fragmentation of decision making that characterizes the permitting system for mining is replicated across other sectors including wind farms, tourism, and infrastructure, each with its own set of agencies, different from those in the minerals sector, handling development applications. Government officials handling one stage of a development application may not be aware of what is happening at a different stage of another project in the same region, or know about planned initiatives in other sectors in that region. As one government officer noted, 'What happens when there are on-going, parallel permit applications? We sit in our respective silos, and have no idea what is going on with the other projects. Different projects have different regulations and time frames to relate to' (cited in Kløcker Larsen et al. 2017: 72). This makes it impossible for Sami communities or regulatory authorities to consider any individual project in the context of the cumulative impact of past approvals and current proposals across multiple sectors. According to Osterlin and Raitio (2020), the overall picture is one of fragmented 'planscapes' that, in turn, result in the creation of fragmented 'landscapes' which render it increasingly difficult for Sami reindeer herding to endure as a viable livelihood. In their words (2020: 3):

> Taken together the increasingly fragmented character of both landscapes and land use planning regulations and practices results in a double pressure on the communities: to adapt their herding practices and allocation of resources to the increasing pressure on their pastures, while needing to simultaneously engage in an increasingly fragmented and complex web of planning and appeal processes under diverse sectoral regulatory regimes.

Impacts of exploration and mining on Sami reindeer herders

Exploration and mining affect reindeer herders in two general ways, first through their impacts on the physical environment and on reindeer behaviour, and second through the demands that engaging with the regulatory system associated with extractive activity makes on Sami time and resources.

In terms of physical impacts, mining can permanently occupy land previously used for grazing or for migration. Mining and exploration activity also leads reindeer to avoid areas where it occurs, removing additional areas from use by reindeer herders. As noted earlier, while the area of land used for mining may be limited, where it occurs on or near key migration routes or pastures of a specific kind that are in limited supply, it can have major adverse impacts (Fohringer et al. 2021; Kløcker Larsen et al. 2022: 4). The scale and severity of these impacts has increased greatly in recent years with the expansion of extractive industry. For example, during 2002–4, fewer than ten exploration permits per year were issued on Sami lands, whereas for 2014–16 the equivalent number was between 40 and 60. During 2001–17, 51 mining concession permits were issued and land designated for mining on traditional Sami territories increased from some 10,000 hectares in 2000 to 20,000 hectares in 2017 (Kløcker Larsen et al. 2018: 377; Osterlin and Raitio 2020: 8–10).

The growing impact of exploration and mining is compounded by the rapid expansion of other industrial activity. Industrial forestry is now practised in many lowland areas, resulting in reduction and fragmentation in the lichen-rich forest that reindeer depend on during winter. The number of wind turbines operating on Sami lands increased from 300 in 2010 to 983 in 2017 (Osterlin and Raitio 2020: 7–8). As large parts of winter grazing areas are particularly suitable for wind energy production, pressure from this source is likely to increase. In 2020 there were 2,035 wind turbines with granted planning applications on traditional Sami territories (Osterlin and Raitio 2020: 10; see also Skarin and Ahman 2014). Damming of lakes and rivers for hydroelectric power, large-scale tourism, and military activities have also had significant negative effects on pasture availability (Ojala and Nordin 2015: 7; Össbo and Lantto 2011). A preliminary mapping of cumulative encroachments from all competing land uses on the grazing lands of one Sami reindeer-herding community found a 54 per cent loss of winter grazing grounds that are critical to reindeer survival (Osterlin and Raitio 2020: 10). Fohringer et al. (2021: 880) report that the community of Laevas has lost use of 34 per cent of its total pasture lands as a result of industrial and infrastructure development. This situation is exacerbated by climate change. Adapting to the shifting climatic conditions requires reindeer herders to have a higher degree of flexibility in their use of the landscape, but encroachment and disturbance from competing land uses reduce flexibility (Osterlin and Raitio 2020: 2, 4).

The Aitik mine, located on the territory of the Gällivare Forest Sami community, provides a concrete illustration of the way in which mining affects Sami livelihoods, documented by Lawrence and Kløcker Larsen (2019) on the basis of consultation with community members. The mine was established in 1968 by Boliden, a Swedish-based multinational company specializing in copper and zinc production and with mines in Sweden, Finland, Norway, and Ireland. Aitik is Sweden's largest open-pit copper mine, employs some 770 people, and in 2020 mined 41.7 million tonnes of ore to produce concentrates containing copper, gold, and silver, and generated a net profit of $254 million (Boliden 2021). Gällivare, like other communities, is subject to a range of existing and proposed industrial impacts, including logging by several forestry companies and a proposed wind farm comprising 150 turbines.

The community opposed the Aitik project from the start but had no capacity to halt it and was not involved in any EIA. From the community's perspective, recent discussions with Boliden involve the provision of information by the company rather than consultation regarding management of the project's impacts. The mine has led directly to loss of pastures, while dust from mining operations has adversely affected other grazing lands. Poorly maintained fencing and gates that Boliden staff have forgotten to close have allowed stray reindeer to wander into the mine area, leading to the loss of many animals, including through drowning in tailings ponds. Boliden pays compensation only where it can be demonstrated that reindeer have been killed in the mine area, and pays no compensation for purchase of supplementary reindeer food to offset the loss of pastures, or for the substantial additional time Sami must devote to herding reindeer around Boliden facilities, monitoring fence lines and roads, and searching for lost reindeer. A number of community members have been forced to give up reindeer herding, with the loss of winter pasture caused by the mine being 'the last straw' (Lawrence and Kløcker Larsen 2019: 57–61).

A second general source of impact is the demands a complex and fragmented regulatory system make on Sami reindeer herders if they are to have any say about the impact of industrial development on their lands and territories. As Sehlin MacNeil notes (2015: 2), 'A deep understanding of the mining industry, the legal processes around mining, as well as the power relations involved, are necessary in order to challenge the mining companies … gaining this information and staying informed is time consuming and further impacts on members of the *sameby*, as their time is needed for reindeer herding.' Sami face a dilemma. If they do not participate, their failure to object to proposed exploration or mining activity may be taken as implied consent by government and companies, and there is little prospect their interests will be considered. If they do participate, there is some limited prospect that this will occur, but participation absorbs time, energy, and money that they need to devote to reindeer herding. Osterlin and Raitio (2020: 13) provide an indication of the scale of the burden facing Sami communities in noting that between 2014 and 2016 a total of 1,181 written statements and appeals would have been required from communities for exploration permit applications and associated work plans alone. Additional commitments would have been required in relation to proposed mining projects, and to participating in face-to-face consultations with project proponents.

These figures relate only to extractive activity. For example, a Sami reindeer-herding community in one region participated in some 20 consultations for wind energy projects alone in 2014. While individual government agencies and developers only need to master regulations for one sector, Sami reindeer-herding communities need to master the different regulations and processes that apply to all the land-use activities that occur in their area (Osterlin and Raitio 2020: 15–16). As one Sami leader noted, 'The degree of exploitation is increasing a lot, and the lands are very fragmented. Before we could think that some exploitation projects did not matter so much, but today we don't have the luxury of not trying to defend our land. But we still have to prioritise what we participate in' (cited in Osterlin and Raitio 2020: 16).

Compounding the difficulty faced by the Sami in participating in regulatory processes is the fact that the legal aid system in Sweden does not provide financial support for Sami people to assert their rights (UNHRC 2016: 11–12).

The difficulties involved in participating effectively in the project approval system has resulted in a growing tendency for Sami people to explore other avenues to influence development on their territories. These have included appeals to international organizations and legal fora, including the UN Human Rights Council; and protests and other forms of opposition to proposed projects, sometimes in conjunction with non-Sami organizations opposed to mining. Such approaches also come with a cost, both in material terms and, in some cases, from the stress associated with a backlash against Sami in the form of hate speech and other expressions of racism (Osterlin and Raitio 2020: 5). In 2014, Stefan Mikaelsson, the President of the General Assembly of the Sametinget, called for an increase in struggle and resistance against mining in what he saw as a desperate situation:

> What we need to do is resist, instead of accepting never-ending negotiations where business as usual leads to further loss of Sámi territory, lands and waters … resistance is the only remaining possibility in a desperate situation. [we have] … already spoken all the words that may be spoken, in documents and statements. So far, none of our actions have had any significant effect on the dominant Swedish society. The colonization and destruction keeps continuing, without any stop. (cited in Ojala and Nordin 2015: 8–9)

I have discussed elsewhere in the book the possible role of negotiated agreements in managing the negative impact of mining on Indigenous lands. Given the state's refusal to acknowledge Sami property rights and the insistence of the Swedish government and developers that mining is not incompatible with reindeer herding, it is unsurprising that while agreements between mining companies and reindeer herders do occur, they have been limited in scope. They do not involve benefit sharing or limits on the scale and form of extractive activity. Rather they focus on mitigation measures such as fencing to keep reindeer away from infrastructure such as roads, and economic compensation for loss of pasture, often in the form of payment for purchase of feed or for transport of animals (Kløcker Larsen et al. 2018: 381–2; Sehlin MacNeil 2015: 2; Tarras-Wahlberg et al. 2017: 657). In this regard, mining is typical of agreements involving Sami communities in other sectors. A recent study indicates that in most cases, agreements involve communities withdrawing appeals against the planned project and/or promising not to not lodge any objections in the future. In return, project developers may pay community representatives a set fee to attend consultations; keep the community informed of activities that might affect reindeer herding; and make modest payments (in one case US$70,000 per annum) to compensate the community for any negative impacts (Kløcker Larsen et al. 2021).

New projects: Kallak and Rönnbäcken

In this section, I discuss two mining projects planned for Sami territories, to assess whether the ability of Sami people to influence development on their lands has increased in recent years.

The first project, the proposed Kallak iron ore project, is being developed by Beowulf Mining plc, a Swedish-owned public company listed on the London and Swedish stock markets. The company has several mining and mineral-processing projects under development, but no operating mines. The existence of the Kallak mineral deposits, located in the county of Norrbotten, has been known since the 1940s, and expenditure by Beowulf of SEK80 million (US$9 million) since it was granted an exploration licence in 2006 has established reserves of some 250 million tonnes of iron ore that can be upgraded to a concentrate with 71 per cent iron. Road and rail infrastructure would be upgraded to ship iron ore to the Swedish port of Luleå and the Norwegian town of Narvik on the Atlantic coast (Beowulf Mining plc 2021a).

Kallak is in the municipality of Jokkmokk, on the reindeer grazing lands of two *samebys*, Sirges and Jåhkågasska, whose members opposed the project believing that it would have severe consequences for their livelihoods. Kallak is located on a peninsula along the river Lilla Luleälven, which contains major reindeer migration routes as well as areas used for resting, gathering, and grazing. The project would cut Jåhkågasska's territory in two, reduce valuable winter pasture, prevent the ability of reindeer to roam, and negatively affect the gathering of reindeer (Forss 2015; Herrmann et al. 2014). One community leader indicated that 'The grazing pastures for the reindeer have already grown smaller … it's hard to say when a point of no return is reached. But with this mine, I personally fear that it will affect my survival as a reindeer herder' (cited in Forss 2015).

In summer 2013, several protests were undertaken by reindeer herders and their allies against the project, and the Sami sought to attract media attention to their cause: for example, circulating photos illustrating Sami use of traditional territories that would be affected by Kallak, including children engaged in berry picking. Sami and non-Sami protestors barricaded the road leading to the site where test drilling was to be conducted, and clashed with police when the latter cleared the way for the mining company's vehicles. Media reports showed how the clashes grew more violent; police were filmed using dogs to intimidate protestors and tearing down towers with protestors still inside. The protests and the police response to them brought national media attention to Kallak and fostered a wider debate in Sweden about the role of mining and its compatibility with Sami reindeer-herding livelihoods and with environmental sustainability (Koivurova et al. 2015: 28; Landén and Fotaki 2018: 28–9; Sehlin MacNeil 2015: 9; Persson et al. 2017: 26). At the same time, the planned mine gained support among politicians and some local residents because of the new job opportunities it offered, while at a national level its supporters argued that the mining industry creates jobs in rural areas and contributes to important technological developments (Labba 2014: 95; Ojala and Nordin 2015: 7).

In July 2015, the CAB for Norrbotten stated that Kallak had a positive economic case, and in October 2015, the Mining Inspectorate recommended to the Swedish government that Beowulf be awarded an exploitation concession. However, in November 2017, the CAB reversed its position and determined that Beowulf should not be granted an exploitation concession, on the basis that reindeer herding was a better use of the land at Kallak. Several state agencies, including the Environmental Protection Agency and the National Heritage Board, advised the government against approving the mine (Anshelm and Haikola 2018: 576). Beowulf argued that the CAB's determination was invalid in part because the Board failed to consider properly the financial health of Jokkmokk Municipalit, noting that 'Over the last two years, the local municipality of Jokkmokks Kommun has been forced to cut its budget by SEK28 million and … desperately needs the economic stimulus, investment, jobs and taxes that Kallak will deliver. … Kallak will bring billions of SEK in investment and hundreds of jobs to Jokkmokk' (Beolwulf 2021a). The company appealed the CAB's decision to the national government and continues to make representations to local and national politicians. As of December 2021, no decision regarding the project's future had been made (Beowulf Mining plc 2021b).

The second project is Rönnbäcken, a planned nickel mine project in Storuman Municipality, Västerbotten County, on the territory of the Vapsten reindeer-herding community. It is regarded as one of the largest undeveloped nickel orebodies in Europe, with measured and estimated reserves of approximately 668 million tonnes with a content of 0.176 per cent nickel. The orebody was originally discovered in the first decade of this century by the Swedish company Nickel Mountain Group AB (NMG), which planned to develop three open-pit mines and produce 26,000 tonnes of high-grade nickel concentrate annually for 20 years, meeting a significant part of Sweden's nickel consumption. The project is now owned by Bluelake Mineral, another Swedish company focused on exploration and mine development in the Nordic region (Bluelake Mineral 2021).

In February 2010, NMG applied for exploitation concessions for two of the three planned open-pit mines, Rönnbäcken No. 1 and Rönnbäcken No. 2. The application documents were sent for comment to affected property owners, including the Vapsten Sami community. Vapsten objected strongly to the grant of the exploitation concessions, arguing that core areas of its pastures would be lost because of the resumption of land for mining and related infrastructure, and the impact of dust generated by the mine on lichen pasture, and that migration routes through the Rönnbäcken area would become unusable. Other industrial projects approved by the state had already made a large part of Vapsten's traditional territories unusable for reindeer husbandry, and the community argued that granting concessions for three open-pit mines would make it impossible to continue traditional livelihoods (CERD 2020: 2; Persson and Öhman 2014). The Västerbotten CAB concluded that there was no impediment to granting the concessions, provided that the mining operations, as far as possible, were adapted to allow continuation of reindeer herding. In June 2010, the Chief Mining Inspector granted the exploitation concessions for Rönnbäcken No. 1 and No. 2, subject to the condition that NMG engage in annual consultations with Vapsten herders to clarify measures required to mitigate disturbances by mining operations.

Vapsten appealed the decision to the government, which rejected the appeal, determining that reindeer husbandry could continue alongside mining operations. The community requested a judicial review by the Supreme Administrative Court, which revoked grant of the concessions on the grounds that due process had not been followed. The Chief Mining Inspector had assumed that coexistence of mining and reindeer herding was possible and had not undertaken, as required by the Swedish Environment Code, an assessment of which of the two, if they were in conflict, should be given priority (Lawrence and Kløcker Larsen 2019: 21). The Court requested a re-examination of the case.

In December 2011, before this reassessment had occurred, NMG applied for an exploitation concession for the third open-pit mine. The application documents were again sent for comment to Vapsten, which again objected to grant of the concession. In October 2012, the Chief Mining Inspector granted the exploitation concession, once more indicating that NMG must engage in annual consultations with the Vapsten Sami and must work to minimize the adverse impact of the mining operations on reindeer husbandry. Vapsten appealed the decision, and requested that the three applications for mining concessions be considered jointly. In August 2013, the government rejected all three appeals, determining that the area available to the Vapsten community for reindeer herding was much larger than that required by NMG and that Vapsten could continue reindeer herding elsewhere. In October 2014, Sweden's Supreme Administrative Court rejected Vapsten's application for a judicial review, finding that the government's decision concerning the three exploitation concessions was lawful (CERD 2020; Persson and Öhman 2014).

In the meantime, in September 2013 Vapsten had lodged, with the support of the Sami Council, the peak representative body for Sami across Sapmi, a complaint against Sweden with the United Nations Committee for the Elimination of Racial Discrimination (CERD). This alleged that Sweden had breached the Convention on the Elimination of All Forms of Racial Discrimination by ignoring its members' property rights through the grant of the three exploitation concessions to NMG without Vapsten's consent, in an area that was Vapsten's traditional property and where its members pursued their livelihood. Vapsten alleged that the concessions granted by Sweden would deprive them of reindeer migration routes, destroy their capacity to pursue their livelihood, and force them to relocate from their traditional territory. Vapsten also claimed that Sweden had breached its right to equal treatment before the law by failing to recognize the unique nature of its property rights as an Indigenous reindeer-herding community (CERD 2020).

On 22 October 2013, CERD requested Sweden to suspend all mining activities in Vapsten's traditional territory while its case was under consideration, a request it reiterated in May 2015. In May 2017, CERD declared Vapsten's complaint admissible. In responding to the complaint, Sweden argued that the Sami's right to pursue reindeer husbandry is not a right of ownership of land, but is rather a usufruct right to utilize land and water for domestic purposes and for reindeer husbandry. Sweden reiterated the justification it provided in approving the exploitation concessions to NMG, that the area affected is small in relation to the total area available to Vapsten for reindeer husbandry, and that 'minerals are located in a certain area and cannot be reallocated elsewhere, whereas reindeer can have a possibility of alternative grazing grounds' (CERD 2020: 4–5). Sweden also argued that the concept of FPIC does not involve 'a collective right to veto', but rather requires that consultations should be undertaken in good faith with the objective of achieving Indigenous consent. Sweden argued that such consultations had been undertaken with Vapsten prior to grant of the exploitation concessions (CERD 2020, 3–4).

In November 2020, CERD rejected Sweden's arguments and found that it had breached the Convention on the Elimination of All Forms of Racial Discrimination and violated the rights of the Vapsten reindeer-herding community. It recommended that Sweden provide 'an effective remedy to the Vapsten Sami Reindeer Herding Community by revising effectively the mining concessions after an adequate process of free, prior and informed consent'. CERD also recommended that Sweden amend its legislation to enshrine the principle of FPIC in its dealings with Sami people (CERD 2020: 16). Sweden has not acted on these recommendations to date. Neither has it sought to progress the Rönnbäcken project.

Conclusion

Until recently, Sami people in Sweden have had no control over mineral development on their traditional territories and have not shared in the economic surpluses it produces. They have had no choice but to try and mitigate its impacts and adjust to them as best they can in seeking to maintain livelihoods based on reindeer husbandry and use of wild resources. These impacts have been greatly magnified because of the cumulative effects of exploration, mining, infrastructure development, wind farms, forestry, and tourism. At the same time, the regulatory systems that Sami must navigate in their attempts to mitigate the impacts of development are fragmented, complex, and time consuming. In combination, the burden of impacts and of trying to mitigate them can be overwhelming. Some Sami have lost the battle to continue their traditional livelihoods and are no longer engaged in reindeer herding. For many others, their capacity to continue reindeer husbandry and maintain its associated cultural and social practices is severely threatened (Kløcker Larsen et al. 2022: 7).

Sami engaged in reindeer herding are primarily concerned with sustaining existing livelihoods, so sharing in economic benefits created by mining has not been a priority for them. In the cases discussed above, they have simply wanted the mining companies to leave them alone so they can maintain reindeer husbandry as a viable way of life. They have negotiated agreements in cases where it has become clear they could not stop mining, with the objective of achieving at least minimal compensation for its effects.

The Sami's negotiating power in dealing with the state and with industry has been weakened by several factors. Sami account for only about 0.2 per cent of Sweden's population, and only a minority of Sami are involved in reindeer herding. The equivalent Indigenous proportion of the population for some other cases discussed in the book is 3–5 per cent (Australia and Canada) and 12 per cent (Chile and the Philippines). Sami reindeer herders live in small communities far from Sweden's major cities, creating further obstacles to their political mobilization and making it very difficult for them to establish a presence on Sweden's 'political radar'. While recent conflicts around mining projects have drawn some media attention, Persson et al. (2017: 26) note, for instance, that during the time when Kallak attracted attention from major media outlets, those same outlets contained more than ten times as many items about the threatened destruction of an old oak tree in Stockholm. In their view, 'questions over mining in Sápmi have routinely been ignored by media … [which] has continuously prevented the Sámi people's opportunities to create a public debate and opinion to facilitate the possibility to influence their situation'. This situation may reflect not just demographic factors, but also reluctance on behalf of Sweden's non-Sami population to acknowledge that Sweden's relationship with Sami people is colonial in nature, and involves denial of human rights when Swedes see themselves as championing human rights in the global arena.

The bargaining position of Sami people has certainly been undermined by the Swedish state's consistent and relentless denial that the Indigenous status of Sami reindeer herders brings with it legal and property rights that would give them a say over whether and in what form industrial development should occur on Sami territories. This is despite the state's obligations, under its own laws, actively to promote the conditions required to maintain Sami culture and to give Sami the opportunity 'to influence issues that concern them'. Sami bargaining positions have also been undermined by the consistent preference the state has afforded to mining interests, and by the reluctance of Sweden's mining industry to afford recognition to Sami interests outside the framework of state policy and legislation, as has occurred in some other countries. The position adopted by state and industry in relation to Sami rights has created an environment hostile to the negotiation of agreements that might include significant benefit sharing for Sami reindeer herders and a capacity for them to help shape the design and management of mining projects. The state's position has also made it difficult for the Sami to take court action on the basis that their rights have been infringed, as opposed to challenging specific administrative decisions on the grounds that state agencies have not followed due legal process. Regulatory and IA processes are fragmented and complex, and offer limited opportunities for Sami participation. Those opportunities that do exist for Sami participation are expensive and time consuming, as barriers are heightened by their inability to access legal aid, by the scant resources available to them compared to government and industry, and by the fact that Sami must navigate different regulatory systems across the multiple industry sectors that impinge on their territories.

There are signs of change. The Kallak and Rönnbäcken cases show that Sami communities, bolstered by their ability to access international legal fora such as CERD and in some cases by support from neighbouring Sami communities and civil society organizations, are now able to slow or halt the progress of new mining projects. It is also notable that certain elements of the state, including CABs and the Environment Department, have taken positions that support Sami interests where these conflict with mining. Kløcker Larsen and Raitio (2019: 19) argue that a 'significant divide seems to exist *within* the state apparatus, i.e. between the national political leadership ... and street-level state officials faced with the consequences of implementation failure in their daily work, e.g. in the form of prolonged permit processes and escalated conflicts' (emphasis in original; see also Anshelm and Haikola 2018).

These changes have not, so far, been accompanied by a willingness on the part of the state or industry to reconsider the fundamental basis of their relationship with Sami reindeer herders. This is indicated by the fact that there has yet to be a case where the final outcome of the permitting system was to deny an extraction concession due to reindeer herding; and that the Swedish government has not ruled out approving projects currently in abeyance at some later date. It is also indicated by the fact that the mining companies developing Kallak and Rönnbäcken continue to press for project approval in the face of strong Sami opposition. Despite the surge of foreign investment in recent years, both the companies involved are Swedish. Multinational firms might be more exposed to changing international norms regarding recognition of Indigenous rights and so be more willing to go beyond what is required by the state.

This situation is not likely to change until there is a basic shift in the attitude of the Swedish state to recognition of inherent Sami ownership rights in their traditional territories and the resources they contain.

17

Analysis and Conclusion

Indigenous peoples and mining: change and continuity

Indigenous peoples are no longer powerless to influence extractive activities on their territories. As is abundantly clear from the history of destruction, dispossession, and marginalization outlined in Chapter 3, no Indigenous peoples in the past were able to stop projects like Pascua Lama and Jabiluka that promised to generate large profits for their investors and large revenues for government. No Indigenous groups were able to shape the design of resources projects in the way the Innu and Inuit did with Voisey's Bay or Aboriginal traditional owners and the Kimberley Land Council (KLC) did with the Browse liquefied natural gas project, or to extract economic benefits from extractive activity on the scale achieved in these two cases or by the Atacameño communities in their agreement with Rockwood. Change has certainly occurred in the relationship between Indigenous peoples, the extractive industry, and the state. As Wanvik and Caine note (2017: 595), 'most academic literature still favours conventional conceptualizations of local indigenous communities as subject to circumstance and which are pushed even further to the fringes of their lands by external forces threatening to extinguish their traditional ways of life'. This characterization does not describe contemporary reality.

Yet change is uneven and in certain respects limited. In few cases do Indigenous peoples have the capacity to exercise free prior and informed consent (FPIC) in relation to proposed projects on their territories. It follows that if they wish to stop projects, they must apply considerable time, resources, and energy, often over many years, and there is no guarantee that they will succeed. Projects continue to be given approval over the opposition of Indigenous landowners. In some cases where Indigenous peoples manage to have projects delayed or shelved, as for example in Sweden and the Philippines, they may be revived later. Indigenous groups that might be prepared to consent to mining if appropriate conditions can be negotiated have, in the absence of FPIC, limited bargaining power because companies know that they can gain project approval in the absence of Indigenous consent. This explains why some Aboriginal communities in Australia sign agreements that offer few economic benefits or additional environmental or cultural protections.

What explains the change that has occurred, and the limited and uneven nature of that change? Reforms in domestic policy and law, brought about by the long-term and relentless efforts of Indigenous peoples, have been critical. As the case studies show, racism and discrimination against Indigenous peoples are still a powerful force in many countries, both in mining companies and in society more broadly.

Indigenous Peoples and Mining. Ciaran O'Faircheallaigh, Oxford University Press. © Ciaran O'Faircheallaigh (2023).
DOI: 10.1093/oso/9780192894564.003.0017

However, in most cases formal constraints on exercise of civil and political rights by Indigenous peoples have been removed and their access to educational opportunities has improved. Recognition of Indigenous identity has occurred in many countries and there has been a slow and uneven but significant increase in the recognition of Indigenous rights in land and resources. Flowing from these fundamental changes, Indigenous peoples have developed a growing capacity to utilize the media, form alliances with non-government organizations (NGOs), and use the courts to push for recognition of their legal rights in relation to existing or proposed mining projects.

The role of the state is critical in explaining the limited and uneven pace of change. In the countries examined, the executive arm of the state—that is, presidents or prime ministers, government ministers, and public servants heading key central and economic agencies—are still overwhelmingly supportive of the extractive industries. They are willing to sacrifice Indigenous rights and interests even where these are recognized in national legislation, if they perceive this is required to allow continuation and expansion of mining, including through violent repression by military and paramilitary forces, as occurred in Chile, Indonesia, and the Philippines. The attitude of the political executive reflects its belief that mining contributes greatly to economic growth and that continued growth is, in turn, essential for their political and bureaucratic careers. The position of political executives also reflects the financial resources available to the mining industry to help reinforce beliefs regarding mining's key economic role, and to undertake lobbying of political decision-makers. In some cases, close personal and financial links between politicians and industry executives also play a part.

That states continue to behave in this way highlights the limitations of changes in international recognition of Indigenous rights reviewed in Chapter 4, at least in the short term. States continue to act in ways manifestly contrary to undertakings they have given in adopting international declarations and conventions. Yet these instruments are not without effect. Indigenous peoples in many countries employ them as one component of their strategies to influence extractive activity and state behaviour. They use international law as external validation for positions they adopt in relation to Indigenous rights, and pressure governments to live up to their commitments under international declarations and covenants. This is exemplified by the extensive references by Atacameño communities in their 2016 agreement with Rockwood to Chile's formal recognition of their rights and its legal obligations under International Labour Organization (ILO) Convention 169. Developments in international law and recognition of Indigenous rights have also been important because they have emerged from the efforts of Indigenous peoples around the globe, in fora such as the United Nations (UN) Permanent Forum on Indigenous Issues (PFII). Those efforts have brought Indigenous peoples together in solidarity, helped strengthen their confidence in pursuing domestic agendas for change, and led to sharing of information on issues related to extractive industries and multinational mining companies. The development of an institutional framework focused on Indigenous issues in the UN has also helped to draw attention to state repression and the failure of state agencies to give effect to Indigenous legal rights: for instance, through the reports of the Special Rapporteur on the Rights of Indigenous Peoples.

All states employ regulatory frameworks whose stated purpose is to identify and manage negative impacts from mining. Environmental impact assessment (EIA) legislation purports to assess whether proposed mining projects are on balance acceptable given their expected environmental impacts, and to identify strategies to mitigate negative impacts if projects are to proceed. EIA systems work to the disadvantage of Indigenous peoples. They understate negative impacts and are biased towards approving projects; discourage Indigenous participation and discount Indigenous knowledge; and focus heavily on impacts on the physical environment, ignoring or discounting the cultural and social effects of mining. Sweden's project approval system, under which fundamental decisions about the desirability and like-lihood of mining are made before affected Sami reindeer herders are consulted, exemplifies the problems that Indigenous peoples face in this area. Similarly, many mineral-producing countries enact legislation whose stated purpose is to protect Indigenous cultural heritage, but which is in reality designed to allow for heritage to be destroyed where it may impede profitable mining operations, as was starkly illus-trated by the destruction of the Juukan Gorge rock shelters in Western Australia in May 2020. States are failing to protect Indigenous peoples against mining's negative impacts.

The case studies also highlight the fact that states are not monolithic and that some state institutions and agencies can be mobilized in support of Indigenous interests. Where the rule of law applies, the judicial branch of the state is playing an especially important role in insisting that the executive respects the legal rights of Indige-nous peoples, and in helping Indigenous peoples to delay, or halt, proposed projects. Law courts do not always function in this manner, as is evident from the Philippines case study, where long delays in judicial processes and reversal of court decisions under political pressure served to deny effective recognition of Indigenous rights. The outcome of litigation is never certain, and as the experience of the San in Botswana shows, the political executive may on occasion ignore court decisions. These factors helps to explain the uneven nature of progress in achieving recognition of Indige-nous rights. Individual administrative agencies may also be aligned with Indigenous interests, as illustrated by the role of Chile's recently created environmental regula-tors in ensuring the success of Indigenous efforts to stop Pascua Lama, and to place limits on water extraction in the Salar de Atacama. Local- or regional-level elements of the state may also be more sympathetic to Indigenous interests, as illustrated by the stand taken recently by some County Administrative Boards in Sweden in defence of Sami reindeer herders. These findings support calls for a more nuanced analysis of the state that pays close attention to specific institutional configurations as these evolve over time (Bainton and Skrzypek 2021).

What of the role of mining companies in bringing about, or inhibiting, change? There has been considerable discussion in recent decades regarding the corporate social responsibility (CSR) policies of mining companies, policies which purport to

ensure that firms take account of the social and cultural welfare of Indigenous communities affected by their operations and to go beyond their legal obligations in doing
so. In addition to the work of individual companies in this area, considerable time
and resources have been committed by industry peak bodies, international financial
institutions, and the UN in developing frameworks for implementing, monitoring,
and evaluating CSR policies (see Chapter 4).

Individual companies have certainly gone beyond their legal obligations in recognizing Indigenous interests. Rio Tinto responded to pressure from Mirrar people not
to proceed with Jabiluka when it had the support of Australian governments to do so.
Albermarle, a US-based multinational corporation (MNC), negotiated a substantial
financial package with the Atacameño communities, in the absence of a legal requirement to do so. Its neighbouring lithium producer, the Chilean-owned Sociedad
Química y Minera de Chile SA, has not undertaken a similar initiative, indicating
that MNCs may be more inclined to take Indigenous interests into consideration.
As against this, Barrick, the world's largest gold producer, assisted individuals and
organizations favourable to the company's Pascua Lama project to gain recognition
as Indigenous and channelled resources in their direction, fomenting division in the
process. Australian and Philippine companies pursued similar tactics in the Philippines with similarly divisive results, and Swedish companies have ignored calls by
Sami reindeer herders to protect their livelihoods. In Australia, individual companies
have negotiated agreements favourable to, and highly unfavourable to, Indigenous
communities for projects governed by the same legislation, indicating that they have
been prepared only to pay what they were compelled to pay to achieve formal project
consents. The 'arrival' of CSR has not led to change across large segments of the
mining industry.

Barrick's behaviour in favouring Indigenous groups whom it considered likely to
support its mine illustrates a wider phenomenon, also evident in state behaviour. This
involves the establishment or co-option of individuals, entities, or processes believed
likely to deliver outcomes favourable to mining. Examples include the role of the
National Commission on Indigenous Peoples, in the Philippines, and the National
Corporation for Indigenous Development, in Chile, in facilitating legal recognition
as 'Indigenous' of individuals and organizations sympathetic to mining; the role of
Toronto Ventures, Inc. (TVI) in funding the takeover of Siocon Subanon Association,
Inc. by pro-mining elements of the Subanon; Western Mining Corporation's practice
of engaging with tribal councils rather than the traditional B'laan leadership; and the
Botswana government's recruitment of a key San leader as part of an effort to establish
a state-controlled consultation forum to manage engagement with the San.

Indigenous agency has been fundamental in bringing about change. Indigenous
action has been central in advancing domestic and international recognition of
Indigenous rights, and Indigenous peoples have delayed and stopped projects where
those rights were not recognized or where they believed mines would inevitably
impose serious costs on them and their territories. They have negotiated agreements

that change the distribution of costs and benefits in fundamental ways, and have created their own impact assessment (IA) processes to help overcome the weaknesses of regulatory EIA.

The exercise of agency implies choice, and a key conclusion from the book is that Indigenous choices and interests in relation to mining are highly diverse. Any assumption that Indigenous peoples are or should be inherently 'anti-mining', or the natural allies of environmental groups opposed to mining, is unfounded. Some Indigenous peoples certainly do simply want miners to 'go away'. These often involve communities which possess economies that are viable in the absence of mining. The Agricultural Community which formed the backbone of the initial opposition to Pascua Lama and Sami reindeer herders are obvious examples. On the other hand, Atacameño peoples in Chile and many Aboriginal people in Australia and Canada wish to capitalize on the economic opportunities provided by mining, while at the same time achieving protection of water and other environmental and cultural resources essential to their livelihoods and well-being. Some groups dealing with poverty and a lack of access to basic services like health and education feel they have little choice but to engage with mining. Peoples who do so are no less 'Indigenous' than the Sami who display little interest in the potential economic benefits of mining or the Diaguita who opposed Pascua Lama.

None of the Indigenous peoples discussed in the book lack interest in economic matters. It is rather that depending on their histories and current situations, they differ in their understanding of how mining relates to their need for viable economic livelihoods. Neither do any of these groups lack a commitment to maintaining the environmental and cultural integrity of their homelands. Some see it as possible, and in some cases essential, to combine this commitment with pursuit of economic opportunities offered by mining. Others do not.

Fundamental attitudes towards mining influence the strategies and tactics that Indigenous peoples use in seeking to influence extractive activity on their territories. Where they have a viable economy and robust social and cultural institutions, they are likely to emphasize protest against and disruption of projects, including through litigation. There is no evidence, for example, that the Diaguita Agricultural Community ever considered negotiating with Barrick regarding Pascua Lama. There was nothing to negotiate about. The aim was simply to stop the project. Where economic imperatives call for engagement with industry, Indigenous peoples are more likely to enter negotiations and to use regulatory and community-controlled IAs to identify ways of maximizing economic opportunities and minimizing environmental and social costs. There are nuances and complexities within this broad picture. Some Indigenous communities may begin to engage with a project with an open mind about its acceptability, but IA and community consultations may reveal that it is unacceptable, and tactics may switch to refusal and litigation. Prevailing legal regimes are also important. It seems apparent that the Sami would prefer the mining industry to leave northern Sweden and let them herd their reindeer in peace. Sweden's legal and policy regime does not admit of such a possibility, and so where case-by-case litigation is unsuccessful in stopping projects, the Sami negotiate agreements to mitigate the impact of mining.

The role of NGOs and civil society more broadly varies depending on the strategies being pursued by Indigenous peoples. Given the limited bargaining power of numerically small Indigenous peoples and their limited financial resources, NGOs can play a key role in supporting protests, helping to finance media campaigns and litigation, putting pressure on shareholders, and raising awareness in the home countries of MNCs about their activities on Indigenous territories. Support in these forms is most relevant, and most likely to be forthcoming, when Indigenous peoples are involved in 'David and Goliath' struggles to stop mining, as for instance with the San in Botswana and the Diaguita in Chile. NGOs are rarely interested in efforts by Indigenous peoples to negotiate stronger agreements or improve IA processes, and if Indigenous peoples decide to switch from a strategy of refusal and protest to one of engagement, NGO support for Indigenous groups may evaporate or even turn into opposition. This occurred in the Philippines when NGOs abandoned the Subanon after their leaders decided the long-term interests of their community required them to engage with the mine operator TVI. The experience of the San shows that there are particular issues in relying on international NGOs, as their support may be vulnerable to changes in NGO priorities and to government action to expel NGO personnel. On the other hand, the position of the Xholobeni was considerably strengthened through their alliances with a diversity of civil society groups, including environmental NGOs, universities, and voluntary legal services.

There is a clear trend across the globe for Indigenous peoples to make greater use of negotiated agreements as part of their strategy for dealing with the mining industry and the state. Opportunities for agreement making have become more widely available with growing national and international recognition of Indigenous rights, increasing Indigenous capacity to stop or delay projects in the absence of agreements, and industry adoption of CSR policies.

Outcomes from negotiations have been highly variable. The general absence of a legal right to stop projects helps explains uneven outcomes. Some Indigenous communities and organizations are in a stronger position than others to overcome or partly compensate for this weak legal position. The most positive outcomes are achieved when Indigenous goals are clearly identified and prioritized through community consultation processes that can also underpin political mobilization; when negotiation is combined with other strategies including litigation and direct action; and when communities have or develop the capacity to obtain and apply relevant technical skills. These conditions are most like to be achieved when individual landowning groups are part of, or supported by, regional Indigenous organizations that can mobilize substantial financial, human, technical, and political resources, as illustrated by the experience of the KLC in Australia, the Innu and Inuit in Canada, and the Consejo de Pueblos Atacameños in Chile. The potential power that can be gained by aggregating individual Indigenous communities based on regions or/and Indigenous nations has also been documented in arenas other than extractive industries (see, for example, Gilbert 2017: 677–8). Aggregation is, of course, not just important for negotiation of agreements. The resources it helps mobilize are equally important for resistance and refusal. However, aggregation of Indigenous landowning groups or communities is not without its challenges. In addition to barriers created by distance, lack of resources, and poor access to communications, group autonomy is a central moral and political principle across many Indigenous societies (see Chapter 5). A key challenge for Indigenous leaders and institutions is to achieve a balance between this principle and the centralization of authority required to achieve concerted action at larger scales.

Achieving positive economic and social impacts from negotiated agreements depends also on effective implementation, which requires allocation of dedicated resources, ongoing monitoring of outcomes, and remedial action where desired outcomes are not being achieved. Specific requirements apply to the management of revenues derived from agreements, where development of clear strategies for investment and application of funds is essential, as is creation of structures and processes that achieve transparency in how revenues are applied and who benefits from them, and accountability on these matters to the members of beneficiary communities. This finding is consistent with the broader literature on mineral resource revenues which suggests that the nature and quality of institutions is critical to whether the 'resource curse' can be avoided.

It has been suggested by James Otto that the state could significantly improve outcomes for Indigenous peoples by mandating through legislation the negotiation of community development agreements (CDAs) for all mining projects and by monitoring agreement implementation. Otto argues that legislation could mandate minimum requirements for CDAs while retaining sufficient flexibility to meet the differing needs of individual communities, and that a corpus of 'best practice' could be developed that would help ensure positive outcomes (Otto 2018). I am sceptical regarding the efficacy of this approach. States have shown little indication of a commitment to reshape the distribution of costs and benefits between mining companies and Indigenous peoples in fundamental ways and it seems likely that any legislation would set the bar at a level that would fail to meet the ambitions and needs of affected Indigenous communities. States have been deficient in enforcing environmental and cultural heritage legislation designed to protect Indigenous interests, and there seems no reason to assume they would be any more diligent in pursuing implementation of CDAs. Further, there is a danger that companies would prove reluctant to go beyond the minimum standards established in law, making it more difficult for Indigenous groups that can exercise significant bargaining power to achieve more favourable outcomes, and stifling innovation and improvement in the terms of agreements over time.

What of the role of Indigenous women in relations between their communities and extractive industry? The extent to which Indigenous women are centrally involved in setting goals and devising and implementing strategies in relation to mining varies considerably. Women are often at the forefront of protest and disruption. This is illustrated, for instance, by the central role of Yvonne Margarula in stopping

the development of the Jabiluka uranium mine and of Xholobeni women in leading litigation and direct action aimed at preventing the plans of Mineral Resources
Commodities to exploit mineral sands on South Arica's Wild Coast. In some cases,
women's roles in spearheading resistance reflects their existing leadership roles in
their communities. The Xholobeni have always operated a hierarchy of dual leadership between men and women, and Aboriginal women in north Australia frequently
play key leadership roles. There is also evidence from the case studies, including
that focusing on the San in Botswana, that extractive activity does affect women or
threaten them in specific ways, which may increase their involvement in resistance
activity.

In some contexts, Indigenous women play little direct role in negotiation of agreements with mining companies, but they may still influence outcomes by shaping
negotiation agendas and strategies, and by taking key roles in implementing agreements. The wide range of women's involvement is illustrated by two of the Indigenous
trusts referred to in discussing the impacts of royalty payments to Indigenous communities. The Ely Trust's directors are all women. There are no women directors
on the board of the Qikiqtani Inuit Association (QIA) Benefits and Legacy Fund.
However, these cases also suggest that the link between the gender of those holding formal positions of authority and outcomes from mining is complex. These
two trusts, while their boards are starkly different in terms of gender composition,
have developed very similar strategies for using their mineral revenues, emphasizing
longer-term and community-wide benefits.

The relevance of theory

What of the theoretical perspectives reviewed at the start of the book? To what extent
are they supported by, or contradicted by, the evidence of the thematic chapters and
the case studies? Modernization theory, with its prediction that the economic benefits
of mining will automatically trickle down to and transform Indigenous communities,
finds little support. Large-scale mineral development generally creates few benefits
for affected Indigenous communities until and unless specific interventions occur: for
example, negotiation of contractual agreements requiring that some of the economic
benefits of mining are shared. In addition, there is no indication that, as modernization theory suggests, market forces will result in the disappearance of Indigenous
economic, cultural, and social formations. These show considerable resilience and
in some cases are being strengthened by the application of resources extracted from
mining projects.

Mining can certainly have devastating effects on Indigenous livelihoods, as suggested by mode of production theory. But those livelihoods cannot accurately be
characterized as equivalent to a 'subsistence mode of production'. Many Indigenous
peoples do still rely to on harvesting wild resources, and connection to country is
central to their social and cultural identity. However, they also engage in producing

food for sale, earn wages or operate businesses in the market economy, or receive cash transfers from mineral royalties or the state. This indicates that engagement with a capitalist economy as such is not fatal to their Indigenous way of life, and indeed may be helping to allow its continuation. This is not to deny that some Indigenous groups believe that *a particular manifestation of capitalism* in the form of massive open-cut mining projects conducted without due regard to their ecological impacts is an existential threat to their existing ways of life. Many Sami reindeer-herding communities in Sweden, for instance, take this view.

This discussion raises the question of whether hybrid theory offers a more satisfactory explanatory framework. There is no question that some Indigenous peoples display behaviour that could be characterized as 'hybrid', as it involves a mix of subsistence activity, market resources, and drawing income from the public sector. For example, hunters in Nunavut who harvest food, sell animal products, and receive support from revenue-sharing income allocated by the QIA Legacy Fund clearly fit this profile. The weakness of the hybrid model is as an explanatory framework. It offers no guide as to how one can explain the wide variety of outcomes that can be observed from Indigenous interactions with subsistence, market, and public economies.

Regulation theory seems more promising in this regard. Regulation theory suggests that communities and peoples do have choices in how they engage with global capitalism and do exercise agency in this engagement. As noted above, the very different responses of Indigenous peoples to extractive industry certainly show agency at work and reveal different modes of engagement. The Diaguita in Chile, the Mirrar in Australia, and the Xholobeni in South Africa have been able to refuse engagement with capitalism in the form of large-scale extractive industry. Other Indigenous peoples, notably in Australia and Canada, have engaged with the mining industry in ways that allow them to shape the design of projects, benefit from employment and training opportunities, and obtain revenue streams that can be applied in pursuing their economic and social priorities.

Regulation theory also argues that the outcomes of engagement with capitalism will be affected by 'modes of social regulation', with 'social regulation' defined as 'a complex of institutions and norms' based on 'such things as habits and customs, social norms, laws and institutional forms' (Hirst and Zeitlin 1991: 19). It proposes that considerable variation can exist in modes of regulation at local, regional, national, and global scales which can explain different outcomes from engagement with capitalism. As noted in Chapter 2, the weakness of regulation theory is that it provides no insight into the implications of specific forms of Indigenous 'social formation' for the success or otherwise of engagements with capitalism.

The ability of Indigenous peoples to exercise choice and the choices they make have certainly been associated with specific 'social formations'. The existence of robust Indigenous economies increases the capacity for refusal, as illustrated by the role of the Agricultural Community in the resistance of Diaguita people to Pascua Lama. The structure of Indigenous political organization, and in particular the link between local and regional levels of organization, is important in allowing Indigenous peoples

290 Indigenous Peoples and Mining

to negotiate favourable agreements with mining companies. Indeed, forms of Indigenous organization are critical to both engagement and refusal, as they shape the capacity, for instance, to mobilize cultural resources, undertake community consultations, establish strategic goals, utilize judicial processes, and to engage with NGOs and direct their efforts. Of fundamental importance is the ability of Indigenous peoples to manage in a productive manner the inevitable tension between the moral principle of autonomy at the local level, and the need for political and organizational aggregation at the regional level. The outcomes of mineral revenues flowing to Indigenous communities is shaped by specific institutional forms, especially by the extent to which these create transparency for and accountability to actual and potential beneficiaries; by the values held by key Indigenous decision-makers; and by the quality of leadership. The way in which these aspects of 'social formation' can vary and interact, and the way in which they can affect outcomes from mineral revenues, are vividly illustrated, for instance, by two contrasting cases from north Australia: manganese mining on Groote Eylandt and bauxite mining in western Cape York.

As race theory and gender theory suggest, social formations in the wider society also influence the pattern of Indigenous engagement with capitalism. Social norms and values such as racism and gender bias have a major impact in many of the case study countries, creating powerful barriers that Indigenous peoples must strive to overcome in pursuing their goals. Legal regimes affecting Indigenous rights and disposition of mineral resources, state institutional structures, specific features of extractive industry sectors, and corporate policies also have a significant impact. These societal variables interact with Indigenous social formations to bring about, as regulation theory suggests, a wide variety of forms of engagement. The extent to which these admit of Indigenous agency varies considerably. The San of the Central Kalahari Game Reserve have faced 'external' social formations that have been unremittingly hostile, and this, combined with the decline of their Indigenous economy and the organizational barriers created by geographical isolation and the dispersion of their communities, has left them engaged in a constant struggle to maintain even a small degree of control over their lives. The fact that legal regimes in Australia and Canada deny Indigenous peoples the right to stop development means some who might prefer to refuse engagement with extractive capitalism have no choice but to accept it and negotiate the best terms they can. For Sami people in Sweden, the terms available are far from acceptable, and many now wonder whether a forced engagement with extractive and other forms of capitalism will mean the end of livelihoods and cultures based on reindeer herding.

Parallel insights can be gained from colonial and postcolonial theory. Political and governing structures created by settler societies such as Australia and Canada certainly involve the denial of sovereignty and help define relations between Indigenous peoples and dominant societies. State rejection of the principle of Indigenous free prior and informed consent is a clear illustration of this denial, as Indigenous peoples are denied the ability to decide whether extractive activity should occur on their territories. The deeply entrenched priority that settler states, and Sweden in its 'settled' north, afford to mining over Indigenous interests is further evidence of the enduring impact of colonialism on Indigenous relations with the extractive sector and the wider society, as is the enduring legacy of racism. The concept of 'refusal', central to the work of postcolonial theorists, also finds support in the case studies, as does the belief that refusal can impose high costs on Indigenous peoples in the short term. These costs not only involve having to forgo the material benefits that engagement would bring, and in some cases suffering repressive responses by the state. They also involve the financial and human resources that must be committed to making refusal effective by denying extractive industry access to Indigenous territories, and the social and cultural impact of divisions that frequently occur in Indigenous communities that adopt a strategy of refusal. The case studies of Chile, the Philippines, and South Africa highlight both the possibility of Indigenous refusal and how substantial its costs can be.

Turning to theories of the state, as noted earlier there is overwhelming evidence that the state, *in general*, acts to support the interests of mining companies, a finding that provides little support for pluralist interpretations of the state. The concept of policy community could be relevant where Indigenous groups combine with elements of civil society including churches, trade unions, and environmental groups to influence specific decisions regarding individual projects. However, there is nothing to suggest that stable policy communities exist that include Indigenous peoples and elements of the state, and which are able to exercise a degree of autonomy from central state direction and routinely achieve policy outcomes consistent with Indigenous interests. On the other hand, the state does not uniformly or always act in a way that suggests, as would Marx and Engels, that it is simply the 'organizing committee' of mining and finance capital. Broad areas of state policy—for instance, domestic and international recognition of Indigenous rights—and the activities of individual state agencies, in particular courts and environmental departments, act to constrain the untrammelled access of extractive capitalism to Indigenous territories. This suggests that the state is also involved in activities designed to establish or maintain its legitimacy in the eyes of both domestic and international audiences, which accords with the more nuanced approach of neo-Marxists such as Poulantzas and Block. The fact that the political executives of states are in most cases strongly responsive to the interests of extractive industry suggests that Poulantzas's 'limited autonomy' may be a more accurate characterization of reality than the more full-blooded independence of societal interests suggested by statist theories. The growing body of international law supporting Indigenous rights suggests that constructivist theory is correct in emphasizing the fact that states do not exist in isolation and that change can emerge from interactions between them in fora such as the PFII and the ILO. The fact that states have no compunction in ignoring their obligations under international law where those obligations might inhibit mining indicates that the practical effect of such change is limited, unless it is reinforced by Indigenous political mobilization in the domestic sphere, designed to force the hand of state actors. Here also Indigenous agency is critical.

There is little to support neo-liberal theories that posit a growing 'absence' of the state and the abandonment of its traditional roles to private capital. To use a sporting analogy, the state may not always be on the playing field, but it is always on the side-lines, and ready to intervene if the Indigenous team seems to be gaining an advantage over the mining industry. State intervention may involve compulsory acquisition of Indigenous rights; blunting the effect of decisions by the courts that favour Indigenous people; or using repression, imprisonment, and violence in efforts to negate Indigenous resistance. The state also, very importantly, writes the rules of the game, in the form of constitutional enactments and statutes which confer structural advantages on the mining industry that are difficult to overcome. These include the 'free entry' system that assumes mining is always the state's preferred land use, a position made explicit by the Swedish state's unbending preference for mining over reindeer herding. This does not mean that Indigenous peoples accept the state's rules, but these rules do frame Indigenous encounters with extractive industry.

The pessimism and discounting of Indigenous agency that characterizes application of neo-liberal governance theory to the engagement of Indigenous peoples with the mining industry also appears unjustified. Indigenous people are certainly not always the winners from that engagement, but neither are they always the losers, as suggested by the critique of negotiated agreements as a neo-liberal technology. This is indicated by the success of Indigenous peoples in using agreements to influence the design of extractive projects and capturing a significant share of the wealth they generate. More generally, every case study illustrates the existence and influence of Indigenous agency, though the end to which agency is exercised and the degree of influence it exerts do vary from case to case.

No single theoretical approach is sufficient to explain the complex and varied patterns that characterize relations between Indigenous peoples and extractive industry across the globe. Neo-Marxist theories offer perhaps the most convincing account of the role of the state in influencing those relations. However, the state's role alone does not explain outcomes. Insights from regulation theory and colonial and postcolonial theory are needed to do so, because they both recognize the structural constraints facing Indigenous peoples in seeking to control their lives, but also recognize the power of Indigenous agency in shaping the way in which Indigenous societies interact with mining and with dominant societies. The impact of Indigenous agency is highly variable, and in some cases still severely constrained. In many other cases, it is on the ascendency, promising hope that in future decades Indigenous peoples across the globe will achieve greater control over extractive industries and the future of their territories and cultures.

A concluding comment

While the histories and priorities of the Indigenous peoples discussed in this book vary, what unites them is a determination to control what happens on their ancestral lands. They may wish to stop mining entirely. They may wish to stop some mining projects and not others. They may be keen to facilitate mining if they can capture an equitable share of its benefits and effectively manage its cultural, social, and environmental impacts. Their key demand is to exercise the right to decide whether to accept extractive projects on their territories. They share a resilience and a determination that bodes well for their ability to achieve this demand in decades to come.

References

AANDC (Aboriginal Affairs and Northern Development Canada), 2014. 'The Government of Canada's Approach to Implementation of the Inherent Right and the Negotiation of Aboriginal Self-Government'. Government of Canada, https://www.rcaanc-cirnac.gc.ca/eng/1100100031843/1539869205136, accessed 28 February 2022.

Abagado, 2020. 'CA Won't Stop Didipio Mine Closure, But Won't Let Oceana Gold Save Face by Withdrawing Case'. Abagado, https://abogado.com.ph/ca-wont-stop-didipio-mine-closure-but-wont-let-oceanagold-save-face-by-withdrawing-case/, accessed 3 June 2021.

Abale, F., 1999. 'The Importance of Consent: Indigenous Peoples' Politics in Canada'. In *Canadian Politics*, 3rd edition, edited by J. Bickerton and A. Gagnon. Peterborough: Broadview, 443–62.

ABC (Australian Broadcasting Commission), 2015a. 'What Has Happened to $34 million Missing from Groote Eylandt Aboriginal Trust?'. ABC, https://www.abc.net.au/7.30/what-has-happened-to-$34-million-missing-from/6913444, accessed 28 February 2022.

ABC, 2015b. 'Bail Refused over Aboriginal Trust Theft'. ABC, http://www.sbs.com.au/news/article/2015/12/18/bail-refused-over-aboriginal-trust-theft, accessed 28 February 2022.

ABS (Australian Bureau of Statistics), 2012. 'Census of Population and Housing: Characteristics of Aboriginal and Torres Strait Islander Australians, 2011'. ABS, http://www.abs.gov.au/ausstats/abs@.nsf/mf/2076.0, accessed 28 January 2019.

ACHPR (African Commission on Human and Peoples' Rights), 2005. *Report of the African Commission's Working Group of Experts on Indigenous Populations/Communities*. ACHPR: Banjul, The Gambia.

Acker, J., 1990. 'Hierarchies, Jobs, Bodies: A Theory of Gendered Organizations'. *Gender and Society* 4(2): 139–58.

Acuna, R. M., 2015 'The politics Politics of extractive Extractive governanceGovernance: Indigenous peoples Peoples and Ssocio-environmental Cconflicts'. *The Extractive Industries and Society*, 2: 85–92.

Åhrén, M., 2004. 'Indigenous Peoples' Culture, Customs, and Traditions and Customary law: The Saami People's Perspective'. *Arizona Journal of International and Comparative Law* 21(1): 63–112.

AIHW (Australian Institute of Health and Welfare), 2022. 'Profile of Indigenous Australians'. AIHW, https://www.aihw.gov.au/reports/australias-welfare/profile-of-indigenous-australians, accessed 4 January 2022.

Aipin, Y., 1989. 'Not by Oil Alone'. *IWGIA Newsletter* 57: 136–43.

Albert, B. 1992. 'Indian Lands, Environmetal Policy and Military Geopolitics in the Development of the Brazilian Amazon: The Case of the Yanomami'. *Development and Change* 23: 35–70.

ALC (Anindilyakwa Land Council), 2015. *Annual Report 2014–2015*. Alyangula: ALC.

Alfred, G. R., 1995. *Heeding the Voices of Our Ancestors: Kahnawake Mohawk Politics and the Rise of Native Nationalism*. Toronto: Oxford University Press.

Alfred, G. R., 1999. *Peace Power and Righteousness: An Indigenous Manifesto*. Toronto: Oxford University Press.

Alfred, G. R., 2009. 'Colonialism and State Dependency'. *Journal of Aboriginal Health* 5(2): 42–60.

Ali, S., and O'Faircheallaigh, C., 2007. 'Extractive Industries, Environmental Performance and Corporate Social Responsibility'. *Greener Management International: Journal of Corporate Environmental Strategy and Practice* 52: 5–16.

Allam, L., and Wahlquist, C., 2020. 'More than 100 Aboriginal Sacred Sites—Some Dating before the Ice Age—Could Be Destroyed by Mining Companies'. *The Guardian*, 28 August, https://www.theguardian.com/australia-news/2020/aug/28/more-than-100-aboriginal-sacred-sites-some-dating-before-the-ice-age-could-be-destroyed-by-mining-companies, accessed 7 April 2021.

Allen, D. W., 2007. 'Information Sharing during the Klondike Gold Rush'. *Journal of Economic History* 67(4): 944–67.

Alternative Law Group Inc., et al., 2009. 'Submission to the [United Nations] Committee on the Elimination of all forms of Racial Discrimination Philippines Indigenous Peoples ICERD Shadow Report'. https://www2.ohchr.org/english/bodies/cerd/docs/ngos/PIP_Philippines75.pdf, accessed 17 May 2021.

Althaus, C., and O'Faircheallaigh, C., 2019. *Leading from Between: Indigenous Leadership and Participation in the Public Service*. Montreal: McGill Queen's University Press.

Altman, J., 1983. *Aborigines and Mining Royalties in the Northern Territory*. Canberra: Australian Institute of Aboriginal Studies.

Altman, J., and Kerins, S. (eds), 2012. *People on Country: Vital Landscapes, Indigenous Future*. Sydney: Federation Press.

Amarshi, A., Good, K., and Mortimer, R., 1979. *Development and Dependency: The Political Economy of Papua New Guinea*. Melbourne: Oxford University Press.

Amengual, M., 2018. 'Buying Stability: The Distributive Outcomes of Private Politics in the Bolivian Mining Industry'. *World Development* 104: 31–45.

Anaya, J., 1997. 'Indigenous Peoples in International Law'. *Cultural Survival Quarterly* 21(2): 58–61.

Anaya, J., 2010. *The Situation of Indigenous Peoples in Botswana: Report by the Special Rapporteur on the Situation of Human Rights and Fundamental Freedoms of Indigenous People, James Anaya*, A/HRC/15. New York: United Nations Human Rights Council.

Anderson, C., 1983. 'Aborigines and Tin Mining in North Queensland: A Case Study in the Anthropology of Contact History'. *Mankind* 13(6): 473–98.

Anderson, K., and Lawrence, B., 2006. *Strong Women Stories: Native Vision and Community Survival*. Toronto: Sumach Press.

Anderson, R. A., Dana, L. P., and Dana, T. E., 2006. 'Indigenous Land Rights, Entrepreneurship, and Economic Development in Canada: "Opting-in" to the Global Economy'. *Journal of World Business* 41: 45–55.

Andreucci, D., and Radhuber, I. R., 2015. 'Limits to "Counter-neoliberal" Reform: Mining Expansion and the Marginalisation of Post-extractivist Forces in Evo Morales's Bolivia'. *Geoforum* 84: 280–91.

Anglo American, 2022. 'Women in Mining: Promoting Human Rights and Economic Development through Gender Equality'. Anglo American, https://www.angloamerican.com/development/emps/~/media/Files/A/Anglo-American-Plc/siteware/docs/mb_women, accessed 15 February 2022.

Anguelovski, I., 2011. 'Understanding the Dynamics of Community Engagement of Corporations in Communities: The Iterative Relationship between Dialogue Processes and Local Protest at the Tintaya Copper Mine in Peru'. *Society and Natural Resources* 24: 384–99.

Anshelm, J., and Haikola, S., 2018. 'Depoliticization, Repoliticization, and Environmental Concerns: Swedish Mining Politics as an Instance of Environmental Politicization'. *ACME: An International Journal for Critical Geographies* 17(2): 561–96.

APWLD (Asia Pacific Forum on Women, Law and Development), 2009. *Mining and Women in Asia: Experiences of Women Protecting Their Communities and Human Rights against Corporate Mining.* Chiang Mai: APWLD.

Australian Government, 2006. 'Mine Closure and Completion: Leading Practice Sustainable Development Program for the Mining Industry'. Canberra https://nt.gov.au/__data/assets/pdf_file/0015/203415/mine-closure-and-completion.pdf, accessed 7 April 2021.

Aylwin, J., 1999. 'Indigenous Rights in Chile: Progress and Contradiction in the Context of Economic Globalisation'. *Indigenous Law Bulletin*, August/September: 23–5.

Babidge, S., 2013. '"Socios": The Contested Morality of "Partnerships" in Indigenous Community–Mining Company Relations, Northern Chile'. *Journal of Latin American and Caribbean Anthropology* 18: 274–93.

Babidge, S., 2015. 'Contested Value and an Ethics of Resources: Water, Mining and Indigenous People in the Atacama Desert, Chile'. *Australian Journal of Anthropology* 27: 84–103.

Babidge, S., 2018. 'Sustaining Ignorance: The Uncertainties of Groundwater and Its Extraction in the Salar de Atacama, Northern Chile'. *Journal of the Royal Anthropological Institute* 25: 83–102.

Babidge, S., and Belfrage, M., 2017. 'Failing Forward: A Case Study in Neoliberalism and Abandonment in Calama'. *Cultural Dynamics* 29(4): 235–54.

Babidge, S., Kalazich, F., Prieto, M., and Yager, K., 2019. '"That's the Problem with that Lake; It Changes Sides": Mapping Extraction and Ecological Exhaustion in the Atacama'. *Journal of Political Ecology* 26: 738–60.

Bainton, N., 2010. *The Lihir Destiny: Cultural Responses to Mining in Melanesia.* Canberra: ANU E-Press.

Bainton, N., and Jackson, R. T., 2020. 'Adding and Sustaining Benefits: Large-Scale Mining and Landowner Business Development in Papua New Guinea'. *Extractive Industries and Society* 7: 366–75.

Bainton, N. A., and Macintyre, M., 2013. '"My Land, My Work": Business Development and Large Scale Mining in Papua New Guinea'. *Research in Economic Anthropology* 33: 139–65.

Bainton, N., and Skrzypek, E., 2021. 'An Absent Presence: Encountering the State through Natural Resources Extraction in Papua New Guinea and Australia'. In *The Absent Presence of the State in Large-Scale Resource Extraction Projects*, edited by N. Bainton and E. E. Skrzypek. Canberra: ANU Press, 1–41.

Bainton, N., Owen, J. R., and Kemp, D., 2020. 'Invisibility and the Extractive-Pandemic Nexus'. *Extractive Industries and Society* 7(3): 841–3.

Baker, J. M., and Westman, C. N., 2018. 'Extracting Knowledge: Social Science, Environmental Impact Assessment, and Indigenous Consultation in the Oil Sands of Alberta, Canada'. *Extractive Industries and Society* 5: 144–53.

Balana, C., 2011. 'Palawan Tribal Folk Hit Use of Fake Leaders'. *Philippine Daily Inquirer*, 7 June.

Ballard, C., 2001. *Human Rights and the Mining Sector in Indonesia: A Baseline Study.* London: International Institute for Environment and Development.

Baluarte, D. C., 2004. 'Balancing Indigenous Rights and a State's Right to Develop'. *Sustainable Development Law and Policy* 4: 9–15.

Bankes, N., 2004. 'Natural Resource Projects, Indigenous Peoples and the Role of International Law'. *Resources* 87: 1–6.

BankTrack, 2016. 'Tampakan Copper and Gold Mine Project Philippines'. BankTrack, https://www.banktrack.org/project/tampakan_copper_and_gold_mine_project, accessed 27 May 2021.

Barker, T., 2006. *Employment Outcomes for Aboriginal People: An Exploration of Experiences and Challenges in the Australian Minerals Industry.* Research Paper No. 6, CSRM, University of Queensland, Brisbane.

Barrick Gold Corporation, 2015. *Annual Report 2014*. Toronto.

Barrick Gold Corportaion, 2020. 'Barrick Accepts Environmental Court Ruling, Continues to Seek New Opportunities in Chile'. Barrick Gold Corporation, https://www.barrick.com/English/news/news-details/2020/barrick-accepts-environmental-court-ruling/default.aspx, accessed 6 September 2020.

Barsh, R. L., 1994. 'Indigenous Peoples in the 1990s: From Object to Subject of International Law'. *Harvard Human Rights Journal* 7: 33–86.

Batise, S., 2016. 'Experiences with Joint Ventures in the Mineral Sector'. Presentation to PDAC 2016. Gogama, Ontario: Warbun Tribal Council.

BBC News, 2020. 'Rio Tinto Chief Jean-Sebastien Jacques to Quit over Aboriginal Cave Destruction'. BBC News, 11 September, https://www.bbc.com/news/world-australia-54112991, accessed 23 March 2021.

Bebbington, A., and Bury, J. (eds), 2013. *Subterranean Struggles: New Dynamics of Mining, Oil and Gas in Latin America*, Austin, TX: University of Texas Press.

Bebbington, A., and Scurrah, M., 2013. 'Hydrocarbon Conflicts and Indigenous Peoples in the Peruvian Amazon: Mobilization and Negotiation along the Rio Corrientes'. In *Subterranean Struggles: New Dynamics of Mining, Oil and Gas in Latin America*, edited by A. Bebbington and J. Bury. Austin, TX: University of Texas Press, 174–96.

Bedi, H., 2008. 'Environmental Mis-assessment'. *Development and Change* 44(1): 101–23.

Belayneh, A., Rodon, T., and Schott, S., 2018. 'Mining Economies: Inuit Business Development and Employment in the Eastern Subarctic'. *Northern Review* 47: 59–78.

Bell, J., 2021. 'Mary River Mine Blockade Highlights Nunavut Agreement's Fatal Flaw'. *Nunatsiaq News*, 12 February, https://nunatsiaq.com/stories/article/mary-river-mine-blockade-highlights-nunavut-agreements-fatal-flaw/, accessed 24 February 2022.

Beowulf Mining plc, 2021a. 'Kallak Iron Ore Project: Mineral Resource Estimate and Exploration Target Upgrade'. Beowolf Mining plc, https://news.cision.com/se/beowulf/r/kallak-iron-ore-project—mineral-resource-estimate-and-exploration-target-upgrade,c3352732, accessed 23 November 2021.

Beowulf Mining plc, 2021b. 'Kallak Update'. Beowulf Mining plc, https://polaris.brighterir.com/public/beowulf_mining_plc/news/rns_widget/story/rd70kmr, accessed 31 December 2021.

Berger, T., 1977. *Northern Frontier, Northern Homeland: The Report of the Mackenzie Valley Pipeline Inquiry*. Vancouver: Douglas & McIntyre.

Berman, M., 2018. 'Resource Rents, Universal Basic Income, and Poverty among Alaska's Indigenous Peoples'. *World Development* 106: 161–72.

Bernauer, W., 2011. 'Uranium Mining, Primitive Accumulation and Resistance in Baker Lake, Nunavut: Recent Changes in Community Perspectives'. MA thesis, Department of Native Studies, University of Manitoba, Winnipeg.

Bhatt, K. L., 2020. *Concessionaires, Financiers and Communities: Implementing Indigenous Peoples' Rights to Land in Transnational Development Projects*. Cambridge: Cambridge University Press.

BHP, 2020a. *BHP Annual Report 2020*. BHP, https://www.bhp.com/-/media/documents/investors/annual-reports/2020/200915_bhpannualreport2020.pdf?la=en, accessed 21 September 2020.

BHP, 2020b. 'Our Contributions'. BHP, https://www.bhp.com/our-approach/our-contributions/, accessed 7 October 2020.

Block, F. L., 1987. *Revising State Theory: Essays in Politics and Postindustrialism*. Philadelphia, PA: Temple University Press.

Bluelake Mineral, 2021. 'Nickel: Rönnbäcken, Bluelake Mineral'. Bluelake Mineral, https://bluelakemineral.com/en/projects/nickel/, accessed 31 December 2021.

Boileau, J., 2016. "'Opening Wealth's Door": Chinese Market Gardening on the Goldfields'. In *Rushing for Gold: Life and Commerce on the Goldfields of New Zealand and Australia*, edited by L. Carpenter and L. Fraser. Dunedin: Otago University Press, 122–32.

Boliden, 2021. 'Boliden Aitik'. Boliden, https://www.boliden.com/operations/mines/boliden-aitik, accessed 31 December 2021.

Bond, C., and Kelly, L., 2021. 'Returning Land to Country: Indigenous Engagement in Mined Land Closure and Rehabilitation'. *Australian Journal of Management* 46(1): 174–92.

Boutet, J-S., 2014. 'Opening Ungava to Industry: A Decentring Approach to Indigenous History in Subarctic Québec, 1937–54'. *Cultural Geographies* 21(1): 79–97.

Bradshaw, B., Fidler, C., and Wright, A., 2016. *Impact and Benefit Agreements and Northern Resource Governance: What We Know and What We Still Need to Figure Out*. Whitehorse: Yukon College.

Brake, J., 2016. 'Elder Speaks Out against Muskrat Falls, Innu Leadership'. *The Independent*, 3 October, https://theindependent.ca/news/elder-speaks-out-against-muskrat-falls-innu-leadership/, accessed 7 January 2022.

Brereton, D., Owen, J., and Kim, J., 2011. *World Bank Extractive Industries Source Book: Good Practice Notes on Community Development Agreements*. Brisbane: CSRM, University of Queensland, https://espace.library.uq.edu.au/view/UQ:254168, accessed 21 February 2022.

Brody, Hugh, 2000. *The Other Side of Eden: Hunters, Framers and the Shaping of the World*. Vancouver: Douglas & McIntyre.

Browne, M. W., and Robertson, K., 2009. *Benefit Sharing Agreements in British Columbia: A Guide for First Nations, Businesses and Governments, Report prepared by Woodward & Company for the Ecosystem-Based Management Working Group*. Victoria: Woodward & Company.

Brubacher & Associates, 2002. *The Nanisivik Legacy in Arctic Bay: A Socio-economic Impact Study*. Department of Sustainable Development, Government of Nunavut, https://assembly.nu.ca/library/GNedocs/2002/000595-e.pdf, accessed 21 April 2021.

Brunnschweiler, C. N., and Bulte, E. H., 2008. 'Linking Natural Resources to Slow Growth and More Conflict'. *Science* (320): 616–17.

Buchanan, G., and May, K., 2012. 'Indigenous Rangers and the Customary Economy'. In *People on Country: Vital Landscapes, Indigenous Future*, edited by J. Altman and S. Kerins. Sydney: Federation Press, 65–81.

Butler, C., Watkinson, B., and Witzke, J., 2021. 'The Immovable Object: Mitigation as Indigenous Conservation'. *Collaborative Anthropologies* 13(2): 1–28.

Butlin, N. G., 1993. *Economics and the Dreamtime: A Hypothetical History*. Cambridge: Cambridge University Press.

Cahir, F., 2012. *Black Gold: Aboriginal People on the Goldfields of Victoria, 1850–1870*. Canberra: Anu E-Press.

Caine, K. J., and Krogman, N., 2010. 'Powerful or Just Plain Power-Full? A Power Analysis of Impact and Benefit Agreements in Canada's North'. *Organization and Environment* 23(1): 76–98.

Calderon, L., 2021 'Tampakan, Other Giant Mines Could Strike Gold in Wake of Duterte's New Order'. CNN Philippines, https://www.cnnphilippines.com/news/2021/4/26/Exclusive—Tampakan—other-giant-mines-could-strike-gold-in-wake-of-Duterte-s-new-order.html, accessed 27 May 2021.

Caliguid, F. A., 2011. 'CHR to Probe Mining "Abuses" in Surigao Provinces'. *Inquirer Mindanao*, 5 June.

Cameron, E., and Levitan, T., 2014. 'Impact and Benefit Agreements and the Neoliberalization of Resource Governance and Indigenous-State Relations in Northern Canada'. *Studies in Political Economy* 93(1): 25–52.

Campbell, J. L., 2007. 'Why Would Corporations Behave in Socially Responsible Ways? An Institution Theory of Corporate Social Responsibility'. *Academy of Management Review* 32(3): 946–67.

Canada, Newfoundland and the LIA (Labrador Inuit Association), 2002. *The Voisey's Bay Interim Measures Agreement*. St John's, Newfoundland.

Canadian Museum of Immigration and the University of Western Ontario, 2020. '"The Crowd of Crazy Fools": The Gold Rush in British Columbia and the Yukon'. Canadian Museum of Immigration, https://pier21.ca/research/immigration-history/the-gold-rush-in-british-columbia-and-the-yukon#:~:text=%22The%20Crowd%20of%20Crazy%20Fools,British%20Columbia%20and%20the%20Yukon&text=It%20was%20a%20strange%20scene,space%20of%20a%20city%20block, accessed 15 July 2020.

Cannon, T., 1992. *Corporate Responsibility*. London: Pitman.

Carmichael, D., Hubert, J., Reeves, B., and Schanche, A. (eds), 1994. *Sacred Sites, Sacred Places*. London and New York: Routledge.

Carpenter, L., 2013. 'Finding "Te Wherro" in Ōtākou: Māori and the Early Days of the Otago Gold Rush'. *MAI: A New Zealand Journal of Indigenous Scholarship* 2(2): 105–20.

Carpenter, L., 2016. 'Finding "Te Wherro" in Otakou: Otago Māori and the Gold Rush'. In *Rushing for Gold: Life and Commerce on the Goldfields of New Zealand and Australia*, edited by L. Carpenter and L. Fraser. Dunedin: Otago University Press, 87–100.

Carreon, E. B., 2009. 'Indigenous Women and Mining'. In *Mining and Women in Asia: Experiences of Women Protecting Their Communities and Human Rights against Corporate Mining*, edited by Asia Pacific Forum on Women, Law and Development (APWLD). Chiang Mai: APWLD, 104–9.

Carrere, M., 2020. 'Chile: ¿Qué está en juego en el Salar de Atacama?' Mongabay, 20 September, https://es.mongabay.com/2020/09/chile-que-esta-en-juego-en-el-salar-de-atacama/, accessed 4 October 2020.

Carroll, A. B., 1999. 'Corporate Social Responsibility'. *Business and Society* 38(3): 268–95.

Carruthers, D., and Rodriguez, P., 2009. 'Mapuche Protest, Environmental Conflict and Social Movement Linkage in Chile'. *Third World Quarterly* 30(4): 743–60.

Caruso, E., Colchester, M., MacKay, F., Hildyard, N., and Nettleton, G., 2003. *Extracting Promises: Indigenous Peoples, Extractive Industries and the World Bank*, Synthesis Report, May 2003. Baguio City: Forest Peoples Program and Tebtebba Foundation.

Carvalho, F. P., 2017. 'Mining Industry and Sustainable Development: Time for Change'. *Food and Energy Security* 6(2): 61–77.

Castillo, E. D., 1998. *Short Overview of Californian Indian History*. California Native American Heritage Commission, http://nahc.ca.gov/resources/california-indian-history/, accessed 15 July 2020.

Cattelino, J., 2010. 'The Double Bind of American Indian Need-Based Sovereignty'. *Cultural Anthropology* 25 (2): 235–62.

Cavallo, G. A., 2013. 'Pascua Lama, Human Rights, and Indigenous Peoples: A Chilean Case through the Lens of International Law'. *Goettingen Journal of International Law* 5(1): 215–49.

Cecco, L., 2021. 'Inuit Hunters Blockade Iron Mine in Freezing Temperatures over Expansion: Standoff Exposes Tensions between Large Inuit Organizations with Power to Approve Permits and Residents of Small Communities'. *The Guardian*, 10 February, https://www.theguardian.com/environment/2021/feb/09/canada-inuit-hunters-blockade-iron-mine-expansion-plan, accessed 22 March 2021.

CERD (Committee on the Elimination of Racial Discrimination), 2020. *Opinion Approved by the Committee under Article 14 of the Convention Concerning Communication No. 54/2013*, CERD/C/102/D/54/2013.

Chance, N. A., and Andreeva, E. N., 1995. 'Sustainability, Equity, and Natural Resource Development in Northwest Siberia and Arctic Alaska'. *Human Ecology* 23(2): 217–40.

Chesterman, J., and Galligan, B., 1997. *Citizens Without Rights: Aborigines and Australian Citizenship*. Melbourne: Cambridge University Press.

Christensen, W., 1990. 'Argyle Impacts: Issues and Concerns'. In *Aborigines and Diamond Mining*, edited by R. Dixon and M. Dillon. Nedlands: University of Western Australia Press, 95–107.

Christian Aid and PIPlinks, 2004. *Breaking Promises, Making Profits: Mining in the Philippines*. London: Christian Aid and PIPlinks.

CIGI (Centre for International Governance Innovation) (ed.), 2018. *UNDRIP Implementation: More Reflections on the Braiding of International, Domestic and Indigenous Laws*. Waterloo, ON: CIGI.

Cocker, M., 1998. *Rivers of Blood, Rivers of Gold: Europe's Conflict with Tribal Peoples*. London: Jonathan Cape.

Collier, P., and Venables, A. J. (eds), 2011. *Plundered Nations? Successes and Failures in Natural Resource Extraction*. Basingstoke: Palgrave Macmillan.

Conservation International, 2022. 'Partnering with Communities'. Conservation International, https://www.conservation.org/priorities/partnering-with-communities, accessed 21 March 2022.

Corbridge, S., 1990. 'Post-Marxism and Development Studies: Beyond the Impasse'. *World Development* 18 (5): 623–39.

Corntassel, Jeff, 2007. 'Partnership in Action? Indigenous Political Mobilization and Co-optation during the First UN Indigenous Decade'. *Human Rights Quarterly* 29: 137–66.

Coumans, C., 2002. 'Mining, Water, Survival and the Diavik Diamond Mine'. In *Moving Mountains: Communities Confront Mining and Globalisation*, edited by G. Evans, J. Goodman, and N. Lansbery. London: Zed, 91–108.

Coumans, C., 2008. 'Realising Solidarity: Indigenous Peoples and NGOs in the Contested Terrain of Mining and Corporate Accountability'. In *Earth Matters: Indigenous Peoples, the Extractive Industries and Corporate Social Responsibility*, edited by C. O'Faircheallaigh and S. Ali. Sheffield: Greenleaf, 42–66.

Cousins, D., and Nieuwenhuysen, J., 1984. *Aboriginals and the Mining Industry*. Sydney: George Allen & Unwin.

Cox, D., and Mills, S., 2015. 'Gendering Environmental Assessment: Women's Participation and Employment Outcomes at Voisey's Bay'. *Arctic* 68(2): 246–60.

Cragg, W., and Greenbaum, A. 2002. 'Reasoning about Responsibilities: Mining Company Managers on What Stakeholders Are Owed'. *Journal of Business Ethics* 39: 319–35.

Craik, N., Gardner, H., and McCarthy, D., 2017. 'Indigenous–Corporate Private Governance and Legitimacy: Lessons Learned from Impact and Benefit Agreements'. *Resources Policy* 52: 379–88.

Crawhall, N., 2011. 'Africa and the UN Declaration on the Rights of Indigenous Peoples'. *International Journal of Human Rights* 15(1): 11–36.

Crawley, A., and Sinclair, A. 2003. 'Indigenous Human Resource Practices in Australian Mining Companies: Toward an Ethical Model'. *Journal of Business Ethics* 45: 361–73.

Cristescu, R. H., Rhodes, J., Frére, C., and Banks, P. B., 2013. 'Is Restoring Flora the Same as Restoring Fauna? Lessons Learned from Koalas and Mining Rehabilitation'. *Journal of Applied Ecology* 50: 423–31.

Cross, H., 2020. 'Former Thalanyji Corporation CEO Paid More than Prime Minister'. *National Indigenous Times*, 2 October, https://nit.com.au/former-thalanyji-corporation-ceo-paid-more-than-prime-minister/, accessed 24 February 2022.

Cross, H., 2021. 'Aboriginal Affairs Portfolio Deserves Sole Focus'. *National Indigenous Times*, 19 February, https://nit.com.au/aboriginal-affairs-portfolio-deserves-sole-focus/, accessed 17 February 2022.

Dahl, J., 1990. 'Introduction'. In *Indigenous Peoples of the Soviet North*, edited by International Working Group on Indigenous Affairs (IWGIA). Copenhagen: IWGIA, 11–22.

Dahl, R. A., 1961. *Who Governs?* New Haven, CT: Yale University Press.

Dalseg, S., Kuokkanen, R., Mills, S., and Simmons, D., 2018. 'Gendered Environmental Assessments in the Canadian North: Marginalization of Indigenous Women and Traditional Economies'. *Northern Review* 47: 135–66.

Dashwood, H. S., 2012. *The Rise of Global Corporate Social Responsibility: Mining and the Spread of Global Norms*. Cambridge: Cambridge University Press.

Davis, S. L., 1998. 'Engaging the Community at the Tampakan Copper Project: A Community Case Study in Resource Development with Indigenous People'. *Natural Resources Forum* 22(4): 233–43.

Day, J. C., and Affum, J., 1995. 'Windy Craggy: Institutions and Stakeholders'. *Resources Policy* 21(1): 21–6.

De Beers, 2008. 'De Beers Response re Botswana'. De Beers, https://media.business-humanrights.org/media/documents/files/reports-and-materials/De-Beers-response-re-Botswana-23-Oct-2008.pdf, accessed 3 February 2022.

De Costa, R., 2006. *A Higher Authority: Indigenous Transnationalism and Australia*. Sydney: UNSW Press.

Deonandan, K., and Bell, C., 2019. 'Discipline and Punish: Gendered Dimensions of Violence in Extractive Development'. *Canadian Journal of Women and the Law* 31(1): 24–57.

Devlin, J. F., and Yap, N. T., 2008. 'Contentious Politics in Environmental Assessment: Blocked Projects and Winning Coalitions'. *Impact Assessment and Project Appraisal* 26(1): 17–27.

DINTEG and KALUHHAMIN, 2015. *Right to Our Mineral Resources in Our Ancestral Territories*. Baguio City and General Santos City: DINTEG and KALUHHAMIN.

Donaldson, T., and Preston, L. E., 1995. 'The Stakeholder Theory of the Corporation: Concepts, Evidence, and Implications'. *Academy of Management Review* 20(1): 65–91.

Doohan, K., 2008. *Making Things Come Good: Relations between Aborigines and Miners at Argyle*. Broome: Backroom Press.

Dowie, M., 2009. 'Nuclear Caribou: On the Front Lines of the New Uranium Rush with the Inuti of Nunavut'. *Orion*, January/February: 20–8.

Doyle, C., 2015. *Indigenous Peoples, Title to Territory, Rights and Resources: The Transformative Role of Free Prior and Informed Consent*. New York: Routledge.

Dyck, N., 1985. 'Introduction'. In *Indigenous Peoples and the Nation-State: Fourth World Politics in Canada, Australia and Norway*, edited by N. Dyck. St John's: Memorial University, 1–26.

Dylan, A., Smallboy, B., and Lightman, E., 2013. '"Saying No to Resource Development Is Not an Option": Economic Development in Moose Cree First Nation'. *Journal of Canadian Studies* 47(1): 59–90.

ELI (Environmental Law Institute), 2004. *Prior Informed Consent and Mining: Promoting the Sustainable Development of Local Communities*. Washington, DC: ELI.

Ellwood, K., 2014. 'Aboriginal Prospectors and Miners of Tropical Queensland, from Pre-Contact Times to ca.1950'. *Journal of Australasian Mining History* 12: 59–80.

Ellwood, K., and Wegner, J., 2019. 'Shared History Forgotten: The Neglected Stories of Aboriginal Miners, Prospectors and Ancillary Workers in the North Queensland Mining Industry'. *Journal of Australasian Mining History* 17: 1–19.

Enbridge, 2011. 'Environmental Performance Overview'. Enbridge, http://csr.enbridge.com/The-Environment/2011-Environmental-Performance-Overview, accessed 14 January 2013.

Environment News, 2005. 'Aboriginal People Win Right to Limit Australian Uranium Mine'. Environment News, http://www.ens-newswire.com/ens/feb2005/2005-02-28-03. asp#:~:text=Aboriginal%20People%20Win%20Right%20to%20Limit%20Australian% 20Uranium%20Mine&text=DARWIN%2C%20Australia%2C%20February%2028%2C, traditional%20lands%20within%20the%20park, accessed 22 March 2021.

Environmental Justice Atlas, 2021. 'Kitchenuhmaykoosib Inninuwug Peoples against Platinum Exploration by Platinex Inc., Ontario, Canada'. Environmental Justice Atlas, https:// www.ejatlas.org/conflict/kitchenuhmaykoosib-inninuwug-peoples-against-platinum-exploration-by-platinex-inc-ontario-canada, accessed 23 March 2021.

ERM (Environmental Resources Management), 2010. *Mining Community Development Agreements: Final Report for the World Bank*. Washington, DC: ERM, https:// documents1.worldbank.org/curated/en/697211468141279238/pdf/712990v30WP0P 10IC00CDA0Report0FINAL.pdf, accessed 21 February 2022.

Esteves, A. M., 2008. 'Women-Owned SMEs in Supply Chains of the Corporate Resources Sector'. In *Gendering the Field: Towards Sustainable Livelihoods for Mining Communities*, edited by K. Lahiri-Dutt. Canberra: ANU E-Press, 133–43.

Evans, G., Goodman, J., and Lansbury, N., 2001. *Moving Mountains: Communities Confront Mining and Globalisation*, London: Zed.

Everingham, J-A., Trigger, D., and Keenan, J., 2021. 'The State's Stakes in the Century Mine'. In *The Absent Presence of the State in Large-Scale Resource Extraction Projects*, edited by N. Bainton and E. E. Skrzypek. Canberra: ANU Press, 279–312.

Faauia, T. N., Morgana, B., and Hikuroab, D., 2017. 'Ensuring Objectivity by Applying the Mauri Model to Assess the Post-disaster Affected Environments of the 2011 MV Rena Disaster in the Bay of Plenty, New Zealand'. *Ecological Indicators* 79: 228–46.

Feldman, A., 2002. 'Making Space at the Nations' Table: Mapping the Transformative Geographies of the International Indigenous Peoples' Movement'. *Social Movement Studies* 1(1): 31–46.

Felton, S., and Becker, H. 2001. *A Gender Perspective on the Status of the San in Southern Africa*. Windhoek: Legal Assistance Centre.

Fernandez, G. R., 2020. 'Neo-extractivism, the Bolivian State, and Indigenous Peasant Women's Struggles for Water in the Altiplano'. *Human Geography* 13(1): 27–39.

Filer, C., 1996. 'Participation, Governance & Social Impact: The Planning of the Lihir Gold Mine'. In *Mining and Mineral Policy Issues in the Asia-Pacific*, edited by D. Denoon, C. Ballard, G. Banks and P. Hancok, Canberra, Australian National University, 67-75.

Finnemore, M., and Sikkink, K., 1998. 'International Norm Dynamics and Political Change'. *International Organization* 52(4): 887–917.

Fohringer, C., Rosqvist, G., Inga, N., and Singh, N. J., 2021. 'Reindeer Husbandry in Peril? How Extractive Industries Exert Multiple Pressures on an Arctic Pastoral Ecosystem'. *People and Nature* 3: 872–86.

Forss, A., 2015. 'A New Era of Exploitation? Mining Sami Lands in Sweden'. *Cultural Survival Quarterly* 40(4): 1–7.

Franciscans International, 2014. *The Tampakan Copper-Gold Project and Human Rights Violations in the South Cotabato, Philippines*. Franciscans International, https:// franciscansinternational.org/fileadmin/media/Business_and_HR/Statements/philippines_ report_tampakancopyrevised_may2014.pdf, accessed 27 May 2021.

Franks, D. M., Davis, R., Bebbington, A. J., Ali, S. H., Kemp, D., and Scurrah, M., 2014. 'Conflict Translates Environmental and Social Risk into Business Costs'. *PNAS* 111(21): 7576–81.

Frederiksen, T., and Himley, M., 2019. 'Tactics of Dispossession: Access, Power, and Subjectivity at the Extractive Frontier'. *Transactions of the Institute of British Geographers* 45(1): 50–64.

Friedman, M., 1990. *Free to Choose: A Personal Statement*. London: Pan.

Gajardo, A., 2018. 'Between Support and Marginalization. The Process of the Diaguita's Reemergence in the Age of Neoliberal Multiculturalism'. *Abya Yala* 2(1): 91–109.

Gajardo, A., 2014. 'Etnicidad, reemergencia indígena y conflict minero. El Proyecto Pascua Lama, el Estado y el proceso de reethnificacion de los Diaguitas del Huasco alto, Chile'. *Anuari del Conflicte Social, 2014*: 73–105.

Gajardo, A., 2018. 'Between Support and Marginalization. The Process of the Diaguita's Reemergence in the Age of Neoliberal Multiculturalism'. *Abya Yala* 2(1): 91–109.

Gajardo, A., 2021. 'Performing the "India Permitida": The Counter-Gift of Indigenous Women Targeted by a Corporate Social Responsibility Programme (Chile)'. *Bulletin of Latin American Research* 40(2): 172–87.

Galbraith, L., Bradshaw, B., and Rutherford, M. D., 2007. 'Towards a New Supraregulatory Approach to Environmental Assessment in Northern Canada'. *Impact Assessment and Project Appraisal* 25(1): 27–41.

Gao, Z., Akpan, G., and Vanjik, J., 2002. 'Public Participation in Mining and Petroleum in Asia and the Pacific: The Ok Tedi Case and Its Implications'. In *Human Rights in Natural Resource Management*, edited by D. N. Zillman, A. R. Lucas, and G. Pring. Oxford: Oxford University Press, 679–93.

Garnett, S., Burgess, N. D., Fa, J. E., Fernández-Llamazares, J., Molnár, Z., Robinson, C. J., and Leiper, I., 2018. 'A Spatial Overview of the Global Importance of Indigenous Lands for Conservation'. *Nature Sustainability* 1: 369–74.

GEAT (Groote Eylandt Aboriginal Trust), 2010. 'Special Purpose Financial Statements and Reports for the Year Ended 30 June 2010'. GEAT: Alyangula.

GEAT, 2011. 'Special Purpose Financial Statements and Reports for the year ended 30 June 2011'. GEAT: Alyangula.

GEAT, 2015. 'Special Purpose Financial Report 31 March 2015'. GEAT: Alyangula.

GEBIE (Groote Eylandt and Bickerton Island Enterprises), 2015. 'Annual Financial Report for the Year Ended 30 June 2015'. Alyangula: GEBIE.

Geoscience Australia, 2022. 'Australian Mineral Facts'. Geoscience Australia, https://www.ga.gov.au/education/classroom-resources/minerals-energy/australian-mineral-facts, accessed 4 January 2022.

Gerbrandt, J. L., and Westman, C. N., 2020. 'When a Pipe Breaks: Monitoring an Emergency Spill in the Oil Sands and Documenting Its Erasure of Indigenous Interests in Land'. *Extractive Industries and Society* 7(4): 1301–8.

GetUp!, 2021. 'Call the Inquiry into Rio's Destruction of Juukan Gorge'. GetUp!, https://www.getup.org.au/campaigns/first-nations-justice-campaigns/heritage-act-contact-ask/call-the-inquiry-into-rio-s-destruction-of-juukan-gorge, accessed 23 March 2021.

Ghostkeeper, E., 2004. '*Weche* Teachings: Aboriginal Wisdom and Dispute Resolution'. In *Intercultural Dispute Resolution in Aboriginal Contexts*, edited by C. Bell and D. Kahahe. Vancouver: UBC Press, 161–75.

Ghuman, G., 2008. 'Aboriginal Protestors Released in Mining Case'. *Toronto Star*, 28 May, https://www.thestar.com/news/ontario/2008/05/28/aboriginal_protesters_released_in_mining_case.html, accessed 23 March 2021.

Gibson, G., 2017. *Cultural and Rights Impact Assessment: A Survey of the Field*. Mikisew Cree First Nation and the Firelight Group, https://firelight.ca/wp-content/uploads/2016/03/MCFN-303_MAPP-Report_Final.pdf, accessed 25 March 2021.

Gibson, G., and O'Faircheallaigh, C., 2015. *IBA Community Toolkit: Negotiation and Implementation of Impact and Benefit Agreements*. Ottawa: Walter & Duncan Gordon Foundation.

Gibson, G., Hoogeveen, D., and MacDonald, A., 2018. *Impact Assessment in the Arctic: Emerging Practices of Indigenous-Led Review*. Gwich'in Council International and Firelight Group, https://gwichincouncil.com/sites/default/files/Firelight%20Gwich%27in%20Indigenous%20led%20review_FINAL_web_0.pdf, accessed 25 March 2021.

Gibson, R., 2006. 'Sustainability Assessment and Conflict Resolution: Reaching Agreement to Proceed with the Voisey's Bay Nickel Mine'. *Journal of Cleaner Production* 14(3/4): 334–48.

Gibson MacDonald, G., Zoe, J. B., and Satterfield, T., 2014. 'Reciprocity in the Canadian Dene Diamond Mining Economy'. In *Natural Resource Extraction and Indigenous Livelihoods: Development Challenges in an Era of Globalization*, edited by E. Gilberthorpe and G. Hilson. London: Ashgate Press, 57–74.

Gilbert, J., 2017. 'Litigating Indigenous Peoples' Rights in Africa: Potentials, Challenges and Limitations'. *International and Comparative Law Quarterly* 66: 657–86.

Gilberthorpe, E., and Rajak, D., 2017. 'The Anthropology of Extraction: Critical Perspectives on the Resource Curse'. *Journal of Development Studies* 53(2): 186–204.

Glynn, T., and Maimunah, S., 2021. 'Unearthing Conscious Intent in Women's Everyday Resistance to Mining in Indonesia'. *Ethnography*, https://doi.org/10.1177/14661381211039372.

Golub, A., 2014. *Leviathons at the Gold Mine: Creating Indigenous and Corporate Actors in Papua New Guinea*. Durham, NC and London: Duke University Press.

Good, K., 2003. Bushmen and Diamonds: (Un)civil Society in Botswana. Discussion Paper No. 23, Nordiska Afrikainstitutet, Uppsala, http://www.diva-portal.org/smash/get/diva2:241418/FULLTEXT01.pdf, accessed 2 February 2022.

Goodland, R. (2012). *Responsible Mining: The Key to Profitable Resource Development*. Burlington: Institute for Environmental Diplomacy and Security, University of Vermont.

Goodland, R., 2009. 'SRK's Impact Assessment: An Overview'. In *Suriname's Bakhuis Bauxite Mine: An Independent Review of SRK's Impact Assessment*, edited by R. Goodland. Paramaribo, Suriname: VIDS, 9–25.

GOS (Government Offices of Sweden), 2013. *Sweden's Minerals Strategy for Sustainable Use of Sweden's Mineral Resources that Creates Growth throughout the Country*. Stockholm: GOS.

Gould, S. F., 2011. 'Does Post-mining Rehabilitation Restore Habitat Equivalent to that Removed by Mining? A Case Study from the Monsoonal Tropics of Northern Australia'. *Wildlife Research* 38: 482–90.

Government of Canada, Office of the Correctional Investigator, 2013. 'Aboriginal Offenders—A Critical Situation'. Office of the Correctional Investigator, https://www.oci-bec.gc.ca/cnt/rpt/oth-aut/oth-aut20121022info-eng.aspx, accessed 4 April 2022.

Govett, M. H., and Govett, G. J. S., 1980. 'The Role of the Australian Minerals Industry in World Mineral Supplies'. *Resources Policy* 6(2): 87–102.

Grand Council of the Cree, 2010. *Cree Nation Mining Policy*. Grand Council of the Cree, https://www.cngov.ca/wp-content/uploads/2018/03/cree_nation_mining_policy-1.pdf, accessed 7 January 2021.

Green, H., 2013. 'State, Company, and Community Relations at the Polaris Mine (Nunavut)'. *Inuit Studies* 37(2): 37–57.

Großmann, K., Padmanabhan, M., and von Braun, K., 2017. 'Contested Development in Indonesia: Rethinking Ethnicity and Gender in Mining'. *Austrian Journal of South East Asian Studies* 10(1): 11–28.

Gunn, B. L., 2018. 'Bringing a Gendered Lens to Implementing the UN Declaration on the Rights of Indigenous Peoples'. In *UNDRIP Implementation: More Reflections on the Braiding of International, Domestic and Indigenous Laws*, edited by Centre for International Governance Innovation. Waterloo, ON: CIGI, 33–9.

Gunningham, N., and Sinclair, D., 2009. 'Organizational Trust and the Limits of Management-Based Regulation'. *Law and Society Review* 43(4): 865–99.

Gustafsson, M-T., and Schilling-Vacaflor, A., 2022. 'Indigenous Peoples and Multiscalar Environmental Governance: The Opening and Closure of Participatory Spaces'. *Global Environmental Politics* 22(2): 1–22.

Hale, C., 2004. 'Rethinking Indigenous Politics in the Era of the "Indio Permitido"'. *NACLA Report on the Americas* 38(2): 16–21.

Haley, S., and Fisher, D., 2014. 'Indigenous Employment, Training and Retention: Successes and Challenges at Red Dog Mine'. In *Natural Resource Extraction and Indigenous Livelihoods: Development Challenges in an Era of Globalization*, edited by E. Gilberthorpe and G. Hilson. Farnham: Ashgate, 11–36.

Hall, R. 2013. 'Diamond Mining in Canada's Northwest Territories: A Colonial Continuity'. *Antipode* 45(2): 376–93.

Hamm, B., Schax, A., and Scheper, C., 2013. *Human Rights Impact Assessment of the Tampakan Copper-Gold Project*. Aachen: Institute for Development and Peace.

Hanna, P., Vanclay, F., Langdon, E. J., and Arts, J., 2015. 'Conceptualizing Social Protest and the Significance of Protest Actions to Large Projects'. *Extractive Industries and Society* 3: 217–39.

Harris, A. S., Sigman, R., Meyer-Sahling, J-H., Mikkelsen, K. S., and Schuster, C., 2020. 'Oiling the Bureaucracy? Political Spending, Bureaucrats and the Resource Curse'. *World Development* 127, https://doi.org/10.1016/j.worlddev.2019.104745, accessed 9 January 2023.

Harvey, B., and Nish, S., 2005. 'Rio Tinto and Indigenous Community Agreement Making in Australia'. *Journal of Energy and Natural Resources Law* 23(4): 499–510.

Haslam, P. A., 2018. 'The Two Sides of Pascua Lama: Social Protest, Institutional Responses, and Feedback Loops'. *European Review of Latin American and Caribbean Studies* 106: 157–82.

Haslam, P. A., 2021. 'The Micro-politics of Corporate Responsibility: How Companies Shape Protest in Communities Affected by Mining'. *World Development* 139, https://doi.org/10.1016/j.worlddev.2020.105322, accessed 9 January 2023.

Havercroft, J., 2010. 'Sovereignty, Recognition and Indigenous Peoples'. In *Moral Limit and Possibility in World Politics*, edited by R. M. Price. Cambridge: Cambridge University Press, 112–36.

Health Council of Canada, 2013. 'Canada's Most Vulnerable: Improving Health Care for First Nations, Inuit and Métis Seniors'. Health Council of Canada, https://www.virtualhospice.ca/Assets/Senior_AB_Report_2013_EN_final_20170609144323.pdf, accessed 28 February 2022.

Hele, K., n.d. 'Native People and the Socialist State: The Native Populations of Siberia and Their Experience as Part of the Union of Soviet Socialist Republics'. *Canadian Journal of Native Studies*, http://www3.brandonu.ca/cjns/14.2/hele.pdf, accessed 4 April 2022.

Herrmann, T. M., Sandström, P., Granqvist, K., D'Astous, N., Vannar, J., Asselin, H., Saganash, N., Mameamskum, J., Guanish, G., Loon, J-B., and Cuciurean, R., 2014. 'Effects of Mining on Reindeer/Caribou Populations and Indigenous Livelihoods: Community-Based Monitoring by Sami Reindeer Herders in Sweden and First Nations in Canada'. *Polar Journal* 4(1): 28–51.

Heywood, A., 2007. *Politics*, 3rd edition. New York: Palgrave Macmillan.

High Court of Botswana, 2006. 'Sesana v. The Attorney General: High Court of Botswana (Dibotelo, Dow and Phumaphi JJ)', 13 December, http://classic.austlii.edu.au/au/journals/AUIndigLawRw/2007/16.html, accessed 4 April 2022.

High Court of South Africa, 2018. 'Beleni and Others v. Minister for Mineral Resources and others: High Court of South Africa', Case No. 73768/2016, 22 November, https://cer.org.za/wp-content/uploads/2018/11/Baleni-and-others-v-Minister-of-Mineral-Resources-and-others.pdf, accessed 9 February 2022.

Hill, C., Madden, C., and Ezpeleta, M., 2016. *Gender and the Extractive Industries: Putting Gender on the Corporate Agenda*. Oxfam, https://policy-practice.oxfam.org/resources/gender-and-the-extractive-industries-putting-gender-on-the-corporate-agenda-620776/, accessed 15 February 2022.

Hipwell, W., Mamen, K., Weitzner, V., and Whiteman, G., 2002. *Aboriginal Peoples and Mining in Canada: Consultation, Participation and Prospects for Changee*. Ottawa: North South Institute.

Hirst, P., and Zeitlin, J., 1991. 'Flexible Specialization versus Post-Fordism: Theory, Evidence and Policy Implications'. *Economy and Society* 20(1): 1–59.

Hitchcock, R. K., Sapignoli, M., and Babchuk, W. A., 2011. 'What About Our Rights? Settlements, Subsistence and Livelihood Security among Central Kalahari San and Bakgalagadi'. *International Journal of Human Rights* 15(1): 62–88.

Hitchcock, R., and Vinding, D. (eds), 2004. *Indigenous Peoples' Rights in Southern Africa*. Copenhagen: IWGIA.

Hitchcock, R. K., and Holm, J. D., 1993. 'Bureaucratic Domination of Hunter-Gatherer Societies: A Study of the San in Botswana'. *Development and Change* 24: 305–38.

Holcombe, S., and Kemp, D., 2018. *Indigenous Employment Futures in an Automated Mining Industry: An Issues Paper and A Case for Research*. Brisbane: CSRM, University of Queensland.

Holcombe, S., and Kemp, D., 2020. 'From Pay-out to Participation: Indigenous Mining Employment as Local Development?' *Sustainable Development* 28(5): 1–14.

Holden, A., 1996. 'Mapoon: "Home to Stay": The Economic and Social Impact of Bauxite Mining and Related Activities on the West Coast of Cape York Peninsula'. Cairns: Cape York Land Council.

Holden, A., and O'Faircheallaigh, C., 1995. *Economic and Social Impact of Mining at Cape Flattery*. Brisbane: Centre for Australian Public Sector Management, Griffith University.

Holden, W., Nadeau, K., and Jacobson, R. D., 2011. 'Exemplifying Accumulation by Dispossession: Mining and Indigenous Peoples in the Philippines'. *Human Geography* 93(2): 141–61.

Hoogeveen, D., 2015. 'Sub-surface Property, Free-Entry Mineral Staking and Settler Colonialism in Canada'. *Antipode* 47 (1): 121–38.

Horowitz, L. S., 2002. 'Daily, Immediate Conflicts: An Analysis of Villagers' Arguments about a Multinational Nickel Mining Project in New Caledonia'. *Oceania* 73: 35–55.

Horowitz, L. S., 2017. '"It Shocks Me, the Place of Women": Intersectionality and Mining Companies' Retrogradation of Indigenous Women in New Caledonia'. *Gender, Place and Culture* 24(10): 1419–40.

Howitt, R., 1990. *'All they get is the dust': Aborigines, Mining and Regional Restructuring in Western Australia's Eastern Goldfields*. Working Paper No. 1, Economic and Regional Restructuring Unit, University of Sydney.

Howitt, R., 2001. *Rethinking Resource Management*. London and New York: Routledge.

Howlett, C., and Lawrence, R., 2019. 'Accumulating Minerals and Dispossessing Indigenous Australians: Native Title Recognition as Settler Colonialism'. *Antipode* 51(3): 818–37.

Howlett, C., Seini, M., McCallum, D., and Osborne, N., 2011. 'Neoliberalism, Mineral Development and Indigenous People: A Framework for Analysis'. *Australian Geographer* 42(3): 309–23.

Hudbay Minerals, 2015. 'Human Rights Policy'. Hudbay Minerals, https://s23.q4cdn.com/405985100/files/doc_downloads/human_right/Human-Rights-Policy.pdf, accessed 4 April 2022.

Human Rights Watch, 2009. 'Peru: Investigate Violence in Bagua'. Human Rights Watch, https://www.hrw.org/news/2009/06/10/peru-investigate-violence-bagua, accessed 22 March 2021.

Hume, M., 2012. 'Enbridge's "Errata" on Caribou Could Prove a Costly Error'. *Globe and Mail*, 12 November: S1–S2.

Humphreys, D., 2000. 'A Business Perspective on Community Relations in Mining'. *Resources Policy* 26: 127–31.

Hunter, B., Howlett, M., and Gray, M., 2015 'The Economic Impact of the Mining Boom on Indigenous and Non-Indigenous Australians'. *Asia and the Pacific Policy Studies* 2(3): 517–30.

ICMM (International Council on Mining and Metals), 2020. 'Mining and Communities'. ICMM, https://www.icmm.com/en-gb/society-and-the-economy/mining-and-communities, accessed 7 October 2020.

ICMM, 2020. *Mining Principles: Performance Expectations*. ICMM, https://www.icmm.com/website/publications/pdfs/mining-principles/mining-principles.pdf, accessed 31 August 2020.

IFC (International Finance Corporation), 2012. 'Performance Standard 7: Indigenous Peoples', 1 January, https://www.ifc.org/wps/wcm/connect/3274df05-7597-4cd3-83d9-2aca293e69ab/PS7_English_2012.pdf?MOD=AJPERES&CVID=jiVQI.D, accessed 31 August 2020.

IGF (Intergovernmental Forum on Mining, Minerals, Metals and Sustainable Development), 2016. 'Gender in Mining Governance: Opportunities for Policy Makers'. IGF, https://www.iisd.org/system/files/2021-03/gender-mining-governance.pdf, accessed 15 February 2022.

Igoe, J., 2006. 'Becoming Indigenous Peoples: Difference, Inequality, and the Globalization of East African Identity Politics'. *African Affairs* 105(420): 399–420.

IIED (International Institute for Environment and Development), 2002. *Breaking New Ground: Mining, Minerals and Sustainable Development: Final Report*. IIED, https://pubs.iied.org/pdfs/9084IIED.pdf, accessed 4 April 2022.

ILO (International Labour Organization), 2013. *Understanding the Indigenous and Tribal Peoples Convention, 1989 (No. 169)*, Geneva: ILO.

Innes, L., 2001. 'Staking Claims: Innu Rights and Mining Claims at Voisey's Bay'. *Cultural Survival Quarterly* 25(1): 12–16.

Innu Nation Task Force on Mining Activities, 1996. *Ntesinan Nteshiniminan Nteniunan: Between a Rock and a Hard Place*. Sheshatshiu: Innu Nation.

Innu Nation, 1999. 'Innu Nation Mounts Court Challenge over Voisey's Bay Project'. Innu Nation press release, 3 September. Goose Bay, Labrador: Innu Nation.

International Association for Impact Assessment (IAIA), 1999. 'Principles of Environmental Impact Assessment Best Practice'. IAIA, https://www.iaia.org/uploads/pdf/principlesEA_1.pdf, accessed 25 March 2021.

IWGIA (International Working Group for Indigenous Affairs), 2011. 'Indigenous Peoples in Botswana'. IWGIA, https://www.iwgia.org/en/botswana/259-central-issues, accessed 14 February 2022.

IWGIA, 2020. *The Indigenous World 2020*. Copenhagen: IWGIA.

IWGIA, 2021. *The Indigenous World 2021*. Copenhagen: IWGIA.

IWIMRA (Indigenous Women in Mining and Resources Australia), 2019. *IWIMRA Report, January–March 2019*, IWIMRA.

Jacka, J. K., 2015. *Alchemy in the Rain Forest: Politics, Ecology and Resilience in a New Guinea Mining Area*. Durham, NC and London: Duke University Press.

Jacka, J. K., 2018. 'The Anthropology of Mining: The Social and Environmental Impacts of Resource Extraction in the Mineral Age'. *Annual Review of Anthropology* 47: 61–77.

Jarroud, M., 2013. 'Chilean Court Suspends Pascua Lama Mine'. Inter Press Service News Agency, 13 April, http://www.ipsnews.net/2013/04/chilean-court-suspends-pascua-lama-mine/, accessed 8 September 2021.

Jenkins, H., and Yakovleva, N., 2006. 'Corporate Social Responsibility in the Mining Industry: Exploring Trends in Social and Environmental Disclosure'. *Journal of Cleaner Production* 14: 271–84.

Jenkins, K., 2017. 'Women Anti-mining Activists' Narratives of Everyday Resistance in the Andes: Staying Put and Carrying On in Peru and Ecuador'. *Gender, Place and Culture* 24(10): 1441–59.

Jensen, T., and Sandström, J., 2020. 'Fly-in/Fly-out and the Fragmentation of Communities: A Case Study of a Uranium Mine on Indigenous Land'. *Journal of Rural Studies* 78: 78–86.

Johnsen, K. I., 2016. 'Land-Use Conflicts between Reindeer Husbandry and Mineral Extraction in Finnmark, Norway: Contested Rationalities and the Politics of Belonging'. *Polar Geography* 39(1): 58–79.

Johnston, B. R., and Garcia-Downing, C., 2004. 'Hydroelectric Development on the Bio-Bio River, Chile: Anthropology and Human Rights Advocacy'. In *In the Way of Development: Indigenous Peoples, Life Projects and Globalization*, edited by M. Blaser, H. A. Feit, and G. McRae. London and New York: Zed, 211–31.

Kalazich, F., 2015. 'Memory as Archaeology: An Experience of Public Archaeology in the Atacama Desert'. *Public Archaeology* 14(1): 44–65.

Katona, J., 2002. 'Mining Uranium and Indigenous Australians: The Fight for Jabiluka'. In *Moving Mountains: Communities, Conflict, Mining and Globalisation*, edited by G. Evans, J. Goodman, and N. Lansbury. London: Zed, 195–206.

Keal, P., 2007. 'Indigenous Self-Determination and the Legitimacy of Sovereign States'. *International Politics* 44: 287–305.

Keeling, A., and Sandlos, J. (eds), 2015. *Mining and Communities in Northern Canada: History, Politics and Memory*. Calgary: University of Calgary Press.

Keenan, K., de Echave, J., and Traynor, K., 2002. *Mining and Communities: Poverty Amidst Wealth*. Amherst, MA: Political Economy Research Institute, University of Massachusetts Amherst.

Kelley, J., 2008. 'Assessing the Complex Evolution of Norms: The Rise of International Election Monitoring'. *International Organization* 62: 221–55.

Kemp, D., and Owen, J., 2013. 'Community Relations and Mining: Core to Business but not "Core Business"'. *Resources Policy* 38: 523–31.

Kemp, D., and Owen, J., 2018. 'The Industrial Ethic, Corporate Refusal and the Demise of the Social Function in Mining'. *Sustainable Development* 26: 491–500.

Kemp, D., and Owen, J., 2020. 'Corporate Affairs and the Conquest of Social Performance in Mining'. *Extractive Industries and Society* 7: 835–7.

Kennett, S. A., 1999. *A Guide to Impact and Benefits Agreements*. Calgary: Canadian Institute of Resources Law.

Ker, P., 2015. 'Oil Contractor Schlumberger to Pay $51m to Settle ATO 'Transfer Pricing' Claim'. *Australian Financial Review*, 15 July, https://www.smh.com.au/money/tax/oil-contractor-schlumberger-to-pay-51m-to-settle-ato-transfer-pricing-claim-20150717-gif426.html, accessed 31 March 2022.

Kidd, R., 1997. *The Way We Civilise: Aboriginal Affairs—The Untold Story*. St Lucia: University of Queensland Press.

KLC (Kimberley Land Council), 2010a. *Kimberley LNG Precinct Strategic Assessment Indigenous Impacts Report, Volume 3: Aboriginal Social Impact Assessment*. KLC, https://www.socialimpactassessment.com/documents/Appendix_E-3.pdf, accessed 22 March 2022.

KLC, 2010b. *Indigenous Impacts Report, Volume 1: Overview and Consolidated Recommendations Report*. KLC, https://jtsi.wa.gov.au/docs/default-source/default-document-library/browse_sar_appendix_e-1_1210.pdf?sfvrsn=25686b1c_10, accessed 22 March 2022.

KLC, 2010c. *Kimberley LNG Precinct Strategic Assessment Indigenous Impacts Report: Six Volumes*. KLC, https://www.jtsi.wa.gov.au/what-we-do/offer-project-support/lng-precincts/

browse-kimberley/browse-lng—environment/appendices-to-strategic-assessment-report/
strategic-assessment-report-appendix-e, accessed 5 April 2022.

KLC, 2010d. *Kimberley LNG Precinct Strategic Assessment Indigenous Impacts Report, Volume 2: Traditional Owner Consent and Indigenous Community Consultation.* KLC, https://www.jtsi.wa.gov.au/docs/default-source/default-document-library/browse_sar_appendix_e-2_1210.pdf?sfvrsn=29686b1c_10, accessed 5 April 2022.

Kløcker Larsen, R., and Raitio, K., 2019. 'Implementing the State Duty to Consult in Land and Resource Decisions: Perspectives from Sami Communities and Swedish State Officials'. *Arctic Review on Law and Politics* 10: 4–23.

Kløcker Larsen, R., Bostrom, M., Muonio Reindeer Herding District, Vilhelmina Sodra Reindeer Herding District, Voernese Reindeer Herding District, and Wik-Karlsson, J., 2022. 'The Impacts of Mining on Sámi Lands: A Knowledge Synthesis from Three Reindeer Herding Districts'. *Extractive Industries and Society*, https://doi.org/10.1016/j.exis.2022.101051.

Kløcker Larsen, R., Osterlin, C., and Guia, L., 2018. 'Do Voluntary Corporate Actions Improve Cumulative Effects Assessment? Mining Companies' Performance on Sami Lands'. *Extractive Industries and Society* 5: 375–83.

Kløcker Larsen, R., Raitio, K., Stinnerbom, M., and Wik-Karlsson, J., 2017. 'Sami–State Collaboration in the Governance of Cumulative Effects Assessment: A Critical Action Research Approach'. *Environmental Impact Assessment Review* 64: 67–76.

Kløcker Larsen, R., Staffansson, J., Omma, I-A., and Lawrenece, R., 2021. 'Avtal mellan samebyar och exploatörer: Hur påverkas renens välmående?' [Agreements between Sami Villagers and Developers: How Is the Reindeer's Well-Being Affected?]. Stockholm Environment Institute, https://doi.org/10.7557/10.6421, accessed 4 April 2022.

Knowles, R., 2021. 'Former Geraldton Deputy Mayor Sentenced for Stealing $3 million from Native Title Fund'. *National Indigenous Times*, 11 November, https://nit.com.au/former-geraldton-deputy-mayor-sentenced-for-stealing-3million-from-native-title-fund/, accessed 24 February 2022.

Koivurova, T. et al., 2015. 'Legal Protection of Sami Traditional Livelihoods from the Adverse Impacts of Mining: A Comparison of the Level of Protection Enjoyed by Sami in Their Four Home States'. *Arctic Review on Law and Politics* 6(1): 11–51.

Kuipers, J. R., Maest, A., MacHardy, K., and Lawson, G., 2006. *Comparison of Predicted and Actual Water Quality at Hardrock Mines: The Reliability of Predictions in Environmental Impact Statements.* Boulder, CO: Buka Environmental.

Kulchyski, P., and Bernauer, W., 2014. 'Modern Treaties, Extraction, and Imperialism in Canada's Indigenous North: Two Case Studies'. *Studies in Political Economy* 93(1): 3–24.

Kunanayagam, R., and Young, K., 1998. 'Mining, Environmental Impact and Dependent Communities: The View from Below in East Kalamintan'. In *The Politics of Environment in Southeast Asia: Resources and Resistance*, edited by P. Hirsch and C. Warren. London and New York: Routledge, 139–58.

Kunkel, T., 2017. 'Aboriginal Values and Resource Development in Native Space: Lessons from British Columbia'. *Extractive Industries and Society* 4: 6–14.

Kuntz, J., 2012. 'Tłı̨chǫ Women and the Environmental Assessment of the NICO Project Proposed by Fortune Minerals Limited'. MA thesis, Department of Anthropology, University of Alberta, Edmonton.

Kuokkanen, R., 2011. 'Indigenous Economies, Theories of Subsistence, and Women: Exploring the Social Economy Model for Indigenous Governance'. *American Indian Quarterly* 35(2): 215–40.

Kuznets, N., 2021. 'Indigenous Groups Say Big Oil's Pollution Threatens Their Existence in Canadian Forest'. *Inside Climate News*, 21 November, https://www.nbcnews.com/news/world/indigenous-groups-say-big-oils-pollution-threatens-existence-canadian-rcna5946, accessed 7 January 2021.

Labba, M. K., 2014. 'Mineral Activities on Sámi Reindeer Grazing Land in Sweden'. *Nordic Environmental Law Journal* 1: 93–8.

Laevas Sami Village, 2012. 'Individual Communication to the United Nations Committee on the Elimination of Racial Discrimination'. Laevas Sami Village, https://uprdoc.ohchr.org/uprweb/downloadfile.aspx?filename=1279&file=Annexe3, accessed 6 March 2022.

Laforce, M., Lapointe, U., and Lebuis, V., 2009. 'Mining Sector Regulation in Quebec and Canada: Is a Redefinition of Asymmetrical Relations Possible?' *Studies in Political Economy* 84(1): 47–78.

Lahiri-Dutt, K., 2011. 'Introduction'. In *Gendering the Field: Towards Sustainable Livelihoods for Mining Communities*, edited by K. Lahiri-Duitt. Canberra: ANU E-Press, 1–20.

Lahiri-Dutt, K. (ed.), 2008. *Gendering the Field: Towards Sustainable Livelihoods for Mining Communities*. Canberra: ANU E-Press.

Landén, A. S., and Fotaki, M., 2018. 'Gender and Struggles for Equality in Mining Resistance Movements: Performing Critique against Neoliberal Capitalism in Sweden and Greece'. *Social Inclusion* 6(4): 25–35.

Lander, J., 2020. *Transnational Law and State Transformation: The Case of Extractive Development in Mongolia*. New York: Routledge.

Lander, J., Hatcher, P., Bebbington, D. H., Bebbington, A., and Banks, G., 2021. 'Troubling the Idealised Pageantry of Extractive Conflicts: Comparative Insights on Authority and Claim-Making from Papua New Guinea, Mongolia and El Salvador'. *World Development* 140, https://doi.org/10.1016/j.worlddev.2020.105372, accessed 9 January 2023.

Langton, M., 2013. *The Quiet Revolution: Indigenous People and the Resources Boom: Boyer Lectures 2012*. Sydney: ABC Books.

Lantto, P., and Mörkenstam, U., 2015. 'Action, Organisation and Confrontation: Strategies of the Sámi Movement in Sweden during the Twentieth Century'. In *Indigenous Politics: Institutions, Representation, Mobilisation*, edited by M. Berg-Nordlie, J. Saglie, and A. Sullivan. Colchester: ECPR Press, 135–63.

Lasley, S., 2019. 'NANA—"Two Worlds, One Spirit"'. *North of 60 Mining News*, https://www.miningnewsnorth.com/story/2019/03/01/in-depth/nana-two-worlds-one-spirit/5630.html, accessed 4 April 2022.

Laurie, V., 2021. 'New Goal for Groote Eylandt's "Ghost Generation"'. *The Australian*, 15 May.

Lawrence, R., and Åhrén, M., 2016. 'Mining as Colonisation: The Need for Restorative Justice and Restitution of Traditional Sami Lands'. In *Nature, Temporality and Environmental Management: Scandinavian and Australian Perspectives on Landscapes and Peoples*, edited by L. Head, S. Saltzman, G. Setten, and M. Stenseke. London: Taylor & Francis, 172–91.

Lawrence, R., and Kløcker Larsen, R., 2017. 'The Politics of Planning: Assessing the Impacts of Mining on Sami Lands'. *Third World Quarterly* 38(5): 1164–80.

Lawrence, R., and Kløcker Larsen, R., 2019. *Fighting to be Herd: Impacts of the Proposed Boliden Copper Mine in Laver, Älvsbyn, Sweden for the Semisjaur Njarg Sami Reindeer Herding Community*. Stockholm: Stockholm Environment Institute.

Lawrence, R., and Mörkenstam, U., 2016. 'Indigenous Self-Determination through a Government Agency: The Impossible Task of the Swedish Samediggi'. *International Journal on Minority and Group Rights* 23(1): 105–28.

Lawrence, R., and Moritz, S., 2019. 'Mining Industry Perspectives on Indigenous Rights: Corporate Complacency and Political Uncertainty'. *Extractive Industries and Society* 6(1): 41–9.

Le Clerc, E., and Keeling, A., 2015. 'From Cutlines to Traplines: Post-industrial Land Use at the Pine Point Mine'. *Extractive Industries and Society* 2: 11–12.

Lebre, E., Owen, J. R., Stringer, M., Kemp, D., and Valenta, R. K., 2021. 'Global Scan of Disruptions to the Mine Life Cycle: Price, Ownership, and Local Impact'. *Environmental Science and Technology*, https://doi.org/10.1021/acs.est.0c08546, accessed 9 January 2023.

Levitus, R., 2009. 'Aboriginal Organizations and Development: The Structural Context'. In *Power, Culture, Economy: Indigenous Australians and Mining*, edited by J. Altman and D. Martin. Canberra: ANU E-Press, 73–98.

Li, F., 2009. 'Documenting Accountability: Environmental Impact Assessment in a Peruvian Mining Project'. *PoLAR: Political and Legal Anthropology Review* 32(2): 218–36.

Li, F., 2015. *Unearthing Conflict: Corporate Mining, Activism and Expertise in Peru*. Durham, NC and London: Duke University Press.

Li, F., 2017. 'Moving Glaciers: Remaking Nature and Mineral Extraction in Chile'. *Latin American Perspectives* 45(5): 102–19.

Library of Congress, 2022. 'Swedish Parliament Adopts Sami Parliament Consultation Order'. Library of Congress, https://www.loc.gov/item/global-legal-monitor/2022-02-03/sweden-swedish-parliament-adopts-sami-parliament-consultation-order/, accessed 27 February 2022.

Limerick, M., Tomlinson, K., Taufatofua, R., Barnes, R., and Brereton, D., 2012. *Agreement Making with Indigenous Groups: Oil and Gas Development in Brisbane*. Brisbane: CSRM, University of Queensland.

Lindblom, C., 1977. *Politics and Markets: The World's Political Economic Systems*. New York: Basic Books.

Lowe, M., 1998. *Premature Bonanza: Standoff at Voisey's Bay*. Toronto: Between the Lines.

Luning, S., 2012. 'Corporate Social Responsibility (CSR) for Exploration: Consultants, Companies and Communities in Processes of Engagements'. *Resources Policy* 37: 205–11.

Lyons, K., 2018. 'Securing Territory for Mining when Traditional Owners Say 'No': The Exceptional Case of Wangan and Jagalingou in Australia'. *Extractive Industries and Society* 6(3): 756–66.

McAteer, E., Cerretti, J., and Ali, S., 2008. 'Shareholder Activism and Corporate Behaviour in Ecuador'. In *Earth Matters: Indigenous Peoples, the Extractive Industries and Corporate Social Responsibility*, edited by C. O'Faircheallaigh and S. Ali. Sheffield: Greenleaf, 180–97.

McGlade, H., 2012. *Our Greatest Challenge: Aboriginal Children and Human Rights*. Canberra: Aboriginal Studies Press.

MacInnes, A., Colchester, M. and Whitmore, A., 2017. 'Free, prior and informed consent: how to rectify the devastating consequences of harmful mining for indigenous peoples'. *Perspetives in Ecology and Conservation* 15: 152-60.

Macintyre, M., 2011. 'Modernity, Gender and Mining: Experiences from Papua New Guinea'. In *Gendering the Field: Towards Sustainable Livelihoods for Mining Communities*, edited by K. Lahiri-Dutt. Canberra: ANU E-Press, 21–32.

MacKay, F., 2002. 'Mining in Suriname: Multinationals, the State and the Maroon Community of Nieuw Koffiekamp'. In *Human Rights and the Environment: Conflicts and Norms in a Globalizing World*, edited by L. Zarsky. London and New York: Earthscan, 57–78.

MacKay, F., 2004. *Indigenous Peoples' Right to Free, Prior and Informed Consent and the World Bank's Extractive Industries Review*. London: Forest Peoples Programme.

MacLean Lane, T., 2018. 'The Frontline of Refusal: Indigenous Women Warriors of Standing Rock'. *International Journal of Qualitative Studies in Education* 31(3): 197–214.

Mahy, P., 2008. 'Sex Work and Livelihoods: Beyond the "Negative Impacts on Women" in Indonesian Mining'. In *Gendering the Field: Towards Sustainable Livelihoods for Mining Communities*, edited by K. Lahiri-Dutt. Canberra: ANU E-Press, 49–65.

Manning, S. M., 2016. 'Intersectionality in Resource Extraction: A Case Study of Sexual Violence at the Porgera Mine in Papua New Guinea'. *International Feminist Journal of Politics* 18(4): 574–89.

Mariqueo, A. A., 2004. 'Chilean Economic Expansion and Mega-development Projects in Mapuche Territories'. In *In the Way of Development: Indigenous Peoples, Life Projects and*

Globalization, edited by M. Blaser, H. A. Feit, and G. McRae. London and New York: Zed, 204–10.

Marshall, D. P., 2002. 'No Parallel: American Settler-Soldiers at War with the Nlaka'pamux of the Canadian West'. In *Parallel Destinies: Canadian–American Relations West of the Rockies*, edited by J. Findlay and K. Coates. Seattle, WA: University of Washington Press, 31–79.

Marx, K., 1972 [1869]. *The Eighteenth Brumaire of Louis Bonaparte*. Moscow: Progress Publishers.

Marx, K., and Engels, F., 1969 [1888]. *The Communist Manifesto*. London: Penguin.

Menton, M., Milanez, F., de Andrade Souza, M., and Cruz, F. S. M., 2021. 'The COVID-19 Pandemic Intensified Resource Conflicts and Indigenous Resistance in Brazil'. *World Development* 138, https://doi.org/10.1016/j.worlddev.2020.105222, accessed 9 January 2023.

Meyer, Y., 2020. '*Baleni v. Minister of Mineral Resources* 2019 2 SA 453 (GP): Paving the Way for Formal Protection of Informal Land Rights'. *Potchefstroom Electronic Law Journal* 23: 1–18.

Midgley, S., 2015. 'Contesting Closure: Science, Politics, and Community Responses to Closing the Nanisivik Mine, Nunavut'. In *Mining and Communities in Northern Canada: History, Politics, and Memory*, edited by A. Keeling and J. Sandlos. Calgary: University of Calgary Press, 293–314.

Milke, M., and Kaplan, L., 2020. 'Canada's Oil Sands and Local First Nations: A Snapshot'. Canada Energy Centre, https://www.canadianenergycentre.ca/research-brief-canadas-oil-sands-and-local-first-nations/, accessed 7 January 2021.

Mining Watch Canada, 2014. 'Barrick Gold Hit with Quebec Class Action—Follows Shareholder Suits in Ontario and US'. Mining Watch Canada, https://miningwatch.ca/news/2014/5/16/barrick-gold-hit-quebec-class-action-follows-shareholder-suits-ontario-and-us, accessed 31 March 2022.

Mirvis, P. H., 2000. 'Transformation at Shell: Commerce and Citizenship'. *Business and Society Review* 105(1): 63–84.

Moeti, S., and Gakelekgolele, G., 2020. 'San Settlement in the Central Kalahari Game Reserve, Botswana'. *Indigenous Negotiations Case Study*, Conservation International, Washington, DC.

Molintas, J. M., 2004. 'The Philippine Indigenous Peoples' Struggle for Land and Life: Challenging Legal Texts'. *Arizona Journal of International and Comparative Law* 21(1): 269–306.

Mongabay, 2021. 'No Safe Space for Philippines' Indigenous Youth as Military Allowed on Campus'. Mongabay, https://news.mongabay.com/2021/01/no-safe-space-for-philippines-indigenous-youth-as-military-allowed-on-campus/, accessed 3 June 2021.

Monosky, M., and Keeling, A., 2021. 'Planning for Social and Community-Engaged Closure: A Comparison of Mine Closure Plans from Canada's Territorial and Provincial North'. *Journal of Environmental Management* 277, https://doi.org/10.1016/j.jenvman.2020.111324, accessed 9 January 2023.

Moody, R. (ed.), 1988. *The Indigenous Voice: Visions and Realities*, Vol. 1. London: Zed.

Moody, R., 1992. *The Gulliver File: Mines, People and Land: A Global Battleground*. London: Minewatch.

Morales, S., 2018. 'Canary in a Coal Mine: Indigenous Women and Extractive Industries in Canada'. In *UNDRIP Implementation: More Reflections on the Braiding of International, Domestic and Indigenous Laws*, edited by Centre for International Governance Innovation. Waterloo, ON: CIGI, 73–84.

Morgan, R., 2004. 'Advancing Indigenous Rights at the United Nations: Strategic Framing and Its Impacts on the Normative Development of International Law'. *Social Legal Studies* 13: 481–500.

Morgan, R., 2007. 'On Political Institutions and Social Movement Dynamics: The Case of the United Nations and the Global Indigenous Movement'. *International Political Science Review* 28: 273–92.

Morrison-Saunders, A., 2018. *Advanced Introduction to Environmental Impact Assessment.* Cheltenham: Elgar.

MRC (Mineral Resources Commodities), 2005. *Annual Report 31 December 2004.* MRC, https://www.mineralcommodities.com/investors-media/annual-reports/, accessed 4 February 2022.

MRC, 2006. *Annual Report 31 December 2005.* MRC, https://www.mineralcommodities.com/investors-media/annual-reports/, accessed 4 February 2022.

MRC, 2011. *Annual Report 2010.* MRC, https://www.mineralcommodities.com/investors-media/annual-reports/, accessed 4 February 2022.

MRC, 2016. 'MRC enters into MOU with BEEE Partner to Divest Interest in Xholobeni project'. MRC, https://www.mineralcommodities.com/wp-content/uploads/2020/10/18-July-2016-MRC-Enters-Into-MOU-With-BEE-Partner-To-Divest-Interest-In-Xholobeni-Mineral-Sands-Project.pdf, accessed 4 February 2022.

MRC, 2020. *Annual Report 2019.* MRC, https://www.mineralcommodities.com/investors-media/annual-reports/, accessed 4 February 2022.

Muehlebach, A., 2003. 'What Self in Self-Determination? Notes from the Frontiers of Transnational Indigenous Activism'. *Identities: Global Studies in Culture and Power* 10: 241–68.

Naipaul, V. S., 1989. *The Loss of Eldorado.* London: Penguin.

Natcher, D., 2019. 'Normalizing Aboriginal Subsistence Economies in the Canadian North'. In *Resources and Sustainable Development in the Arctic*, edited by C. Southcott, F. Abele, D. Natcher, and B. Parlee. New York: Routledge, 219–33.

Natural Resources Canada, 2020. 'Land and Minerals Sector: Indigenous Mining Agreements'. Natural Resources Canada, https://atlas.gc.ca/imaema/en/, accessed 6 January 2022.

Nelson, P., and Dorsey, E., 2007. 'New Rights Advocacy in a Global Public Domain'. *European Journal of International Relations* 13(2): 187–216.

New Internationalist, 2009. 'Brutality in Bagua'. New Internationalist, https://newint.org/blog/editors/2009/06/17/brutality-in-bagua, accessed 21 March 2022.

Newfoundland and the Innu Nation, 2002. 'Memorandum of Agreement Concerning the Voisey's Bay Project'. St John's, Newfoundland.

Nightingale, E., Czyzewski, K., Tester, F., and Aaruaq, N. 2017. 'The Effects of Resource Extraction on Inuit Women and Their Families: Evidence from Canada'. *Gender and Development* 25(3): 367–85.

NNTT (National Native Title Tribunal), 2022. 'Native Title Determinations and Claimant Applications as at 1 January 2022'. NNTT, http://www.nntt.gov.au/Maps/Schedule_and_Determinations_map.pdf, accessed 6 March 2022.

Nolen, S., 2014. 'Behind Barrick's Pascua-Lama Meltdown in the Atacama Desert'. *Report on Business Magazine*, https://www.theglobeandmail.com/report-on-business/rob-magazine/high-and-dry/article18134225/, accessed 8 September 2021.

Norris, R., 2010. *The More Things Change …: The Origins and Impact of Australian Indigenous Economic Exclusion.* Brisbane: Post Pressed.

NWT and Nunavut Chamber of Mines, 2015. *Measuring Success 2014: NWT Diamond Mines Continue to Create Benefits: The Positive Impact of Diamond Mining in the Northwest Territories, 1998–2013.* NWT and Nunavut Chamber of Mines, https://www.miningnorth.com/_rsc/site-content/library/publications/Measuring_Success_NWT_Diamond_Mining.pdf, accessed 22 April 2021.

Nygaard, V., 2016. 'Do Indigenous Interests Have a Say in Planning of New Mining Projects? Experiences from Finnmark, Norway'. *Extractive Industries and Society* 3: 17–24.

O'Faircheallaigh, C., 1995. 'Long Distance Commuting in Resource Industries: Implications for Native Peoples in Australia and Canada'. *Human Organization* 54(2): 205–13.

O'Faircheallaigh, C., 1999. 'Making Social Impact Assessment Count: A Negotiation-Based Approach for Indigenous Peoples'. *Society and Natural Resources* 12: 63–80.

O'Faircheallaigh, C., 2002a. 'Implementation: The Forgotten Dimension of Agreement-Making in Australia and Canada'. *Indigenous Law Bulletin* 5: 4–17.

O'Faircheallaigh, C., 2002b. *A New Model of Policy Evaluation: Mining and Indigenous People*. Aldershot: Ashgate Press.

O'Faircheallaigh, C., 2004. 'Denying Citizens their Rights? Indigenous People, Mining Payments and Service Provision'. *Australian Journal of Public Administration* 63(2): 42–50.

O'Faircheallaigh, C., 2006. 'Mining Agreements and Aboriginal Economic Development in Australia and Canada'. *Journal of Aboriginal Economic Development* 5(1): 74–91.

O'Faircheallaigh, C., 2007. 'Environmental Agreements, EIA Follow-up and Aboriginal Participation in Environmental Management: The Canadian Experience'. *Environmental Impact Assessment Review* 27(4): 319–42.

O'Faircheallaigh, C., 2008. 'Negotiating Protection of the Sacred? Aboriginal–Mining Company Agreements in Australia'. *Development and Change* 39(1): 25–51.

O'Faircheallaigh, C., 2010a. 'Aboriginal Investment Funds in Australia'. In *The Political Economy of Sovereign Wealth Funds*, edited by X. Yi-chong and G. Bahgat. London: Palgrave Macmillan, 157–76.

O'Faircheallaigh, C., 2010b. 'Aboriginal–Mining Company Contractual Agreements in Australia and Canada: Implications for Political Autonomy and Community Development'. *Canadian Journal of Development Studies* 30(1–2): 69–86.

O'Faircheallaigh, C., 2011. 'Green–Black Conflict over Gas Development in the Kimberley: A Sign of Things to Come?' *The Conversation*, 18 October, https://theconversation.com/green-black-conflict-over-gas-development-in-the-kimberley-a-sign-of-things-to-come-3539, accessed 23 March 2021.

O'Faircheallaigh, C., 2012a. 'International Recognition of Indigenous Rights, Indigenous Control of Development and Domestic Political Mobilization'. *Australian Journal of Political Science* 47 (4): 531–46.

O'Faircheallaigh, C., 2012b. 'Curse or Opportunity? Mineral Revenues, Rent Seeking and Development in Aboriginal Australia'. In *Community Futures, Legal Architecture: Foundations for Indigenous People in the Global Mining Boom*, edited by M. Langton and J. Longbottom. Abingdon and New York: Routledge, 45–58.

O'Faircheallaigh, C., 2013a. 'Women's Absence, Women's Power: Indigenous Women and Mining Negotiations in Australia and Canada'. *Ethnic and Racial Studies* 36(11): 1789–1807.

O'Faircheallaigh, C., 2013b. 'Community Development Agreements in the Mining Industry: An Emerging Global Phenomena'. *Community Development* 44(2): 222–38.

O'Faircheallaigh, C., 2013c. 'Extractive Industries and Indigenous Peoples: A Changing Dynamic?' *Journal of Rural Studies* 30: 20–30.

O'Faircheallaigh, C., 2015. 'ESD and Community Participation: The Strategic Assessment of the Proposed Kimberley LNG Precinct, 2007–2013'. *Australasian Journal of Environmental Management* 22(1): 46–61.

O'Faircheallaigh, C., 2016. *Negotiations in the Indigenous World: Aboriginal Peoples and Extractive Industry in Australia and Canada*. New York: Routledge.

O'Faircheallaigh, C., 2017. 'Mining Royalty Payments and the Governance of Aboriginal Australia'. Distinguished Lecture 2017, delivered at Griffith University South Bank campus, 9 August, http://www.concernedaustralians.com.au/media/distinguished-lecture-paper-2017.pdf, accessed 3 September 2020.

O'Faircheallaigh, C., 2018. 'Using Revenues from Indigenous Impact and Benefit Agreements: Building Theoretical Insights'. *Canadian Journal of Development Studies* 39(1): 101–18.

O'Faircheallaigh, C., 2020. 'Impact and Benefit Agreements as Monitoring Instruments in the Minerals and Energy Industries'. *Extractive Industries and Society* 7: 1338–46.

O'Faircheallaigh, C., 2021. 'Explaining Outcomes from Negotiated Agreements in Australia and Canada'. *Resources Policy* 70: 1–7, https://doi.org/10.1016/j.resourpol.2020.101922, accessed 9 January 2023.

O'Faircheallaigh, C., and Ali, S. (eds), 2008. *Earth Matters: Indigenous Peoples, Extractive Industries and Corporate Social Responsibility*. Sheffield: Greenleaf.

O'Faircheallaigh, C., and Babidge, S., forthcoming. 'Negotiated agreements, Indigenous Peoples and Extrative Industry in the Salar de Atacama, Chile: When is an Agreement More then a Contract?' *Development and Change*, https://doi.org/10.1111/dech.12767.

O'Faircheallaigh, C., and Corbett, T., 2005. 'Indigenous Participation in Environmental Management of Mining Projects: The Role of Negotiated Agreements'. *Environmental Politics* 14(5): 629–47.

O'Faircheallaigh, C., and Gibson, G., 2012. 'Economic risk and mineral taxation on Indigenous lands'. Resources Policy 37(1): 10–18.

O'Faircheallaigh, C., and Kelly, R., 2002. 'Corporate Social Responsibility and Native Title Agreement Making'. In *Development and Indigenous Land: A Human Rights Approach*. Sydney: Human Rights and Equal Opportunity Commission and Griffith University, 9–16.

O'Faircheallaigh, C., and Langton, M., 2008. *Report to Rio Tinto Iron Ore, Pilbara Native Title Services and Marnda Mia Central Negotiating Committee*. Brisbane: Griffith University.

O'Faircheallaigh, C., and Lawrence, R., 2019. 'Mine Closure and the Aboriginal Estate'. *Australian Aboriginal Studies* (1): 65–81.

O'Neill, E., 2014. 'Chile Finally Gets Tough on Mining Industry'. *Earth Island Journal*, 26 March, https://www.earthisland.org/journal/index.php/articles/entry/chile_finally_gets_tough_on_mining_industry/, accessed 7 September 2021.

O'Neill, L., 2019. 'The *Bindunbur* "Bombshell": The True Traditional Owners of James Price Point and the Politics of the Anti-gas Protest'. *University of New South Wales Law Journal* 42(2): 597–617.

O'Neill, L. M., 2016, 'A Tale of Two Agreements: Negotiating Aboriginal Land Access Agreements in Australia's Natural Gas Industry'. PhD thesis, University of Melbourne.

OECD (Organisation for Economic Cooperation and Development), 2019. *Linking the Indigenous Sami People with Regional Development in Sweden*. Paris: OECD Publishing.

Ojala, C-G., and Nordin, J. M., 2015. 'Mining Sápmi: Colonial Histories, Sámi Archaeology, and the Exploitation of Natural Resources in Northern Sweden'. *Arctic Anthropology* 52(2): 6–21.

OPIC (Overseas Private Investment Corporation). 2016. 'Strategic Sustainability Performance Plan'. Washington, DC: OPIC, https://www.dfc.gov/media/reports/archived, accessed 4 November 2020.

Orihuela, J. C., 2012. 'The Making of Conflict-Prone Development: Trade and Horizontal Inequalities in Peru'. *European Journal of Development Research* 24 (5): 688–705.

Össbo, A., and Lantto, P., 2011. 'Colonial Tutelage and Industrial Colonialism: Reindeer Husbandry and Early 20th-Century Hydroelectric Development in Sweden'. *Scandinavian Journal of History* 36(3): 324–48.

Osterlin, C., and Raitio, K., 2020. 'Fragmented Landscapes and Planscapes: The Double Pressure of Increasing Natural Resource Exploitation on Indigenous Sámi Lands in Northern Sweden'. *Resources* 9(104): 1–27.

Ostrow, M., 2015. 'Barrick Gold's Pascua Lama Drama: Costs and Bonds in Chile's Regulator-Driven Mining Monitoring System'. Brown-Watson Case 15-03, https://gps.ucsd.edu/_files/faculty/gourevitch/gourevitch_cs_ostrow.pdf, accessed 6 September 2021.

Otto, J., 2018. 'How Do We Legislate for Improved Community Development?'. In *Extractive Industries: The Management of Resources as a Driver of Economic Development*, edited by A. Addison and A. R. Roe. Oxford: Oxford University Press, 1-1-23.

Overud, J., 2019. 'Memory-Making in Kiruna: Representations of Colonial Pioneerism in the Transformation of a Scandinavian Mining Town'. *Culture Unbound: Journal of Current Cultural Research* 11(1): 104-23.

Owen, J., and Kemp, D., 2013. 'Social Licence and Mining: A Critical Perspective'. *Resources Policy* 38(1): 29-35.

Papillon, M., and Rodon, T., 2017. 'Proponent–Indigenous Agreements and the Implementation of the Right to Free, Prior, and Informed Consent in Canada'. *Environmental Impact Assessment Review* 62: 216-24.

Papillon, M., and Rodon, T., 2019. 'The Transformative Potential of Indigenous-Driven Approaches to Implementing Free, Prior and Informed Consent: Lessons from Two Canadian Cases'. *International Journal on Minority and Group Rights* 27: 314-35.

Parlee, B., 2015. 'Avoiding the Resource Curse: Indigenous Communities and Canada's Oil Sands'. *World Development* 74: 425-36.

Parliament of the Commonwealth of Australia, 2020. *Never Again: Inquiry into the Destruction of 46,000 Year Old Caves at the Juukan Gorge in the Pilbara Region of Western Australia: Interim Report*. Australian Parliament, https://parlinfo.aph.gov.au/parlInfo/download/committees/reportjnt/024579/toc_pdf/NeverAgain.pdf;fileType=application%2Fpdf, accessed 7 April 2021.

Pearson, C. A. L., and Helms, K., 2013. 'Indigenous Social Entrepreneurship: The Gumatj Clan Enterprise in East Arnhem Land'. *Journal of Entrepreneurship* 22(1): 43-70.

Peletz, N., Hanna, K., and Noble, B., 2020. 'The Central Role of Inuit Qaujimaningit in Nunavut's Impact Assessment Process'. *Impact Assessment and Project Appraisal* 38(5): 412-26.

Perry, R. J., 1996. *From Time Immemorial: Indigenous Peoples and State Systems*. Austin, TX: University of Texas Press.

Persson, M., and Öhman, M., 2014. 'Visions for a Future at the Source: The Battle against the Rönnbäck Nickel Mining Project'. In *Mindings: Co-constituting Indigenous/Academic/Artistic Knowledges*, edited by J. Gärdebo, M-B. Öhman, and H. Maruyama. Uppsala: Hugo Valentin Centre, 103-19.

Persson, S., Harnesk, D., and Islar, M., 2017. 'What Local People? Examining the Gállok Mining Conflict and the Rights of the Sámi Population in Terms of Justice and Power'. *Geoforum* 86: 20-9.

PH-EITI (Philippines Extractive Industries Transparency Initiative), 2019. *Synergizing Transparency for Sustainability: The Sixth PH-EITI Report (FY2018)*. Manila: PH-EITI.

Philippine Daily Inquirer, 2011. 'Illegal Mining in Zamboanga del Sur Closed: Subanen Leader Rejoices over Province Decision vs "Stubborn" Company'. *Philippine Daily Inquirer*, 3 June.

Pika, A., and Bogoyavlensky, D., 1995. 'Yamal Peninsula: Oil and Gas Development and Problems of Demography and Health among Indigenous Populations'. *Arctic Anthropology* 32(2): 61-74.

Pika, A., and Prokhorov, B., 1989. 'Soviet Union: The Big Problems of Small Ethnic Groups'. *IWGIA Newsletter* 57: 123-36.

PIPlinks 2011. 'TVIRDI Admits Fault and Performs Cleansing Ritual'. PIPlinks, http://www.piplinks.org/Timuay+Jose+Boy+Anoy.html, accessed 18 May 2021.

Pitty, R., and Smith, S. 2011. 'The Indigenous Challenge to Westphalian Sovereignty'. *Australian Journal of Political Science* 46: 121-40.

PIWC (Pauktuutit, Inuit Women of Canada), 2015. *The Impact of Resource Extraction on Inuit Women and Families in Qamani'tuaq, Nunavut Territory: A Qualitative Assessment*. PIWC, https://www.pauktuutit.ca/project/the-impact-of-resource-extraction-on-inuit-women-and-families-in-qamanituaq-nunavut-territory-a-qualitative-assessment/, accessed 11 January 2022.

PIWC, 2016. *The Impact of Resource Extraction on Inuit Women and Families in Qamani'tuaq, Nunavut Territory: A Quantitative Assessment.* PIWC, https://www.pauktuutit.ca/wp-content/uploads/Quantitative-Report-Final.pdf, accessed 11 January 2022.

Polsby, N., 1971. *Community Power and Political Theory.* New Haven, CT: Yale University Press.

Poulantzas, N., 1969. 'The Problem of the Capitalist State'. *New Left Review* 58(1): 67–78.

Procter, A., 2020. 'Elsewhere and Otherwise: Indigeneity and the Politics of Exclusion in Labrador's Extractive Resource Governance'. *Extractive Industries and Society* 7(4): 1292–300.

Prokhorov, B., 1989. 'USSR: How to Save Yamal'. *IWGIA Newsletter* 58: 113–28.

Protestbarrick.net, 2015. 'Chile'. http://protestbarrick.net/section.php@id=14&all=1.html, accessed 6 September 2021.

QIA (Qikiqtani Inuit Association), 2020. *Benefits and Legacy Fund 2019–2020 Annual Report.* QIA, https://www.qia.ca/wp-content/uploads/2020/10/qia-benefits-funds-report-19-20-final_web.pdf, accessed 6 January 2022.

QIA, 2021. *Benefits and Legacy Fund 2020–2021 Annual Report.* QIA, https://www.qia.ca/wp-content/uploads/2021/10/qia-benefits-funds-report-20-21-final-web.pdf, accessed 6 January 2022.

Queensland, 2018. *Social Impact Assessment Guideline.* Queensland Government, https://www.statedevelopment.qld.gov.au/__data/assets/pdf_file/0017/17405/social-impact-assessment-guideline.pdf, accessed 21 March 2022.

Quinteros, J. A., 2020. 'Decolonizing Indigenous Law: Self-Determination and Vulnerability in the Mapuche Case'. In *Education, Human Rights and Peace in Sustainable Development,* edited by M. Nugmanova, Intech Open, 1–10, https://www.intechopen.com/chapters/68963, accessed 9 August 2021.

Raitio, K., Allard, C., and Lawrence, R., 2020. 'Mineral Extraction in Swedish Sápmi: The Regulatory Gap between Sami Rights and Sweden's Mining Permitting Practices'. *Land Use Policy* 99, https://doi.org/10.1016/j.landusepol.2020.105001, accessed 9 January 2023.

Rajak, D., 2007. '"Uplift and Empower": The Gift, the Market and CSR on South Africa's Platinum Belt'. *Research in Economic Anthropology* 28: 297–324.

Ramos, A. R., 1994. 'The Hyperreal Indian'. *Critique of Anthropology* 14(2): 153–71.

Rawls, J. J., 1976. 'Gold Diggers: Indian Miners in the California Gold Rush'. *California Historical Quarterly* 55(1): 28–45.

RDS (Royal Dutch Shell PLC), 2012. *Sustainability Report 2011.* Rotterdam: Royal Dutch Shell PLC.

Regan, A. J., 1998. 'Causes and Course of the Bougainville Conflict'. *Journal of Pacific History* 33(3): 269–85.

Regan, A. J., 2017. 'Bougainville: Origins of the Conflict, and Debating the Future of Large-Scale Mining'. In *Large-Scale Mines and Local-Level Politics: Between New Caledonia and Papua New Guinea,* edited by C. Filer and P-V. Le Meur. Canberra: ANU E-Press, 353–414.

Ren, X., 2013. Implementation of EIA in China'. *Journal of Environmental Assessment Policy and Management* 15(3): 1–20.

Republic of the Philippines, 2016. *2016 Philippine Statistical Yearbook.* Manila: Philippine Statistical Authority.

Rescan. 2012. *KSM Project: Impacts of Mining Operations on Aboriginal Communities in the Northwest Territories and Labrador: Case Studies and Literature Review.* Vancouver: Rescan.

Responsible Mining Foundation, 2020. *Mining and the SDGs: A 2020 Status Update.* RMF, https://www.responsibleminingfoundation.org/mining-and-the-sdgs/, accessed 6 November 2020.

Richards, J., 2006. 'The Application of Sustainable Development Principles in the Minerals Industry'. *International Journal of the Interdisciplinary Social Sciences* 1: 57–67.

Richards, P., 2013. *Race and the Chilean Miracle: Neoliberalism, Democracy, and Indigenous Rights*. Pittsburg, PA: University of Pittsburg Press.

Richardson, E., McLennan, S., and Meo-Sewabu, L., 2019. 'Indigenous Well-Being and Development: Connections to Large-Scale Mining and Tourism in the Pacific'. *Contemporary Pacific* 31(1): 1–34.

Rights and Democracy 2007. *Human Rights Impact Assessments for Foreign Investment Projects Learning from Community Experiences in the Philippines, Tibet, the Democratic Republic of Congo, Argentina, and Peru*. Montreal: International Centre for Human Rights and Democratic Development.

Rio Tinto, 2016. *Why Agreements Matter: A Resource Guide for Integrating Agreements into Communities and Social Performance Work at Rio Tinto*. Rio Tinto, https://www.riotinto.com/-/media/Content/Documents/Sustainability/Corporate-policies/RT-Why-agreements-matter.pdf, accessed 18 February 2022.

Rio Tinto, 2019. 'Voluntary Principles on Security and Human Rights Report'. Rio Tinto, https://www.riotinto.com/search#main-search_q=UN%20Principles&main-search_e=0?main-search_q=UN%20Principles&main-search_e=0, accessed 28 August 2020.

Rio Tinto, 2020. 'Communities'. https://www.riotinto.com/sustainability/communities, accessed 7 October 2020.

Rio Tinto, 2022. *Report into Workplace Culture at Rio Tinto*. Rio Tinto, https://www.riotinto.com/-/media/Content/Documents/Sustainability/People/RT-Everyday-respect-report.pdf, accessed 15 February 2022.

Ritsema, R., Dawson, J., Jorgensen, M., and Macdougall, B., 2015. '"Steering Our Own Ship?" An Assessment of Self-Determination and Self-Governance for Community Development in Nunavut'. *Northern Review* 41: 157–80.

Ritter, D., 2003. 'Trashing Heritage: Dilemmas of Rights and Power in the Operation of Western Australia's Aboriginal Heritage Legislation'. *Studies in Western Australian History* 23: 195–209.

Rodriguez, P., and Carruthers, D., 2008. 'Testing Democracy's Promise: Indigenous Mobilization and the Chilean State'. *European Review of Latin American and Caribbean Studies* 85: 3–21.

Rodríguez-Garavito, C., 2011. 'Global Governance, Indigenous Peoples, and the Right to Prior Consultation in Social Minefields'. *Indiana Journal of Global Legal Studies* 18(1): 263–305.

Rose, D. B., 1984. 'The Saga of Captain Cook: Morality in Aboriginal and European Law'. *Australian Aboriginal Studies* (2): 24–39.

Rose, D. B., 1996. *Nourishing Terrains: Australian Aboriginal Views of Landscape and Wilderness*. Canberra: Australian Heritage Commission.

Rovillos, R. D., and Tauli-Corpuz, V., 2012. 'Development, Power and Identity Politics in the Philippines'. In *The Politics of Resource Extraction: Indigenous Peoples, Multinational Corporations, and the State*, edited by S. Sawyer and E. T. Gomez. London: Palgrave Macmillan/UNRISD, 129–52.

Rowley, C., 1970. *The Destruction of Aboriginal Society: Aboriginal Policy and Practice*, Vol. 1. Canberra: Australia National University Press.

Ruggie, J., 2011. *Report of the Special Representative of the Secretary-General on the Issue of Human Rights and Transnational Corporations and Other Business Enterprises*. UN Human Rights Council, A/HRC/17/31, https://www.ohchr.org/Documents/Issues/TransCorporations/A.HRC.17.32.pdf, accessed 28 August 2020.

Ruin, P., 2021. 'Girjas Sami Village vs. the Swedish State: Breakthrough for Indigenous People'. *Baltic Worlds* 14(1–2): 4–11.

Russell, P., 2005. *Recognising Aboriginal Title: The Mabo Case and Indigenous Resistance to English-Settler Colonialism*. Sydney: UNSW Press.

Salmond, A., 2017. *Tears of Range: Experiments Across Worlds*. Auckland: Auckland University Press.

Samson, C., 2017. 'The Idea of Progress, Industrialization, and the Replacement of Indigenous Peoples'. *Social Justice* 44(4): 1–26.

Sánchez-Vázquez, L., and Leifsen, E., 2019. 'Resistencia antiminera en espacios formales de gobernanza: El caso de CASCOMI en Ecuador'. *European Review of Latin American and Caribbean Studies* 108: 65–86.

Santoyo, G. M., 2002. *Possibilities and Perspectives of Indigenous Peoples with Regard to Consultations and Agreements within the Mining Sector in Latin America and the Caribbean*. Ottawa: North South Institute.

Sanz, P., 2007. 'The Politics of Consent: The State, Multinational Capital and the Subanon of Canatuan'. In *Negotiating Autonomy: Case Studies on Philippine Indigenous Peoples' Land Rights*, edited by A. B. Gatmaytan. Quezon City/Copenhagen: IWGIA, 109–35.

Sanz, P., 2019. 'Mining in Other People's Land: The Unintended Consequences of Mineral Liberalization in Subanon Land in Mindanao, Philippines'. PhD thesis, University of Saskatchewan, Saskatoon.

Sapignoli, M., and Hitchcock, R. K., 2013. 'Chronology of the Central Kalahari Game Reserve: Update III, 2002–2012'. *Botswana Notes and Records* 45: 52–65.

Sarker, T. K., 2013. 'Voluntary Codes of Conduct and Their Implementation in the Australian Mining and Petroleum Industries: Is There a Business Case for CSR?' *Asian Journal of Business Ethics* 2(2): 205–24.

Sarmiento, B. S., 2012. 'Mining Firm, Not Tribesmen, to Blame for Atrocities in Tampakan'. *Minda News*, 1 July, https://www.mindanews.com/top-stories/2012/07/mining-firm-not-tribesmen-to-blame-for-atrocities-in-tampakan/, accessed 27 May 2021.

Sarmiento, B. S., 2020. 'Church-Led Group Revives Campaign vs South Cotabato Mining Project'. *Inquirer Mindanao*, 17 October, https://newsinfo.inquirer.net/1349129/church-led-group-revives-campaign-vs-south-cotabato-mining-project, accessed 7 June 2021.

Saugestad, S., 2011. 'Impact of International Mechanisms on Indigenous Rights in Botswana'. *International Journal of Human Rights* 15(1): 37–61.

Sawchuk, J., 1998. *The Dynamics of Native Politics: The Alberta Métis Experience*. Saskatoon: Purich Publishing.

Sawyer, S., 2004. *Crude Chronicles: Indigenous Politics, Multinational Oil and Neoliberalsim Policies in Ecuador*. Durham, NC and London: Duke University Press.

Sawyer, S., and Gomez, E. T. (eds), 2012. *The Politics of Resource Extraction: Indigenous Peoples, Multinational Corporations, and the State*. Basingstoke: Palgrave Macmillan.

Saxinger, G., forthcoming. 'The FIFO Social Overlap: Success and Pitfalls of Long-Distance Commuting in the Mining Sector'. In *Extractive Industry and the Sustainability of Canada's Arctic Communities*, edited by C. Southcott, F. Abele, D. Natcher, and B. Parlee. Montreal: McGill-Queen's University Press.

Schilling-Vacaflor, A., and Eichler, J., 2017. 'The Shady Side of Consultation and Compensation: "Divide-and-Rule" Tactics in Bolivia's Extraction Sector'. *Development and Change* 48(6): 1439–63.

Schott, S., Belayneh, A., Boutet, J-S., Rodon, T., and Seguin, J-M., forthcoming. 'Mining Economies, Mining Families: The Impacts of Extractive Industries on Economic and Human Development in the Eastern Sub-Arctic'. In *Extractive Industry and the Sustainability of Canada's Arctic Communities*, edited by C. Southcott, F. Abele, D. Natcher, and B. Parlee. Montreal: McGill-Queen's University Press.

Scobie, W., and Rodgers, K., 2019. 'Diversions, Distractions, and Privileges: Consultation and the Governance of Mining in Nunavut'. *Studies in Political Economy* 100(3): 232–51.

Scott, D. N., 2020. 'Extraction Contracting: The Struggle for Control of Indigenous Lands'. *South Atlantic Quarterly* 119(2): 269–99.

Sehlin Macneil, K., 2015. 'Shafted: A Case of Cultural and Structural Violence in the Power Relations between a Sami Community and a Mining Company in Northern Sweden'. *Ethnologia Scandinavica* 45: 1–15.

Sehlin Macneil, K., 2017. *Extractive Violence on Indigenous Country Sami and Aboriginal Views on Conflicts and Power Relations with Extractive Industries.* Umeå: Umeå University.

Siakwah, P., 2017. 'Are Natural Resource Windfalls a Blessing or a Curse in Democratic Setting?' *Resources Policy* 52: 122–33.

Simons, P., and Handl, M., 2019. 'Relations of Ruling: Feminist Critique of the United Nations Guiding Principles on Business and Human Rights and Violence against Women in the Context of Resource Extraction'. *Canadian Journal of Women and the Law* 31(1): 113–50.

Simpson, A., 2017. 'The Ruse of Consent and the Anatomy of "Refusal": Cases from Indigenous North America and Australia'. *Postcolonial Studies* 20(1): 18–33.

Simpson, J., 2013. 'Hunted by Their Own Government—The Fight to Save Kalahari Bushmen'. *The Independent*, 5 October, https://www.independent.co.uk/news/world/africa/hunted-by-their-own-government-the-fight-to-save-kalahari-bushmen-8904934.html, accessed 3 February 2022.

Simpson, L. B., 2017. *As We Have Always Done: Indigenous Freedom through Radical Resistance.* Minneapolis, MN and London: University of Minnesota Press.

Skarin, A., and Ahman, B., 2014. 'Do Human Activity and Infrastructure Disturb Domesticated Reindeer? The Need for the Reindeer's Perspective'. *Polar Biology* 37: 1041–54.

Skocpol, T., 1981. 'Political Response to Capitalist Crisis: Neo-Marxist Theories of the State and the Case of the New Deal'. *Politics and Society* 10: 155–201.

SMI (Sagittarius Mines Inc.), 2011. '*SMI Consults Stakeholders on Its Proposed Tampakan Copper-Gold Mining Operation*'. Press release, 14 June. Manila: SMI.

SMI ICE Chile and Cuatro Vientos, 2020. *Study for Evaluation and Analysis of the Implementation of the Cooperation, Sustainability, and Mutual Benefit Agreement between the Atacamenos Peoples Council (CPA), the 18 Communities and Albemarle Limitada: Preliminary Results Report.* Santiago: SMI ICE Chile and Cuatro Vientos.

Smith, L. T., 2021. *Decolonizing Methodologies: Research and Indigenous Peoples*, 3rd edition. London: Zed.

Smith, M. L., 1989. 'Changing Agendas and Policy Communities: Agricultural Issues in the 1930s and the 1980s'. *Public Administration* 67(2): 149–65.

Smith, M. L., 1990. 'Pluralism, Reformed Pluralism and Neopluralism: The Role of Pressure Groups in Policy-Making'. *Political Studies* 38: 302–22.

Smith, M. L, 1991. 'From Policy Community to Issue Network: Salmonella in Eggs and the New Politics of Food'. *Public Administration* 69(2): 235–56.

Soares, A., 2004. 'The Impact of Corporate Strategy on Community Dynamics: A Case Study of the Freeport Mining Company in West Papua, Indonesia'. *International Journal on Minority and Group Rights* 11: 115–42.

Söderholm, P., and Svahn, N., 2015. 'Mining, Regional Development and Benefit-Sharing in Developed Countries'. *Resources Policy* 45: 78–91.

Southcott, C., 2015. *Northern Communities Working Together: The Social Economy of Canada's North.* Toronto: University of Toronto Press.

Southcott, C., and Natcher, D., 2018. 'Extractive Industries and Indigenous Subsistence Economies: A Complex and Unresolved Relationship'. *Canadian Journal of Development Studies* 39(1): 137–54.

Sovacool, B. K., 2010. 'The Political Economy of Oil and Gas in Southeast Asia: Heading towards the Natural Resource Curse?' *Pacific Review* 23(2): 225–59.

Spoerer, M., 2014. 'Paradoxes of Participatory Democracy: Citizen Participation, Collective Action and Political Influence in a Chilean Environmental Conflict'. *Nuevo Mundo*, https://journals.openedition.org/nuevomundo/67153, accessed 5 April 2022.

Stammler, F., and Ivanova, A., 2016. 'Confrontation, Coexistence or Co-ignorance? Negotiating Human-Resource Relations in Two Russian regions'. *Extractive Industries and Society* 3: 60–72.

Starr, K., 1998. 'The Gold Rush and the California Dream Author'. *California History* 77(1): 56–67.

State of Western Australia, Goolarabooloo Jabirr Jabirr Peoples, Woodside Energy Limited, Broome Port Authority, and LandCorp, 2011. *Browse LNG Precinct Project Agreement.* https://www.wa.gov.au/system/files/2019-06/Browse%20Precinct%20Project%20Agreement.pdf, accessed 4 April 2022.

Statistics Canada, 2018. 'Aboriginal Peoples Highlight Tables, 2016 Census'. Statistics Canada, https://www12.statcan.gc.ca/census-recensement/2016/dp-pd/hlt-fst/abo-aut/index-eng.cfm, accessed 28 February 2022.

St-Laurent, G. P., and Le Billon, P., 2015. 'Staking Claims and Shaking Hands: Impact and Benefit Agreements as a Technology of Government in the Mining Sector'. *Extractive Industries and Society* 2: 590–602.

Stoffle, R. W., and Evans, M. J., 1990. 'Holistic Conservation and Cultural Triage: American Indian Perspectives on Cultural Resources'. *Human Organization* 49(2): 91–9.

Stokes, D. B., Marshall, B. G., and Veiga, M. M., 2019. 'Indigenous Participation in Resource Developments: Is It a Choice?' *Extractive Industries and Society* 6: 50–7.

Strelein, L. M., 2003. 'Yorta Yorta v. Victoria—Comment'. *Land Rights Laws: Issues of Native Title* (21): 1–8.

Superior Court of Ontario, 2013. 'Choc v. Hudbay Minerals Inc., 2013 ONSC 1414'. https://www.americanbar.org/content/dam/aba/administrative/environment_energy_resources/Events/Summit/course_materials/1_choc_v_hudbay-minerals-inc.pdf, accessed 4 April 2022.

Supervising Scientist, 1997. *Kakadu Region Social Impact Study: Report of the Aboriginal Project Committee.* Environment Australia, http://www.environment.gov.au/ssd/publications/krsis-reports/project-committee/index.html, accessed 22 March 2021.

Supreme Court of the Northern Territory, 2014. *Groote Eylandt Aboriginal Trust Incorporated (Statutory Manager Appointed) v. Skycity Darwin Pty Ltd* [2014] NTSC 28.

Szablowski, D., 2002. 'Mining, Displacement and the World Bank: A Case Analysis of Compania Minera Antamina's Operations in Peru'. *Journal of Business Ethics* 39(3): 247–53.

Szablowski, D., 2007. *Transnational Law and Local Struggles: Mining, Communities and the World Bank.* Oxford and Portland, OR: Hart Publishing.

Szablowski, D., 2010. 'Operationalizing Free, Prior and Informed Consent in the Extractive Industry Sector? Examining the Challenges of a Negotiated Model of Justice'. *Canadian Journal of Development Studies* 30(1–2): 111–30.

Tahltan First Nation/IISD (International Institute for Sustainable Development), 2004. *Out of Respect: The Tahltan, Mining and the Seven Questions to Sustainability.* Dease Lake: Tahltan First Nation and IISD.

Taksami, C., 1990. 'Opening Speech at the Congress of the Small Peoples of the Soviet North'. In *Indigenous Peoples of the Soviet North, edited by International Working Group on Indigenous Affairs (IWGIA).* Copenhagen: IWGIA, 23–44.

Tan, A. K., 2006, 'All That Glitters: Foreign Investment in Mining Trumps the Environment in the Philippines'. *Pace Environmental Law Review* 23(1): 182–208.

Tarras-Wahlberg, N. H., Cronjé, F., Reyneke, S., and Sweet, S., 2017. 'Meeting Local Community Needs: The Cases of Iron Ore Mining in Sweden and South Africa'. *Extractive Industries and Society* 4: 652–60.

Taylor, I., and Mokhawa, G., 2003. 'Not Forever: Botswana, Conflict Diamonds and the Bushmen'. *African Affairs* 102(407): 261–83.

Tlale, M. T., 2020. 'Conflicting Levels of Engagement under the *Interim Protection of Informal Land Rights Act* and the *Minerals and Petroleum Development Act*: A Closer Look at the Xholobeni Community Dispute'. *Potchefstroom Electronic Law Journal* 23: 1–32.

Tlicho Investment Corporation, 2015. *Tlicho Investment Corporation Board Report 2015*. Tlicho, http://tlicho.ub8.outcrop.com/sites/default/files/900T-Board_Report_2015-web.pdf, accessed 22 April 2021.

Tonnies, F., 1887/2001. *Community and Civil Society*. Cambridge, Cambridge University Press.

Torrado, N. R. T., 2022. 'Overcoming Silencing Practices: Indigenous Women Defending Human Rights from Abuses Committed in Connection to Mega-Projects: A Case in Colombia'. *Business and Human Rights Journal* 7: 29–44.

Toscano, N., 2021. '"I Am Ultimately Accountable": Rio Tinto Chairman to Stand Down after Cave Blast Disaster'. *Sydney Morning Herald*, 3 March, https://www.smh.com.au/business/companies/i-am-ultimately-accountable-rio-tinto-chairman-to-stand-down-after-cave-blast-disaster-20210303-p577bv.html#:~:text=Rio%20Tinto%20chairman%20Simon%20Thompson%20has%20announced%20he%20will%20step,at%20Western%20Australia's%20Juukan%20Gorge, accessed 22 March 2021.

Trebeck, K., 2007. 'Tools for the Disempowered? Leverage over Mining Companies'. *Australian Journal of Political Science* 42(4): 541–62.

Tsuji, L. J. S., McCarthy, D. D., Whitelaw, G. S., and McEachren, J., 2011. 'Getting Back to Basics: The Victor Diamond Mine Environmental Assessment Scoping Process and the Issue of Family-Based Traditional Land versus Registered Traplines'. *Impact Assessment and Project Appraisal* 29(1): 37–47.

Tulele, L., 2020. '*Employer Attitude/Behaviour Matters: Impact of Employer Attitude/Behaviour on Indigenous Employees' Skill Acquisition and Employment Experience in the Australian Mining and Finance/Banking Sectors*'. PhD thesis, Griffith University, Brisbane.

Tully, J., 2000. 'The Struggles of Indigenous Peoples for and of Freedom'. In *Political Theory and the Rights of Indigenous Peoples*, edited by D. Ivison, P. Patton, and W. Sanders. Cambridge: Cambridge University Press, 36–59.

Turner, D. H., 1996. *Return to Eden: A Journey through the Aboriginal Promised Landscape of Amagalyuagba*. New York: P. Lang.

TVI Resources Development Inc., 2009. 'Tribal Leaders Reconcile the Past, Unite for the Future'. TVI, https://tvird.com.ph/tribal-leaders-reconcile-the-past-unite-for-the-future/, accessed 18 May 2021.

Tysiachniouk, M., Henry, L. A., Lamers, M., and van Tatenhove, J. P. M., 2018. 'Oil and Indigenous People in Sub-Arctic Russia: Rethinking Equity and Governance in Benefit Sharing Agreements'. *Energy Research and Social Science* 37: 140–52.

United Nations 2010. 'The UN "Protect, Respect and Remedy": Framework for Business and Human Rights'. United Nations, https://media.business-humanrights.org/media/documents/files/reports-and-materials/Ruggie-protect-respect-remedy-framework.pdf, accessed 28 August 2020.

UNDESA (United Nations Department of Economic and Social Affairs), 2004. *An Overview of the Principle of Free, Prior and Informed Consent and Indigenous Peoples in International and Domestic Law and Practice*, PFII/2004/WS.2/8. New York: UNDESA.

UNESC (United Nations Economic and Social Council), 2002. *Workshop on Indigenous Peoples, Private Sector Natural Resource, Energy and Mining Companies, and Human Rights*, UN Document E/CN.4/Sub.2/AC.4/2002/3. New York: UNESC.

UNESC, 2004a. *Standard Setting: Preliminary Working Paper on the Principle, of Free, Prior and Informed Consent of Indigenous Peoples*, E/CN.4/Sub.2/AC.4/2004/4. New York: UNESC.

UNESC, 2004b. *Indigenous Peoples' Permanent Sovereignty over Natural Resources: Final Report of the Special Rapporteur,* E/CN.4/Sub.2/2004/30. New York: UNESC.

UNESCO (United Nations Educational Scientific and Cultural Organization), 2022. 'Indigenous Peoples'. UNESCO, http://www.unesco.org/new/en/indigenous-peoples/, accessed 3 April 2022.

UNHRC (United Nations Human Rights Council), 2011. *Report of the Special Rapporteur on the Rights of Indigenous Peoples: The Situation of the Sami People in the Sápmi Region of Norway, Sweden and Finland.* UNHCR, http://unsr.jamesanaya.org/docs/countries/2011-report-sapmi-a-hrc-18-35-add2_en.pdf, accessed 31 March 2022.

UNHRC, 2016. *Report of the Special Rapporteur on the Rights of Indigenous Peoples on the Human Rights Situation of the Sami People in the Sápmi region of Norway, Sweden and Finland.* UNHRC, https://digitallibrary.un.org/record/847081?ln=en, accessed 25 October 2021.

UNOHCHR (United Nations Office of the High Commissioner for Human Rights), 2011. *Guiding Principles on Business and Human Rights: Implementing the United Nations, Respect, Protect and Remedy Framework,* https://www.ohchr.org/documents/publications/guidingprinciplesbusinesshr_en.pdf, accessed 28 August 2020.

UNOHCHR, 2014. *Frequently Asked Questions about the Guiding Principles on Business and Human Rights.* UNOHCHR, https://www.ohchr.org/Documents/Publications/FAQ_PrinciplesBussinessHR.pdf, accessed 28 August 2020.

Urkidi, L., 2010. 'A Glocal Environmental Movement against Gold Mining: Pascua–Lama in Chile'. *Ecological Economics* 70: 219–27.

Urkidi, L., and Walter, M., 2011. 'Dimensions of Environmental Justice in Anti-gold Mining Movements in Latin America'. *Geoforum* 42: 683–95.

Usher, P., 1997. 'Common Property and Regional Sovereignty: Relations between Aboriginal Peoples and the Crown in Canada'. In *The Governance of Common Property in the Pacific Region,* edited by P. Lamour. Canberra: Australian National University, 103–22.

Vakhtin, N. B., 1998. 'Indigenous People of the Russian Far North: Land Rights and the Environment'. *Polar Geography* 22(2): 79–104.

Vanclay, F., and Hanna, P., 2019. 'Conceptualizing Company Response to Community Protest: Principles to Achieve a Social License to Operate'. *Land* 8 (101): 1–31, https://doi.org/10.3390/land8060101, accessed 9 January 2023.

VBNC (Voisey's Bay Nickel Company), 1997. *Voisey's Bay Mine/Mill Project Environmental Impact Statement.* St John's: VBNC.

Vel, C., 2014. 'Respecting the "Guardians of Nature:" Chile' s Violations of the Diaguita Indigenous Peoples' Environmental and Human Rights and the Need to Enforce Obligations to Obtain Free, Prior, and Informed Consent'. *American Indian Law Journal* 2(2): 641–80.

Visaya, V., 2020. 'Police Dismantle Human Barricade'. *Manila Times,* 8 April, https://www.manilatimes.net/2020/04/08/news/regions/police-dismantle-human-barricade/711197/, accessed 3 June 2021.

Wanvik, T., and Caine, K., 2017. 'Understanding Indigenous Strategic Pragmatism: Métis Engagement with Extractive Industry Developments in the Canadian North'. *Extractive Industries and Society* 4: 595–605.

Warden-Fernandez, J., 2001. *Indigenous Communities and Mineral Development.* London: International Institute for Environment and Development.

Watego, C., 2021. *Another Day in the Colony.* Brisbane: University of Queensland Press.

Weitzner V., 2008. *Missing Pieces: An Analysis of the Draft Environmental and Social Impacts Reports for the Bakhuis Bauxite Project, West Suriname.* Ottawa: North-South Institute.

Welker, M., 2014. *Enacting the Corporation: An American Mining Firm in Post-authoritarian Indonesia.* Berkeley, CA: University of California Press.

Westman, C. N., 2013. 'Cautionary Tales: Making and Breaking Community in the Oil Sands Region'. *Canadian Journal of Sociology* 38(2): 211–31.

Westman, C. N., Joly, T. L., and Gross, L. (eds), 2020. *Home in the Oil Sands: Settler Colonialism and Environmental Change in Subarctic Canada*. London and New York: Routledge.

Wetzlmaier, M., 2012. 'Cultural Impacts of Mining in Indigenous Peoples' Ancestral Domains in the Philippines'. *Austrian Journal of South-East Asian Studies* 5(2): 335–44.

Wiebe, A., 2015. 'A Problematic Process: The Memorandum of Understanding between Barrick Gold and Diaguita Communities of Chile'. Mining Watch Canada and Observatorio Latinoamericano de Conflictos Ambientales, https://media.business-humanrights.org/media/documents/files/documents/barrick_mou_pascua_lama_eng_15sep1015.pdf, accessed 9 August 2021.

Wild, K., 2014. 'Groote Eylandt Aboriginal Trust Sues Auditor for Failing to Detect Millions in Alleged Fraud'. ABC News, https://www.abc.net.au/news/2014-09-19/groote-eylandt-aboriginal-trust/5756978, accessed 28 February 2022.

Wilkes, R., 2006. 'The Protest Actions of Indigenous Peoples: A Canadian–US Comparison of Social Movement Emergence'. *American Behavioral Scientist* 50 (4): 510–55.

Wilson, J., 1998. *The Earth Shall Weep: A History of Native America*. London: Icador.

Woodside Energy Ltd, 2007. *Pluto LNG Development: Burrup LNG Park Social Impact Study*. Woodside Energy, http://www.woodside.com.au/Working-Sustainably/Communities/Social-Contribution/Documents/Pluto%20LNG%20Development%20-%20Social%20Impact%20StudyJune2007.pdf.

World Bank, 1991. *Operational Directive Indigenous Peoples OD 4.20*. World Bank, https://www.ifc.org/wps/wcm/connect/4da94701-07cc-4df3-9798-947704a738d4/OD420_IndigenousPeoples.pdf?MOD=AJPERES&CVID=jqewORB, accessed 31 August 2020.

World Bank, 2007. *Indigenous Peoples Rights Act: Legal and Institutional Frameworks, Implementation and Challenges in the Philippines*. Washington, DC: World Bank.

World Bank. 2011. *Implementation of the World Bank's Indigenous Peoples Policy: A Learning Review (FY 2006–2008)*, OPCS Working Paper, August. Washington, DC: World Bank.

World Bank. 2013. *OP 4.10—Indigenous Peoples, Revised April 2013*. Washington, DC: World Bank.

Xanthaki, A. 2017. 'International Instruments on Cultural Heritage: Tales of Fragmentation'. In *Indigenous Peoples' Cultural Heritage, Rights, Debates, Challenges*, edited by A. Xanthaki, S. Valkonen, L. Heinämäki, L., and P. Nuorgam. Leiden and Boston, MA: Brill/ Nijhoff, 1–19.

Yakovleva, N., 2011. 'Oil Pipeline Construction in Eastern Siberia: Implications for Indigenous People'. *Geoforum* 42: 708–19.

Yakovleva, N. P., Alabaster, T., and Petrova, P. G., 2000. 'Natural Resource Use in the Russian North: A Case Study of Diamond Mining in the Republic of Sakha'. *Environmental Management and Health* 11(4): 318–36.

Yi-chong, X., and Bahgat, G., 2010. *The Political Economy of Sovereign Wealth Funds*. London: Palgrave Macmillan.

York, G., 1990. *The Dispossessed: Life and Death in Native Canada*. London: Vintage UK.

Ziff, B., and Hope, M., 2008. 'Unsitely: The Eclectic Regimes that Protect Aboriginal Culture and Places in Canada'. In *Protection of First Nations Cultural Heritage: Laws, Policy, and Reform*, edited by C. Bell and R. Patterson. Vancouver: UBC Press, 181–202.

Zukulu, S., 2020. 'Mining in the Eastern Cape Province, South Africa '. *Indigenous Negotiations Case Study*, Conservation International, Washington, DC.

Index

For the benefit of digital users, indexed terms that span two pages (e.g., 52–53) may, on occasion, appear on only one of those pages.

Afar peoples, forcing from territories 100
Africa
  Barabaig people 101
  illegality of shifting cultivation 101
  San and Xholobeni 201
    outcomes 216
    shared features 218
  Tswana-speaking people 203–204
  see also Botswana; South Africa
agreements *see* negotiated agreements
Alaska, conflicting government energy
    policies 99–100
Algeria, Amazigh populations, state
    repression 101
Amadiba Crisis Committee (ACC), South
    Africa 213
AmaMpondo, South Africa 214
Amazigh populations, Algeria and Tunisia 101
Amazon, resistance tactics, shareholder
    activism 133
Amungme people, Papua New Guinea 33–34
ARCO 88
Argyle diamond mine, Western Australia 67–68
Asia Indigenous Peoples Pact 43
Atacameño, Chile 176, 285
  Council of Atacamanian Peoples (CPA) 176,
    189–194
Australia
  45 agreements 116–117, 245
  Aboriginal Heritage Act 147–148
  Aboriginal Land Rights
    Northern Territory 111, 247–248
    Queensland 247–248
  Aboriginal population
    1992 *Mabo* judgment 108
    Anindilyakwa people 249
    decline 69
    Eastern Guruma people 147–148
    extinguishment of native title rights 242–243
    Indigenous peoples 'defined out of
      existence' 60
    Jidi Jidi people's resistance tactics,
      shareholder activism 132–133
    Mirrar people's opposition to
      Jabiluka 122–123, 125–127,
      132–133

Puutu Kunti Kurrama and Pinikura (PKKP)
    peoples 148
  recognition of inherent Indigenous rights in
    land 241
  ultimate impact of mining on
    well-being 248–253
Argyle diamond mine, Western
    Australia 67–68
Aurukun 31–32
bauxite mining 30–32, 71–72
  Authorities to Prospect (ATPs) 31
  Comalco 31
  Special Bauxite Mining Leases (SBMLs) 31
  Weipa township 31
  women and 71–72
Broken Hill Proprietary (BHP) 188–189
Cape York region 31–32, 71–72, 143
Consolidated Zinc merger with Rio-Tinto
    (Conzinc Rio Tinto of Australia,
    CRA) 26
Groote Eylandt 249–250, 252–253, 289–290
history of mining 25–28, 31–32
Hope Vale and Mitsubishi Corporation 164
Indigenous Impacts Report, Kimberley Land
    Council 146
Jabiluka uranium project 122–123, 125
  Mirrar people's opposition 122–123,
    125–127
  Yvonne Margarula and 125–127
Kakadu National Park, uranium 122–123,
    125–127
liquefied natural gas
  Browse LNG project 144, 146, 162, 245,
    256–257, 281
  Kimberley Land Council 109–110, 122–123,
    125–127, 144, 146, 245–248
  Woodside Energy Ltd 145
Mapoon 31–32
Mineral Resources Commodities (MRC) 213
  see also Botswana
Napranum 31–32
Native Title Act and Right to Negotiate 243
North Ethical Shareholders group 126
North Ltd, plans to develop Jabiluka 126–127
political environment 253–257

Australia (*Continued*)
Puutu Kunti Kurrama and Pinikura (PKKP) peoples 148
Queensland coal 112
racist and discriminatory government policies 240–241
Ranger and Jabiluka uranium projects 122–123, 125
responsibility for Indigenous affairs 99–100
Rio Tinto, destruction of Juukan Gorge rock shelters 133–134, 148
settlement history 239
summary/conclusion 257
Traditional Owner Task Force (TOTF) 144–145
Weipa (bauxite) township 31
Western Cape Communities Coexistence (WCCC) Agreement 110
Authorities to Prospect (ATPs) 31
Awis Tingi people, Nicaragua 45

Bangladesh
state repression of Indigenous culture 101
violence used 100
Barabaig Indigenous people, in Namibia 101
Barrick Gold Ltd
Pascua Lama gold project 180–186
abandonment 107, 184–185
bauxite
Australia 30–32, 71–72
Authorities to Prospect (ATPs) 31
Comalco 31
Special Bauxite Mining Leases (SBMLs) 31
Weipa township, Australia 31
BHP Billiton 78–79, 207–209
biodiversity 44–45, 196
Bonn Guidelines on Access to Genetic Resources 44–45
Convention on Biological Diversity (1992) 44–45
B'laan Indigenous peoples, Philippines 230
Block, F., on neo-Marxist theories 91–93
Bolivia
Hydrocarbon Law 101–102
women in Kanak society 72, 74
Bonn Guidelines on Access to Genetic Resources 44–45
Botswana 200–211
BHP Billiton 207–209
Central Kalahari Game Reserve (CKGR) 205–217
coverage by exploration licences 207
De Beers mining 203–204, 207
dispossession and removal of groups 204–205
San resettlement from (map) 206
shutdown of all services (2002) 205–206

Ditshwanelo, human rights centre 207
environmental impact assessment (EIA) 202, 213
Kalahari San 201–218, 290
First People of the Kalahari (1993) 207, 209
effectively defunct (2006) 210
High Court decision 2006 208
present marginalization 211
reluctance to consider recognition of Indigenous identities 204
and Xholobeni (SA), shared features 218
Mineral Resources Commodities (MRC) 213–217
Transworld Energy and Mineral Resources (TEM) 213
Tswana-speaking people 203–204
Bougainville copper/gold deposit, Papua New Guinea 127–128, 143
Conzinc Rio Tinto of Australia (CRA) 127–128
Panguna mine 127–129
Bougainville Revolutionary Army (BRA) 128–129
Broken Hill Proprietary (BHP) 79, 83, 86, 188–189, 208
business, United Nations and 50–52

Canada
British Columbia
colonial contexts and British Crown 240
employment figures 98
exemption from protection examples 148
gold rushes 25, 29
oil pipeline 87
Squamish Nation (SN) and 256
Tlingit First Nation and 135–136
Tulsequah Chief old mine 135–136
Calder case 242–243, 253
Canadian First Peoples 240
change to Constitution 242–243
diamond mines in Northwest Territories 247
Enbridge, caribou, impact assessment of pipeline 87
Hudbay Minerals 86
Indigenous peoples 'defined out of existence' 61
Indigenous rights 244
Inuit communities 71–72
recognition of inherent Indigenous rights in land 242
ultimate impact of mining on well-being 248–253
Kitchenuhmaykoosib Inninuwug 135
public protests 135
Metis communities, strategic pragmatists 117
negotiated agreements, content 112, 243–244
Newfoundland, Voisey's Bay nickel deposit 129–133
Nunavut Territory 169, 251–252, 289

Ontario, protests against platinum
    exploration 135
political environment 253–257
racist and discriminatory government
    policies 240–241
responsibility for Indigenous affairs 99–100
settlement history 239–240
summary/conclusion 257
Tlingit First Nation 135–136
Toronto Ventures Inc. (TVI) 284
Voisey's Bay Ni deposit,
    Newfoundland 129–132
    combining resistance and engagement 248
capitalist system, long-term requirements 92
caribou
    impact assessment of pipeline, Enbridge 87
    see also reindeer herding
Chile 175–200
    Agricultural Community 180–185, 199, 285
    Atacameño communities 110, 147, 281–285
    Broken Hill Proprietary (BHP) 188–189
    CONADI (National Corporation for Indigenous
        Development) 177–178, 182, 185–186,
        189
    declaratory provisions 194
    economic liberalization 68
    economic policies 107
    environmental litigation 197
    Escondida (Minera Escondida Limitada
        MEL) 188–190, 192, 197–200
    Huasco valley 180–184
    'Indigenous Law' 177–178
    Indigenous peoples 176–180
        Atacameño 176
        Diaguita 180, 182–186
        measures to improve status 177
    Mapuche 68, 176–179
        waves of dispossession 68
    National Corporation for Indigenous Devel-
        opment (CONADI) 177–178, 182,
        185–186, 189
    National Lithium Commission 195
    Pascua Lama 180–187
        Barrick Gold Ltd 175, 180–187
        Diaguita Indigenous people 180–187,
            289–290
        NGOs and 185
        summary/conclusion 185–187
    Peine community, BHP Escondida
        mine 189–192, 198
    ratifying ILO C169 (Indigenous and Tribal
        Peoples Convention 1989) 186
    Salar de Atacama 187–200
        Atacama–Rockwood agreement 175, 191
        Council of Atacamanian Peoples
            (CPA) 187–200

map 188
placing limits on extraction 283
private water rights 198
summary/conclusion 198–200
structural racism 179–180
summary/conclusion 185, 198, 199
Superintendency of the Environment
    (SMA) 183–185
Water Code 195
Chumbivilcas, Peru 120
civil society, role for Indigenous people 286
Colombia, resistance to mining, Indigenous
    women and 124–127
colonization
    experiences of 68–71
    racism and 69–71
Comalco Ltd
    bauxite 31
    Special Bauxite Mining Leases (SBMLs) 31
CONADI (National Corporation for Indigenous
    Development) 177–178, 182, 185–186,
    189
Congo, Democratic Republic of, amended
    Constitution 102
consent, Indigenous free prior and informed
    consent (IFPIC) 45–46, 74, 234–235,
    253
Conservation International 108
Consolidated Zinc, merger with Rio Tinto
    Mining 31
Convention on Biological Diversity (1992) 44–45
Conzinc Rio Tinto of Australia Ltd 31
copper and gold, Tampakan 230, 235
corporate social responsibility (CSR) 49–50, 77,
    82, 108–109, 148–149, 155–156, 182
    see also multinational corporations (MNCs)
cultures, Indigenous people 63–68

Dahl, Robert, pluralist theories 61, 93, 94
De Beers
    Botswana mining 203–204, 207
        CKGR 208
        Debswana 203–204
    diamond mining, Ontario 159
    SI picketing 209
Diaguita peoples, Chile 180, 182–186
diamond mines
    Northwest Territories, Canada 247
    Ontario 159
    prospecting, Botswana 207
diamonds, oil and gas in Soviet Union 34–36

employment in mining 153–156
Enbridge, caribou, impact assessment of
    pipeline 87

environmental impact assessment (EIA) 138,
140–142, 144–145, 151–152
  Botswana 202, 213
  community-controlled impact
    assessment 143–146
  Indigenous women 233
  limited opportunity for consultations with
    affected First Nations 254
  summary/conclusion 283
  Swedish Sami (SSR) 241, 269–270, 272–273
  Tampakan, Philippines 233
Eritrea, forcing Afar and Kunama Indigenous
    peoples from their territories 100
Evenki landowners, gas pipeline, Siberia 115

FECONACO (Federation of Native Communities
    of Rio Corrientos) 117–119
financial institutions 52–53
Freeport McMoran 32–34
  Papua New Guinea 32–34
Freeport (US, Indonesia), Ertsberg/Grassberg
    copper 32–34

Glencore 78, 232–233
Global South 108
gold
  Bougainville copper/gold deposit 127–128, 143
  Indonesia 32–34
  small-scale mining 79
gold rushes 22–29, 66–67
Groote Eylandt, Australia 249–250, 252–253,
    289–290
Guyana, negotiation training workshops 108

history of mining 22–23
  adverse social and cultural impacts 25
  Australia
    Queensland 31–32
    Victoria 25–28
  copper and gold in Indonesia 32–34
  diamonds, oil and gas in Soviet Union 36
  forces for change 39–40
  gold rushes 22–29
    British Columbia 25, 29, 30
    California 23–26
    state and 29–30
  New Zealand 28
  oldest mines identified in Australia 23
  post-Second World War mining boom 23,
    30–31, 37
  summary/conclusion 36–38
Hope Vale, and Mitsubishi Corporation 164
Hudbay Minerals, Canada 86–87, 120
human rights advocacy, censure/publicity
    principal weapons 39–40
Hydrocarbon Law 101–102

India, Supreme Court evictions 101
Indigenous controlled impact assessment
    (ICIA) 143–145
  potential to help manage negative impacts of
    mining 146
  vs conventional IA 145
Indigenous cultural heritage 63–68
  exemption from protection 148
  impacts on 145–146
  land, kinship and social relations 63
  protecting 146–149
  spirituality 64–65
  three categories 146–147
  weakness of legislation 148–149
Indigenous free prior and informed consent
    (IFPIC) 45–46, 74, 234–235, 253
Indigenous peoples/communities
  analysis and conclusion 281–293
  cosmologies and ontologies 67
  and cultures 63–68
  definitional issues 59–63
  employment in mining 153–156
  experiences of colonization 68–71
  increase in workforce 155–156
  institutional arrangements 98–100
  IPRA 221
  land and kinship 63–65
  law and morality 64–65
  motivation for engaging in resistance 122–123
  negotiation and agreements 107
  numbers 59
  opposition 122–137
  resistance tactics 132–137
  self-identification 61
  shared characteristics 59–63
  state policies 100–102
  summary/conclusion 75–76, 137
  supplying goods and services 157
  see also Indigenous women
Indigenous rights
  ancestral lands 45
  cultural traditions 48
  Draft Declaration (1994) 46–47
  enforcement, implementation, and private
    sector 49–50
  establishment in international fora 42–45
  free prior and informed consent 45–46
  and international law 40–45
  legal instruments dealing with 39
  political freedom 41–42
  pre-Second World War 39
  spiritual relationship with lands 48
  status of international legal instruments 39–40
  summary/conclusion 55–56
  undermining by racism 69–71
Indigenous traditional owners 62

Indigenous women
  and agreement making 120–121
  Bougainville Island, PNG 71–72
  environmental impact assessment (EIA) 233
  exclusion from decision making 74
  gender bias 81
  impacts or risks of impacts 73
  Kanak society, Bolivia 72, 74
  mining and 71–75
  resistance and 124–127
  response to mining in contrast with men 72–75
  social and political influence 73
Indonesia
  copper and gold 32–34
  see also Papua New Guinea
Innu/Inuit, Labrador, Voisey's Bay, combining
    resistance and engagement 129–133
institutional arrangements, for Indigenous
    peoples 98–100
International Convention on Elimination of
    All Forms of Racial Discrimination
    (ICERD) 40, 42
International Conventions, listed 40
International Council on Mining and Metals
    (ICMM)
  Indigenous cultural heritage policy publication
    (three of 27) 148–149
  key principles 74
  level of protection offered 149
  mine 'closure' and continuing legacy of
    mining 149–151
  no engagement with communities as policy
    development or review 148–149
International Covenant on Civil and Political
    Rights (ICCPR) 40
International Covenant on Economic Social and
    Cultural Rights (ICESCR) 40
International Finance Corporation (IFC) 52
international financial institutions (IFIs) 52–53
International Indian Treaty Council (US) 42
International Labour Organization (ILO)
  Convention C107 on Indigenous and Tribal
    Populations 41
  second Convention C169 on Indigenous and
    Tribal Populations 44, 108
international law, fora, establishment of
    indigenous rights 40–45
International Monetary Fund 223
International Working Group on Indigenous
    Affairs (IWGIA) 42, 100
  NGOs 207
Inuit Circumpolar Conference 43
Inuit people, Voisey's Bay,
    Newfoundland 129–132
iron ore, dominant companies 78

Jidi Jidi people, resistance tactics, shareholder
    activism 132–133

Kakadu National Park, World Heritage value,
    uranium mining 122–123, 125–127
Kalahari
  De Beers, mining exploration start 207
  see also Botswana
Kallak, Swedish new mining project 275
Kamoro people, Papua New Guinea 33–34
Kanak society
  New Caledonia 72
  Vale's static vision of Kanak women 74
Kenya, negotiation training workshops 108
Kimberley Land Council (KLC), Indigenous
    Impacts Report 146
Kitchenuhmaykoosib Inninuwug, Ontario, public
    protests 135
Kunama peoples, forcing from territories 100

Labrador Inuit Association, Voisey's Bay nickel
    deposit, combining resistance and
    engagement 129–133
land, kinship and social relations 63
Lindblom, C, Privileged Position of Business,
    The 94
liquefied natural gas (LNG), Australia 146, 160,
    162, 245, 256–257, 281
lithium 3, 107, 110, 155, 175, 188–190, 195, 198,
    284
  National Lithium Commission, Chile 195
litigation, public protests 135–136

Maasai peoples, Tanzania 61–62
Marcopper mine, Philippines, Marinduque 220
Margarula, Y 125–127, 129, 287–288
Marxist theories 9–10, 91, 97
  neo-Marxist theories 91–93, 100, 291
Mayan people, Hudbay and 87
media campaigns 133
Minera Escondida Limitada (MEL) 188–189
Mineral Resources Commodities (MRC) see
    Australia; Botswana
mineral sand mining, titanium 211
mining industry
  'closure' and continuing legacy of
    mining 149–151
  corporate decision making 80–81
  economic disadvantage of Indigenous
    peoples 153
  economic opportunities 153
    curse or opportunity? 170
    mining revenues 159–166
    monetary benefits 166–168
    supplying goods and services 157–158

mining industry (*Continued*)
  tensions and dilemmas in managing
      payments 168–170
  employment 153–156
  gender and *see* Indigenous women
  human rights reputation and 81
  impact assessment, vs Indigenous controlled
      impact assessment (ICIA) 145
  initiatives, engagement with Indigenous
      peoples 53–55
  life cycle of mine 78
  summary/conclusion 171
  see also bauxite mining; corporate social
      responsibility; history of mining;
      negative effects of extractive industry;
      negotiated agreements;
Mining Minerals and Sustainable Development
      (MMSD), key principles 53–54
Mirrar people, Jabiluka uranium project 125–126
Mitsubishi Corporation 119, 164
Mongolia 108
Moro Islamic Liberation Front (MILF) 219–220,
      228
Mount Isa Mines 78
multinational corporations (MNCs) 284, 286
  see also corporate social responsibility (CSR)

Namibia, Barabaig Indigenous people 101
National Commission on Indigenous Peoples
      (NCIP), Philippines 222–235
negative effects of extractive industry 138–140
  community-controlled impact
      assessment 143–146
  continuing legacy of mining 149–151
  environmental, social, cultural, economic
      impacts 138–152
  impacts of mining on Indigenous
      lands/peoples 138–152
  protecting Indigenous cultural
      heritage 146–149
  summary/conclusion 151–152
negotiated agreements
  study of 45 agreements, Australia 116–117, 245
  contending perspectives 107
  content 112
  factors driving agreement making 108–109
  Forgotten Dimension of Agreement Making 119
  implementation 107, 119–121
  Indigenous women and 120–121
  instrument of neo-liberal governance 114–115
  numbers 107
  parties and processes 109–111
networks and alliances 134
New Caledonia, Kanak society 72, 74
New People's Army (NPA), Philippines 219–220,
      232, 234

Newfoundland, Innu and Labrador Inuit people,
      Voisey's Bay 129–133
Newmont 78
Nicaragua, Awis Tingi people 45
nickel
  Rönnbäcken, Vapsten community lands,
      Sweden 267, 276
  Voisey's Bay, Newfoundland 122–123, 129–132
nongovernmental organisations (NGOs)
  and acceptance of international norms 96–97
  alliances with affected communities 89,
      117–118, 131, 181–182, 207
  Barrick Gold and 199
  civil society and 286, 289–290
  International Working Group on Indigenous
      Affairs (IWGIA) 207
  Pascua Lama and 185
  permission to submit formal proposals 46–47
  role for Indigenous people 286
  San and 209–211, 217
  Subanon and 229
  UN Working Group on Indigenous Peoples
      (WGIP) and 43
  withdrawal of financial and political support 66
Normandy Ltd 78
North Ethical Shareholders group, Australia 126
North Ltd, Australia 126–127, 132–133
Nunavut Territory, Canada 169, 251–252, 289

Occidental Petroleum Company (OPC),
      Peru 117–118
Oceania Gold 220
Ontario, Kitchenuhmaykoosib Inninuwug, public
      protests 135
Organization of American States 42

Papua New Guinea
  Amungme and Kamoro people 33–34
  Bougainville Copper Agreement (BCA) 128,
      143
      Panguna copper mine 6, 71–72, 109,
      122–124, 127–129
  Bougainville copper/gold deposit 127–128, 143
  government 128–129
  Indigenous peoples, defined 60
  as state 90
  West Papua Liberation movement, Indonesia
      attack on 33–34
  see also Indonesia
Pascua Lama *see* Chile
Pasminco Ltd 78
Peine community *see* Chile
Peru
  Chumbivilcas, Hudbay Minerals 120
  Federation of Native Communities of Rio
      Corrientos (FECONACO) 117–119

Occidental Petroleum Company
    (OPC) 117–118
Peruvian Amazon, Rio Corrientes region,
    Plus-petrol 117
Philippines 219–237
    Certificates of Ancestral Domain Title
        (CADTs) 221
    Duterte ban on open-cut mines 220
    economic challenges 220
    environmental impact assessment (EIA) 233
    Indigenous Peoples' Rights Act (1997) 220,
        223, 225–227
    liberalization of mining legislation 223
    Marcopper mine 220
    Marinduque, Marcopper mine 220
    Mindanao 224–225, 230
    Mineral Production Sharing Agreement
        (MPSA) 225–226
    Mining Act 223, 226, 231
    Moro Islamic Liberation Front
        (MILF) 219–220, 228
    National Commission on Indigenous Peoples
        (NCIP) 222–235
        Ancestral Domains Office 222
        Council of Elders 224, 227
    negotiation training workshops 108
    New People's Army (NPA) 219–220, 232, 234
    Siocon 224
    Siocon Subanon Association 284
    state's support for mining 235–236
    Subanon and Toronto Ventures Inc 224
    summary/conclusion 235
    Tampakan copper and gold deposit 230, 235
    World Bank 223
Pinikura (PKKP) peoples, Australia 148
platinum extraction, Ontario,
        Kitchenuhmaykoosib, public
        protests 135
pluralist theories 93–94, 96, 97, 103, 291
Polsby, R, on pluralist theories 93–94
Poulantzas, N, neo-Marxist theories 91–93, 291
production/mode of production theory 9–13, 17,
    19–21, 91, 96–97
public awareness, and public protests 135
Puutu Kunti Kurrama and Pinikura (PKKP),
    Australia 148

racism, colonization and 69–71
regulation theory 12
reindeer herding, Sweden 259
resistance tactics 132–137
    Indigenous women and 124–127
    litigation 135–136
    shareholder activism 132–133
    summary/conclusion 137

Rio Tinto 78, 112, 113–114, 119, 127–128, 148,
    155–156, 250–251, 253, 255, 284
    Jabiluka mine and 122–123, 125–127, 284
    restructure of company internal
        governance 133–134
    takeover of North Ltd 127
    workplace culture 81
Rio Tinto Iron Ore (RTIO)
    destruction of Juukan Gorge rock
        shelters 133–134, 148
    workforce 155–156
Rio Tinto-Zinc Corporation, London 31
Rönnbäcken, Swedish new mining project 275
Russia
    diamonds, oil and gas (in Soviet Union) 34–36
    Indigenous peoples 'defined out of existence' 61
    Indigenous peoples of North 34–35
    Shakalin Island, Indigenous Peoples 115–116
    Siberia, Evenki landowners, gas pipeline 115,
        141–142
    Yakutia, indigenous rights ignored 35–36
    Yamal peninsula, lack of compensation for
        destruction 36

Sagittarius Mines, Inc. (SMI) 232–235
Salar de Atacama see Chile
Sami and reindeer herding see Sweden, Sami
San people see Botswana, Kalahari San
San people, see also South Africa
self-determination 40–41
Shakalin Island, Russia 115–116
Siberia
    Evenki landowners, gas pipeline 115
    see also Russia
Siocon
    Toronto Ventures Inc. (TVI) 284
    see also Philippines
'social Darwinism' 23
South Africa 108, 211–216
    Amadiba Crisis Committee (ACC) 213
    AmaMpondo, autonomous governance
        structures 214
    apartheid past 216–217
    Department of Mineral Resources (DMR),
        MRC mining rights 214
    Interim Protection of Informal Land Right Act
        (1996) 212
    San and Xholobeni
        outcomes 216
        shared features 218
    summary/conclusion 216
    Transworld Energy and Mineral Resources
        (TEM) 213
    Xholobeni community 201, 218, 286, 289
        location 212
        mineral sand mining 211

South Africa (*Continued*)
  NGOs and 213
  women's central role in opposition to
    mining 216
Soviet Union *see* Russia
state, concept of 90
  autonomy 90–96, 103
  central coordination activity 90–91
  common organizational form 90–91
  Indigenous peoples *in* the state 97–98
  Indigenous policies 98, 100–102
  institutional arrangements 98–100
  level of responsibility for Indigenous affairs 99
  potential errors 91
  preferred outcomes 91–92
  protecting interests of capital 93
  role of state 93–95
  State Indigenous policies 100
  summary/conclusion 102–103
  theories of the state 91–97, 291
Subanon/Siacon Association, Toronto Ventures
    Inc. (TVI) 284
Sweden, Sami
  denial of Sami ownership of/control over
      territories occupied by Sami 81
    denial of transgression of Sami rights 81
  ethnicity and number 259–260
    National Union of the Swedish Sami
        (SSR) 262–263
    pastoral activity 78
    refusal of recognition of ownership of Sami
        traditional territories 261–263
  Reindeer Grazing Act (1886), transgression of
      Sami rights 81
  reindeer herding 259, 290
    economic activity, estimated
        turnover 261–262
    map 262
    requirement of access to specific types of
        pasture 260
  Reindeer Herding Act (1971), slaughter
      regulations 82
  rights, and mineral development 263
  sameby communities 261
  Sametinget 263
  see also Sweden, state
Sweden, state
  Aitik mine, Gallivare Sami lands 272–273
  Boliden Laver copper mine 269, 272–273
  discrimination and racism by 261–262
  interpretation of free prior and informed
      consent (FPIC) 81
  Mineral Inspectorate, granting of exploitation
      concessions 85–87

mining
  fragmentation of decision making/permitting
      system for mining 87
  impacts of exploration/mining on Sami
      herders 271
  mineral policy and mining regulatory
      system 267
    new projects: Kallak and Rönnbäcken 275
  reindeer herding, alternative forms of land use
      by non-Sami 266–267
  summary/conclusion 278
  support of Christion missionaries in prohibition
      of Sami culture 263–264
  see also Sweden, Sami

Tampakan
  copper and gold deposit, Philippines 230, 235
  Western Mining Corporation 78, 230, 284
Tanzania, Maasai peoples 61–62
Tembagapura, Papua New Guinea 32–34
theoretical perspectives
  colonialism and postcolonialism 16–17
  gender theory 17–18
  Marxism and modes of production 10–11
  modernization theory and
      developmentalism 11–12
  neo-liberal governance theory 14–15
  racism and whiteness 15–16
  regulation and 'hybrid' theories 12–14
  structure and agency 19–20
titanium, mineral sand mining 211
Toronto Ventures Inc. (TVI) 284
trade unions 93–94, 134, 248, 291
Traditional Owner Task Force (TOTF) 144–145
Transworld Energy and Mineral Resources
      (TEM) 213
  mineral sand mining 211
  subsidiary of Mineral Resources Commodities
      (*qv*) 213
Tunisia
  Amazigh populations 101
  state repression of Indigenous culture 101

UN Climate Change Conference, on
    environmental damage in
    Chile 199–200
UN Decade of the World's Indigenous Peoples
    (1995–2004) 43
UN Declaration on the Rights of Indigenous
    Peoples (UNDRIP) 46–47, 101–102
UN Economic and Social Council (UNESC) 42
UN Permanent Forum on Indigenous Issues
    (PFII) 42–43
UN Sub-Commission on Prevention of
    Discrimination and Protection of
    Minorities 46–47

Articles 26, 32 47–48
Draft Declaration (1994) 46–48
UN Voluntary Fund for Indigenous Peoples 43
UN Working Group on Indigenous Peoples
(WGIP), NGOs and 43
United Nations (UN)
business and 50–52
status/compliance with international legal
instruments 39–40
United States (US)
Alaska, conflicting government energy
policies 99–100
American Convention on Human Rights 45
California, Indian population decline 69
Organization of American States 42–43, 48
Universal Declaration of Human Rights (UDHR)
(1948) 40, 42
uranium mining, Mirrar people's opposition to
Jabiluka 122–123, 125–127

Vale 78
iron ore 78
static vision of Kanak women 74
violence against mining companies or state
personnel/property 136–137

Voisey's Bay Nickel Company (VBNC),
Newfoundland 129–133
Voisey's Bay/Innu Rights Coalition, nickel
deposit 131–132

water extraction 187–188, 195, 283
Weipa (bauxite) township, Australia 31
Western Mining Corporation, Tampakan 78, 230,
284
workforce, increase in Indigenous
territories 155–156
Working Group on Indigenous Peoples
(WGIP) 42–43, 68
World Bank 52–53
impact assessments of projects 141
Philippine Mining Act 223
structural adjustment programme,
Philippines 223
World Council of Churches 42
World Council of Indigenous Peoples 42

Xholobeni community 201, 218, 286, 289
San and Xholobeni, shared features 218
see also South Africa
Xstrata 78, 232–233